BMA's

TALENT & OLYMPIAD

EXAMS RESOURCE BOOK

CLASS VIII

BRAIN MAPPING
A C A D E M Y
Mapping Your Future

www.bmatalent.com

Published by:

Brain Mapping Academy

#16-11-16/1/B, First Floor, Farhath Hospital Road,
Saleem Nagar, Malakpet, Hyderabad-500 036.
© 040-66135169, 65165169.
E-mail: info@bmatalent.com
Website: www.bmatalent.com

ISBN: 978-81-906877-5-1

Disclaimer

Every care has been taken by the compilers and
publishers to give correct, complete and updated information.
In case there is any omission, printing mistake or any
other error which might have crept in inadvertently,
neither the compiler / publisher nor any of the
distributors take any legal responsibility.

*In case of any dispute, all matters are subjected to the exclusive
jurisdiction of the courts in Hyderabad only.*

First Edition   : 2003

Revised Edition

Printed at:
Sri Vinayaka Art Printers, Hyderabad.

Publisher's Note

Sometimes the understanding of fundamental concepts alone does not help the students to crack the competitive exams as most of them are objective in structure. Students need rigorous training to familiarize themselves to the style of the exams they are attempting. The board exams which are of qualifying, but not competitive, nature do not completely address the needs of students in testing them in objective type format.

To bridge this gap and to enable the students to face the reality of competitive exams, Brain Mapping Academy, decided to bring out an all-objective questions reference book at the secondary level education.

A crisp summary of the topics and useful equations were provided at the beginning of each chapter so that the students can memorize the important points.

Care has been taken to design thought-provoking questions. These should help students to attain a deeper understanding of principles. The questions have been reviewed to fill the gaps in problem coverage and to build the confidence in the students. They have also been expanded to impart reasoning/logical/analytical skills. Hints have been provided for the difficult questions that stimulate the mental muscles.

This book will cater all the requirements of the students who are approaching national/state level talent search examinations and all Olympiad exams. This book also complements the additional preparation needs of the students for the regular board exams.

We took utmost care to make this the best resource book available for the talent exams aspirants. We welcome criticism from the students, teacher community and educators, especially concerning any errors and deficiencies which may have remained in this edition and the suggestions for improvement for the next edition.

NATIONAL LEVEL SCIENCE TALENT SEARCH EXAMINATION

Aim of this examination

The focus on fundamentals at the secondary level is so important that without a firm understanding of them, a child cannot be expected to face the reality of the competitive world once he/she finishes the formal education. Even while opting for higher studies the student has to go through a complete scan of what he/she knows. Exams like IIT-JEE, AIEEE, AIIMS, AFMC, CAT, SAT, GRE, GMAT, etc. are so designed to test the fundamental strength of a student. Hence the need of the hour is building the fundamental base as strong as possible.

A successful life emerges out from healthy and sound competition. Competition is the only way for the students to shake lethargy. It's the only way to get introduced for manly worthiness. Firm standards in education and competition are the tonic for a promising and talented future.

This exactly is the philosophy behind the Unified Council's NSTSE.

Organisation

National Science Talent Search Examination is conducted by Unified Council. Unified Council is India's first ISO 9001 certified organisation in the educational testing and assessment sector. It is a professionally managed progressive organisation in the field of education established in the year 1994 by eminent personalities and academicians from diverse domains of education. Since its inception, Unified Council has put together the best brains in an endeavour to make the younger generation fundamentally stronger and nourish their brains for a bright and enterprising future.

Eligibility : Students of classes 2, 3, 4,5,6,7,8,9,10,11&12 are eligible to participate in this examination.

Medium & Syllabus: This exam is conducted in only English medium and is suitable for all the students following CBSE/ICSE/State Board Syllabi.

Examination Pattern

There will be a separate question paper for each class. All questions are objective-type multiple choice with no negative marking for wrong answers.

No. of Questions: 50   **Marks:** 50 (for 2nd class)

No. of Questions: 75   **Marks:** 75 (for 3rd class)

No. of Questions: 100   **Marks:** 100 (for classes 4th to 12th)

Duration: 90 minutes

Date : Conducted every year on the last Sunday of January.

Test Centres : Spread across the country.

DIVISION OF MARKS

FOR CLASS II

Mathematics	:	25 marks
General Science	:	25 Marks

FOR CLASS III

Mathematics	:	40 marks
General Science	:	35 Marks

FOR CLASSES IV & V

Mathematics	:	45 marks
General Science	:	45 Marks
General Questions	:	10 marks

FOR CLASSES VI TO X

Mathematics	:	25 marks
Physics	:	25 marks
Chemistry	:	20 marks
Biology	:	20 marks
General Questions	:	10 marks

FOR CLASS XI & XII(PCM)

Mathematics	:	40 marks
Physics	:	25 marks
Chemistry	:	25 marks
General Questions	:	10 marks

FOR CLASS XI & XII(PCB)

Biology	:	40 marks
Physics	:	25 marks
Chemistry	:	25 marks
General Questions	:	10 marks

Infrastructure

The Council makes use of ultra-modern equipment such as **Optical Mark Recognition (OMR)** *equipment to evaluate the answer papers to proficiently assess students' performance. The examination procedure is* **completely computerised.**

Unique Service from Unified Council:

Unique analysis reports like Student's Performance Report for students, General School Report & Individual School Report for schools will be provided. These reports will be very much helpful for students & schools to analyse their strengths and weaknesses.

General School Report (GSR) analyses the performance of students participating in the exam (subject-wise and class-wise). The report, in graphical format will have Ogive and Histogram Graphs, which are useful to schools that wish to improve their students' performance by benchmarking the areas of weaknesses and building upon them. This report is provided free of cost.

Individual School Report (ISR) analyses the performance of your school when compared to the rest of the students participating in this examination (subject-wise, class-wise and question-wise). This report acts as a tool for the schools to improve their students' performance in the future by benchmarking the areas of weaknesses and building upon them. ISR is also provided free of cost.

Awards & Scholarships:

Top 100 members in each class will be awarded with Scholarships, Cash Awards & Rewards etc.

Presentation Ceremony:

The awards for the toppers and Institutional Awardees will be presented by eminent personalities at a grand celebration in Hyderabad before an impressive gathering of thousands of students, parents& teachers.

For further details write to **Unified Council**

#16-11-16/1/B, Farhath Hospital Road, Saleem Nagar, Malakpet, Hyderabad-500 036
Phones : 040-24557708, 24545862, 66139917
E-mail: exam@unifiedcouncil.com, Website: www.unifiedcouncil.com

CONTENTS

Mathematics

1. Rational Numbers 1
2. Linear Equations in one Variable 10
3. Understanding Quadrilaterals 20
4. Practical Geometry 34
5. Data Handling 38
6. Squares and Square Roots 50
7. Cubes and Cube Roots 61
8. Comparing Quantities 66
9. Algebraic Expressions and Identities 83
10. Visualising Solid Shapes 95
11. Mensuration 100
12. Exponents and Powers 122
13. Direct and Inverse Proportions 130
14. Factorisation 139
15. Introduction to Graphs 151
16. Playing with Numbers 162
    Crossword Puzzle – I 166
    MODEL TEST PAPER 167

Physics

1.	Force & Pressure	171
2.	Friction	180
3.	Sound	186
4.	Chemical Effects of Electric Current	193
5.	Some Natural Phenomena	199
6.	Light	206
7.	Stars and The Solar System	213
Crossword Puzzle – II		220
	MODEL TEST PAPER	221

Chemistry

1.	Synthetic Fibres and Plastics	227
2.	Metals and Non-metals	232
3.	Coal and Petroleum	242
4.	Combustion and Flame	250
5.	Pollution of Air and Water	259
Crossword Puzzle – III		266
	MODEL TEST PAPER	267

Biology

1.	Food Production and Management	271
2.	Cell	279
3.	Microorganisms	288
4.	Conservation of Plants and Animals	300
5.	Reproduction in Animals	307
6.	Reaching the Age of Adolescence	316
	Crossword Puzzle – IV	323
	MODEL TEST PAPER	324
	Answers to Crossword Puzzles	329

MATHEMATICS

Chapter 1

Rational Numbers

Get It Right

Error in finding number of rational numbers between two given rational numbers.

e.g. find the number of rational numbers between $\dfrac{2}{10}$ and $\dfrac{4}{10}$.

✗ Incorrect	**✓ Correct**
There is only one rational number between $\dfrac{2}{10}$ and $\dfrac{4}{10}$ i.e., $\dfrac{3}{10}$ such that $$\dfrac{2}{10} < \dfrac{3}{10} < \dfrac{4}{10}$$	There are infinite number of rational numbers between $\dfrac{2}{10}$ and $\dfrac{4}{10}$. ∵ if we write $\dfrac{2}{10}$ as $\dfrac{20000}{100000}$ and $\dfrac{4}{10}$ as $\dfrac{40000}{100000}$ we get rational numbers $\dfrac{21000}{100000}, \dfrac{22000}{100000}$, ------- in between $\dfrac{2}{10}$ and $\dfrac{4}{10}$. Again many rational numbers are there between $\dfrac{21000}{100000}, \dfrac{22000}{100000}$.

Synopsis

Natural numbers

♦ 1, 2, 3, 4, ... etc., are called natural numbers denoted by N.

Whole numbers

♦ All natural numbers together with zero are called whole numbers denoted by W.

W = 0, 1, 2, 3, 4, ...

Integers (Z)

♦   . . . . . –4, –3, –2, –1, 0 1, 2, 3, 4, . . .
♦   (i) –1, –2, –3, –4, ... are called negative integers.
♦   (ii) 1, 2, 3, 4, ... are called positive integers.

Note :

♦   Zero is neither positive nor negative.

♦   The numbers of the form $\dfrac{a}{b}$, where a and b are natural numbers are called fractions.

Eg : $\dfrac{3}{5}, \dfrac{7}{11}, \dfrac{13}{213}, \ldots$ etc.

♦   The numbers of the form $\dfrac{p}{q}$, where p and q are integers and $q \neq 0$ are called rational numbers.

Eg : $\dfrac{-3}{5}, \dfrac{7}{-11}, \dfrac{-13}{-213}, \ldots$ etc.

♦   If the denominator of a rational number has no prime factors other than 2 (or) 5, then and only then it is expressible as a <u>terminating decimal</u>. Ex. 3/4 = 0.75   8/10 = 0.8
♦   Every rational number is always expressible in the form of a terminating (or) a <u>repeating decimal</u>. Ex 8/11 = 0.727272...

Properties of all real numbers

Closure property of addition:

♦   The sum of two rational numbers is always a rational number.

Commutative law for addition:

♦   a + b = b + a, $\forall$ rational numbers 'a' and 'b'.

Associative law for addition:

♦   (a + b) + c = a + (b + c), $\forall$ rational numbers a, b and c.

Existence of additive identity:

♦   Zero is the additive identity.

a + 0 = 0 + a = a, $\forall$ rational numbers a .

Existence of additive inverse

♦   For each rational number 'a', there exists a rational number '–a' such that
a + (–a) = (–a) + a = 0.

Closure property for multiplication:

♦   The product of two rational numbers is a rational number.

Commutative law of multiplication:

♦   ab = ba, $\forall$ rational numbers a and b.

Associative law of multiplication:

♦   (ab)c = a(bc), ∀ rational numbers a, b and c.

Existence of multiplicative identity:

♦   1 is called the multiplicative identity.

      1.a = a.1 = a, ∀ rational numbers a.

Existence of multiplicative inverse:

♦   Every non–zero rational number 'a' has its multiplicative inverse $\dfrac{1}{a}$.

Distributive law of multiplication over addition:

♦   a(b + c) = ab + ac, ∀ rational numbers a, b and c.

♦   Zero is a rational number which has no multiplicative inverse.

Multiple Choice Questions

1. The additive inverse of $\dfrac{-a}{b}$ is:

   (A) $\dfrac{a}{b}$ (B) $\dfrac{b}{a}$

   (C) $\dfrac{-b}{a}$ (D) $\dfrac{-a}{b}$

2. Multiplicative inverse of '0' is:

   (A) $\dfrac{1}{0}$ (B) 0

   (C) does not exist   (D) $\dfrac{0}{0}$

3. Which of the following statement is false?
   (A) Every fraction is a rational number
   (B) Every rational number is a fraction
   (C) Every integer is a rational number
   (D) All the above

4. A rational number can be expressed as a terminating decimal if the denominator has factors:
   (A) 2 or 5   (B) 2 ,3 or 5
   (C) 3 or 5   (D) none of these

5. Express 0.75 as rational number.

   (A) $\dfrac{75}{99}$ (B) $\dfrac{75}{90}$

   (C) $\dfrac{3}{4}$ (D) None of these

6. Express $0.\overline{75}$ as rational number.

   (A) $\dfrac{75}{90}$ (B) $\dfrac{25}{33}$

   (C) $\dfrac{3}{4}$ (D) None of these

7. Express $0.3\overline{58}$ as rational number.

   (A) $\dfrac{358}{1000}$ (B) $\dfrac{358}{999}$ (C) $\dfrac{355}{990}$ (D) All

8. Which of the following statements is true?

   (A) $\dfrac{5}{7} < \dfrac{7}{9} < \dfrac{9}{11} < \dfrac{11}{13}$ (B) $\dfrac{11}{13} < \dfrac{9}{11} < \dfrac{7}{9} < \dfrac{5}{7}$

   (C) $\dfrac{5}{7} < \dfrac{11}{13} < \dfrac{7}{9} < \dfrac{9}{11}$ (D) $\dfrac{5}{7} < \dfrac{9}{11} < \dfrac{11}{13} < \dfrac{7}{9}$

9. A rational number between $\frac{1}{4}$ and $\frac{1}{3}$ is:

   (A) $\frac{7}{24}$ (B) 0.29

   (C) $\frac{13}{48}$ (D) all the above

10. Which step in the following problem is wrong?

   $a = b = 1$

   $a = b$

   step–1 : $a^2 = ab$

   step–2 : $a^2 - b^2 = ab - b^2$

   step–3 : $(a + b)(a - b) = b(a - b)$

   step 4 : $a + b = \dfrac{b(a - b)}{a - b}$

   $a + b = b$

   $1 + 1 = 1$

   $2 = 1$

   (A) Step–4   (B) Step–3
   (C) Step–2   (D) Step–1

11. The value of $1.\overline{34} + 4.1\overline{2}$ is :

   (A) $\frac{133}{99}$ (B) $\frac{371}{90}$

   (C) $\frac{5169}{990}$ (D) $\frac{5411}{990}$

12. The value of $4 - \dfrac{5}{1 + \dfrac{1}{3 + \dfrac{1}{2 + \dfrac{1}{4}}}}$ is:

   (A) $\frac{40}{31}$ (B) $\frac{4}{9}$ (C) $\frac{1}{8}$ (D) $\frac{31}{40}$

13. The sum of the additive inverse and multiplicative inverse of 2 is:

   (A) $\frac{3}{2}$ (B) $\frac{-3}{2}$ (C) $\frac{1}{2}$ (D) $\frac{-1}{2}$

14. If p:every fraction is a rational number and q:every rational number is a fraction, then which of the following is correct?
   (A) p is true and q is false.
   (B) p is false and q is true.
   (C) Both p and q are true.
   (D) Both p and q are false.

15. Which of the following is a rational number (s) ?

   (A) $\frac{-2}{9}$

   (B) $\frac{4}{-7}$

   (C) $\frac{-3}{-17}$

   (D) All the three given numbers.

16. $\frac{-5}{0}$ is a _____.

   (A) positive rational number.
   (B) negative rational number.
   (C) either positive or negative rational number.
   (D) neither positive nor negative rational number.

17. A rational number equivalent to $\frac{-5}{-3}$ is:

   (A) $\frac{-25}{15}$ (B) $\frac{25}{-15}$

   (C) $\frac{25}{15}$ (D) none of these

18. $\frac{-2}{-19}$ is a :

(A) positive rational number.

(B) negative rational number.

(C) either positive or negative number.

(D) has neither a positive numerator nor a negative number.

19. Which of the following rational numbers is in the standard form?

(A) $\dfrac{8}{-36}$

(B) $\dfrac{-7}{53}$

(C) $\dfrac{3}{-4}$

(D) None of these

20. If $\dfrac{-3}{x} = \dfrac{x}{27}$, then the value of 'x' is ____.

(A) a rational number.

(B) not a rational number.

(C) an integer.

(D) a natural number.

21. The given rational numbers are $\dfrac{1}{2}, \dfrac{4}{-5}, \dfrac{-7}{8}$. If these numbers are arranged in the ascending order or descending order, then the middle number is:

(A) $\dfrac{1}{2}$

(B) $\dfrac{-7}{8}$

(C) $\dfrac{4}{-5}$

(D) None of these

22. The average of the middle two rational numbers if $\dfrac{4}{7}, \dfrac{1}{3}, \dfrac{2}{5}, \dfrac{5}{9}$ are arranged in ascending order is:

(A) $\dfrac{86}{90}$ (B) $\dfrac{86}{45}$ (C) $\dfrac{43}{45}$ (D) $\dfrac{43}{90}$

23. The difference between the greatest and least numbers of $\dfrac{5}{9}, \dfrac{1}{9}, \dfrac{11}{9}$ is:

(A) $\dfrac{2}{9}$

(B) $\dfrac{4}{9}$

(C) $\dfrac{10}{9}$

(D) $\dfrac{2}{3}$

24. For any two rational numbers x and y, which of the following properties are correct ?

(i) x < y

(ii) x = y

(iii) x > y

(A) Only (i) and (ii) are correct.

(B) Only (ii) and (iii) are correct.

(C) Only (ii) is correct.

(D) All (i), (ii), (iii) are correct.

25. If A : The quotient of two integers is always a rational numbers and R : $\dfrac{1}{0}$ is not rational, then which of the following statements is true?

(A) A is true and R is correct explanation of A..

(B) A is false and R is the correct explanation of A.

(C) A is true and R is false.

(D) Both A and R are false.

26. If A : Every whole number is a natural number and R : 0 is not a natural number, Then which of the following statement is true ?

(A) A is false and R is the correct explanation of A.

(B) A is true and R is the correct explanation of A.

(C) A is true and R is false.

(D) Both A and R are true.

27. By what rational number should $\dfrac{-8}{39}$ be multiplied to obtain 26 ?

(A) $\dfrac{507}{4}$ (B) $\dfrac{-507}{4}$

(C) $\dfrac{407}{4}$ (D) None of these

28. Which property of multiplication is illustrated by: $\dfrac{-4}{3} \times \left(\dfrac{-6}{5} + \dfrac{8}{7} \right) =$

$\left(\dfrac{-4}{3} \times \dfrac{-6}{5} \right) + \left(\dfrac{-4}{3} \times \dfrac{8}{7} \right)$

(A) Associative property
(B) Commutative property
(C) Distributive property
(D) None of these

Previous Contest Questions

1. Which of the following is not a rational number?

(A) $\dfrac{3}{17}$ (B) $\dfrac{-4}{19}$ (C) $\dfrac{0}{8}$ (D) $\dfrac{3}{0}$

2. If p : All integers are rational numbers and q : every rational number is an integer then which of the following statement is correct ?

(A) p is false and q is true
(B) p is true and q is false
(C) Both p and q are true.
(D) Both p and q are false.

3. If $\dfrac{-3}{5} = \dfrac{-24}{x}$, then x = _____

(A) 40   (B) –40

(C) ±40   (D) None of these

4. Which of the following statement is true about a rational number $\dfrac{-2}{3}$?

(A) It lies to the left side of '0' on the number line.

(B) It lies to the right side of '0' on the number line.

(C) It is not possible to represent on the number line.

(D) It cannot be determined on which side the number lies.

5. Out of the rational numbers $\dfrac{-5}{11}, \dfrac{-5}{12}, \dfrac{-5}{17}$, which is greater ?

(A) $\dfrac{-5}{11}$ (B) $\dfrac{5}{-12}$

(C) $\dfrac{-5}{17}$ (D) None of these

6. Arrange the following numbers in descending order.

$-2, \dfrac{4}{-5}, \dfrac{-11}{20}, \dfrac{3}{4}$

(A) $\dfrac{3}{4} > -2 > \dfrac{-11}{20} > \dfrac{4}{-5}$

(B) $\dfrac{3}{4} > \dfrac{-11}{20} > \dfrac{4}{-5} > -2$

(C) $\dfrac{3}{4} > \dfrac{4}{-5} > -2 > \dfrac{-11}{20}$

(D) $\dfrac{3}{4} > \dfrac{4}{-5} > \dfrac{-11}{20} > -2$

7. What is the percentage of least number in the greatest number if $\dfrac{3}{5}, \dfrac{9}{5}, \dfrac{1}{5}, \dfrac{7}{5}$ are arranged in ascending or descending order?

(A) $11\frac{1}{9}$ % (B) 10 % (C) 20 % (D) 25 %

8. $2-\frac{11}{39}+\frac{5}{26}=$ _____ .

(A) $\frac{149}{39}$ (B) $1+\frac{71}{78}$

(C) $\frac{149}{76}$ (D) $\frac{149}{98}$

9. The sum of two rational number is –3 .

If one of the nubmers is $\frac{-7}{5}$, then the other number is:

(A) $\frac{-8}{5}$ (B) $\frac{8}{5}$ (C) $\frac{-6}{5}$ (D) $\frac{6}{5}$

10. The product of two rational numbers is $\frac{-9}{16}$. If one of the numbers is $\frac{-4}{3}$, then the other number is:

(A) $\frac{36}{48}$ (B) $\frac{25}{64}$ (C) $\frac{27}{49}$ (D) $\frac{27}{64}$

⊘ Answers ⊘

Multiple Choice Questions

1. A	2. C	3. B	4. A	5. C	6. B	7. C	8. A	9. D	10. A
11. D	12. C	13. B	14. A	15. D	16. D	17. C	18. A	19. B	20. B
21. C	22. D	23. C	24. D	25. B	26. A	27. B	28. C		

Previous Contest Questions

1. D	2. B	3. A	4. A	5. C	6. B	7. A	8. B	9. A	10. D

Explanatory Answers

1. (A) ∵ P + (–P) = (–P) + P = 0 is the additive inverse property.

So additive inverse of $\frac{-a}{b}$ is $\frac{a}{b}$.

2. (C) Does not exist since division by zero is not defined.

3. (B) Every rational number is not a fraction. Since in rational numbers, we use integers and in fractions, we use only natural numbers.

4. (A) When the denominator has factors 2 (or) 5, then only a rational number is expressible as a terminating decimal.

5. (C) $0.75 = \frac{75}{100} = \frac{3}{4}$

6. (B) $0.\overline{75} = \frac{75}{99} = \frac{25}{33}$

7. (C) $0.3\overline{58} = \frac{358-3}{990} = \frac{355}{990}$

8. (A) $\frac{5}{7} = 0.71$; $\frac{7}{9} = 0.77$

$\frac{9}{11} = 0.81$; $\frac{11}{13} = 0.84$

So $\frac{5}{7} < \frac{7}{9} < \frac{9}{11} < \frac{11}{13}$.

9. (D) $\frac{1}{4} = 0.25 ; \frac{1}{3} = 0.33$

$\frac{7}{24} = 0.29 ; \frac{13}{48} = 0.27$

So $\dfrac{7}{24}, \dfrac{13}{48}$ and 0.29 are lying

between $\dfrac{1}{4}$ & $\dfrac{1}{3}$.

10. (A) $\because a = b = 1 \Rightarrow a - b = 0$
Division by zero is not defined.
So we cannot divide by $(a - b)$.

11. (D) $1.\overline{34} = \dfrac{133}{99}$

$4.1\overline{2} = \dfrac{371}{90}$

$1.\overline{34} + 4.1\overline{2} = \dfrac{133}{99} + \dfrac{371}{90}$

$= \dfrac{4081 + 1330}{990} = \dfrac{5411}{990}$

13. (B) $-2 + \dfrac{1}{2} = \dfrac{-3}{2}$

15. (D) $\because$ In all fractions, both numerator and denominator are integers.

16. (D) $\because$ Denominator is '0', it is not a rational number.

17. (C) $\because \dfrac{-5}{-3} = \dfrac{-5}{-3} \times \dfrac{-5}{-5} = \dfrac{25}{15}$

18. (A) $\because$ Both numerator and denominator are negative (i.e., same sign)

19. (B) $\because$ In (A) and (C), the denominator is negative.

20. (B) $\dfrac{-3}{x} = \dfrac{x}{27}$

$x \times x = -3 \times 27$

$\Rightarrow x^2 = -81 \Rightarrow x^2 = -81$

$x = \sqrt{-81}$, which is not a rational number.

21. (C) The descending order is $\dfrac{1}{2}, \dfrac{-4}{5}, \dfrac{-7}{8}$

so middle number is $\dfrac{-4}{5}$.

22. (D) $\dfrac{4}{7}, \dfrac{1}{3}, \dfrac{2}{5}, \dfrac{5}{9}$

The above numbers in ascending order are:

$\dfrac{1}{3} < \dfrac{2}{5} < \dfrac{5}{9} < \dfrac{4}{7}$

Middle two numbers are $\dfrac{2}{5}$ and $\dfrac{5}{9}$.

$\therefore$ Average $= \dfrac{2/5 + 5/9}{2} = \dfrac{43}{90}$

23. (C) The ascending order of given numbers is $\dfrac{1}{9}, \dfrac{5}{9}, \dfrac{11}{9}$

$\therefore$ Required difference

$= \dfrac{11}{9} - \dfrac{1}{9} = \dfrac{10}{9}$

25. (B) $\because \dfrac{1}{0}$ is not rational, the quotient of two integers is not rational.

26. (A) Zero (0) is a whole number but not a natural number.

27. (B) $x \times \dfrac{-8}{39} = 26$

$\Rightarrow x = \dfrac{26}{-8/39} \Rightarrow 26 \times \dfrac{39}{-8}$

$= \dfrac{-507}{4}$

28. (C) $\because a \times (b + c) = (a \times b) + (a \times c)$ is distributive.

Previous Contest Questions

3. (A) $\dfrac{-3}{5} = \dfrac{-24}{x} \Rightarrow -3 \times x = -24 \times 5$

$x = \dfrac{-24 \times 5}{-3} = 40$

5. (C) $\dfrac{-5}{11}, \dfrac{-5}{12}, \dfrac{-5}{17}$

∵ All have same numerator. So the rational number having the least denominator is the greatest. But here all have negative sign. So, the number having greatest denominator is greater. Hence,

$\dfrac{-5}{17}$ is greater.

7. (A) The given numbers can be arranged in the ascending order as :

$\dfrac{1}{5} > \dfrac{3}{5} > \dfrac{7}{5} > \dfrac{9}{5}$

Greatest number = $\dfrac{9}{5}$;

Least number = $\dfrac{1}{5}$

We have $\dfrac{9}{5} \times \dfrac{x}{100} = \dfrac{1}{5}$

$x = \dfrac{100}{9} = 11\dfrac{1}{9}\%$

8. (B) $\dfrac{2}{1} - \dfrac{11}{39} + \dfrac{5}{26}$

$= \dfrac{156 - 22 + 15}{78} = \dfrac{149}{78}$

$= 1\dfrac{71}{78} = 1 + \dfrac{71}{78}$

9. (A) Let x be the required number.

So, $x + \left(\dfrac{-7}{5}\right) = -3$

$x = -3 + \dfrac{7}{5} = \dfrac{-15 + 7}{5} = \dfrac{-8}{5}$

10. (D) $x \times \dfrac{-4}{3} = \dfrac{-9}{16}$

$x = \dfrac{-9/16}{-4/3} = \dfrac{-9}{16} \times \dfrac{-3}{4} = \dfrac{27}{64}$

Chapter 2 — Linear Equations in One Variable

Get It Right

A. Error in recognising whether an equation is a linear equation.

e.g. Which of the following is not a linear equation ?

A) $4x + 1 = -x$ B) $\dfrac{5}{3}y + y = 4$ C) $-pq + 5 = -3$ D) None of these

✗ Incorrect

'D' is true as all the three equations are linear equations.

✓ Correct

'C' is correct.

∵ $-pq + 5 = -3$ is not a linear equation.

B. Error in solving linear equations.

e.g. $4 + \dfrac{x}{3} = 5$

✗ Incorrect

$4 + \dfrac{x}{3} = 5$

$4 + x = 15$

$x = 15 - 4 = 11$

4 is not multiplied by 3.

✓ Correct

$4 + \dfrac{x}{3} = 5$

$\dfrac{12 + x}{3} = 5$

$12 + x = 15$

$x = 3$

4 is multiplied by 3

$\dfrac{x}{3} = 5 - 4$

$\dfrac{x}{3} = 1$

$x = 3$

Synopsis

Equation:

An equation is a statement of equality of two algebraic expressions involving one or more unknown quantities.

Linear equation:

An equation involving only linear polynomials is called a linear equation.

Transposition:

Any term of an equation may be taken to the other side by changing sign. This process is called transposition.

Multiple Choice Questions

1. If the digit 1 is placed after a two digit number whose tens digit is 't' and units digit is 'u', the new number is:
   (A) $10t + u + 1$ (B) $100t + 10u + 1$
   (C) $t + u + 1$ (D) none of these

2. The solution of $\dfrac{x-5}{2} - \dfrac{x-3}{5} = \dfrac{1}{2}$ is:
   (A) $x = 7$ (B) $x = 9$
   (C) $x = 8$ (D) $x = 5$

3. The solution of $\dfrac{2x+1}{3x-1} = \dfrac{3}{2}$ is:
   (A) $x = 1$ (B) $x = -1$
   (C) $x = 2$ (D) $x = -3$

4. In an examination a student was asked to find $\dfrac{3}{14}$ th of a certain number. By mistake, he found $\dfrac{3}{4}$ of it. His answer was 150 more than the correct answer. The number given him is:
   (A) 290 (B) 280
   (C) 240 (D) 180

5. $\dfrac{2}{3}$ rd of a number when multiplied by $\dfrac{3}{4}$ th of the same number make 338. The number is:
   (A) 18 (B) 24 (C) 36 (D) 26

6. A man is 5 years older than his wife and the wife is now thrice as old as their daughter, who is 10 years old. How old was the man when his daughter was born?
   (A) 20 years (B) 23 years
   (C) 25 years (D) 30 years

7. Twenty years ago, my age was $\dfrac{1}{3}$ rd of what it is now. My present age is:
   (A) 66 years (B) 30 years
   (C) 33 years (D) 36 years

8. If $3\dfrac{1}{x} \times 3\dfrac{3}{4} = 12\dfrac{1}{2}$, then the value of 'x' is:
   (A) 1 (B) $\dfrac{1}{3}$ (C) 2 (D) 3

9. There were only two candidates in an election. One got 62% votes and was elected by a margin of 144 votes. The total number of voters were:
   (A) 500 (B) 600 (C) 700 (D) 800

10. When 75% of a number is added to 75 the result is the number again. The number is:
(A) 150   (B) 300   (C) 100   (D) 450

11. A student has to secure 40% marks to pass. He got 40 marks and failed by 40 marks. The maximum number of marks is:
(A) 160   (B) 180   (C) 200   (D) 320

12. If the sum of three consecutive even numbers is 234, then the smallest among them is:
(A) 76   (B) 78
(C) 80   (D) none of these

13. Two angles in a triangle are in the ratio 4 : 5. If the sum of these angles is equal to the third angle, then the third angle is:
(A) 180^0 (B) 40^0 (C) 50^0 (D) 90^0

14. The ratio of number of males to number of females in a club are 7 : 4. If there are 84 males in the club, the total number of members in the club are:
(A) 126   (B) 132   (C) 136   (D) 148

15. The prices of a scooter and cycle are in the ratio 9 : 5. If a scooter costs Rs. 4,200 more than a cycle. The price of cycle is:
(A) Rs. 5,250   (B) Rs. 5,200
(C) Rs. 5,000   (D) Rs. 4,800

16. The ratio of two numbers is 3 : 8 and their difference is 115. The largest number is:
(A) 69   (B) 115   (C) 184   (D) 230

17. A number 351 is divided into two parts in the ratio 2 : 7. Find the product of the numbers.
(A) 20,294   (B) 21,294
(C) 25,295   (D) 31,294

18. A boat goes downstream and covers the distance between two ports in 4 hrs while it covers the same distance upstream in 5 hrs. If the speed of the stream is 2 kmph, the speed of the boat in still water is:
(A) 15 km/hr   (B) 20 km/hr
(C) 24 km/hr   (D) 18 km/hr

19. If $\frac{2}{3}$ of a number is 20 less than the original number, then the number is:
(A) 60   (B) 40   (C) 80   (D) 120

20. If 10 is added to four times a certain number the result is 5 less than five times the number. The number is:
(A) 10   (B) 15   (C) 20   (D) 25

21. If a number increased by 8% of itself gives 135, then that number is:
(A) 112   (B) 100
(C) 125   (D) none of these

22. A number consists of two digits whose sum is 8. If 18 is added to the number, its digits are interchanged. Find the number.
(A) 53   (B) 35   (C) 92   (D) 63

23. How much pure alcohol should be added to 400 ml of strength 15% to make its strength 32%?
(A) 50 ml   (B) 75 ml
(C) 100 ml   (D) 150 ml

24. By selling a bicycle for Rs. 1,885, a man gains 16%. At what price did he buy the bicycle?
(A) Rs. 1,625   (B) Rs. 1,825
(C) Rs. 2,000   (D) None of these

25. X and Y together can do a piece of work in 8 days, which X alone can do in 12 days. In how many days can Y do the same work alone?
(A) 12 days   (B) 24 days
(C) 36 days   (D) 16 days

26. A man can row at 8 kmph in still water. If the river is running at 2 kmph, it takes him 48 minutes to row to a place and back. How far is the place?
(A) 1 km   (B) 2 km (C) 3 km (D) 4 km

27. The solution of $(x+4)^2 - (x-5)^2 = 9$ is:
    (A) 1   (B) 2   (C) 3   (D) 4

28. If the angles of a triangle are in the ratio 2 : 3 : 4, then the difference between the greatest and smallest angles is:
    (A) 10^0 (B) 20^0 (C) 30^0 (D) 40^0

29. The consecutive multiples of 3 whose sum is 51 are:
    (A) 24, 27   (B) 20, 31
    (C) 40, 11   (D) 25, 26

30. The value of x for which open sentence $x+3=5$ is true.
    (A) 0   (B) 1   (C) 2   (D) 3

31. The value of x for which the open sentence $x+6=7$ is true.
    (A) 1   (B) 2   (C) 3   (D) 4

32. $\dfrac{x}{5}=2$ is true when value of x is:
    (A) 5   (B) 10   (C) 15   (D) 20

33. If $2-\dfrac{x}{3}=4$, then the value of x is:
    (A) –6   (B) 6   (C) –4   (D) 4

34. If $2x+3 = x-4$, then the value of x is:
    (A) –4   (B) –7   (C) –9   (D) –10

35. The solution for $\dfrac{2x}{5}=\dfrac{10}{3}$ is:
    (A) $\dfrac{25}{3}$ (B) $\dfrac{35}{3}$ (C) $\dfrac{45}{2}$ (D) $\dfrac{55}{2}$

36. If $9-7x=5-3x$, then the value of x is:
    (A) 0   (B) $\dfrac{1}{4}$ (C) $\dfrac{1}{2}$ (D) 1

37. If $\dfrac{x}{3}+\dfrac{x}{2}=5$, then the value of x is:
    (A) 2   (B) 4
    (C) 6   (D) None of these

38. If $4x = 15-3x$, then the value of x is:
    (A) $\dfrac{15}{7}$ (B) $\dfrac{14}{5}$ (C) $\dfrac{13}{6}$ (D) $\dfrac{12}{5}$

39. If $\dfrac{50}{x}+3=13$, then the value of x is:
    (A) 2   (B) 4   (C) 5   (D) 8

40. Sum of two numbers is 35 and their difference is 13. Then the numbers are:
    (A) 10, 25 (B) 22, 13 (C) 24, 11 (D) 20, 15

41. The sum of a two digit number and the number obtained by reversing the order of its digits is 121, and the two digits differ by 3. Then the number is/are:
    (A) 34 or 33   (B) 47 or 74
    (C) 36 or 63   (D) None of these

42. The twice the son's age in years is added to the father's age, the sum is 70. But if twice the father's age is added to the son's age, the sum is 95. Then the ages of father and son respectively are:
    (A) 30 yrs, 10 yrs   (B) 40 yrs, 15 yrs
    (C) 45 yrs, 20 yrs   (D) None of these

43. 4 chairs and 3 tables cost Rs. 2100 and 5 chairs and 2 table cost Rs. 1750 then the costs of a chair and a table separately are:
    (A) Rs. 150, Rs. 500 (B) Rs. 100, Rs. 450
    (C) Rs. 200, Rs. 600 (D) None of these

44. A fraction is such that if the numerator is multiplied by 3 and the denominator is reduced by 3, we get 18/11, but if the numerator is increased by 8 and the denominator is doubled, we get 2/5. Then the fraction is:
    (A) $\dfrac{16}{25}$ (B) $\dfrac{12}{25}$ (C) $\dfrac{20}{25}$ (D) $\dfrac{22}{25}$

45. In a two digit number, the tens digit is three times the units digit. When the number is decreased by 54, the digits are reversed. Then the number is:
    (A) 36   (B) 39   (C) 93   (D) 96

Previous Contest Questions

1. Solve $5 - \dfrac{2d + 7}{9} = 0$.

   (A) 19   (B) 14
   (C) 9   (D) 7

2. Given that $\dfrac{-6p - 9}{3} = \dfrac{2p + 9}{5}$, find the value of p.

   (A) −4   (B) −2
   (C) 3   (D) 5

3. When a certain number, m, is divided by 5 and added to 8, the result is equal to 3m subtracted from 4. The value of m is:

   (A) 2   (B) $\dfrac{4}{3}$

   (C) $-\dfrac{1}{3}$ (D) $-\dfrac{5}{4}$

4. Kiran scored 80 marks in his Science test which is $\dfrac{5}{6}$ of the total marks. What are the total marks for the test?
   (A) 96   (B) 100
   (C) 104   (D) 108

5. If the total of four consecutive odd numbers is 40, the smallest number is:
   (A) 7   (B) 9
   (C) 11   (D) 13

6. The figure shows a rectangle with a perimeter of 60 cm.

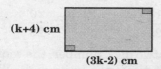

   (k+4) cm
   (3k-2) cm

What is the value of k?
(A) 7   (B) 9
(C) 12   (D) 29

7. The figure shows a cuboid with a volume of 180 cm^3.

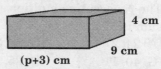

   4 cm
   9 cm
   (p+3) cm

What is the value of p?
(A) 72   (B) 36
(C) 18   (D) 2

8. If $26 - (7m - 9) = -2m$, then m=____.

   (A) $\dfrac{9}{17}$ (B) $\dfrac{35}{9}$

   (C) 7   (D) 9

9. Given that $5x - 2(6 + 7x) = 15$, the value of x is:

   (A) $1\dfrac{13}{14}$ (B) $1\dfrac{8}{19}$

   (C) $\dfrac{1}{3}$ (D) −3

10. Given that $\dfrac{3x - 4}{4x + 3} = 2$, find the value of x.
    (A) −3   (B) −2
    (C) 2   (D) 3

⊘ Answers ⊘

Multiple Choice Questions

1. B	2. C	3. A	4. B	5. D	6. C	7. B	8. D	9. B	10. B
11. C	12. A	13. D	14. B	15. A	16. C	17. B	18. D	19. A	20. B
21. C	22. B	23. C	24. A	25. B	26. C	27. A	28. D	29. A	30. C
31. A	32. B	33. A	34. B	35. A	36. D	37. C	38. A	39. C	40. C
41. B	42. B	43. A	44. B	45. C					

Previous Contest Questions

1. A	2. B	3. D	4. A	5. A	6. A	7. D	8. C	9. D	10. B

Explanatory Answers

1. **(B)** Placing the '1' as indicated in the problem, shifts the given digits to the left, so that 't' is now the hundred's digit and 'u' is now the ten's digit.

   $\therefore 100t + 10u + 1$

2. **(C)** $\dfrac{x-5}{2} - \dfrac{x-3}{5} = \dfrac{1}{2}$

   $\dfrac{5x - 25 - 2x + 6}{10} = \dfrac{1}{2}$

   $3x - 19 = 5$

   $3x = 24$

   $x = 8$

3. **(A)** $\dfrac{2x+1}{3x-1} = \dfrac{3}{2}$

   $4x + 2 = 9x - 3$

   $5x = 5$

   $x = 1$

4. **(B)** Let the required number be x.
   We have,

   $\dfrac{3x}{4} - \dfrac{3x}{14} = 150$

   $\dfrac{21x - 6x}{28} = 150$

   $x = \dfrac{150 \times 28}{15} = 280$

5. **(D)** Let the number be x.

   $\dfrac{2x}{3} \times \dfrac{3x}{4} = 338$

   $\Rightarrow x^2 = 676$

   $x = \sqrt{676} = 26.$

6. **(C)** Let the age of daughter be x yrs.
   Age of wife = 3x
   Age of the man = 3x + 5
   Given that x = 10
   $\Rightarrow$ age of man = 3(10) + 5 = 35 years
   $\therefore$ Age of the man when his daughter was born
   = 35 – 10 = 25 yrs

7. **(B)** Let the present age be 'x' years.
   We have,

   $x - 20 = \dfrac{x}{3}$

   $\dfrac{2x}{3} = 20$

   $x = 30$ years

8. **(D)** $3\dfrac{1}{x} \times 3\dfrac{3}{4} = 12\dfrac{1}{2}$

   $\dfrac{3x+1}{x} \times \dfrac{15}{4} = \dfrac{25}{2}$

$10x = 9x + 3$

$x = 3$

9. **(B)** Let the total number of votes be x.

$$\frac{62x}{100} - \frac{38x}{100} = 144$$

$$\frac{24x}{100} = 144$$

$x = 600$

10. **(B)** Let the number be x.

We have,

$$\frac{75x}{100} + 75 = x$$

$$\frac{25x}{100} = 75$$

$x = 300$

11. **(C)** Let the maximum number of marks be x.

We have,

$$\frac{40x}{100} = 40 + 40$$

$x = 200$

12. **(A)** Let the three consecutive even numbers be

$2x - 2, 2x, 2x + 2$

We have,

$(2x - 2) + 2x + (2x + 2) = 234$

$6x = 234$

$x = 39$

∴ Least even number

$= 2x - 2 = 2(39) - 2 = 76$

13. **(D)** Let the angles be 4x and 5x.

Third angle = $4x + 5x = 9x$

We have

$4x + 5x + 9x = 180^0$

$x = 10^0$

∴ Third angle = $9x = 9 \times 10^0 = 90^0$

14. **(B)** Let the number of males = 7x

and number of Females = 4x

Given that,

$7x = 84 \Rightarrow x = 12$

Total number of members

$= 7x + 4x = 11x = 11 \times 12 = 132$

15. **(A)** Let cost of scooter = 9x

and Let cost of cycle = 5x

We have,

$9x - 5x = 4,200$

$x = 1,050$

∴ cost price of cycle = $5 \times 1,050$

$= Rs. 5,250$

16. **(C)** Let the numbers be 3x and 8x.

We have,

$8x - 3x = 115$

$x = 23$

Largest number = $8x = 8 \times 23$

$= 184$

17. **(B)** Let the numbers be 2x and 7x.

$2x + 7x = 351$

$x = 39$

Product = $2x \times 7x = 14x^2$

$= 14 \times (39)^2$

$= 21,294$

18. **(D)** Let the speed of the boat in still water be x km/hr.

The speed downstream

$= (x + 2)$ km/hr

The speed upstream

$= (x - 2)$ km/hr

We have,

$4(x + 2) = 5(x - 2)$

$x = 18$ km/hr

19. **(A)** Let the number be x.

$$\frac{2}{3}x = x - 20$$

$x = 60$

20. **(B)** Let the number be x.

$4x + 10 = 5x - 5$

$x = 15$

21. (C) $x + 8\%$ of $x = 135$

$$\frac{108x}{100} = 135$$

$$x = 135 \times \frac{100}{108} = 125$$

22. (B)

10	1
x	y

The number is $10x + y$
When digits are reversed, the number becomes $10y + x$.
We have,
$x + y = 8$ -----(1)
$10x + y + 18 = 10y + x$
$x - y + 2 = 0$ ---- (2)
Solving (1) and (2) we get
$x = 3, y = 5$
∴ The number is 35.

23. (C) $\frac{15}{100} \times 400 = 60$ ml

$$\frac{60 + x}{400 + x} \times 100 = 32$$

$$\frac{60 + x}{400 + x} = \frac{32}{100} = \frac{8}{25}$$

$x = 100$ ml

24. (A)   Let $CP = x$

Gain $= \frac{16}{100}x = \frac{4x}{25}$

SP $= \frac{4x}{25} + x = \frac{29x}{25}$

$$\frac{29x}{25} = 1,885$$

$x = $ Rs. 1,625.

25. (B) $\frac{1}{12} + \frac{1}{x} = \frac{1}{8}$

$$\frac{1}{x} = \frac{1}{8} - \frac{1}{12} = \frac{1}{24}$$

∴ $x = 24$ days

26. (C)   Speed of the man in still water
= 8 kmph.
Speed of the river = 2 kmph
Downstream = 8 + 2 = 10 kmph
Upstream = 8 – 2 = 6 kmph

$$\frac{x}{10} + \frac{x}{6} = \frac{48}{60}$$

$8x = 24$
$x = 3$ km

27. (A) $(x + 4)^2 - (x - 5)^2 = 9$
$x^2 + 8x + 16 - x^2 - 25 + 10x = 9$
$\qquad\qquad 18x = 18$
$\qquad\qquad\quad x = 1$

28. (D) $2x + 3x + 4x = 180^0$
$9x = 180^0$
$x = 20^0$
Difference
$= 4x - 2x = 2x = 2 \times 20^0 = 40^0$

29. (A) $3x + (3x + 3) = 51$
$x = 8$
∴ The two numbers are 24, 27.

30. (C) $x + 3 = 5$
If $x = 1$ then $1 + 3 = 5$ (False)
If $x = 2$ then $2 + 3 = 5$ (True)
∴ The value of $x = 2$

31. (A) $x + 6 = 7$
If $x = 1$ then $1 + 6 = 7$ (true)
∴ The value of $x = 1$

32. (B) $\frac{x}{5} = 2$

If x= 1, 2, 3, 4, 5, 6, 7, 8, 9 the open sentence is (false)

If x = 10 then $\frac{10}{5} = 2$

∴ The value of x is 10

33. (A) $2 - \frac{x}{3} = 4$

$-\frac{x}{3} = 4 - 2 \Rightarrow -\frac{x}{3} = 2 \Rightarrow -x = 2 \times 3$

$\Rightarrow x = -6$

34. (B) $2x + 3 = x - 4 \Rightarrow 2x - x = -4 - 3$

$\Rightarrow x = -7$

35. (A) $\dfrac{2x}{5} = \dfrac{10}{3}$

On cross multiplying we get

$6x = 50 \quad \therefore x = \dfrac{50}{6} = \dfrac{25}{3}$

36. (D) $9 - 7x = 5 - 3x$

$-7x + 3x = 5 - 9 \Rightarrow -4x = -4$

$x = \dfrac{-4}{-4} = 1$

37. (C) $\dfrac{x}{3} + \dfrac{x}{2} = 5 \Rightarrow \dfrac{2x + 3x}{6} = 5$

$2x + 3x = 5 \times 6 \Rightarrow 5x = 30$

$\Rightarrow x = \dfrac{30}{5} = 6$

38. (A) $4x = 15 - 3x \Rightarrow 4x + 3x = 15$

$7x = 15 \Rightarrow \therefore x = \dfrac{15}{7}$

39. (C) $\dfrac{50}{x} + 3 = 13 \Rightarrow \dfrac{50}{x} = 13 - 3$

$\Rightarrow \dfrac{50}{x} = 10$

$\Rightarrow 10x = 50 \Rightarrow x = \dfrac{50}{10} \Rightarrow x = 5$

40. (C) Let the two numbers be x and y.
Then, $x + y = 35$ -------(1)

$x - y = 13$ --------(2)

Adding equations (1) and (2) we get
$2x = 48 \Rightarrow x = 24$
Subtracting equation (2) from (1)
we get $2y = 22 \Rightarrow y = 11$

Hence the two numbers are 24 and 11

41. (B) Let the digit in the units place be x and the digit at the ten's place be y.

Then number = $10y + x$
The number obtained by reversing the order of the digits is $10x + y$
According to the given conditions, we have

$(10y + x) + (10x + y) = 121$

$\Rightarrow 11(x + y) = 121 \Rightarrow x + y = 11$

and $x - y = \pm 3$

($\because$ difference of digits is 3)
Thus, we have the following sets of simultaneous equations

$x + y = 11$ -------(1) $x - y = 3$ ------(2)

$x + y = 11$ -------(3) $x - y = -3$ ----(4)

on solving equations (1) & (2) we get
x = 7, y = 4 on solving equations (3) & (4) we get x = 4. y = 7
When x = 7, y = 4 we have number
$= 10y + x = 10 \times 4 + 7 = 47$
When x = 4, y = 7, we have number
$= 10y + x = 10 \times 7 + 4 = 74$
Hence the required number is either 47 or 74

42. (B) Suppose fathers age (in years) be x and that of sons be y. Then
$x + 2y = 70$ and $2x + y = 95$ and this system of equations may be written as $x + 2y - 70 = 0$

$2x + y - 95 = 0$

By cross multiplying we get

$$\frac{x}{2 \times -95 - (-70)} = \frac{-y}{1 \times -95 \times -2 \times -70}$$

$$\frac{1}{1 \times 1 - 2 \times 2}$$

$$\Rightarrow \frac{x}{-190 + 70} = \frac{-y}{-95 + 140} = \frac{1}{-3}$$

$$\Rightarrow \frac{x}{-120} = \frac{-y}{-45} \frac{1}{-3} \Rightarrow x = \frac{-120}{-3}$$

and $y = \dfrac{-45}{-3} = 15$

Hence father's age is 40 years and the son's age is 15 years

43. **(A)** Let the cost of a chair be Rs. x and that of a table be Rs. y. Then,

$4x + 3y = 2100$ and $5x + 2y = 1750$

This system of equations can be written as $4x + 3y - 2100 = 0$,

$5x + 2y - 1750 = 0$ By using cross multiplication, we have

$$\frac{x}{3 \times -1750 - 2 \times -2100}$$

$$= \frac{-y}{4 \times -1750 - 5 \times -2100}$$

$$= \frac{1}{4 \times 2 - 3 \times 5}$$

$$\Rightarrow \frac{x}{-5250 + 4200} = \frac{-y}{-7000 + 10500}$$

$$= \frac{1}{8 - 15}$$

$$\Rightarrow \frac{x}{-1050} = \frac{y}{-3500} = \frac{1}{-7}$$

$$\Rightarrow x = \frac{-1050}{-7} = 150 \quad \text{and}$$

$$y = \frac{-3500}{-7} = 500$$

Hence, cost of one chair = Rs. 150 and cost of one table = Rs. 500

44. **(B)** Let the fraction be $\dfrac{x}{y}$

Then according to the given conditions, we have $\dfrac{3x}{y-3} = \dfrac{18}{11}$

and $\dfrac{x+8}{2y} = \dfrac{2}{5}$ or

$11x = 6y - 18$ and $5x + 40 = 4y$

$\Rightarrow 11x - 6y + 18 = 0$ and

$5x - 4y + 40 = 0$

By cross multiplication, we have

$$\frac{x}{-6 \times 40 - (-4) \times 18} = \frac{-y}{11 \times 40 - 5 \times 18}$$

$$= \frac{1}{11 \times -4 - 5 \times -6} \Rightarrow \frac{x}{-240 + 72}$$

$$= \frac{-y}{440 + 30} = \frac{1}{-44 + 30} \Rightarrow \frac{x}{-168} = \frac{y}{-360}$$

$$= \frac{1}{-14} \Rightarrow x = \frac{-168}{-14} \text{ and } y = \frac{-350}{-14}$$

$\Rightarrow x = 12$ and $y = 25$,

Hence the fraction is $\dfrac{12}{25}$

45. **(C)** Let the digit in the units place be x and the digit in the ten's place by y. Then number = 10y +x

According to the given condition, we have $y = 3x$ ------(1)

Number obtained by reversing the digits = 10x + y

If the number is decreased by 54, the digits are reversed

∴ number - 54 = Number obtained by reversing the digits

$\Rightarrow 10y + x - 54 = 10x + y$

$\Rightarrow 9x - 9y = -54 \Rightarrow x - y = -6$ --(2)

Putting y = 3x in equation (2), we get

$x - 3x = -6 \Rightarrow x = 3$

Putting x = 3 in equation (1), we get y = 9

hence number

$= 10y + x = 10 \times 9 + 3 = 93$

Chapter 3

Understanding Quadrilaterals

Get It Right

Error in recognising interior and exterior angles of a quadrilateral.

e.g. find the value of 'y' in the following figure.

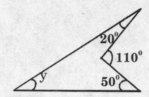

20^0

110^0

50^0

y

✗ Incorrect

✓ Correct

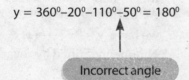

$y = 360^0 - 20^0 - 110^0 - 50^0 = 180^0$

Incorrect angle

$y = 360^0 - 20^0 - (360^0 - 110^0) - 50^0$

$= 360^0 - 20^0 - 250^0 - 50^0 = 40^0$

Synopsis

Quadrilateral

◆ A closed figure bounded by four line segments is called a quadrilateral.

Types of quadrilaterals

Parallelogram : In a parallelogram

◆ The opposite sides are equal,

◆ The opposite angles are equal,

◆ Each diagonal bisects the other.

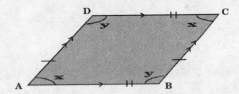

Rectangle:

♦ A parallelogram is a rectangle if each of its angles is a right angle. A rectangle obeys all the properties of a parallelogram.

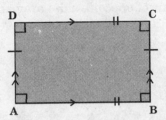

Square :

A rectangle having all its sides equal is called a square.

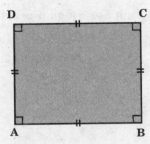

Rhombus :

A parallelogram having all sides equal is called a rhombus.

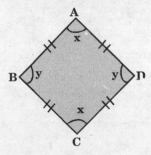

Kite :

Kite is a quadrilateral formed by two isosceles triangles standing on the opposite sides of a common base.

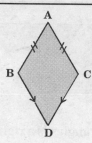

Trapezium :

A quadrilateral in which one pair of opposite sides are parallel is called a trapezium.

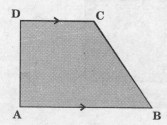

NOTE :

If the non-parallel sides of a trapezium are equal, it is called an isosceles trapezium.

S.No.	Property	Parallelogram	Rhombus	Rectangle	Square	Trapezium	Kite
1.	Diagonals bisect each other	yes	yes	yes	yes	Not always	yes
2.	Each diagonal bisects each pair of opposite angles	Not always	Not always	Not always	yes	Not always	Not always
3.	The diagonals form four congruent triangles	Not always	Not always	Not always	yes	Not always	Not always
4.	The diagonals are perpendicular to each other	Not always	yes	Not always	yes	Not always	yes
5.	The diagonals are equal	yes	Not always	yes	yes	Not always	Not always
6.	Diagonals are equal and right bisectors of each other	Not always	Not always	Not always	yes	Not always	Not always

Multiple Choice Questions

1. ABCD is a quadrilateral. If AC and BD bisect each other then ABCD must be :
   (A) square   (B) rectangle
   (C) parallelogram   (D) rhombus

2. ABCD is a parallelogram. The angle bisectors of $\angle A$ and $\angle D$ meet at O. The measure of $\angle AOD$ is:
   (A) 45^0
   (B) 90^0
   (C) dependent on the angles A and D
   (D) cannot be determined from given data

3. The diameter of circumcircle of a rectangle is 10 cm and breadth of the rectangle is 6 cm. Its length is:
   (A) 6 cm   (B) 5 cm
   (C) 8 cm   (D) none of these

4. ABCD is a quadrilateral. AB = BC = CD = DA and $\angle A = \angle B = \angle C = \angle D = 90^0$. Then ABCD can be called as:
   (A) rectangle
   (B) square
   (C) trapezium
   (D) None of these

5. The sum of the angles of a quadrilateral is:
   (A) 180^0
   (B) 360^0
   (C) 270^0
   (D) depends on the quadrilateral

6. RSTU is a parallelogram as shown in the figure below. Then the shown angles x and y are related as:

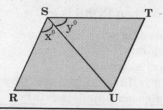

(A) x = y
(B) x < y
(C) x > y
(D) cannot be determined from given data

7. ABCD and MNOP are quadrilaterals as shown in the figure below. Then

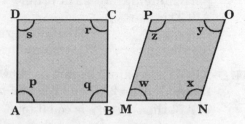

(A) p + q + r + s = w + x + y + z
(B) p + q + r + s < w + x + y + z
(C) p + q + r + s > w + x + y + z
(D) none of the foregoing

8. A parallelogram which has equal diagonals is a :
   (A) square   (B) rectangle
   (C) rhombus   (D) none

9. If ABCD is a parallelogram, then $\angle A - \angle C$ is :
   (A) 180^0 (B) 0^0 (C) 360^0 (D) 90^0

10. In a square ABCD, the diagonals bisect at "O". Then triangle AOB is :
    (A) an equilateral triangle.
    (B) an isosceles but not a right angled triangle.
    (C) a right angled but not an isosceles triangle.
    (D) an isosceles right angled triangle.

11. The perimeter of a parallelogram is 180 cm. One side exceeds another by 10 cm. The sides of the parallelogram are:
    (A) 40 cm, 50 cm
    (B) 45 cm each
    (C) 50 cm each
    (D) cannot be determined

12. One of the diagonals of a rhombus is equal to a side of the rhombus. The angles of the rhombus are:
(A) 60^0 and 80^0 (B) 60^0 and 120^0
(C) 120^0 and 240^0 (D) 100^0 and 120^0

13. In the quadrilateral ABCD, the diagonals AC and BD are equal and perpendicular to each other. Then ABCD is a:
(A) square   (B) parallelogram
(C) rhombus   (D) trapezium

14. ABCD is a parallelogram as shown in figure. If AB = 2AD and P is mid-point of AB, then $\angle$CPD is equal to:

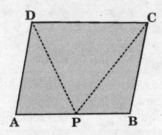

(A) 90^0 (B) 60^0 (C) 45^0 (D) 135^0

15. In a parallelogram ABCD, if AB = 2x+ 5, CD = y + 1, AD = y + 5 and BC = 3x – 4 then ratio of AB : BC is:

(A) 71 : 21 (B) 12 : 11 (C) 31 : 35 (D) 4 : 7

16. If ABCD is an isosceles trapezium, $\angle$C is equal to:
(A) $\angle$B   (B) $\angle$A   (C) $\angle$D   (D) 90^0

17. The diagonals of a parallelogram ABCD intersect at O. If $\angle$BOC = 90^0 and $\angle$BDC = 50^0, then $\angle$OAB is:
(A) 10^0 (B) 40^0 (C) 50^0 (D) 90^0

18. A diagonal of a rectangle is inclined to one side of the rectangle at 25^0. The acute angle between the diagonals is:
(A) 25^0 (B) 40^0 (C) 50^0 (D) 55^0

19. ABCD is a rhombus. If $\angle$ACB = 40^0, then $\angle$ADB is:
(A) 40^0 (B) 45^0 (C) 50^0 (D) 60^0

20. The quadrilateral formed by joining the mid-points of the sides of a quadrilateral PQRS, taken in order, is a rectangle if:
(A) PQRS is a rectangle
(B) PQRS is a parallelogram
(C) diagonals of PQRS are perpendicular
(D) diagonals of PQRS are equal

21. The quadrilateral formed by joining the mid-points of the sides of a quadrilateral PQRS, taken in order, is a rhombus if:
(A) PQRS is a rhombus
(B) PQRS is a parallelogram
(C) diagonals of PQRS are perpendicular
(D) diagonals of PQRS are equal

22. If angles P, Q, R and S of the quadrilateral PQRS, taken in order, are in the ratio 3 : 7 : 6 : 4 then PQRS is a:
(A) rhombus   (B) parallelogram
(C) trapezium   (D) kite

23. If PQ and RS are two perpendicular diameters of a circle, then PRQS is a:
(A) rectangle
(B) trapezium
(C) square
(D) rhombus but not square

24. If bisectors of $\angle$A and $\angle$B of a quadrilateral ABCD intersect each other at P, that of $\angle$B and $\angle$C at Q, that of $\angle$C and $\angle$D at R, and that of $\angle$D and $\angle$A at S, then PQRS is a:
(A) rectangle
(B) rhombus
(C) parallelogram
(D) quadrilateral whose opposite angles are supplementary

25. AB and CD are diameters. Then ACBD is :

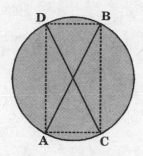

(A) square
(B) trapezium
(C) isosceles trapezium
(D) rectangle

26. ABCD is a square E, F, G, H are the mid-points of the four sides. Then the figure EFGH is:
(A) square   (B) rectangle
(C) trapezium   (D) parallelogram

27. If a quadrilateral has two adjacent sides equal and the other two sides equal, then it is called:
(A) parallelogram   (B) square
(C) rectangle   (D) kite

28. Choose the correct statement.

(A) The diagonals of a parallelogram are equal.

(B) The diagonals of a rectangle are perpendicular to each other.

(C) If the diagonals of a quadrilateral intersect at right angles, it is not necessarily a rhombus.

(D) Every quadrilateral is either a trapezium or a parallelogram or a kite.

29. If two adjacent angles of a parallelogram are in the ratio 3 : 2, then the measure of the angles are :
(A) $108^0, 72^0$ (B) $72^0, 36^0$
(C) $100^0, 80^0$ (D) $144^0, 36^0$

30. ABC and DEF are straight lines. Find the value of x

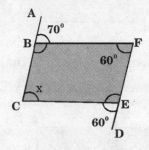

(A) 60^0 (B) 70^0 (C) 80^0 (D) 85^0

31. In the given diagram, find the value of x.

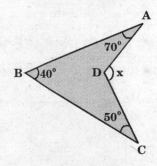

(A) 60^0 (B) 80^0 (C) 160^0 (D) 180^0

32. The area of the trapezium shown is:

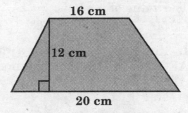

(A) $206 \, cm^2$ (B) $216 \, cm^2$
(C) $200 \, cm^2$ (D) $224 \, cm^2$

33. Given that the area of parallelogram ABCD is $50\,cm^2$. Then the length of AD in the diagram is:

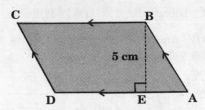

(A) 10 cm (B) 20 cm (C) 15 cm (D) 25 cm

34. The area of shaded region is:

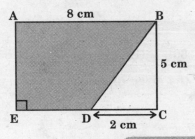

(A) $25\,cm^2$ (B) $35\,cm^2$

(C) $45\,cm^2$ (D) None of these

35. The diagram, ABCD is a parallelogram and ADE is a straight line. Given that the area of the triangle CDE is $10\,cm^2$, then the area of the whole diagram in cm^2 is:

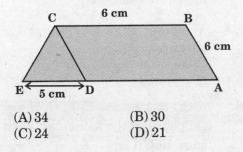

(A) 34   (B) 30
(C) 24   (D) 21

Previous Contest Questions

1. In the diagram, ABCD is a rhombus.

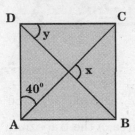

The value of $x - y$ is:
(A) 50^0 (B) 40^0 (C) 30^0 (D) 20^0

2. In the diagam, ABCD is a rhombus. AEC and BED are straight lines.

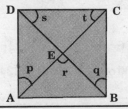

$p + q + r + s + t = ?$
(A) 200^0 (B) 270^0 (C) 360^0 (D) 540^0

3. The measures of the angles of a quadrilateral ABCD are respectively in the ratio $1 : 2 : 3 : 4$. Then which of the following is true.
(A) AC = BC   (B) AB || DC
(C) AD ||BC   (D) None of these

4. In a trapezium ABCD, AB is parallel to CD and the diagonals intersect each other at O. In this case, the ratio OA/OC is equal to:

(A) $\dfrac{OB}{OD}$ (B) $\dfrac{BC}{CD}$ (C) $\dfrac{AD}{AB}$ (D) $\dfrac{AC}{BD}$

5. In a $\triangle ABC$, P and Q are the midpoints of AB and AC, PQ is produced to R such that PQ = QR, then PRCB is:
(A) Rectangle   (B) Square
(C) Rhombus   (D) Parallelogram

6. If the lengths of two diagonal of a rhombus are 12 cm and 16 cm, then the length of each side of the rhombus are:
    (A) 10 cm
    (B) 14 cm
    (C) Can not determined
    (D) None of these

7. One side of a rectangular field is 4 metres and its diagonal is 5 metres. The area of the field is _____.
    (A) $12\,m^2$

    (B) $15\,m^2$

    (C) $20\,m^2$

    (D) $4\sqrt{5}\,m^2$

8. The diagonal of rectangle is thrice its smaller side. The ratio of its sides is___.
    (A) $\sqrt{2}:1$ (B) $2\sqrt{2}:1$
    (C) $3:2$ (D) $\sqrt{3}:1$

9. The following figure shows a polygon with all its exterior angles.

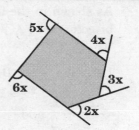

The value of x is:
(A) 10^0 (B) 18^0 (C) 20^0 (D) 36^0

10. In the figure given below, PTU is a straight line.

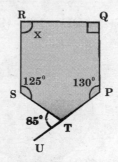

What is the value of x ?
(A) 100^0 (B) 110^0 (C) 120^0 (D) 130^0

Explanatory Answers

1. (C) Since, diagonals of a parallelogram bisect each other, ABCD must be a parallelogram.
        Also square, rhombus and rectangle are types of parallelogram.

2. (B)

As shown in the figure the angle bisectors of $\angle A$ and $\angle D$ meet at "O".

Let $\angle A = x^0$; $\angle D = (180 - x)^0$

$\therefore \dfrac{\angle A}{2} = \dfrac{x}{2}$ and

$\dfrac{\angle D}{2} = \dfrac{180 - x}{2} = 90 - \dfrac{x}{2}$.

$\angle AOD = 180 - \left(\dfrac{x}{2} + 90 - \dfrac{x}{2}\right)$

or $\angle AOD = 180 - (90) = 90^0$

3.   (C)

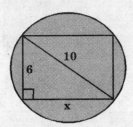

As shown in the diagram, we have a right angled triangle. Let the length of rectangle be x. Then $x^2 + 6^2 = 10^2$ or x = 8 cm

5.   (B)

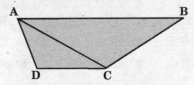

Let us divide a quadrilateral ABCD into two triangles as shown in figure below. Sum of the angles of a triangle is 180^0. Hence the sum of angles in both triangles = 360^0. Hence sum of angles in a quadrilateral is 360^0.

6.   (D)   As seen in the diagram given, triangle RSU and triangle STU are congruent. But x and y are not corresponding angles.

7.   (A)   The sum of the angles of a quadrilateral is 360^0.

8.   (B)   A square and a rectangle are both parallelograms which have equal diagonals. However (B) is the more appropriate choice since all squares are also rectangles.

9.   (B)   We know that opposite angles of a parallelogram are equal. Hence $\angle A - \angle C = 0$

10.   (D)   Since diagonals of a square are equal and bisect at right angles, triangle AOB is an isosceles right angled triangle.

11.   (A)   Let one side be x cm. Then adjacent side is (x + 10) cm

$\therefore$ x + (x + 10) + x + (x + 10) =180

$\Rightarrow$ 4x + 20 = 180 or x = 40 cm

$\therefore$ x + 10 = 50 cm

12.   (B)

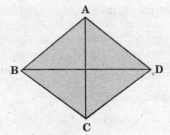

As shown in figure, let BD = AB = AD. Then ABD is an equilateral triangle and all its angles = 60^0.

$\therefore \angle A = 60^0$. Also $\angle C = 60^0$.

But $\angle B = \angle D$ and

$\angle A + \angle B + \angle C + \angle D = 360^0$

$\therefore \angle B = \angle D = 120^0$.

14.   (A)   As shown in the figure, since P is the midpoint of AB and AB = 2AD. We have AB = 2AP = 2AD

or AP = AD

i.e., triangle ADP is isosceles triangle. $\angle ADP = x$ and $\angle APD = x$ then,

$\angle A = 180 - 2x$

By some argument, since

$\angle B = 2x$,

$\angle CPB = \angle PCB = 90 - x$

Since $\angle APB = 180^0$,

$\angle CPD = 90^0$

15. (C) We know that in a parallelogram opposite sides are equal.

$\therefore$ AB = CD or $2x + 5 = y + 1$
and $y + 5 = 3x - 4$
$2x - y = -4$ ....(i)
$y - 3x = -9$ .....(ii)
Adding, $-x = -13$ or $x = 13$ and $y = 30$
Substituting we have,
AB = 31 cm and BC = 35 cm

16. (C)

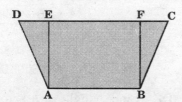

From definition, we know that in an isosceles trapezium the non-parallel sides are equal or AD = BC in the figure. Drop perpendiculars AE and BF to CD. Triangles ADE and BFC are congruent by RHS congruency. Hence $\angle D = \angle C$.

17. (B)

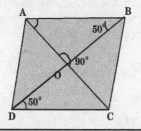

Since alternate angles are equal, we have $\angle DBA = 50^0$. Also or $\angle AOB = 90^0$.

$\therefore$ In triangle OAB, since sum of angles is 180^0, we have $\angle OAB = 40^0$

18. (C)

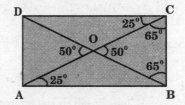

Since $\angle CAB = 25^0$, clearly $\angle OCB = 65^0$. Let diagonals meet at "O". Triangle OCB is an isosceles triangle.

$\therefore \angle OBC = 65^0$

$\therefore \angle BOC = 50^0$.

19. (C) We know that diagonals of a rhombus bisect each other at right angles. Also AB = BC.

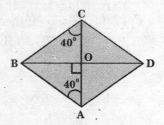

$\therefore$ ABC is an isosceles triangle. Hence $\angle BAC = 40^0$. Let diagonals meet at "O". Then $\angle AOB = 90^0$. $\angle ABO = 50^0$.

But AB = AD and hence ABD is an isosceles triangle.

$\angle ADB = 50^0$

20. (C) We know that the line joining midpoints of two sides of a

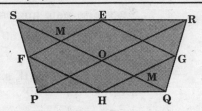

triangle is half the third side and parallel to third side.

$$\therefore \; EF = \frac{1}{2}PR \;\; \text{and} \;\; HF = \frac{1}{2}QS$$

or EF = HG also HF = EG.

Clearly EFHG is a parallelogram.

If it is to be a rectangle, the diagonals should cut at right angles

$$\therefore \;\; \angle ROQ = 90^0 \Rightarrow \angle EMO = 90^0$$

$$\Rightarrow \angle MEG = 90^0 \text{ and}$$

$$\angle E = \angle F = \angle G = \angle H = 90^0.$$

$$\Rightarrow PR \perp QS$$

21. (D) We know from problem 20 (Refer solution 20) that PQRS is a parallelogram. If diagonals of PQRS are equal then

EF = EG = HG = FH or EFGH is a rhombus.

22. (C) Let the angles be 3x, 7x ,6x and 4x.

$$\therefore \; 3x + 7x + 6x + 4x = 360^0 \text{ or}$$

$20x = 360^0$ or $x = 18^0$. The angles are $54^0, 126^0, 108^0, 72^0$. We see that adjacent angles are supplementary but opposite angles are not equal. Clearly, it is a trapezium.

23. (C) Let the diagonals meet at "O" as shown in figure.

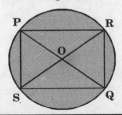

∠POS = ∠ROQ = 90⁰

$\angle POS = \angle ROQ = 90^0$

Also PO = OQ = OS = OR, i.e., the diagonals are equal and bisect at right angles. Clearly, PRQS is a square.

24. (D)

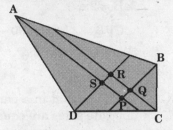

As shown in above figure,

$$\angle S = 180 - \left(\frac{\angle A}{2} + \frac{\angle D}{2} \right) \text{ and}$$

$$\angle Q = 180 - \left(\frac{\angle B}{2} + \frac{\angle C}{2} \right). \text{ Clearly}$$

Clearly, $\angle S + \angle Q$

$$= 360 - \frac{(\angle A + \angle B + \angle C + \angle D)}{2}$$

$$= 360 - \frac{360}{2} = 360^0 - 180^0 = 180^0$$

25. (D) Since, angle in a semicircle is a right angle. Clearly

$$\angle A = \angle C = \angle B = \angle D = 90^0$$

The diagonals (diametres) are equal but they are not intersecting (bisecting) at right angles. Hence, it is not a square and can be only a rectangle.

26. (A) We know that the line joining the midpoints of two sides of a triangle is half the third side and parallel to third side.

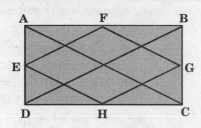

∴ In triangle ADB, EF = $\frac{1}{2}$ DB

Also, EH = $\frac{1}{2}$ AC

But DB = AC. ∴ EF = EH

Also, EF = HG = FG = EH

Also, since AEF and BFG are isosceles triangles.

∠AEF = ∠AEF $- 45^0$

= ∠BFG = ∠FGB

But ∠AFB = 180^0 or

∠EFG = 90^0 similarly,

∠H = ∠G = ∠E = ∠F = 90^0

Hence, EFGH is a square.

28. (C)   If the diagonals of a quadrilateral intersect at right angles, it is not necessarily a rhombus.

29. (A)   Let the angles be 3x and 2x.

We have,

3x + 2x = 180^0

5x = 180^0

x = 36^0

∴ The angles are 36 × 3, 36 × 2

= $108^0, 72^0$.

30. (B)   In the given figure

∠ABF + ∠FBC = 180^0

70° + ∠FBC = 180^0

⇒ ∠FBC = $180^0 - 70^0 = 110^0$

Now, ∠DEC + ∠CEF = 180^0

60° + ∠CEF = 180^0

∠CEF = $180^0 - 60^0 = 120^0$

Now, ∠FBC + ∠BCE + ∠CEF

                          +∠BFE = 360^0

110^0 + x + 120^0 + 60^0 = 360^0

290^0 + x = 360^0 ⇒ x = 70^0

31. (C)   In quadrilateral ABCD,

∠ABC + ∠BCD + ∠CDA +∠DAB

                          = 360°

(Sum of angles of a quadrilateral)

40^0 + 50^0 + ∠CDA + 70^0 = 360°

⇒ ∠CDA + 160° = 360°

⇒ ∠CDA = $360^\circ - 160^\circ = 200^\circ$

Now, ∠CDA + ∠ADC = 360°

(∵ Angle at a point)

200° + x = 360° ⇒ x = $360^\circ - 200^\circ$

x = 160^0

32. (B)   Area of trapezium = $\frac{1}{2}(a+b) \times h$

= $\frac{1}{2}(16+20) \times 12$

= 36 × 6

= 216 cm^2

33. (A)   Area = AD × BE

50 = AD × 5

∴ AD = 10 cm

34. (B) Area of shaded region = Area of trapezium ABDE

$$= \frac{1}{2} \times (8+6) \times 5 = \frac{1}{2} \times 14 \times 5$$

$$= 35\, cm^2$$

35. (A) Area of $\triangle$CDE = 10 cm^2

$$= \frac{1}{2} \times 5 \times h = 10 \Rightarrow h = \frac{10 \times 2}{5}$$

h = 4 cm

∴ Total area of the whole diagram = Area of trapezium ABCE

$$= \frac{1}{2} \times (6+11) \times 4 = 34\, cm^2$$

Previous Contest Questions

1. (B)

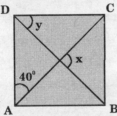

x = 90^0
(∵ diagonals of rhombus bisect each other at right angles.)
Now, in $\triangle$ADC, AD = DC (sides of rhombus)
∴ ∠DAC = ∠ACD = 40^0
(∵ equal sides have equal angles opposite to them)
Now in $\triangle$OCD,
y = $180^0 - (90^0 + 40^0)$
$= 180^0 - 130^0 = 50^0$
∴ x − y = $90^0 - 50^0 = 40^0$

2. (B) In rhombus ABCD,
∠A + ∠B + ∠C + ∠D = $360°$
$$\Rightarrow \frac{\angle A}{2} + \frac{\angle B}{2} + \frac{\angle C}{2} + \frac{\angle D}{2} = \frac{360°}{2}$$
p + q + s + t = 180 ---------(1)

(∵ diagonals of rhombus are angle bisectors)
Now ∠r = 90^0 --------------------(2)
(∵ diagonals of rhombus bisect the diagonals at right angles)
Adding (1) and (2), we get
p + q + r + s + t = $180^0 + 90^0$
∴ p + q + r + s + t = 270^0

3. (B)

∵ ∠A, ∠B, ∠C and ∠D are in the ratio 1 : 2 : 3 : 4, So ∠A = 36^0,
∠B = 72^0, ∠C = 108^0, ∠D = 144^0
$\Rightarrow$ ∠A + ∠D = 180^0 and
∠B + ∠C = 180^0 $\Rightarrow$ AB || DC

4. (A) In $\triangle$OAB and $\triangle$OCD ;
∠AOB = ∠COD
(vertically opposite angle)
∠ABD = ∠BDC and
∠BAC = ∠ACD
$\triangle$OAB ≅ $\triangle$OCD
$\Rightarrow$ OA/OC = OB/OD = AB/CD

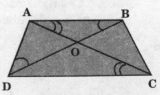

5. (D) ∵ P and Q are mid points of AB and AC then, PQ = $\frac{1}{2}$BC and PQ||BC

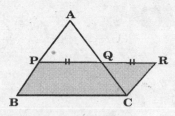

So, BC = 2PQ = PR

Hence, PRCB is a parallelogram.

6. (A) We have,
Sum of squares of diagonals of rhombus = sum of squares of its sides

Let each side of rhombus be a.

$\Rightarrow 4a^2 = d_1^2 + d_1^2$

$\Rightarrow 4a^2 = (12)^2 + (16)^2$

$\qquad = 144 + 256 = 400$

$\Rightarrow a^2 = \dfrac{400}{4} = 100$ or

$a = \sqrt{100} = 10cm$

7. (A) Let the other side of rectangle be x m.
∵ the sides of rectangle are perpendicular

$\therefore 4^2 + x^2 = 5^2$ (By pythogoras theorem)

$16 + x^2 = 25 \Rightarrow x^2 = 25 - 16 = 9$

$\therefore x = \sqrt{9} = 3$ m

$\therefore$ Area of rectangle = $3 \times 4 = 12m^2$

8. (B)

Let the smaller side of rectangle be x.

Let the length be l.

$\therefore$ Diagonal = 3x

Now, since the sides of rectangle are perpendicular,

$(3x)^2 = l^2 + x^2$

$\qquad$ (By pythogoras theorm)

or

$l^2 = 9x^2 - x^2 = 8x^2$

$l = 2\sqrt{2}x$,

$\therefore$ ratio of sides = $2\sqrt{2}x / x = 2\sqrt{2} : 1$

9. (B) The sum of all exterior angles of a polygon = $360°$

$\therefore 2x + 3x + 4x + 5x + 6x = 360^0$

$20x = 360^0$

$x = \dfrac{360^0}{20} = 18^0$

10. (A) $\angle STP = 180^0 - 85^0 = 95^0$

We have, sum of all interior angles of " n" sided polygon

$= (n-2) \times 180^0$

$= (5-2) \times 180^0$

$= 3 \times 180^0 = 540^0$

$\Rightarrow x + 90^0 + 125^0 + 130^0 + 95^0$

$\qquad\qquad\qquad = 540^0$

$\Rightarrow x + 440^0 = 540^0$

$\Rightarrow x = 540^0 - 440^0 = 100^0$

✧ ✧ ✧

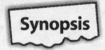 4 Practical Geometry

Get It Right

Error in applying properties of quadrilaterals.

e.g. Can you construct a quadrilateral PQRS with the given measurements?

PQ = 7 cm, $\angle P = 100°$, $\angle Q = 125°$, $\angle R = 100°$, and $\angle S = 75°$

 Incorrect

 **Correct**

Yes, we can construct a quadrilateral with the above given constructions.

No, it is not possible to construct a quadrilateral with given measurements as here,

sum of angles $\neq 360°$

$\because 100° + 125° + 100° + 75°$

$= 400° \neq 360°$

Synopsis

Quadrilateral:

The figure formed by four line segments is called a quadrilateral.

- A quadrilateral has four sides, four angles and two diagonals.

Convex Polygon:

A quadrilateral in which the measure of each angle is less than $180°$ is known as a convex quadrilateral.

Concave Polygon:

A quadrilateral in which one of the angles measures more than $180°$ is known as a concave quadrilateral.

- The sum of all angles in a quadrilateral is $360°$.

- To construct a quadrilateral, we need five measurements.

Multiple Choice Questions

1. If one of the angle measures more than 180^0 in a quadrilateral, then that is known as:
    (A) a parallelogram
    (B) a concave quadrilateral
    (C) a convex quadrilateral
    (D) a trapezium

2. A quadrilateral which has exactly one pair of parallel sides is called:
    (A) a parallelogram (B) a rectangle
    (C) a trapezium   (D) a kite

3. Which of the following statements is true?

    (A) The diagonals of a rectangle are perpendicular
    (B) The diagonals of a rhombus are equal
    (C) Every square is a rhombus
    (D) None of these

4. The number of measurements required to construct a quadrilateral is:
    (A) 5   (B) 4
    (C) 3   (D) 2

5. To construct a parallelogram, the minimum number of measurements required is:
    (A) 2   (B) 3   (C) 4   (D) 1

6. The minimum number of dimensions needed to construct a rectangle is:
    (A) 1   (B) 2   (C) 3   (D) 4

7. The minimum number of measu-rements needed to construct a square is:
    (A) 1   (B) 2   (C) 3   (D) 4

8. In a quadrilateral PQRS, if $\angle P = \angle R = 100^0$ and $\angle S = 75^0$, then $\angle Q = $ _____ .
    (A) 50^0 (B) 85^0 (C) 120^0 (D) 360^0

9. The sum of the angles in a quadrilateral is equal to _____ .
    (A) 2 right angles   (B) 3 right angles
    (C) 4 right angles   (D) 360 right angles

10. If the lengths of two diagonals of a rhombus are 12 cm and 16 cm, then the length of each side of the rhombus is:
    (A) 10 cm
    (B) 14 cm
    (C) cannot be determined
    (D) none of these

Previous Contest Questions

1. The diagram shows the construction of a parallelogram KLMN. The width of the compasses for step I and step II are the same. $\angle KLM = $ _____ .

    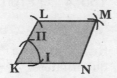

    (A) 45^0 (B) 60^0 (C) 120^0 (D) 135^0

2. In the diagram, KLMN is a constructed parallelogram. The value of $\angle KLM$ is:

    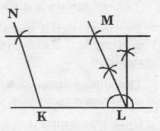

    (A) 15^0 (B) 30^0 (C) 45^0 (D) 60^0

3.   The diagram shows the construction of:

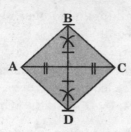

(A) a trapezium   (B) a rhombus
(C) a rectangle   (D) a kite

4.   To construct a parallelogram, the minimum number of measurements required is _____.
(A) 5   (B) 3   (C) 2   (D) 1

5.   Two adjacent angles of a parallelogram are in the ratio 1 : 2. The angles are:
(A) 20^0 and 40^0 (B) 30^0 and 60^0
(C) 60^0 and 120^0 (D) None of these

6.   In a trapezium ABCD, AB||CD. If $\angle A = 60^0$ then $\angle D = ?$
(A) 110^0 (B) 120^0 (C) 70^0 (D) 300^0

7.   Two adjacent sides of a parallelogram are 6 cm and 8 cm. Its perimeter is:
(A) 28 cm   (B) 26 cm
(C) 14 cm   (D) None of these

8.   In a parallelogram ABCD, diagonals AC and BD intersect at O. If AO = 6 cm then AC = _____.
(A) 5 cm (B) 10 cm (C) 12 cm (D) 14 cm

9.   In a parallelogram, the sum of adjacent angles is:
(A) 90^0 (B) 180^0 (C) 270^0 (D) 360^0

10.   In a parallelogram, if $\angle A = 65^0$, then $\angle B$, $\angle C$ and $\angle D$ are respectively:
(A) $115^0, 65^0, 115^0$ (B) $112^0, 65^0, 112^0$
(C) $110^0, 60^0, 110^0$ (D) None of these

⊘ Answers ⊘

Multiple Choice Questions

1. B	2. C	3. C	4. A	5. B	6. B	7. A	8. B	9. C	10. A

Previous Contest Questions

1. C	2. C	3. B	4. B	5. C	6. B	7. A	8. C	9. B	10. A

Explanatory Answers

2.   (C)   ∵ Trapezium is having exactly one pair of parallel sides.

3.   (C)   ∵ Every square is a rhombus.

5.   (B)   To construct a parallelogram minimum 3 measurements are required.

6.   (B)   Two dimensions are sufficient to construct a rectangle.

7.   (A)   Only 1 measurement is sufficient to construct a square.

8.   (B)   We have,

$$\angle P + \angle Q + \angle R + \angle S = 360^0$$

$$100^0 + \angle Q + 100^0 + 75^0 = 360^0$$

$$\angle Q = 360^0 - 275^0 = 85^0$$

9.   (C)   Sum of the angles in a quadrilateral $= 360^0$

$$= 4 \times 90^0$$

$$= 4 \text{ right angles}$$

10. (A)   Length of the each side of a rhombus

$$= \sqrt{\left(\frac{d_1}{2}\right)^2 + \left(\frac{d_2}{2}\right)^2}$$

$$= \sqrt{\left(\frac{12}{2}\right)^2 + \left(\frac{16}{2}\right)^2}$$

$$= \sqrt{6^2 + 8^2}$$

$$= \sqrt{100}$$

$$= 10 \text{ cm}$$

Previous Contest Questions

5. (C)   The sum of adjacent angles $= 180^0$

The angles are:

$$180^\circ \times \frac{1}{3} = 60^0 \text{ and}$$

$$180^\circ \times \frac{2}{3} = 120^0$$

6. (B) $\because$ AB || CD, we have

$\angle A + \angle D = 180^0$ ($\because$ angles at the same side of transversal)

$\Rightarrow \angle D = 180^0 - 60^0 = 120^0$

7. (A) $\because$ Opposite sides of a parallelogram are equal. So, perimeter

$$= 6 + 8 + 6 + 8 = 28 \text{ cm}.$$

8. (C) $\because$ Diagonals of parallelogram bisect each other. we have

$$AC = 2 \times AO = 2 \times 6 = 12 \text{ cm}.$$

9. (B)   The sum of adjacent angles of parallelogram = 180^0.

10. (A) $\because$ In a parallelogram, opposite angles are equal. So,

$$\angle A = \angle C = 65^0$$

Also $\angle B = \angle D$ we have

$$\angle A + \angle B + \angle C + \angle D = 360^0$$

$$\Rightarrow 65^0 + \angle B + 65^0 + \angle B = 360^0$$

$$\Rightarrow 2\angle B = 360^0 - 130^0$$

$$\Rightarrow 2\angle B = 230^0$$

$$\Rightarrow \angle B = \frac{230^0}{2} = 115^0$$

$$\therefore \quad \angle B = \angle D = 115^0$$

Chapter 5 Data Handling

Error in reading the data.

e.g. The double bar graph shows the number of pineapples and durians sold at two fruit stalls, M and K.

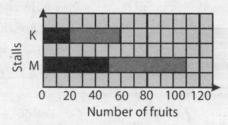

Pineapples ▮ Durians

What is the difference in the number of durians sold between stalls M and K ?

✗ Incorrect

Difference in the number of durians sold
= 110 − 60 = 50

↑

These are total fruits sold, not only durians

✓ Correct

Difference in the number of durians sold
= (110 − 50) − (60 − 20) = 20

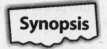
Synopsis

Collection and tabulation of data

Data:

The word data means information in the form of numerical figures or a set of given information.

Raw Data:

Data obtained in the original form is called a raw data.

Array:

Arranging the numerical figures of a data in ascending or descending order is called an array.

Tabulation:

Arranging the data in a systematic tabular form is called tabulation or presentation of the data.

Observation:

Each numerical figure in a data is called an observation.

Frequency:

The number of times a particular observation occurs is called its frequency.

Range:

The difference between the highest and lowest values of the observations in a given data is called its range.

Frequency Distribution:

A table showing the frequencies of various observations of data is called a frequency distribution or simply a frequency table.

Tally marks:

♦ When the number of observations is large, we make use of tally marks to find the frequencies.

♦ Tallies are usually marked in a bunch of five for the case of counting.

Grouped Data:

♦ When the list of observations is long, the data is usually organised into groups called class intervals and the data so obtained is called a grouped data.

♦ The lower value of a class interval is called its lower limit and the upper value is called its upper limit.

- The difference between the upper and lower class limits is called the width or the size of the class interval.

- The mid-value of a class interval is called its class mark.

Graphical representation

- A histogram is a pictorial representation of the grouped data in which class intervals are taken along the horizontal axis and class frequencies along the vertical axis and for each class a rectangle is constructed with base as the class interval and height determined from the class frequency.

- In a bar graph, bars of uniform width are drawn with various heights. The height of a column represents the frequency of the corresponding observation.

- In a pie-chart the values of different components are represented by the sectors of a circle. The total angle of 360^0 at the centre of a circle is divided according to the values of the components.

    Central angle for a component

    $$= \frac{\text{value of the component}}{\text{total value}} \times 360^0$$

Pie chart:

Pie Chart represents data in relative quantities by using the areas of sectors in a circle.

- In pie chart , quantities of data are related to the size of angles of sectors.

- The formula to find the size of the angle of a sector is:

    $$\text{Angle of sector} = \frac{\text{Quantity represented by the sector}}{\text{Total quantity}} \times 360^0$$

Experiment:

An experiment is a situation involving chance or probability that leads to results called outcomes.

Outcome:

An outcome is the result of a single trial of an experiment.

Event:

An event is one or more outcomes of an experiment.

Probability:

Probability is the measure of how likely an event is.

- The probability of event A is the number of ways A can occur divided by the total number of possible outcomes.

♦ $P(A) = \dfrac{\text{The number of ways event 'A' can occur}}{\text{The total number of possible outcomes}}$

Random Experiment:

A random experiment is one whose outcomes have an equal chance of occuring.

Equally Likely Outcomes:

The outcomes of an event with same probability to occur are known as equally likely outcomes.

Multiple Choice Questions

1. From the frequency table, the percentage of families with less than 3 children is $\dfrac{x}{40} \times 100$. Find the value of 'x'

Number of children	0	1	2	3	4
Number of families	2	5	11	15	7

   (A) 7   (B) 15   (C) 11   (D) 18

2. A group of 20 participants entered a quiz competition. Their scores are given in the table below. Calculate the percentage of the participants who scored more than 2 points.

Score	0	1	2	3	4
Number of participants	3	5	7	4	1

   (A) 5%   (B) 15%   (C) 25%   (D) 60%

3. A survey was carried out for the purpose of determining the number of children in each family. The results are shown in the table below. Calculate the percentage of families which have more than 2 children.

Number of children	0	1	2	3	4
Frequency	1	4	7	6	2

   (A) 35%   (B) 40%   (C) 60%   (D) 75%

4. The scores obtained by a group of participants in a game are shown in the table. A participant who scores more than 3 points receives a hamper. If the number of participants who do not receive hampers is twice the number of those who do, find the value of y.

Score	2	3	4	5
Number of participants	104	16	y	34

   (A) 2   (B) 26   (C) 32   (D) 68

5. The frequency table shows the marks obtained by a group of students in a monthly test. Calculate the percentage of students who failed the test if 40 is the passing mark.

Marks	Number of students
0-19	5
20-29	7
40-59	14
60-79	11
80-99	3

   (A) 3%   (B) 12%   (C) 15%   (D) 30%

6. The table shows the distribution of marks in an English test. Grade B is given to marks ranging from 40 to 54. Calculate the percentage of pupils who obtained a grade B.

Marks	Frequency
30-34	2
35-39	8
40-44	13
45-49	8
50-54	5
55-59	4

(A) 26%   (B) 52%   (C) 65%   (D) 75%

7. The table shows the number of handphones sold by Ramesh over a period of 3 days. Given that he sold 150 more handphones on Tuesday than on Wednesday, which of the following pictograms represents the sales over the 3 days ?

Day	Number of hand phones
Monday	200
Tuesday	
Wednesday	150

(A)
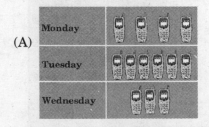

Key: 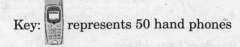 represents 50 hand phones

(B)

Key: represents 50 hand phones

(C)
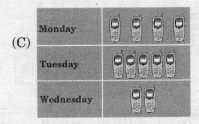

Key: represents 50 hand phones

(D)
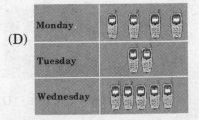

Key: represents 50 hand phones

8. The table shows the type and number of cakes sold by a bakery. In a pictograph, one symbol ◺ represents

5 cakes. How many symbols are required to represent the number of the best-selling type of cake?

Types of cakes	Number of cakes
P	50
Q	35
R	45

(A) 5   (B) 9   (C) 10   (D) 15

9. The pictogram shows the number of pupils who cycle to school. What is the total number of pupils who cycle to school?

Key: represents 30 pupils.

(A) 15   (B) 300   (C) 420   (D) 450

10. The pictogram shows the number of visitors to an exhibition in a particular week. The number of visitors recorded after Wednesday is:

Monday	😊😊😊😊😊
Tuesday	😊😊
Wednesday	😊😊😊
Thursday	😊😊😊😊😊😊
Friday	😊😊😊😊

Key: 😊 represents 6 visitors.

(A) 10   (B) 18   (C) 60   (D) 70

11. The pictogram shows the number of calculators sold by a shop over three days. A total of Rs. 600 was collected from the sale of calculators on Monday. Which of the following statements is correct?

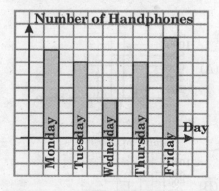

Key: △ represents 5 calculators

(A) The price of each calculator is Rs. 50

(B) The total sales made over the 3 days amounted to Rs. 1800

(C) 60 calculators were sold on Tuesday.

(D) The difference between the sales on Tuesday and Wednesday is Rs. 200

12. The bar chart shows the number of handphones sold by a shop in 5 days of a certain week. The difference between the highest number and the lowest number of handphones sold is 15. Find the number of handphones sold on Thursday.

Number of Handphones

(A) 6   (B) 12   (C) 18   (D) 24

13. The bar chart shows the number of television sets sold by a shop in 5 months. The sales in May, as a percentage of the total sales in the 5 months is:

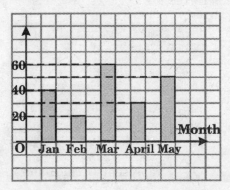

(A) 25%

(B) $33\frac{1}{3}\%$

(C) 50%

(D) $66\frac{2}{3}\%$

14. P, Q and R are three shops selling computers. The sales made by shop P is $\frac{2}{3}$ of the sales made by shop R. The volume of sales by shop Q is twice the volume made by shop P. Shop R sold 600 computers. Which of the following bar charts correctly represent the sales of computers by shops, P, Q and R ?

(A)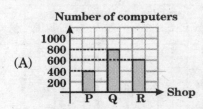

(B)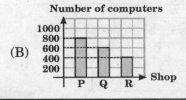

(C)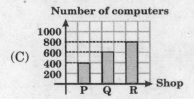

(D)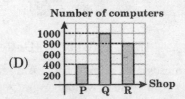

15. The pie chart shows four different modes of transport to school for a group of students. Calculate the percentage of students who go to school by bus.

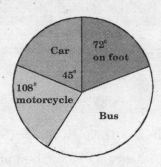

(A) 13.5%   (B) 34.7%
(C) 37.5%   (D) 40.3%

16. The table shows the frequency distribution of grades obtained by 120 students. The data is represented in the following pie chart. Which sector is incorrectly labelled ?

Grade	A	B	C	D
Frequency	20	50	45	5

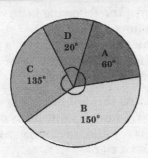

(A) A   (B) B   (C) C   (D) D

17. The table shows the number of cups of four different beverages sold by a coffee shop in a certain day. The angle of sector in a pie chart representing tea is:

Beverage	Number of cups
Coffee	60
Tea	75
Hot chocolate	25
Milk	40

(A) 40⁰   (B) 72⁰   (C) 108⁰   (D) 135⁰

18. The pie chart shows the examination grades obtained by a group of students. Which of the following statements about the pie chart is true ?

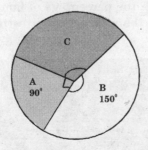

(A) 15% of the students scored grade B
(B) 90% of the students scored grade A

(C) $\frac{1}{4}$ of the students scored grade B

(D) $\frac{1}{3}$ of the students scored grade C

19. The pie chart shows the number of participants from four countries P, Q, R and S taking part in a tennis tournament. Given that there are 18 participants from country S, find the number of participants from country R.

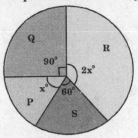

(A) 18   (B) 21   (C) 27   (D) 42

20. The table shows the number of three different brands of laptops sold by a certain store. The data are respresented by the pie chart which shows a semicircle divided into six equal sectors. The angle of sector representing the number of Bell laptops sold is:

Brand	Number of laptops
Ace	60
Bell	40
Compact	20

(A) ∠POR   (B) ∠ROV
(C) ∠QOT   (D) ∠POU

21. The pie chart shows the distribution of grades obtained by a group of students in a test. The number of students who scored grade C is twice the number who

scored grade B, and $\frac{3}{5}$ of the students scored grades B and C. Find the angle of sector which represents grade C.

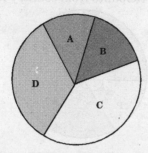

(A) 108⁰

(B) 144⁰

(C) 216⁰

(D) 288⁰

22. Which of the following is an experiment?
(A) Tossing a coin
(B) Rolling a single 6-sided die.
(C) Choosing a marble from a jar.
(D) All of the above

23. Which of the following is an outcome?
(A) Rolling a pair of dice
(B) Landing on red
(C) Choosing 2 marbles from a jar.
(D) None of the above.

24. Which of the following experiments does NOT have equally likely outcomes?
(A) Choose a number at random from 1 to 7
(B) Toss a coin.
(C) Choose a letter at random from the word SCHOOL.
(D) None of the above

25. What is the probability of choosing a vowel from the alphabet?
(A) $\frac{21}{26}$　　　　(B) $\frac{5}{26}$

(C) $\frac{1}{21}$　　　　(D) None of these

26. A number from 1 to 11 is chosen at random. What is the probability of choosing an odd number?
(A) $\frac{1}{11}$　　　　(B) $\frac{5}{11}$

(C) $\frac{6}{11}$　　　　(D) None of these

Previous Contest Questions

1. The frequency table shows the number of passengers in each of the 40 taxis that were inspected during a police road-block. Find the value of 'x'.

Number of Passengers	0	1	2	3	4
Number of taxis	3	8	10	x	7

(A) 2　　　(B) 3　　　(C) 12　　　(D) 22

2. The table shows the number of children in each of the 35 families surveyed. Which of the following workings to cal-

culate the percentage of families with more than 3 children, is correct ?

Number of Children	Tally
2	IIII
3	HHT HHT
4	HHT II
5	HHT III
6	HHT I

(A) $\frac{10}{35}\times100$ (B) $\frac{14}{35}\times100$

(C) $\frac{21}{35}\times100$ (D) $\frac{31}{35}\times100$

3. The pictogram shows the number of houses sold by a developer over a period of 3 months. Which of the following statements is correct ?

January	
February	
March	

key: represents 30 houses

(A) 50 houses were sold in January

(B) The highest number of houses sold in a month is 5

(C) 60 houses more we sold in February than in March

(D) The total number of houses sold in the 3 months is 110.

4. The pictogram shows the number of pupils who cycle to school. On the whole, what is the percentage of class 2 pupils who cycle to school ?

Class 1	
Class 2	
Class 3	

key: represents 30 pupils

(A) 10%   (B) 25%   (C) $37\frac{1}{2}$% (D) 50%

5. The bar chart represents the data given in the frequency table shown below. The bar for which year is incorrectly drawn ?

Year	Number of Computers sold
1995	‖‖‖ ‖‖‖ ‖‖‖ |||
1996	‖‖‖ |||
1997	‖‖‖ ‖‖‖
1998	‖‖‖	

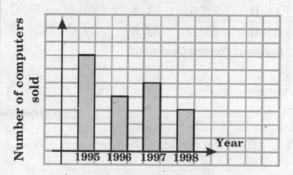

(A) 1995   (B) 1996
(C) 1997   (D) 1998

6. A school has strength of 2000 students. The following pie graph shows the interests of students in different subjects. The number of students interested in Maths is:

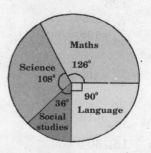

(A) 700

(B) 600

(C) 200

(D) 500

7.   The pie chart shows the number of fruits sold in a store. Given that the number of apples is 180 and number of oragnes is 400, the value of x, in degress, is:

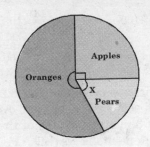

(A) 60   (B) 70   (C) 160   (D) 200

Answers

Multiple Choice Questions

1. D	2. C	3. B	4. B	5. D	6. C	7. A	8. C	9. D	10. C
11. B	12. C	13. A	14. A	15. C	16. D	17. D	18. D	19. D	20. B
21. B	22. D	23. B	24. C	25. B	26. C				

Previous Contest Questions

1. C	2. C	3. C	4. D	5. A	6. A	7. B

Explanatory Answers

1.   (D) $2 + 5 + 11 = 18$

2.   (C) $\dfrac{5}{20} \times 100 = 25\%$

3.   (B) $\dfrac{8}{20} \times 100 = 40\%$

4.   (B) $120 = 2(y + 34)$

$\Rightarrow y = \dfrac{120}{2} - 34$

$= 26$

5.   (D) $\dfrac{12}{40} \times 100 = 30\%$

6.   (C) $\dfrac{26}{40} \times 100 = 65\%$

8.   (C) $\dfrac{50}{5} = 10$

9.   (D) $15 \times 30 = 450$

10.   (C) $10 \times 6 = 60$

13.   (A) $\dfrac{50}{200} \times 100 = 25\%$

15.   (C) $\dfrac{135}{360} \times 100 = 37.5\%$

16.   (D) $5 \times \dfrac{360}{120} = 15^0$

17.   (D) $\dfrac{75}{200} \times 360 = 135^0$

19.   (D) $x + 90 + 2x + 60 = 360$

$\Rightarrow x = 70^0$

$R = 2x = 140^0$

$60^0 - 18$

$140^0 - ?$

$\dfrac{140 \times 18}{60} = 42$

21. (B) $360 \times \dfrac{3}{5} = 216^0$

$\because$ B = x and C = 2x,
We have,

Angle made by $C^0 = 216 \times \dfrac{2}{3} = 144^0$

Previous Contest Questions

1. (C) $3 + 8 + 10 + x + 7 = 40$
             $x = 40 - 28 = 12$

4. (D) $\dfrac{210}{420} \times 100 = 50\%$

6. (A) $\dfrac{126}{360} \times 2000 = 700$

7. (B) $90^0 \underline{\qquad} 180$
             $? \underline{\qquad} 400$

$400 \times \dfrac{90}{180} = 200$

Angle of sector showing oranges
$= 200^0$
we have,
$90^0 + 200^0 + x^0 = 360^0$
$\Rightarrow x = 360 - 290$
$= 70^0$

6 Squares and Square Roots

Get It Right

A   Error in calculating the square roots of fractions.

e.g. Calculate the value of $\sqrt{\dfrac{9}{49}}$.

✗ Incorrect

$$\sqrt{\dfrac{9}{49}} = \dfrac{3}{49}$$

Only the square root of the numerator was calculated.

✓ Correct

$$\sqrt{\dfrac{9}{49}} = \dfrac{\sqrt{9}}{\sqrt{49}} = \dfrac{3}{7}$$

The numerator and denominator were separated before working out the square root.

B.   Error in calculating the square of decimals.

e.g. $(0.02)^2 =$ _____

✗ Incorrect

$(0.02)^2 = 0.004$

✓ Correct

$(0.02)^2 = 0.\underline{0004}$

4 decimal places.

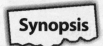
Synopsis

Square:

Square is obtained when a number is multiplied by itself twice.

Perfect Square:

A natural number is called a perfect square if it is the square of some natural number.

Properties of squares

♦   A number ending in 2, 3, 7 (or) 8 is never a perfect square.

♦   A number ending in an odd number of zeroes is never a perfect square.

♦   Squares of even numbers are even.

♦   Squares of odd numbers are odd.

♦   For every natural number 'n',

we have

$(n + 1)^2 - n^2 = (n + 1) + n$

Eg : $9^2 - 8^2 = 9 + 8 = 17$.

♦   A triplet (a, b, c) of three natural numbers a, b and c is called a pythagorean triplet if $a^2 + b^2 = c^2$.

♦   The square of a natural number 'n' is equal to the sum of the first 'n' odd numbers.

♦   There are no natural numbers 'm' and 'n' for which $m^2 = 2n^2$.

♦   The square root of a number 'x' is that number which when multiplied by itself gives 'x' as the product. We denote the square root of x by $\sqrt{x}$.

♦   For any positive numbers 'a' and 'b', we have,

(i) $\sqrt{ab} = \sqrt{a} \times \sqrt{b}$

(ii) $\sqrt{\dfrac{a}{b}} = \dfrac{\sqrt{a}}{\sqrt{b}}$

Multiple Choice Questions

1.   The square root of 1,764 is:
     (A) 32   (B) 42   (C) 48   (D) 38

2.   The square root of 53,361 is:
     (A) 231   (B) 211   (C) 261   (D) 249

3.   The least perfect square which is divisible by 2, 4 and 6 is:
     (A) 36   (B) 64   (C) 16   (D) 18

4.   The square root of 3,90,625 is:
     (A) 645   (B) 225   (C) 735   (D) 625

5.   The least perfect square exactly divisible by each of the numbers 6, 9, 15 and 20 is:
     (A) 3,600   (B) 900   (C) 400   (D) 225

6.   The sides of a rectangular field are 80 m and 18 m respectively. The length of the diagonal is:
     (A) 84 m   (B) 98 m   (C) 82 m   (D) 86 m

7. The least number of 4 digits which is a perfect square is:
    (A) 1,000   (B) 1,004
    C) 1,016   (D) 1,024

8. The least number which must be subtracted from 2,509 to make it a perfect square is:
    (A) 6   (B) 9   (C) 12   (D) 14

9. The value of $\sqrt{0.9}$ is (approx.):
    (A) 0.3   (B) 0.6   (C) 0.9   (D) 0.4

10. The square root of $42\dfrac{583}{1369}$ is:

    (A) $6\dfrac{19}{37}$ (B) $4\dfrac{2}{11}$

    (C) $7\dfrac{2}{121}$ (D) none of these

11. The square root of $\dfrac{441}{961}$ is:

    (A) $\dfrac{21}{39}$ (B) $\dfrac{37}{21}$ (C) $\dfrac{21}{31}$ (D) $\dfrac{11}{13}$

12. If M is a square number, then the next immediate square number is:
    (A) M + 5   (B) $M + 2\sqrt{M} + 1$
    (C) $M^2 + 2M$ (D) none of these

13. $\sqrt{\dfrac{1}{16} + \dfrac{1}{9}} =$ _____

    (A) $\dfrac{7}{12}$ (B) $\dfrac{25}{144}$

    (C) $\dfrac{5}{12}$ (D) none of these

14. If $\sqrt{1 + \dfrac{27}{169}} = 1 + \dfrac{x}{13}$, then x = _____

    (A) 1
    (B) 14
    (C) cannot be determined
    (D) none of these

15. The square root of
    $71 \times 72 \times 73 \times 74 + 1$ is:
    (A) 9,375   (B) 9,625
    (C) 5,625   (D) 5,255

16. If a square number ends in 6, the preceeding figure is:
    (A) an even number.
    (B) an odd number.
    (C) a prime number.
    (D) a composite number.

17. The value of $\sqrt{(-1)} \cdot \sqrt{(-1)}$ is:
    (A) –1   (B) +1
    (C) ± 1 (D) none of these

18. The value of $(501)^2 - (500)^2$ is:
    (A) 1   (B) 101
    (C) 1,001   (D) none of these

19. Which of the following is a Pythagorean triplet?
    (A) (6, 8, 10)   (B) (3, 4, 7)
    (C) (5, 12, 18)   (D) none of these

20. The value of
    $1 + 3 + 5 + 7 + 9 + \ldots + 25$ is:
    (A) 196   (B) 625   (C) 225   (D) 169

21. The smallest number by which 396 must be multiplied so that the product becomes a perfect square is:
    (A) 5   (B) 11   (C) 3   (D) 2

22. The value of $\sqrt{99} \times \sqrt{396}$ is:
    (A) 208   (B) 198
    (C) 254   (D) none of these

23. Square root of
    $\dfrac{0.081}{0.0064} \times \dfrac{0.484}{6.25} \times \dfrac{2.5}{12.1}$ is:
    (A) 0.45   (B) 0.75   (C) 0.95   (D) 0.99

24. $\sqrt{1 + \sqrt{1 + \sqrt{1 + ...}}}$ = _____
    (A) equals 1
    (B) lies between 0 and 1
    (C) lies between 1 and 2
    (D) is greater than 2

25. The value of $\dfrac{1 + \sqrt{0.01}}{1 - \sqrt{0.1}}$ is close to___.

    (A) 0.6   (B) 1.1
    (C) 1.6   (D) 1.7

26. If $x * y = \sqrt{x^2 + y^2}$, then the value of

    $\left(1 * 2\sqrt{2}\right)\left(1 * -2\sqrt{2}\right)$ is: ·
    (A) – 7   (B) 0   (C) 2   (D) 9

27. $\sqrt{41 - \sqrt{21 + \sqrt{19 - \sqrt{9}}}}$ = _____
    (A) 3   (B) 6   (C) 5   (D) 6.4

28. A number added to its square gives 56. The number is:
    (A) 12   (B) 9   (C) 8   (D) 7

29. The least number which must be subtracted from 6,156 to make it a perfect square is:
    (A) 62   (B) 72   (C) 52   (D) 82

30. A four digit perfect square number whose first two digits and last two digits taken seperately are also perfect squares is:
    (A) 1,681   (B) 1,636
    (C) 3,664   (D) 6,481

31. The square of a natural number subtracted from its cube is 48. The number is:
    (A) 6   (B) 5   (C) 4   (D) 8

32. The smallest natural number which when added to the difference of squares of 17 and 13 gives a perfect square is:
    (A) 1   (B) 5   (C) 11   (D) 24

33. If $\sqrt{\dfrac{16}{49}} = \dfrac{x}{49}$ then x = _____ .

    (A) 4   (B) 7   (C) 16   (D) 28

34. The square root of a perfect square containing 'n' digits has _____ digits.
    (A) $\dfrac{n+1}{2}$ (B) $\dfrac{n}{2}$

    (C) A or B   (D) none of these

35. The area of a square field is $80\dfrac{244}{729}$ sq m. The length of each side of the field is:
    (A) 8.96 m   (B) 10.26 m
    (C) 13.54 m   (D) none of these

36. If $\sqrt{2^n} = 64$, then the value of "n" is:
    (A) 2   (B) 4   (C) 6   (D) 12

37. If $\sqrt{6} = 2.55$, then the value of

    $\sqrt{\dfrac{2}{3}} + 3\sqrt{\dfrac{3}{2}}$ is:

    (A) 4.48   (B) 4.49
    (C) 4.50   (D) none of these

38. $\sqrt{\dfrac{36.1}{102.4}} = ?$

    (A) $\dfrac{29}{32}$ (B) $\dfrac{19}{72}$

    (C) $\dfrac{19}{32}$ (D) $\dfrac{29}{62}$

39. $\dfrac{?}{\sqrt{2.25}} = 550$

    (A) 825   (B) 82.5
    (C) 3666.66   (D) 2

40. $\dfrac{\sqrt{32} + \sqrt{48}}{\sqrt{8} + \sqrt{12}} = ?$

    (A) $\sqrt{2}$ (B) 2   (C) 4   (D) 8

41. If $\sqrt{24} = 4.899$, then the value of $\sqrt{\dfrac{8}{3}}$ is:

   (A) 0.544   (B) 2.666
   (C) 1.633   (D) 1.333

42. If $\sqrt{2} = 1.4142$, then the approximate value of $\sqrt{\dfrac{2}{9}}$ is:

   (A) 0.2321   (B) 0.4714
   (C) 0.3174   (D) 0.4174

43. $\sqrt{\dfrac{4}{3}} - \sqrt{\dfrac{3}{4}} = ?$

   (A) $\dfrac{1}{2\sqrt{3}}$ (B) $-\dfrac{1}{2\sqrt{3}}$

   (C) 1   (D) $\dfrac{5\sqrt{3}}{6}$

44. The least perfect square number divisible by 3, 4, 5, 6 and 8 is:
   (A) 900   (B) 1200
   (C) 2500   (D) 3600

45. $\sqrt{0.0009} \div \sqrt{0.01} = ?$
   (A) 3   (B) 0.3
   (C) $\dfrac{1}{3}$ (D) none of these

46. $\sqrt{0.01 + \sqrt{0.0064}} = ?$
   (A) 0.3   (B) 0.03
   (C) $\sqrt{0.18}$ (D) none of these

47. If $\sqrt{2401} = \sqrt{7^x}$, then the value of 'x' is:
   (A) 3   (B) 4
   (C) 5   (D) 6

48. The value of $\sqrt{0.9}$ is (approximately):
   (A) 0.3   (B) 0.03
   (C) 0.33   (D) 0.94

49. The value of $\sqrt{0.064}$ is:
   (A) 0.8   (B) 0.08
   (C) 0.008   (D) 0.252

50. The value of $\sqrt{\dfrac{0.16}{0.4}}$ is:

   (A) 0.2   (B) 0.02
   (C) 0.63   (D) $\dfrac{2\sqrt{5}}{5}$

51. The smallest number of 4 digits, which is a perfect square, is:
   (A) 1000   (B) 1016
   (C) 1024   (D) 1036

52. The least number by which 216 must be divided to make the result a perfect square, is:
   (A) 3   (B) 4   (C) 6   (D) 9

53. The least number to be subtracted from 16800 to make it a perfect square, is:
   (A) 249   (B) 159
   (C) 169   (D) 219

54. A gardner wants to plant 17956 trees and arranges them in such a way that there are as many rows as there are trees in a row. The number of trees in a row is:
   (A) 144   (B) 136
   (C) 154   (D) 134

55. A group of students decided to collect as many paise from each member of the group as is the number of members. If the total collection amounts to Rs.22.09, the number of members in the group is:
   (A) 37   (B) 47   (C) 107   (D) 43

56. A general wishes to draw up his 36562 soldiers in the form of a solid square. After arranging them, he found that some of them are left over. How many are left?
   (A) 36   (B) 65
   (C) 81   (D) 97

Previous Contest Questions

1. $\sqrt{\dfrac{0.289}{0.00121}} = ?$

   (A) $\dfrac{1.7}{11}$ (B) $\dfrac{17}{11}$ (C) $\dfrac{170}{11}$ (D) $\dfrac{17}{110}$

2. If $\sqrt{75.24 + x} = 8.71$, then the value of x is:

   (A) 0.6241   (B) 6.241
   (C) 62.41   (D) none of these

3. If $\sqrt{3} = 1.732$, then the approximate value of $\dfrac{1}{\sqrt{3}}$ is:

   (A) 0.617   (B) 0.313
   (C) 0.577   (D) 0.173

4. If $\sqrt{0.04 \times 0.4 \times a} = 0.4 \times 0.04 \times \sqrt{b}$, then the value of $\dfrac{a}{b}$ is:

   (A) 0.016   (B) 1.60
   (C) 0.16   (D) none of these

5. $\sqrt{\left(12 + \sqrt{12 + \sqrt{12 + \ldots}}\right)} = ?$

   (A) 3   (B) 4
   (C) 6   (D) greater than 6

6. Which of the following numbers, where some of the digits have been suppressed by symbols, can possibly be the perfect square of a 3 digit odd number?

   (A) 65 x x x 1   (B) 9 x x 1
   (C) 10 x x x 4   (D) 9 x x x x x x 5

7. $\sqrt{2\sqrt{2\sqrt{2\sqrt{2\sqrt{2}}}}} = ?$

   (A) 0   (B) 1   (C) 2   (D) $2^{31/32}$

8. The largest number of 5 digits, which is perfect square is:

   (A) 99999   (B) 99764 (C) 99976 (D) 99856

9. What smallest number must be added to 269 to make it a perfect square:

   (A) 31   (B) 16   (C) 7   (D) 20

10. The least number by which 176 be multiplied to make the result a perfect square, is:

    (A) 8   (B) 9   (C) 10   (D) 11

⊘ Answers ⊘

Multiple Choice Questions

1. B	2. A	3. A	4. D	5. B	6. C	7. D	8. B	9. C	10. A
11. C	12. B	13. C	14. A	15. D	16. B	17. A	18. C	19. A	20. D
21. B	22. B	23. A	24. C	25. C	26. D	27. B	28. D	29. B	30. A
31. C	32. A	33. D	34. C	35. A	36. D	37. D	38. C	39. A	40. B
41. C	42. B	43. A	44. D	45. B	46. A	47. B	48. D	49. D	50. C
51. C	52. C	53. B	54. D	55. B	56. C				

Previous Contest Questions

1. C	2. A	3. C	4. A	5. B	6. A	7. D	8. D	9. D	10. D

Explanatory Answers

1. **(B)** $1764 = 4 \times 7 \times 7 \times 9 = 2^2 \times 7^2 \times 3^2$

$$\therefore \sqrt{1764} = \sqrt{2^2 \times 7^2 \times 3^2}$$
$$= 2 \times 7 \times 3$$
$$= 42$$

2. **(A)** $53361 = 11 \times 11 \times 21 \times 21$
$$= 11^2 \times 21^2$$

$$\therefore \sqrt{53361} = \sqrt{11^2 \times 21^2}$$
$$= 11 \times 21 = 231$$

3. **(A)**

2	2, 4, 6
	1, 2, 3

$\therefore$ LCM of 2, 4, 6 =
$2 \times 1 \times 2 \times 3 = 12$

Least perfect square which is a multiple of 12 is 36.

4. **(D)**

	625
6	$3906\overset{\cdot}{2}5$
	36
122	306
	244
1245	6225
	6225
	0

5. **(B)**

3	6, 9, 15, 20
5	2, 3, 5, 20
2	2, 3, 1, 4
	1, 3, 1, 2

$\therefore$ LCM $= 3 \times 5 \times 2 \times 3 \times 2 = 180$.
The least multiple of 180 which is a perfect square is
$180 \times 5 = 900$

6. **(C)** $\sqrt{80^2 + 18^2} = \sqrt{6724} = 82$ m

7. **(D)**   By trial and error method,
(A), (B) and (C) are not perfect squares. $1024 = 32 \times 32 = 32^2$

8. **(B)**

	50
5	$2\overset{\cdot}{5}0\overset{\cdot}{9}$
	25
100	09
	00
	09

Hence 9 is the smallest number to be subtracted from 2509 to make it a perfect square.

9. **(C)** $\because$ $0.9 \times 0.9 = 0.81$

10. **(A)** $\sqrt{42\dfrac{583}{1369}} = \sqrt{\dfrac{58081}{1369}}$

$$= \frac{\sqrt{58081}}{\sqrt{1369}}$$

$$= \frac{241}{37} = 6\frac{19}{37}$$

11. **(C)** $\sqrt{\dfrac{441}{961}} = \dfrac{\sqrt{441}}{\sqrt{961}} = \dfrac{21}{31}$

12. **(B)** $M + 2\sqrt{M} + 1$
Eg : take $M = 4$, a square number.
$M + 2\sqrt{M} + 1 = 4 + 2\sqrt{4} + 1$
$= 4 + 2 \times 2 + 1 = 9$

13. **(C)** $\sqrt{\dfrac{1}{16} + \dfrac{1}{9}} = \sqrt{\dfrac{25}{144}} = \dfrac{5}{12}$

14. **(A)** $\sqrt{1 + \dfrac{27}{169}} = \sqrt{\dfrac{196}{169}} = \dfrac{14}{13} =$

$$1\frac{1}{13} = 1 + \frac{1}{13}$$

$$\therefore \ x = 1$$

15. (D)   We have,

$$\sqrt{a\,(a+1)\,(a+2)\,(a+3)+1}$$

$$= a^2 + 3a + 1$$

$$\sqrt{(71)\,(72)\,(73)\,(74)+1}$$

$$= (71)^2 + 3(71) + 1$$

$$= 5255$$

16. (B)   Let us take some square numbers ending with 6. Ex: 36, 196, 256, 676, ...

By observation, the preceeding digit is an odd number.

17. (A)   We define $\sqrt{-a}$ as the quantity which is being multiplied by itself (or) squared become equal to '–a'.

So $\sqrt{-a} \times \sqrt{-a} = \left(\sqrt{-a}\right)^2 = -a$

$$\therefore \ \sqrt{-1} \times \sqrt{-1} = -1$$

18. (C)   We have,

$$(n+1)^2 - n^2 = (n+1) + n$$

So, $(501)^2 - (500)^2 = 501 + 500$

$$= 1,001$$

19. (A)   General form is

$(2m,\ m^2 - 1,\ m^2 + 1)$

Put m = 3

So $2m = 6,\ m^2 - 1 = 3^2 - 1 = 8,$

$m^2 + 1 = 3^2 + 1 = 10$

$\therefore$ (6, 8, 10) is a Pythagorean triplet.

20. (D)   Here we have to find the sum of 13 odd numbers.

So, $13^2 = 169$

21. (B) $396 = 2 \times 2 \times 3 \times 3 \times 11$

So 396 should be multiplied by 11 to make the product a perfect square.

22. (B) $\sqrt{99} \times \sqrt{396} = \sqrt{99 \times 396}$

$$= \sqrt{3 \times 3 \times 11 \times 3 \times 3 \times 2 \times 2 \times 11}$$

$$= 3 \times 3 \times 2 \times 11 = 198$$

23. (A) $\sqrt{\dfrac{0.081}{0.0064} \times \dfrac{0.484}{6.25} \times \dfrac{2.5}{12.1}}$

$$= \sqrt{\frac{810}{64} \times \frac{484}{6250} \times \frac{25}{121}}$$

$$= \sqrt{\frac{81}{64} \times \frac{484}{625} \times \frac{25}{121}}$$

$$= \frac{9}{8} \times \frac{22}{25} \times \frac{5}{11} = 0.45$$

24. (C)   Let $x = \sqrt{1 + \sqrt{1 + \sqrt{1 + \ldots}}}$

$$x = \sqrt{1 + x}$$

Squaring on both sides

$x^2 = 1 + x$

$x^2 - x - 1 = 0$

Solving we get $x = \dfrac{1 \pm \sqrt{5}}{2}$

$\therefore$ x value lies between 1 and 2.

25. (C) $\dfrac{1 + \sqrt{0.01}}{1 - \sqrt{0.1}} = \dfrac{1 + 0.1}{1 - 0.32} = \dfrac{1.1}{0.68} = 1.6$

26. (D)

$1 * 2\sqrt{2} = \sqrt{(1)^2 + \left(2\sqrt{2}\right)^2} = \sqrt{1+8} = 3$

$1 * -2\sqrt{2} = \sqrt{(1)^2 + \left(-2\sqrt{2}\right)^2} = \sqrt{1+8} = 3$

$\left(1 * 2\sqrt{2}\right)\left(1 * -2\sqrt{2}\right) = (3)(3) = 9$

27. (B) $\sqrt{41 - \sqrt{21 \div \sqrt{19 - \sqrt{9}}}}$

$$= \sqrt{41 - \sqrt{21 + \sqrt{16}}}$$

$$= \sqrt{41 - \sqrt{21 + 4}}$$

$$= \sqrt{41 - 5} = \sqrt{36} = 6$$

28. (D) Let the number be x.

$x^2 + x = 56$

$x^2 + x - 56 = 0$

$(x + 8)(x - 7) = 0$

$x = -8$ or 7

29. (B)

$$7 \begin{array}{|c|} \overset{\cdot \quad \cdot}{6156} \\ \underline{49} \\ 1256 \\ \underline{1184} \\ 72 \end{array} 78$$

148

∴ 72 must be subtracted from 6156 to make it a perfect square.

30. (A) By checking the answers only (A) is satisfying the given conditions.

31. (C) $x^3 - x^2 = 48$

$x^2(x - 1) = 48 = 4^2(4 - 1)$

∴ $x = 4$

32. (A) $17^2 - 13^2 = 289 - 169 = 120$

$120 + 1 = 121 = 11^2$

33. (D) $\sqrt{\dfrac{16}{49}} = \dfrac{4}{7} = \dfrac{x}{49}$

$\Rightarrow x = 28$

34. (C) If 'n' is even then square root will contain $\dfrac{n}{2}$ digits.

If 'n' is odd then square root will contain $\dfrac{n+1}{2}$ digits.

35. (A) Length of each side

$= \sqrt{80\dfrac{244}{729}} = \sqrt{\dfrac{58564}{729}}$

$= \dfrac{242}{27} = 8.96$ m

36. (D) $\sqrt{2^n} = 64 = 2^6 \Rightarrow 2^{n/2} = 2^6$

So, $\dfrac{n}{2} = 6$ or $n = 12$.

37. (D) $\sqrt{\dfrac{2}{3}} + 3.\sqrt{\dfrac{3}{2}}$

$= \dfrac{\sqrt{2}}{\sqrt{3}} \times \dfrac{\sqrt{3}}{\sqrt{3}} + 3 \times \dfrac{\sqrt{3}}{\sqrt{2}} \times \dfrac{\sqrt{2}}{\sqrt{2}}$

$= \dfrac{\sqrt{6}}{3} + \dfrac{3\sqrt{6}}{2} = \dfrac{2.55}{3} + \dfrac{3 \times 2.55}{2}$

$\dfrac{2.55}{3} + \dfrac{7.65}{2} = \dfrac{5.10 + 22.95}{6}$

$= \dfrac{28.05}{6} = 4.675$

38. (C) $\sqrt{\dfrac{36.1}{102.4}} = \sqrt{\dfrac{361}{1024}} = \dfrac{\sqrt{361}}{\sqrt{1024}} = \dfrac{19}{32}$

39. (A) Let $\dfrac{x}{\sqrt{2.25}} = 550$.

Then, $\dfrac{x}{1.5} = 550$.

∴ $x = (550 \times 1.5) = \left(\dfrac{550 \times 15}{10}\right) = 825$.

40. (B) $\dfrac{\sqrt{32} + \sqrt{48}}{\sqrt{8} + \sqrt{12}} = \dfrac{\sqrt{16 \times 2} + \sqrt{16 \times 3}}{\sqrt{4 \times 2} + \sqrt{4 \times 3}}$

$\dfrac{4\sqrt{2} + 4\sqrt{3}}{2\sqrt{2} + 2\sqrt{3}} = \dfrac{4\left(\sqrt{2} + \sqrt{3}\right)}{2\left(\sqrt{2} + \sqrt{3}\right)} = 2$

41. (C) $\sqrt{\dfrac{8}{3}} = \dfrac{\sqrt{8}}{\sqrt{3}} \times \dfrac{\sqrt{3}}{\sqrt{3}} = \dfrac{\sqrt{24}}{3} = \dfrac{4.899}{3} = 1.633$.

42. (B) $\sqrt{\dfrac{2}{9}} = \dfrac{\sqrt{2}}{\sqrt{9}} = \dfrac{\sqrt{2}}{3} = \dfrac{1.4142}{3} = 0.4714$.

43. (A) $\dfrac{\sqrt{4}}{\sqrt{3}} - \dfrac{\sqrt{3}}{\sqrt{4}} = \dfrac{2}{\sqrt{3}} - \dfrac{\sqrt{3}}{2} = \dfrac{4-3}{2\sqrt{3}} = \dfrac{1}{2\sqrt{3}}$

44. (D) L.C.M. of 3, 4, 5, 6, 8 is 120.

Now, $120 = 2 \times 2 \times 2 \times 3 \times 5$

∴ Required number =

$120 = 2 \times 2 \times 2 \times 3 \times 5 \times 2 \times 3 \times 5$

$= 3600.$

```
3 | 1000(31
  |  9
61|  100
  |   61
  |   39
```

∴ Required number = $(32)^2 = 1024.$

45. (B) Given expression = $\dfrac{\sqrt{0.0009}}{\sqrt{0.01}}$

$= \dfrac{\sqrt{0.0009}}{\sqrt{0.0100}} = \sqrt{\dfrac{9}{100}}$

$= \dfrac{\sqrt{9}}{\sqrt{100}} = \dfrac{3}{10} = 0.3$

52. (C) $216 = 2 \times 2 \times 2 \times 3 \times 3 \times 3.$

Clearly, in order to make it a perfect

square, it must be divided by 2×3 i.e., 6.

47. (A) $\sqrt{2401} = \sqrt{7^x} \Rightarrow 7^x = 2401 \Rightarrow x = 4$

48. (D) $\sqrt{0.9} = \sqrt{0.90} = \sqrt{\dfrac{90}{100}} = \dfrac{\sqrt{90}}{10}$

$= \dfrac{9.4}{10} = 0.94.$

53. (B)
```
  1  | 16800(129
     | 1
 22  | 68
     | 44
249  | 2400
     | 2241
     |  159
```

∴ Required number to be subtracted = 159.

49. (D) $\sqrt{0.064} = \sqrt{0.0640}$

$= \sqrt{\dfrac{640}{10000}} = \dfrac{\sqrt{640}}{100}$

$= \dfrac{25.2}{100} = 0.252.$

54. (D)
```
  1  | 17956(134
     | 1
 23  | 79
     | 69
264  | 1056
     | 1056
     |    0
```

∴ Number of trees in a row = 134.

50. (C) $\sqrt{\dfrac{0.16}{0.4}} = \sqrt{\dfrac{0.16}{0.40}} = \sqrt{\dfrac{16}{40}} = \sqrt{\dfrac{4}{10}}$

$\sqrt{0.4} = \sqrt{0.40} = \sqrt{\dfrac{40}{100}} = \dfrac{\sqrt{40}}{10}$

$= \dfrac{6.3}{10} = 0.63.$

51. (C) The smallest number of 4 digits = 1000.

55. (B) Number of members

$= \sqrt{2209} = 47 \cdot$

56. (C)

$$
\begin{array}{r|l}
1 & \overset{\bullet}{3}6\overset{\bullet}{5}6\overset{\bullet}{2}(191 \\
 & 1 \\
29 & \overline{265} \\
 & 261 \\
381 & \overline{462} \\
 & 381 \\
 & \overline{81}
\end{array}
$$

∴ Number of soldiers left = 81

Previous Contest Questions

1. (C) $\sqrt{\dfrac{0.289}{0.00121}} = \sqrt{\dfrac{0.28900}{0.00121}} = \sqrt{\dfrac{28900}{121}}$

   $= \dfrac{\sqrt{28900}}{\sqrt{121}} = \dfrac{170}{11}.$

2. (A) $75.24 + x = 8.71 \times 8.71$

   $\Rightarrow x = 0.6241.$

3. (C) $\dfrac{1}{\sqrt{3}} = \dfrac{1}{\sqrt{3}} \times \dfrac{\sqrt{3}}{\sqrt{3}} = \dfrac{\sqrt{3}}{3} = \dfrac{1.732}{3} = 0.577.$

4. (A) $\sqrt{0.04 \times 0.4 \times a} = 0.4 \times 0.04 \times \sqrt{b}$

   $\Rightarrow \sqrt{0.016a} = 0.016 \times \sqrt{b}$

   $\Rightarrow \dfrac{\sqrt{a}}{\sqrt{b}} = \dfrac{0.016}{\sqrt{0.016}} = \sqrt{0.016}$

   $\Rightarrow \sqrt{\dfrac{a}{b}} = \sqrt{0.016}$

   $\Rightarrow \dfrac{a}{b} = 0.016.$

5. (B) Let $\sqrt{\left(12 + \sqrt{12 + \sqrt{12 + \ldots\ldots}}\right)} = x.$

   Then, $\sqrt{12 + x} = x \Rightarrow 12 + x = x^2$

   ∴ $x^2 - x - 12 = 0$ or

   $(x-4)(x+3) = 0$

   So, $x = 4$ (neglecting $x = -3$).

6. (A) The square of an odd number

can not have 4 as the unit digit. The square of a 3 digit number will have at least 5 digits and at the most 6 digits. So, option (A) is correct answer.

7. (D) Given Expression =

   $$\sqrt{2 \times \sqrt{2 \times \sqrt{2 \times \sqrt{2 \times 2^{1/2}}}}}$$

   $$= \sqrt{2 \times \sqrt{2 \times \sqrt{\left(2 \times 2^{3/4}\right)}}}$$

   $$= \sqrt{2 \times \sqrt{2 \times 2^{7/8}}} = \sqrt{2 \times 2^{15/16}} = 2^{31/32}$$

8. (D) The largest number of 5 digits = 99999.

$$
\begin{array}{r|l}
3 & \overset{\bullet}{9}9\overset{\bullet}{9}9\overset{\bullet}{9}(316 \\
 & 9 \\
61 & \overline{99} \\
 & 61 \\
626 & \overline{3899} \\
 & 3756 \\
 & \overline{143}
\end{array}
$$

∴ Required number

   $= (99999 - 143) = 99856.$

9. (D)

$$
\begin{array}{r|l}
1 & \overset{\bullet}{2}6\overset{\bullet}{9}(16 \\
 & 1 \\
26 & \overline{169} \\
 & 156 \\
 & \overline{13}
\end{array}
$$

∴ Required number to be added

   $= (17)^2 - 269 = 20.$

10. (D) $176 = 2 \times 2 \times 2 \times 2 \times 11.$

   So, in order to make it a perfect square, it must be multiplied by 11.

Chapter 7 Cubes and Cube Roots

Get It Right

A Error in calculating the cube root of negative numbers.

e.g. Calculate the value of $\sqrt[3]{-125}$

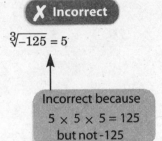

✗ **Incorrect**

$\sqrt[3]{-125} = 5$

Incorrect because

$5 \times 5 \times 5 = 125$
but not -125

✓ **Correct**

$\sqrt[3]{-125} = -5$

Correct because

$(-5) \times (-5) \times (-5) = -125$
The cube root of a negative
number is always negative.

B. Error in calculating cube root of a mixed fraction

e.g. $\sqrt[3]{27\dfrac{1}{8}} =$ _____

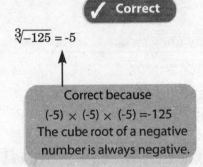

✗ **Incorrect**

$\sqrt[3]{27\dfrac{1}{8}} = 3\dfrac{1}{2}$

✓ **Correct**

$\sqrt[3]{27\dfrac{1}{8}} = \sqrt[3]{\dfrac{217}{8}}$

Change the mixed number into an
improper fraction before finding
its cube root.

Synopsis

Cube:

Cube is obtained when a number is multiplied by itself three times.

Perfect Cube:

A natural number is said to be a perfect cube if it is the cube of some natural number.

◆   Cubes of all even natural numbers are even.

◆   Cubes of all odd natural numbers are odd.

◆   Cubes of negative integers are negative.

Cube root:

The cube root of a number x is that number whose cube gives x. It is denoted by $\sqrt[3]{x}$.

◆   For any positive integer x, we have

$$\sqrt[3]{-x} = -\sqrt[3]{x}$$

◆   For any integers a and b, we have

(i) $\sqrt[3]{ab} = \sqrt[3]{a} \times \sqrt[3]{b}$

(ii) $\sqrt[3]{\dfrac{a}{b}} = \dfrac{\sqrt[3]{a}}{\sqrt[3]{b}}$

Multiple Choice Questions

1. If 72K is a perfect cube, then the value of K is:
    (A) 1   (B) 2   (C) 3   (D) 4

2. The cube root of 27^2 is:
    (A) 27   (B) 9
    (C) 3   (D) none of these

3. If $a^3 = b^3 + c^3 + d^3$, the least value of 'a' is:
    (A) 6   (B) 9
    (C) 3   (D) none of these

4. The cube of 0.9 is:
    (A) 72.9   (B) 0.729
    (C) 7.29   (D) none of these

5. The number which is not a perfect cube among the following is:
    (A) 1,331   (B) 216   (C) 243   (D) 512

6. Which of the following statement is true?
    (A) Cubes of all even natural numbers are even.
    (B) Cubes of all odd natural numbers are odd.
    (C) Cubes of negative integers are negative.
    (D) All the above

7. The smallest number by which 2560 must be multiplied so that the product is a perfect cube is:
    (A) 5   (B) 25   (C) 10   (D) 15

8. The smallest number by which 8,788 must be divided so that the quotient is perfect cube is:
    (A) 4   (B) 12   (C) 16   (D) 32

9. The cube root of 1.331 is:
    (A) 0.11   (B) 0.011
    (C) 11   (D) 1.1

10. The cube root of $\dfrac{-512}{729}$ is:

   (A) $\dfrac{4}{7}$ (B) $\dfrac{8}{9}$

   (C) $\dfrac{-8}{9}$ (D) none of these

11. The value of $\sqrt[3]{343} \times \sqrt[3]{-64}$ is:
   (A) 28   (B) –28   (C) 18   (D) –18

12. The length of each side of the cubical box is 2.4 m. Its volume is:
   (A) 13.824 cu m   (B) 13.824 cu cm
   (C) 13.824 m²   (D) 13.824 cm²

13. The cube of a number is 8 times the cube of another number. If the sum of the cubes of numbers is 243, the difference of the numbers is:
   (A) 3   (B) 4
   (C) 6   (D) none of these

14. The square of a natural number subtracted from its cube is 48. The number is:
   (A) 6   (B) 5   (C) 4   (D) 8

15. Which of the following numbers are perfect cubes?
   (A) 108   (B) 343 (C) 243   (D) 5,324

16. Which of the following is the cube of even natural number?
   (A) 729   (B) 3,375 (C) 1,331 (D) 13,824

17. Which of the following is the cube of odd natural number?
   (A) 32,768   (B) 4,096
   (C) 6,859   (D) 1,728

18. The cube root of 0.001728 is:
   (A) 0.12   (B) 1.2
   (C) 12   (D) none of these

19. $\sqrt[3]{-2,744} \div \sqrt[3]{0.008}$ = _____
   (A) 70   (B) – 70
   (C) 14   (D) – 14

Previous Contest Questions

1. $\sqrt[3]{3 - \dfrac{17}{27}}$ = _____

   (A) $\dfrac{4}{3}$ (B) $\dfrac{3}{4}$ (C) $-\dfrac{3}{4}$ (D) $-\dfrac{4}{3}$

2. $\sqrt[3]{0.125} + 3$ = _____
   (A) 8   (B) 3.5   (C) 2   (D) 0.35

3. $\sqrt[3]{-3\dfrac{3}{8}}$ = _____

   (A) $\dfrac{3}{2}$ (B) $\dfrac{3}{4}$ (C) $-\dfrac{3}{4}$ (D) $-\dfrac{3}{2}$

4. Calculate the value of $\sqrt[3]{-64} + \sqrt{9^2}$.
   (A) –4   (B) 3
   (C) 5   (D) 77

5. Calculate the value of $\sqrt[3]{\dfrac{-192}{81}}$.

   (A) $-\dfrac{5}{3}$ (B) $\dfrac{-4}{3}$ (C) $\dfrac{3}{2}$ (D) $\dfrac{13}{9}$

6. $\sqrt[3]{216}$ is:
   (A) Less than 6   (B) Greater than 6
   (C) Equal to 6   (D) Equal to 9

7. Given that $512 = 8^3$ and $3.375 = 1.5^3$, find the value of $\sqrt[3]{512} \times \sqrt[3]{3.375}$.
   (A) 12   (B) 9.5
   (C) 8   (D) 1.5

8. Given that $\sqrt[3]{x} = -6$, find the value of x.
   (A) 216   (B) 18
   (C) –18   (D) –216

9. $9 + \sqrt[3]{-343} =$ _____
       (A) 16   (B) 11
       (C) 2   (D) –7

10.   The length of each edge of a cube is 9 m,
       The volume of the cube, in m^3, is:
       (A) 27   (B) 81
       (C) 108   (D) 729

✎ Answers ✎

Multiple Choice Questions

| 1. C | 2. B | 3. A | 4. B | 5. C | 6. D | 7. B | 8. A | 9. D | 10. C |
| 11. B | 12. A | 13. A | 14. C | 15. B | 16. D | 17. C | 18. A | 19. B | |

Previous Contest Questions

| 1. A | 2. B | 3. D | 4. C | 5. B | 6. C | 7. A | 8. D | 9. C | 10. D |

Explanatory Answers

1. (C) $72 = 2 \times 2 \times 2 \times 3 \times 3$
          If K = 3 then
          $72 K = 72 \times 3 = 216 = 6^3$ is a
          perfect cube.

2. (B) $27 = 3 \times 3 \times 3 = 3^3$
          $27^2 = \left(3^3\right)^2 = \left(3^2\right)^3 = 9^3$
          $\therefore$ cube root of $27^2 = 9$

3. (A)   a = 6
          $6^3 = 3^3 + 4^3 + 5^3$

4. (B) $(0.9)^3 = 0.9 \times 0.9 \times 0.9 = 0.729$

6. (D)   All the given statements are true.

7. (B) $2,560 = 2 \times 2 \times 2 \times 4 \times 4 \times 4 \times 5$
          Clearly, on multiplication, by
          $5 \times 5 = 25$, it becomes a perfect
          cube.

8. (A) $8,788 = 4 \times 13 \times 13 \times 13$
          On division by 4 it becomes a
          perfect cube.

9. (D) $\sqrt[3]{1.331} = \sqrt[3]{(1.1)^3} = 1.1$

10. (C) $\sqrt[3]{\dfrac{-512}{729}} = \dfrac{\sqrt[3]{-512}}{\sqrt[3]{729}} = \dfrac{-8}{9}$

11. (B) $\sqrt[3]{343} \times \sqrt[3]{-64} = \sqrt[3]{343 \times -64}$

          $= -\sqrt[3]{7 \times 7 \times 7 \times 4 \times 4 \times 4}$
          $= -7 \times 4 = -28$

12. (A)   a = 2.4 m
          Volume = $a^3 = (2.4)^3$
          $= 2.4 \times 2.4 \times 2.4$
          $= 13.824$ cu m

13. (A) $x^3 = 8y^3$ ......(1)
          $x^3 + y^3 = 243$ ....(2)
          Solving (1) & (2) we get
          x = 6, y = 3
          $\therefore$ Difference = 6 – 3 = 3

14. (C)   Let the number be x.
          $x^3 - x^2 = 48$
          $x^2(x - 1) = 48 = 4^2(4 - 1)$
          $\therefore$ x = 4.

15. (B) $\because 343 = 7^3$.

16. (D)   Since $13,824 = 24^3$ and 24 is an
          even number.

17. (C)   Since $6,859 = 19^3$ and 19 is an odd
          number.

18. (A) $\sqrt[3]{0.001728} = \sqrt[3]{(0.12)^3} = 0.12$

19. (B) $\sqrt[3]{-2744} \div \sqrt[3]{0.008} = -14 \div 0.2$
          $= -70$

Previous Contest Questions

1. (A) $\sqrt[3]{\dfrac{27\times 3-17}{27}} = \sqrt[3]{\dfrac{81-17}{27}} = \sqrt[3]{\dfrac{64}{27}}$

   $= \sqrt[3]{\dfrac{(4)^3}{(3)^3}} = \dfrac{4}{3}$

2. (B) $\sqrt[3]{0.125} + 3 = 0.5 + 3 = 3.5$

3. (D) $\sqrt[3]{-3\dfrac{3}{8}} = \sqrt[3]{\dfrac{-27}{8}} = \sqrt[3]{\dfrac{-3^3}{2^3}} = \dfrac{-3}{2}$

4. (C) $\sqrt[3]{-64} + \sqrt{9^2} = -4 + 9 = 5$

5. (B) $\sqrt[3]{\dfrac{-192}{81}}$

   $= \sqrt[3]{\dfrac{(-2)\times(-2)\times(-2)\times 2\times 2\times 2\times 3}{3\times 3\times 3\times 3}}$

   $= \dfrac{-2\times 2}{3} = \dfrac{-4}{3}$

6. (C) $\sqrt[3]{216} = 2\times 3 = 6$

7. (A) $\sqrt[3]{512} \times \sqrt[3]{3.375} = 8\times 1.5 = 12$

8. (D) $\sqrt[3]{x} = -6$

   $x = (-6)^3 = (-6)\times(-6)\times(-6) = -216$

9. (C) $9 + \sqrt[3]{-343}$

   $= 9 + \sqrt[3]{(-7)\times(-7)\times(-7)}$

   $= 9 + (-7) = 2$

10. (D) Volume of cube $= 9\times 9\times 9\,m^3$

    $= 729\,m^3$

✧ ✧ ✧

Chapter 8

Comparing Quantities

Get It Right

A Error in calculating compound interest.

e.g. A sum of money at CI amounts to thrice itself in 3 years. In how many years wil it be 9 times itself ?

 Incorrect

$\because$ The sum is getting thrice in 3 years

$\therefore$ Number of years to get 9 times of the amount $= 3 \times 3 = 9$ years.

 Correct

It will take $3 \times 2 = 6$ years to get 9 times of the amount.

$\because$ If a certain amount becomes N times in T years then same amount will be N^2 times in T × 2 years, N^3 times in T × 3 years and N^x times in T × x years.

B Error in finding profit or loss percent.

e.g. A shopkeeper marks his goods at 10% above the cost price and allows a discount of 10% on the marked price. What is his gain or loss percent ?

 Incorrect

Shopkeeper neither gain nor loss.

Correct

If goods incur a gain of x % and other a loss of x %, then overall he gets loss %

$$= \frac{x^2}{100}\% = \frac{10^2}{100}\% = 1\%$$

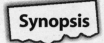
Synopsis

Compound Interest:

- $$A = P\left(1 + \frac{R}{100}\right)^n$$

Where,
A – amount,
P – principle,
R – rate of interest,
n – time
- Compound interest = A – P
- In case of depreciation (or) decay,

$$A = P\left(1 - \frac{R}{100}\right)^n$$

- If the rates be p%, q% and r% during 1st, 2nd and 3rd years respectively, then the population

after 3 years $= P\left(1 + \dfrac{p}{100}\right)\left(1 + \dfrac{q}{100}\right)\left(1 + \dfrac{r}{100}\right)$

- If principle = Rs. P, rate = R% per annum and time = n years then,
  (a) amount after "n" years (compounded annually)

$$A = P\left(1 + \frac{R}{100}\right)^n$$

  (b) Amount after "n" years (compounded half–yearly)

$$A = P\left(1 + \frac{R}{2 \times 100}\right)^{2n}$$

  (c) Amount after "n" years (compounded quarterly)

$$A = P\left(1 + \frac{R}{4 \times 100}\right)^{4n}$$

- When T = 2 years and n = 1, then

$$CI - SI = \frac{R \times S.I.}{2 \times 100} = P\left(\frac{R}{100}\right)^2$$

- When T = 3 years and n = 1, then

$$CI - SI = \frac{SI}{3}\left[\left(\frac{R}{100}\right)^2 + 3\left(\frac{R}{100}\right)\right]$$

- If a certain amount becomes N times in T years,
  then same amount will be N^2 times in T $\times$ 2 years, N^3 times in T $\times$ 3 years and N^x times in T $\times$ x years.

PROFIT AND LOSS:

Cost price (CP) :

The price at which an article is purchased is called its cost price.

Selling price (SP):

The price at which an article is sold is called its selling price.

(a) If SP > CP, there is a gain and Gain = SP – CP.

(b) If SP < CP, there is a loss and   Loss = CP – SP.

Profit and loss percentage:

(i) Profit % = $\dfrac{\text{profit}}{\text{CP}} \times 100$

(ii) Loss % = $\dfrac{\text{loss}}{\text{CP}} \times 100$

NOTE : Profit and loss percentage are reckoned on cost price.

Important formulae:

(i) $SP = \left(\dfrac{100 + \text{gain}\%}{100}\right) \times CP$

(ii) $SP = \left(\dfrac{100 - \text{loss}\%}{100}\right) \times CP$

(iii) $CP = \left(\dfrac{100}{100 + \text{gain}\%}\right) \times SP$

(iv) $CP = \left(\dfrac{100}{100 - \text{loss}\%}\right) \times SP$

Discount

In order to give a boost to the sales of an item or to clear the old stock, articles are sold at reduced prices. This reduction is given on the Marked Price (MP) of the article and is known as discount.

(i) SP = MP – discount

(ii) Discount = MP – SP

(iii) Discount % = $\dfrac{MP - SP}{MP} \times 100$

Multiple Choice Questions

1. A sum of money, at compound interest, yields Rs. 200 and Rs. 220 at the end of first and second year respectively. The rate % is:
   (A) 20   (B) 15   (C) 10   (D) 5

2. A sum of money at CI amounts to thrice itself in 3 years. In how many years will it be 9 times itself?
   (A) 18   (B) 12   (C) 9   (D) 6

3. The CI on a certain sum for 2 years is Rs. 41 and SI is Rs. 40. Then the rate percent per annum is:
   (A) 4%   (B) 5%   (C) 6%   (D) 8%

4. The difference in SI and CI on a certain sum of money in 2 years at 15% p.a. is Rs. 144. The sum is:
   (A) Rs. 6,000   (B) Rs. 6,200
   (C) Rs. 6,300   (D) Rs. 6,400

5. In what time will a sum of Rs. 800 at 5% p.a. CI amounts to Rs. 882?
   (A) 1 year   (B) 5 years
   (C) 4 years   (D) 2 years

6. The CI on Rs. 8000 for 1 year at 5% p.a. payable half-yearly is:
   (A) Rs. 800   (B) Rs. 810
   (C) Rs. 400   (D) Rs. 405

7. The SI on a sum of money for 3 years is Rs. 240 and the CI on the sum at same rate for 2 years is Rs. 170. The rate % p.a. is:
   (A) 16%   (B) 8%
   (C) $12\frac{1}{2}\%$ (D) $8\frac{1}{3}\%$

8. What sum lent out at CI will amount to Rs. 968 in 2 years at 10% p.a. interest?
   (A) Rs. 800   (B) Rs. 1000
   (C) Rs. 1200   (D) None of these

9. If the difference between SI and CI on a certain sum of money for 3 years at 10% p.a. is Rs. 15.50. The sum is:
   (A) Rs. 1,000   (B) Rs. 500
   (C) Rs. 1,500   (D) Rs. 2,000

10. Raghu borrowed Rs. 25,000 at 20% p.a. compounded half–yearly. What amount of money will discharge his debt after $1\frac{1}{2}$ years?
    (A) Rs. 28,275   (B) Rs. 36,275
    (C) Rs. 33,275   (D) None of these

11. The CI on Rs. 16, 000 at 15% p.a. for $2\frac{1}{3}$ years is:
    (A) Rs. 6,418   (B) Rs. 5,000
    (C) Rs. 22,218   (D) Rs. 6,218

12. In what time will Rs. 1000 amount to Rs. 1331 at 10% p.a. in CI?
    (A) 4 years   (B) 3 years
    (C) 2 years   (D) 1 year

13. The present population of a town is 25,000. It grows at 4%, 5% and 8% during first year, second year and third year respectively, the population after 3 years is:
    (A) 29,484   (B) 28,696
    (C) 24,576   (D) 30,184

14. The value of an article which was purchased 2 years ago, depreciates at 12% per annum. If its present value is Rs. 9680, the price at which it was purchased is:
    (A) Rs. 10,000   (B) Rs. 12,500
    (C) Rs. 14,575   (D) Rs. 16,250

15. The cost of a vehicle is Rs. 1,75,000. If its value depreciates at the rate of 20% per annum, then the total depreciation after 3 years was:

(A) Rs. 86,400   (B) Rs. 82,500
(C) Rs. 84,500   (D) Rs. 85,400

16. The CI on a certain sum for 2 years is Rs. 410 and SI is Rs. 400. The rate of interest per annum is:
(A) 10% (B) 8% (C) 5% (D) 4%

17. The CI on a certain sum for 2 years at 10% per annum is Rs. 525. The SI on the same sum for double the time at half the rate percent per annum is:
(A) Rs. 400   (B) Rs. 500
(C) Rs. 600   (D) Rs. 800

18. On a sum of money the SI for two years is Rs. 660, while CI is Rs. 696.30, the rate of interest being the same in both the cases. The rate of interest is:

(A) 10%   (B) $10\frac{1}{2}$ % (C) 12% (D) 11%

19. A man borrowed Rs. 3125 for CI and it amounted to Rs. 4500 in 2 years. The rate of CI per annum is:
(A) 30%   (B) 25% (C) 20% (D) 15%

20. A sum of money doubles itself in 3 years at CI, when the interest is compounded annually. In how many years will it amount to 16 times of itself?
(A) 6 years   (B) 8 years
(C) 12 years   (D) 16 years

21. The CI on a certain sum at 5% for 2 years is Rs. 328. The SI for that sum at the same rate and for the same period will be:
(A) Rs. 320   (B) Rs. 322
(C) Rs. 325   (D) Rs. 326

22. A sum lent at CI amounts in 2 years to Rs. 578.40 and in 3 years to Rs. 614.55. Find the rate of interest.

(A) 5%   (B) $6\frac{1}{4}$ % (C) 7% (D) $12\frac{1}{2}$ %

23. Find the amount on Rs. 12,500 for 2 years compounded annually, the rate of interest being 15% for the first year and 16% for the second year.
(A) Rs. 16,500   (B) Rs. 16,750
(C) Rs. 16,675   (D) None of these

24. The gain or loss percent when a carriage, which cost Rs. 4000, is sold for Rs. 5000 is:
(A) 10% loss   (B) 25% loss
(C) 25% profit   (D) none of these

25. Sugar is bought at Rs. 16.20 per kg and sold at Rs. 17.28 per kg. The gain percent is:

(A) $6\frac{2}{3}$ %   (B) $3\frac{1}{3}$ %

(C) 10%   (D) $10\frac{2}{3}$ %

26. A merchant buys a 50 litre cask of wine for Rs. 6250 and sells it at Rs. 130 per litre. His loss or gain percent is:

(A) $3\frac{11}{50}$ % loss   (B) 4% profit

(C) 25% profit   (D) 8% gain

27. A woman bought two parcels of toffees, the same number in each parcel. She bought the first pack at 25 paise per each toffee and the second pack at 3 toffees for 65 paise. She mixed them together and sold at Rs. 3.50 a dozen. Her gain percent is:

(A) 15%   (B) 25% (C) $16\frac{2}{3}$ % (D) 12%

28. The selling price of goods which cost Rs. 10 and were sold at a gain of 10% is:
(A) Rs. 12   (B) Rs. 18
(C) Rs. 11   (D) Rs. 11.10

29. The selling price when goods which cost Rs. 65 are sold at a loss of 10% is:
(A) Rs. 71.50   (B) Rs. 58.50
(C) Rs. 59.75   (D) Rs. 66.50

30. A man bought 542 kg of sugar for Rs.7560.90 and sold it so as to gain 20%. The selling price per kilogram of sugar is:
(A) Rs. 16.74   (B) Rs. 22.92
(C) Rs. 31.46   (D) Rs. 12.24

31. A man sells a mare for Rs. 1085 making a profit of $8\frac{1}{2}$%. The cost of the mare is:
(A) Rs. 982   (B) Rs. 999.50
(C) Rs. 927.75   (D) Rs. 1000

32. A trader marks his goods 30 % above the cost price but makes a reduction of $6\frac{1}{4}$% on the marked price for ready money. His gain percent is:
(A) 23.75%   (B) 23.25%
(C) 21.875%   (D) 20%

33. A publisher sells books to a retail dealer at Rs. 5 a copy but allows 25 copies to be counted as 24. If the retailer sells each of the 25 copies at Rs. 6, his profit percent is:
(A) 20%   (B) 25% (C) 24%   (D) 40%

34. A trader marks his goods at 25% above his cost price and allows a discount of $12\frac{1}{2}$% on purchases for cash payment. The profit percent he makes is:
(A) $9\frac{3}{8}$%   (B) $11\frac{2}{3}$%

(C) $7\frac{1}{3}$%   (D) $4\frac{1}{11}$%

35. The percentage equivalent to $\frac{3}{8}$ is:
(A) 37.5%   (B) 0.375%
(C) 40%   (D) 3.75%

36. If the discount is 10%, an item bought for Rs. 9 is priced at:
(A) Rs. 11   (B) Rs. 10
(C) Rs. 8.10   (D) Rs. 12

37. A cask containing 425 litres lost 8% by leakage and evaporation. The number of litres left in the case were:
(A) $\frac{425 \times 8}{100}$ (B) $425 - \frac{425 \times 8}{100}$

(C) $425 + \frac{425 \times 8}{100}$ (D) $425 \times \frac{425 \times 8}{100}$

38. $12\frac{1}{2}$ % of Rs. 50 is equal to:
(A) Rs. 6.25   (B) Rs. 6.15
(C) Rs. 6.75   (D) Rs. 6.45

39. 8% of Rs. 625 is equal to:
(A) Rs. 50   (B) Rs. 75
(C) Rs. 80   (D) Rs. 100

40. 0.9 percent can be expressed as:
(A) 0.009 (B) .09   (C) .0009 (D) .9

41. A producer blends two qualities of rice. One costing Rs. 12.50 per kg and the other costing Rs. 14 per kg in the ratio 4: 5. Find his profit percent if he sells the mixture at the rate of Rs. 16 per kg.
(A) 25%   (B) 15% (C) 20%   (D) 10%

42. Ravi sold an article to Sudhir at a profit of 6% who in turn sold that to Gopal at a loss of 5%. If Gopal paid Rs. 2,014 for the article, find the cost price of the article for Ravi.
(A) Rs. 2,020   (B) Rs. 2,000
(C) Rs. 1,900   (D) Rs. 2,011

43. If a merchant estimates his profits as 20% of the selling price, what is his real profit percent.
(A) 25%   (B) 20% (C) 22%   (D) 30%

44. Karuna bought a car for a certain sum of money. She spent 10% of the cost on repairs and sold the car for a profit of Rs. 11,000. How much did she spend on repairs, if she made a profit of 20%?
    (A) Rs. 4,000   (B) Rs. 4,400
    (C) Rs. 5,500   (D) Rs. 5,000

45. An article when sold at a gain of 5% yield Rs. 15 more than when sold at a loss of 5%. Its cost price would be:
    (A) Rs. 150   (B) Rs. 200
    (C) Rs. 250   (D) Rs. 300

46. A man bought goods worth Rs. 6,000 and sold half of them at a gain of 10%. At what gain percent must he sell the remainder to get a gain of 25% on the whole?
    (A) 40%   (B) 25% (C) 25%   (D) 20%

47. A shopkeeper fixes the MP of an item 35% above its CP. The percentage of discount allowed to gain 8% is:
    (A) 43%   (B) 30% (C) 20%   (D) 31%

48. A shopkeeper marks his goods at 40% above the cost price and allows a discount of 40% on the marked price. His loss or gain is:
    (A) no loss and no gain
    (B) 16% loss
    (C) 16% gain
    (D) 20% gain

49. If SP of an article is $\frac{4}{3}$ of its CP then the profit in the transaction is:
    (A) $\frac{1}{3}\%$ (B) $20\frac{1}{2}\%$

    (C) $33\frac{1}{3}\%$ (D) $25\frac{1}{2}\%$

50. If 5% more is gained by selling an article for Rs. 350 than by selling it for Rs. 340, the cost of the article is:

(A) Rs. 50   (B) Rs. 160
(C) Rs. 200   (D) Rs. 225

51. A cycle is sold for Rs. 880 at a loss of 20%. For how much should it be sold to gain 10%?
    (A) Rs. 1400   (B) Rs. 1210
    (C) Rs. 1100   (D) Rs. 1000

52. If a company sells a car with a marked price of Rs. 2,72,000 and gives a discount of 4% on Rs. 2,00,000 and 2.5% on the remaining amount of Rs. 72,000, then the actual price charged by the company for the car is:
    (A) Rs. 2,50,000   (B) Rs. 2,55,000
    (C) Rs. 2,60,100   (D) Rs. 2,62,200

53. Garima purchased a briefcase with an additional 10% discount on the reduced price after deducting 20% on the labelled price, If the labelled price was Rs. 1400, at what price did she purchase the briefcase?
    (A) Rs. 980   (B) Rs. 1008
    (C) Rs. 1056   (D) Rs. 1120

54. A bag marked at Rs. 80 is sold for Rs. 68. The rate of discount is:
    (A) 12%   (B) 15%

    (C) $17\frac{11}{17}\%$ (D) 20%

55. A pair of articles was bought for Rs.37.40 at a discount of 15%. What must be the marked price of each of the articles?
    (A) Rs. 11   (B) Rs. 22
    (C) Rs. 33   (D) Rs. 44

56. A shopkeeper gives 12% additional discount on radio after giving an initial discount of 20% on the labelled price of

a radio. If the final selling price of the radio is Rs. 704, then what is its labelled price?

(A) Rs. 844.80   (B) Rs. 929.28

(C) Rs. 1000   (D) Rs. 1044.80

57. A fan is listed at Rs. 1500 and a discount of 20% is offered on the list price. What additional discount must be offered to the customer to bring the net price to Rs. 1104 ?

(A) 8%   (B) 10% (C) 12% (D) 15%

58. A discount of 15% on one article is the same as a discount of 20% on another article. The costs of the two articles can be:

(A) Rs. 40, Rs. 20   (B) Rs. 60, Rs. 40

(C) Rs. 80, Rs. 60   (D) Rs. 60, Rs. 40

59. What will be the list price of an article which is sold for Rs. y after giving a discount of x% ?

(A) $\dfrac{100y}{100-x}$ (B) $\dfrac{100y}{1-x}$

(C) $\dfrac{100y}{1-(x/100)}$ (D) None of these

60. Jatin bought a refrigerator with 20% discount on the labelled price. If he woud have bought it with 25% discount, he could have saved Rs. 500. At what price did he buy the refrigerator?

(A) Rs. 5,000   (B) Rs. 10,000

(C) Rs. 12,500   (D) Rs. 15,000

61. The selling price of 4 articles is same as the C.P of 5 articles. Then profit percent is _____.

(A) 25%   (B) 20%

(C) 18%   (D) None of these

62. By selling 20 mangoes a person recovers price of 25 mangoes. Then profit percentage is:

(A) 20%   (B) 25% (C) 27.5% (D) 22.5%

63. The shopkeeper gives a discount of 12% on the pair of shoes marked as for Rs. 1425, then S.P is:

(A) Rs. 1245   (B) Rs. 1425

(C) Rs. 1524   (D) Rs. 1254

64. If a refrigerator is marked at Rs. 13750 and sold for Rs. 12100, then discount is:

(A) Rs. 1560   (B) Rs. 1650

(C) Rs. 1600   (D) None of these

65. A book is marked at Rs. 880 and sold for Rs. 770, then discount percentage is:

(A) 20%   (B) 25%

(C) 12.5%   (D) None of these

66. The discount percentage is 25% what is the fraction multiplied with marked price to find selling price?

(A) $\dfrac{1}{4}$ (B) $\dfrac{3}{4}$ (C) $\dfrac{125}{100}$ (D) $\dfrac{100}{75}$

67. The marked price of an article is Rs. x, and selling price is Rs. y, then the discount percentage is:

(A) $\dfrac{(x-y)100}{x}$ (B) $\dfrac{(y-x)100}{x}$

(C) $\left(\dfrac{y-x}{y}\right)100$ (D) $\dfrac{x-y}{100}$

68. The selling price and cost price of an article differ by Rs. 240. If the profit percentage is 20, then selling price is:

(A) Rs. 1440   (B) Rs. 1200

(C) Rs. 1420   (D) None of these

69. What is a single discount equivalent to a series discount of 20%, 10% and 5%?

(A) 81%   (B) 31.4%

(C) 31.6%   (D) None of these

70. A shopkeeper allows a discount of 10% on the marked price. How much above the cost price must he mark his goods to gain 8%?

(A) 20%   (B) 100%

(C) 80%   (D) None of these

Previous Contest Questions

1. A man sells two articles for the same price for Rs. 640. He earns 20% profit on the first and 10% profit on the second. Find the over all percent profit.
    (A) 14.78%   (B) 14.08%
    (C) 14.58%   (D) 14.68%

2. By selling 33 acres of land, one gains about the selling price of 11 acres. Find the gain percent.
    (A) 20%   (B) 40% (C) 50%   (D) 22%

3. The cost price of 9 articles is equal to the selling price of 11 articles. Then the loss percentage is:
    (A) $18\frac{2}{11}$% (B) $2\frac{9}{11}$% (C) $15\frac{1}{2}$% (D) $16\frac{1}{2}$%

4. Profit earned by selling an article for Rs. 1,060 is 20% more than the loss incurred by selling the article for Rs. 950. At what price should the article be sold to earn 20% profit?
    (A) Rs. 1000   (B) Rs. 1150
    (C) Rs. 1,250   (D) Rs. 1,200

5. The compound interest on Rs. 24,480 at $6\frac{1}{4}$% per annum for 2 years 73 days, is:
    (A) Rs. 2,929
    (B) Rs. 3,000
    (C) Rs. 3,131
    (D) Rs. 3,636

6. Sam invested Rs. 15000 at the rate of 10% per annum for one year. If the interest is compounded half-yearly, then the amount received by Sam at the end of the year will be:
    (A) Rs. 16,500   (B) Rs. 16,525.50
    (C) Rs. 16,537.50   (D) Rs. 18,150

7. What is the difference between the compound interests on Rs. 5,000 for $1\frac{1}{2}$ years at 4% per annum compounded yearly and half-yearly?
    (A) Rs. 2.04   (B) Rs. 3.06
    (C) Rs. 4.80   (D) Rs. 8.30

8. What will be the difference between simple and compound interest at the rate of 10% per annum on a sum of Rs. 1,000 after 4 years?
    (A) Rs. 31   (B) Rs. 32.10
    (C) Rs. 40.40   (D) Rs. 64.10

9. The present worth of Rs. 169 due in 2 years at 4% per annum compounded interest is:
    (A) Rs. 150.50   (B) Rs. 154.75
    (C) Rs. 156.25   (D) Rs. 158

10. In how many years will a sum of Rs. 800 at 10% per annum compounded, semi-annually become Rs. 926.10?
    (A) $1\frac{1}{3}$ (B) $1\frac{1}{2}$ (C) $2\frac{1}{3}$ (D) $2\frac{1}{2}$

⊘ Answers ⊘

Multiple Choice Questions

1. C	2. D	3. B	4. D	5. D	6. D	7. C	8. A	9. B	10. C
11. D	12. B	13. A	14. B	15. D	16. C	17. B	18. D	19. C	20. C
21. A	22. B	23. C	24. C	25. A	26. B	27. B	28. C	29. B	30. A
31. D	32. C	33. B	34. A	35. A	36. B	37. B	38. A	39. A	40. A
41. C	42. B	43. A	44. D	45. A	46. A	47. C	48. B	49. C	50. C
51. B	52. D	53. B	54. B	55. B	56. C	57. A	58. C	59. A	60. B
61. A	62. B	63. D	64. B	65. C	66. B	67. A	68. A	69. C	70. A

Previous Contest Questions

1. A	2. C	3. A	4. D	5. A	6. C	7. A	8. D	9. C	10. B

Explanatory Answers

1. (C) A = Rs. 220; P = Rs. 200; R = ?
   n = 1 year.

   $$A = P\left(1 + \frac{R}{100}\right)^n$$

   $$220 = 200\left(1 + \frac{R}{100}\right)^1$$

   $$1 + \frac{R}{100} = \frac{220}{200}$$

   R = 10%

3. (B) $CI - SI = \frac{R \times SI}{2 \times 100}$

   $$41 - 40 = \frac{R \times 40}{2 \times 100}$$

   R = 5%

4. (D) $CI - SI = \frac{R \times SI}{2 \times 100}$

   $$144 = \frac{15 \times SI}{200}$$

   SI = Rs. 1,920

   $$\frac{PTR}{100} = Rs.\,1,920$$

   $$\frac{P \times 2 \times 15}{100} = 1,920$$

   P = Rs. 6,400

5. (D) $882 = 800\left(1 + \frac{5}{100}\right)^n$

   $$\left(\frac{105}{100}\right)^n = \frac{882}{800}$$

   n = 2 years

6. (D) $A = 8000\left(1 + \frac{5}{2 \times 100}\right)^2$

   = Rs. 8405
   CI = A – P = 8405 – 8000 = Rs. 405

7. (C) SI for 1st year = Rs. 80
                   = CI for 1st year
   CI for 2 years = 170
   = CI for 1st year + CI for 2nd year
   ∴ CI for 2nd year
   = Interest on Rs. 80 for 1 year
   = 90 – 80 = 10
   ∴ Rate of interest

   $$= \frac{10}{80} \times 100 = 12\frac{1}{2}\%$$

8. (A) $A = P\left(1 + \frac{R}{100}\right)^n$

   $$968 = P\left(1 + \frac{10}{100}\right)^2$$

   $$968 = P\left(\frac{11}{10}\right)^2$$

   P = Rs. 800

9. (B) CI – SI =

   $$P\left[\left(\frac{R}{100}\right)^3 + 3\left(\frac{R}{100}\right)^2\right]$$

   $$15.50 = P\left[\left(\frac{10}{100}\right)^3 + 3\left(\frac{10}{100}\right)^2\right]$$

   $$P = 15.50 \times \frac{1000}{31} = Rs. 500$$

10. (C) $A = 25000\left(1 + \frac{20}{200}\right)^3$

    $$= 25000 \times \left(\frac{11}{10}\right)^3$$

    = Rs. 33,275

11. (D) $A = P\left(1 + \frac{R}{100}\right)^n\left(1 + \frac{TR}{100}\right)$

$$A = 16000 \times \left(1 + \frac{15}{100}\right)^2 \times \left(1 + \frac{\frac{1}{3} \times 15}{100}\right)$$

= Rs. 22,218.

∴ CI = 22,218 – 16,000 = Rs. 6218

12. **(B)** $1331 = 1000\left(1 + \frac{10}{100}\right)^n$

$$\frac{1331}{1000} = \left(\frac{11}{10}\right)^n$$

$$\left(\frac{11}{10}\right)^3 = \left(\frac{11}{10}\right)^n \Rightarrow n = 3 \text{ years}$$

13. **(A)** Population after 3 years

$$= p\left(1 + \frac{p}{100}\right)\left(1 + \frac{q}{100}\right)\left(1 + \frac{r}{100}\right)$$

$$= 25000 \times \left(1 + \frac{4}{100}\right) \times \left(1 + \frac{5}{100}\right) \times \left(1 + \frac{8}{100}\right)$$

$$= 25000 \times \frac{26}{25} \times \frac{21}{20} \times \frac{27}{25} = 29,484$$

14. **(B)** $\because A = P\left(1 - \frac{R}{100}\right)$

$$9680 = P\left(1 - \frac{12}{100}\right)^2$$

$$P = 9680 \times \frac{25}{22} \times \frac{25}{22}$$

= Rs. 12,500

15. **(D)** Value of the vehicle after 3 years

$$= 1,75,000 \times \left(1 - \frac{20}{100}\right)^3$$

$$= 1,75,000 \times \frac{4}{5} \times \frac{4}{5} \times \frac{4}{5}$$

= Rs. 89, 600

∴ Total depreciation

= 1,75,000 – 89,600

= Rs. 85,400

16. **(C)** Using $CI - SI = \frac{R \times SI}{2 \times 100}$

$$410 - 400 = \frac{R \times 400}{2 \times 100}$$

$$R = \frac{10}{2} = 5\%$$

17. **(B)** $P\left[\left(1 + \frac{10}{100}\right)^2 - 1\right] = 525$

$$P \times \frac{21}{100} = 525$$

$$\Rightarrow P = Rs. 2500$$

$$SI = \frac{2500 \times 4 \times 5}{100} = Rs.500$$

18. **(D)** $CI - SI = \frac{R \times SI}{2 \times 100}$

$$696.30 - 660 = \frac{R \times 660}{2 \times 100}$$

$$36.30 = \frac{R \times 660}{2 \times 100}$$

$$R = \frac{36.30 \times 200}{660} = 11\%$$

19. **(C)** $A = P\left(1 + \frac{R}{100}\right)^n$

$$4500 = 3125\left(1 + \frac{R}{100}\right)^2$$

$$\left(1 + \frac{R}{100}\right)^2 = \frac{4500}{3125} = \frac{144}{100}$$

$$1 + \frac{R}{100} = \frac{12}{10}$$

R = 20%

20. **(C)** $2P = P\left(1 + \frac{R}{100}\right)^3$

$$1 + \frac{R}{100} = 2^{\frac{1}{3}} \text{-----}(1)$$

Suppose the money becomes 16 times itself in n years.

$$16P = P\left(1 + \frac{R}{100}\right)^n$$

$$1 + \frac{R}{100} = 2^{\frac{4}{n}} \text{-----}(2)$$

From (1) and (2)

$$2^{\frac{1}{3}} = 2^{\frac{4}{n}}$$

$$\frac{1}{3} = \frac{4}{n}$$

n = 12 years

21. (A) $$328 = P\left[\left(1 + \frac{5}{100}\right)^2 - 1\right]$$

$$328 = P \times \frac{41}{400}$$

P = Rs. 3200

$$SI = \frac{3200 \times 5 \times 2}{100} = Rs.320$$

22. (B) ∵ S.I for 1 year = C.I for 1 year
CI for 1 year = 614.55 − 578.40
= Rs. 36.15
SI for 1 year = Rs. 36.15

$$R = \frac{100 \times I}{P \times T}$$

$$= \frac{100 \times 36.15}{578.40 \times 1} = 6\frac{1}{4}\%$$

23. (C) $$A = p\left(1 + \frac{p}{100}\right)\left(1 + \frac{q}{100}\right)$$

$$A = 12500 \times \left(1 + \frac{15}{100}\right) \times \left(1 \times \frac{16}{100}\right)$$

$$= 12500 \times \frac{115}{100} \times \frac{116}{100}$$

$$= Rs. 16,675$$

24. (C) Profit % = $\dfrac{SP - CP}{CP} \times 100$

$$= \frac{5000 - 4000}{4000} \times 100 = 25\%$$

25. (A) Profit % = $\dfrac{SP - CP}{CP} \times 100$

$$= \frac{17.28 - 16.20}{16.20} \times 100 = 6\frac{2}{3}\%$$

26. (B) Cost per litre of wine =

$$\frac{6250}{50} = 125$$

$$gain\% = \frac{SP - CP}{CP} \times 100$$

$$= \frac{130 - 125}{125} \times 100 = 4\%$$

27. (B) If she bought 3 at 25 paise each, she spent 75 paise and 3 for 65 paise, then totally for 6 she spent 1.40 or for a dozen she spent 2.80 and sold the dozen at Rs. 3.50.

$$\therefore \ gain\% = \frac{0.70}{2.80} \times 100 = 25\%$$

28. (C) Gain = $0.1 \times 10 = Re.1$
∴ SP = CP + gain = 10 + 1 = Rs. 11

29. (B) Loss = $\dfrac{10}{100} \times 65 = 6.50$
∴ SP = CP − loss = 65 − 6.50 = 58.50

30. (A) SP = CP(1+gain%)
The cost of sugar per kilogram

$$= \frac{7560.90}{542} = 13.95$$

S.P. at 20% profit
= 13.95 × 1.2 = Rs. 16.74

31. (D) CP = SP(1+gain%)
Let CP of mare be Rs. 100 then

SP = Rs. 108.50 at $8\frac{1}{2}\%$ profit

If SP is Rs. 1085, then

$$CP = \frac{1085}{108.5} \times 100 = Rs.1000$$

32. (C) Gain% = $\dfrac{SP - CP}{CP} \times 100$

Let cost price be Rs. 100. The MP is

Rs. 130. After discount of $6\dfrac{1}{4}\%$ the

SP is Rs. $130\left(\dfrac{93.75}{100}\right) = Rs.\,121.875$

Gain % =

$\dfrac{121.875 - 100}{100} \times 100 = 21.875\%$

33. (B) Gain% = $\dfrac{SP - CP}{CP} \times 100$

The cost of 25 copies to the retailer
= $5 \times 24 = Rs.\,120$.
The SP of 25 copies = $6 \times 25 = $ Rs. 150

Profit % = $\dfrac{150 - 120}{120} \times 100 = 25\%$

34. (A) Gain% = $\dfrac{SP - CP}{CP} \times 100$

Let cost price be Rs.100.
Then MP = Rs. 125
The SP = 125 (.875) = 109.375
The gain = Rs. 9.375

Gain % = $\dfrac{9.375}{100} \times 100 = 9.375\% = 9\dfrac{3}{8}\%$

35. (A) $\dfrac{3}{8} = \dfrac{3}{8} \times \dfrac{100}{100} = \dfrac{37.5}{100} = 37.5\%$

36. (B) Let MP be Rs. 100. Then
SP = Rs. 90 @ 10% discount. But SP is Rs. 9.
∴ MP is Rs.10.

37. (B) Capacity of cask = Leakage + evaporation + remaining liquid.
The liquid lost by leakage and

evaporation = $\dfrac{8}{100} \times 425$

∴ Remaining = = $425 - \dfrac{8}{100} \times 425$

38. (A) $12\dfrac{1}{2}\%$ of Rs. 50 = $\dfrac{1}{8} \times 50 = 6.25$

39. (A) 8% of Rs. 625 = $\dfrac{8}{100} \times 625 = Rs.50$

40. (A) $0.9\% = \dfrac{0.9}{100} = 0.009$

41. (C) Profit % = $\dfrac{Profit}{CP} \times 100$

CP = $12.50 \times 4x + 14 \times 5x = 120x$
SP = $16 \times 9x = 144x$
Gain = SP – CP = $144x - 120x = 24x$

Gain % = $\dfrac{gain}{CP} \times 100 = \dfrac{24x}{120x} \times 100 = 20\%$

42. (B) Let the CP of the article = Rs. x.

SP for Ravi = $CP \times \dfrac{100 + g}{100} = \dfrac{106}{100}x$

∴ CP for Sudhir = $\dfrac{106x}{100}$

SP of Sudhir = $\dfrac{106x}{100} \times \dfrac{95}{100}$

CP of Gopal = $\dfrac{106x}{100} \times \dfrac{95}{100}$

We have, $\dfrac{106x}{100} \times \dfrac{95}{100} = 2,014$

x = Rs. 2,000

43. (A) Suppose SP = Rs. 100
Profit = Rs. 20
CP = 100 – 20 = Rs. 80

Profit% = $\dfrac{profit}{CP} \times 100 = \dfrac{20}{80} \times 100$

= 25%

44. (D) Let CP of car be Rs. x.

Cost on repair = $\dfrac{x}{10}$

Total cost = $x + \dfrac{x}{10} = \dfrac{11x}{10}$

We have, $\dfrac{11x}{10} \times \dfrac{20}{100} = \dfrac{11x}{50} = 11,000$

$x = 50,000$

Cost on repair = $\dfrac{x}{10} = \dfrac{50,000}{10}$

$= $ Rs. 5000

45. **(A)** Suppose the CP of the article
$= $ Rs. 100
I case :   Profit = 5%
      SP = 100 + 5 = Rs. 105
II case : Loss = 5%
      SP = CP – loss = 100 – 5
             = Rs. 95
Difference between two SP's
           = 105 – 95 = Rs. 10
If the difference = Rs. 10 then
           CP = Rs. 100
If the difference = Rs. 15 then
           CP = Rs. 150

46. **(A)** Total CP = Rs. 6,000
Profit = 25%
Overall SP =

$6000 \times \dfrac{100 + 25}{100} = $ Rs.7,500

SP of half of the goods

$= 3000 \times \dfrac{100 + 10}{100} = $ Rs.3,300

SP of remaining half goods
= 7,500 – 3,300 = Rs. 4,200
Profit on remaining half goods
costing Rs. 3000
= Rs. 4200 – Rs. 3000 = Rs. 1,200

Profit % = $\dfrac{1200}{3000} \times 100 = 40$

47. **(C)** Let CP of article = Rs. 100

MP = $100 \times \dfrac{135}{100} = $ Rs.135

SP required = $100 \times \dfrac{108}{100} = $ Rs.108

On Rs. 135 discount allowed
= Rs. 135 – Rs. 108 = Rs. 27
Hence on Rs. 100 discount allowed

is $\dfrac{27}{135} \times 100 = 20\%$

48. **(B)** Let the CP of articles be Rs. 100

Loss % = $\dfrac{40 \times 40}{100} = 16\%$

49. **(C)** Suppose CP of article = Rs. 100

SP = $100 \times \dfrac{4}{3} = $ Rs. $\dfrac{400}{3}$

Profit = SP – CP =

     $\dfrac{400}{3} - 100 = $ Rs. $\dfrac{100}{3}$

Profit % = $\dfrac{\dfrac{100}{3}}{100} \times 100 = 33\dfrac{1}{3}\%$

50. **(C)** Difference between
SP = Rs. 350 – Rs. 340 = Rs. 10
5% of CP = Rs. 10

100% of CP = $\dfrac{100}{5} \times 10 = $ Rs.200.

51. **(B)** SP of cycle = Rs. 880
Loss = 20%
CP of cycle =

$880 \times \dfrac{100}{100 - 20} = $ Rs.1100

If gain required is 10% then

SP = $1100 \times \dfrac{100 + 10}{100} = $ Rs.1210

52. **(D)** M.P. = Rs. 2,72,000.
Discount = Rs. [(4% of 2,00,000)
+ (2.5% of 72,000)]
= Rs. (8,000 + 1,800)
= Rs. 9,800.
∴ Actual price
= Rs. (2,72,000 – 9,800)
= Rs. 2,62,200.

53. **(B)** C.P = 90% of 80% of Rs. 1400

$$= Rs. \left(\frac{90}{100} \times \frac{80}{100} \times 1400\right)$$

$$= Rs. \ 1008.$$

54. **(B)** Rate of discount

$$= \left(\frac{12}{80} \times 100\right)\% = 15\%$$

55. **(B)** S.P. of each article $= Rs. \left(\frac{37.40}{2}\right)$

$= Rs. \ 18.70.$
Let M.P. be Rs. x.
Then, 85% of x = 18.70

$$\Rightarrow \ x = \left(\frac{18.70 \times 100}{85}\right) = 22.$$

56. **(C)** Let the labelled price be Rs x.
88 % of 80% of x = 704

$$\Rightarrow x = \left(\frac{704 \times 100 \times 100}{80 \times 88}\right) = 1000.$$

57. **(A)** S.P. after 1st discount

$$= Rs. \left(\frac{80}{100} \times 1500\right) = Rs. \ 1200.$$

Net S.P. = Rs. 1104.
Discount on Rs. 1200 = Rs. 96.
∴ Required discount =

$$\left(\frac{96}{1200} \times 100\right)\% = 8\%.$$

58. **(C)** Let the costs of the two articles be x
and y. Then, 15% of x = 20% of y

$$\Rightarrow \frac{x}{y} = \frac{20}{15} = \frac{4}{3}$$

So, x and y must be in the ratio of
4 : 3.

59. **(A)** Let the list price be Rs. z.

$$\therefore (100 - x)\% \ of \ z = y$$

$$\Rightarrow \left(\frac{100 - x}{100}\right) \times z = y$$

$$\Rightarrow z = \left(\frac{100y}{100 - x}\right)$$

60. **(B)** Let the labelled price be Rs. x.
Then, (80% of x) - (75% of x) = 500
$\Rightarrow$ 5% of x = 500

$$\Rightarrow x = \left(\frac{500 \times 100}{5}\right) = 10000.$$

61. **(A)** Let C.P of 1 article is Rs x.
$\Rightarrow$ C.P of 5 articles = Rs. 5x
Given C.P of 5 articles = S. P of 4
articles $\Rightarrow$ S.P of 4 articles = Rs. 5x

$$\Rightarrow S. \ P \ of \ 1 \ articles = Rs. \ \frac{5}{4}x$$

$$Profit = \frac{5}{4}x - x = Rs \ \frac{x}{4}$$

$$Profit \% = \left(\frac{\frac{x}{4}}{x} \times 100\right)\% = 25\%$$

62. **(B)** Let S.P of 20 mangoes = C.P of 25
mangoes = Rs. 100

$$S.P \ of \ 1 \ mango = Rs \ \frac{100}{20} = Rs. \ 5$$

$$and \ C.P \ of \ 1 \ mango = Rs \ \frac{100}{25}$$

$$= Rs. \ 4 \ Profit = Rs \ (5 - 4) = Rs. \ 1$$

$$Profit\% = \frac{1}{4} \times 100 = 25\%$$

63. **(D)** Given M.P = Rs 1425, Discount

$$= 12\% \ of \ Rs \ 1425 = \frac{12}{100} \times 1425$$

$= Rs. \ 171$ Selling price of shoes = Rs.
$(1425 - 171) = Rs. \ 1254$

64. **(B)** Given M.P= Rs. 13750, S.P
= Rs. 12100 Discount = M.P – S.P
$= Rs. (13750 - 12100) = Rs. \ 1650$

65. **(C)** Given M.P = Rs. 880, S.P = Rs. 770
Discount = M.P – S.P = Rs.
$(880 - 770) = Rs. \ 110$ Discount%

$$= \frac{\text{Discount}}{\text{M.P}} \times 100$$

$$= \frac{110}{880} \times 100 = 12.5\%$$

66. (B) Given discount = 25%

$$\text{S.P} = \frac{\text{M.P}(100 - d\%)}{100}$$

$$= \frac{\text{M.P}(100 - 25)}{100}$$

$$\text{M.P} \times \frac{75}{100} \Rightarrow \text{M.P} \times \frac{3}{4}$$

$\therefore \dfrac{3}{4}$ should be multiplied with M.P

to get S.P

68. (A) Let the cost price of the article be Rs. x Selling price is 1.2 x (at a gain of 20%) Given S.P – C.P = Rs. 240

$$1.2x - x = 240 \Rightarrow 0.2x = 240$$

$$\Rightarrow x = \frac{240}{0.2} = 1200$$

Selling price = 1.2 × 1200 = Rs. 1440

69. (C) Let the original price of an article be Rs. 100
Reduced price after a series of successive discount of 20%, 10% and 5%

$$= 100 \times 80\% \times 90\% \times 95\%$$

$$= 100 \times 0.8 \times 0.9 \times 0.95 = 68.4$$

∴ Single discount =

$$(100 - 68.4) = 31.6\%$$

70. (A) Let C.P be Rs 100 ⇒ S.P is Rs. 108
Let the M.P of the goods be Rs. x
Since he allows a discount of 10% on M.P and sells at 8% gain
∴ 90% of x = Rs. 108

$$x = 108 \times \frac{100}{90} = \text{Rs. } 120$$

Previous Contest Questions

1. (A) C.P of item sold at a profit of 20%

$$= \frac{640}{1.2} = \text{Rs. } 533.33$$

C.P of the item sold at a profit of

$$10\% = \frac{640}{1.1} = \text{Rs. } 581.81$$

Total C.P = Rs.1115.14,
Total S.P = Rs.1,280

$$\text{Profit}\% = \frac{164.86}{1115.14} \times 100 = 14.78\%$$

2. (C) SP of 33 acres of land = CP of 33 acres + gain SP of 33 acres of land = CP of 33 acres + SP of 11 acres
∴ SP if 22 acres = CP of 33 acres =

$$\text{SP of 1 acre} = \text{Re } \frac{1}{22}$$

$$\text{CP of 1 acre} = \text{Re } \frac{1}{33}$$

$$\text{Profit} = \text{Re } \left(\frac{1}{22} - \frac{1}{33} \right)$$

$$= \text{Re } \left(\frac{11}{22 \times 33} \right)$$

$$= \text{Re } \frac{1}{66}.$$

$$\text{Profit}\% = \frac{1}{66} \times \frac{33}{1} \times \frac{100}{1} = 50\%$$

3. (A) Let CP of 9 articles = SP of 11 articles = Re 1

$$\therefore \text{CP of 1 article} = \text{Re } \frac{1}{9},$$

$$\text{SP of 1 article} = \text{Re } \frac{1}{11}$$

$$\therefore \text{Loss} = \text{Re } \left(\frac{1}{9} - \frac{1}{11} \right) = \text{Re } \frac{2}{99} \text{ and}$$

$$\text{Loss}\% = \frac{\text{Loss}}{\text{CP}} \times 100$$

$$=\frac{\frac{2}{99}}{1/9}\times100=18\frac{2}{11}\%$$

5. (A) Time $=2\frac{73}{365}$ years $=2\frac{1}{5}$ years.

∴ Amount = Rs.

$$\left[20480\times\left(1+\frac{25}{4\times100}\right)^{2}\left(1+\frac{\frac{1}{5}\times\frac{25}{4}}{100}\right)\right]$$

$$=\text{Rs.}\left(20480\times\frac{17}{16}\times\frac{17}{16}\times\frac{81}{80}\right)$$

$$=\text{Rs. }23{,}409$$

∴ C.I.Rs.$(23409-20480)=$ Rs. 2,929.

6. (C) P = Rs. 15000; R = 10% p.a = 5% per half-year; T = 1 year = 2 half-years.

$$\therefore \text{ Amount}=\left[15000\times\left(1+\frac{5}{100}\right)^{2}\right]$$

$$=\text{Rs.}\left(15000\times\frac{21}{20}\times\frac{21}{20}\right)$$

$$=\text{Rs. }16{,}537.50$$

7. (A) C.I. when interest is compounded yearly

$$=\text{Rs.}\left[5000\times\left(1+\frac{4}{100}\right)\times\left(1+\frac{\frac{1}{2}\times4}{100}\right)\right]$$

$$=\text{Rs.}\left(5000\times\frac{26}{25}\times\frac{51}{50}\right)=\text{Rs. }5{,}304$$

C.I. when interest is compounded half-yearly

$$=\text{Rs.}\left[5000\times\left(1+\frac{2}{100}\right)^{3}\right]$$

$$=\text{Rs.}\left(5000\times\frac{51}{50}\times\frac{51}{50}\times\frac{51}{50}\right)$$

$$=\text{Rs. }5{,}306.04.$$

∴ Difference

$$=\text{Rs. }(5306.04-5304)$$

$$=\text{Rs. }2.04.$$

8. (D) S.I. = Rs. $\left(\frac{1000\times10\times4}{100}\right)=$ Rs. 400

$$\text{C.I. = Rs.}\left[1000\times\left(1+\frac{10}{100}\right)^{4}-1000\right]$$

$$=\text{Rs. }464.10$$

∴ Difference = Rs. $(464.10-400)$

$$=\text{Rs. }64.10.$$

9. (C) Present worth

$$=\text{Rs.}\left[\frac{1}{\left(1+\frac{4}{100}\right)^{2}}\right]\times169$$

$$=\text{Rs.}\left(169\times\frac{25}{26}\times\frac{25}{26}\right)=\text{Rs. }156.25$$

10. (B) Let the time be n years. Then,

$$800\times\left(1+\frac{5}{100}\right)^{2n}=926.10$$

$$\text{or }\left(1+\frac{5}{100}\right)^{2n}=\frac{9261}{8000}$$

$$\text{or }\left(\frac{21}{20}\right)^{2n}=\left(\frac{21}{20}\right)^{3}$$

or $2n=3$ or $n=\frac{3}{2}$

∴ $n=1\frac{1}{2}$ years.

Get It Right

A Error in adding and subtracting algebraic fractions.

e.g. (a) Simplify $\dfrac{1}{x} + \dfrac{2}{3x}$

 Incorrect

$$\frac{1}{x} + \frac{2}{3x} = \frac{1+2}{x+3x} = \frac{1}{4x}$$

> Incorrect because the LCM of x and 3x is 3x.

 Correct

$$\frac{1}{x} + \frac{2}{3x} = \frac{1(\times 3)}{x(\times 3)} + \frac{2}{3x} = \frac{3+2}{3x} = \frac{5}{3x}$$

B Error while dividing algebraic fractions.

e.g. Simplify $\dfrac{2x}{y} \div xy$

 Incorrect

$$\frac{2x}{y} \div xy = 2x^2$$

> Incorrect because the reciprocal of xy is $\dfrac{1}{xy}$.

 Correct

$$\frac{2x}{y} \div xy = \frac{2x}{y} \times \frac{1}{xy} = \frac{2}{y^2}$$

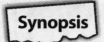

Algebraic Expression:

A combination of constants and variables connected by $+$, $-$, $\times$ and $\div$ is known as an algebraic expression.

Eg : $2 - 3x + 5x^{-2}y^{-1} + \dfrac{x}{3y^3}$

Polynomial:

An algebraic expression in which the variables involved have only non-negative integral powers is called a polynomial.

Eg : $2 - 3x + 5x^2y - \dfrac{1}{3}xy^3$

Degree of a Polynomial:

♦   In case of a polynomial in one variable, the highest power of the variable is called the degree of the polynomial.

Eg : $5x^3 - 7x + \dfrac{3}{2}$ is a polynomial in x of degree 3.

♦   In case of polynomial in more than one variable, the sum of the powers of the variables in each term is taken up and the highest sum so obtained is called the degree of the polynomial.

Eg : $5x^3 - 2x^2y^2 - 3x^2y + 9y$ is a polynomial of degree 4 in x and y.

Linear Polynomial:

A polynomial of degree 1 is called a linear polynomial.

Quadratic Polynomial:

A polynomial of degree 2 is called a quadratic polynomial.

Cubic Polynomial:

A polynomial of degree 3 is called a cubic poynomial.

Biquadratic Polynomial:

A polynomial of degree 4 is called a biquadratic polynomial.

Monomial:

A polynomial containing 1 term is called a monomial.

Binomial:

A polynomial containing 2 terms is called a bionomial.

Trinomial:

A polynomial containing 3 terms is called a trinomial.

Constant Polynomial:

A polynomial containing one term consisting of a constant is called a constant polynomial.

♦   The degree of a constant polynomial is zero.

♦   The terms of a polynomial are said to be in ascending (or) descending order if they increase (or) decrease in degrees respectively.

Eg : (1) $3 - 7x + 5x^2 - 2x^3$ is in ascending order

(2) $-2x^3 + 5x^2 - 7x + 3$ is in descending order.

♦   Terms with same variables and which have the same exponent are called like or similar terms, otherwise they are called unlike (or) dissimilar terms.

Eg : (1) $3x^3, \dfrac{1}{2}x^3, -9x^3, ...$ etc, are like terms

(2) $x^2y, 3xy^2, -4x^3, ...$etc, are unlike terms.

♦   Dividend = (Divisor $\times$ Quotient) + Reminder

Some important identities:

♦ $(a + b)^2 = a^2 + 2ab + b^2$

♦ $(a - b)^2 = a^2 - 2ab + b^2$

♦ $(a + b)(a - b) = a^2 - b^2$

♦ $(a + b + c)^2 = a^2 + b^2 + c^2 + 2ab + 2bc + 2ca$

♦ $(a + b)^3 = a^3 + b^3 + 3ab(a + b) = a^3 + b^3 + 3a^2b + 3ab^2$

♦ $(a - b)^3 = a^3 - b^3 - 3ab(a - b) = a^3 - b^3 - 3a^2b + 3ab^2$

♦ $a^3 + b^3 = (a + b)(a^2 - ab + b^2)$

♦ $a^3 - b^3 = (a - b)(a^2 + ab + b^2)$

♦ $(x + a)(x + b) = x^2 + (a + b)x + ab$

♦ $a^3 + b^3 + c^3 - 3abc = (a + b + c)(a^2 + b^2 + c^2 - ab - bc - ca)$

♦   If $a + b + c = 0$ then $a^3 + b^3 + c^3 = 3abc$

Multiple Choice Questions

1. Which of the following expressions is a polynomial?

   (A) $3x^{\frac{1}{2}} - 4x + 3$

   (B) $4x^2 - 3\sqrt{x} + 5$

   (C) $3x^2y - 2xy + 5x^4$

   (D) $2x^4 + \dfrac{3}{x^2} - 1$

2. The degree of the polynomial

   $5x^3 - 6x^3y + 4y^2 - 8$ is:
   (A) 3
   (B) 4
   (C) 2
   (D) can't be determined

3. What must be added to $x^3 + 3x - 8$ to get $3x^3 + x^2 + 6$?
   (A) $2x^3 + x^2 - 3x + 14$
   (B) $2x^2 + x^2 + 14$
   (C) $2x^3 + x^2 - 6x - 14$
   (D) None of these

4. What must be subtracted from

   $x^3 - 3x^2 + 5x - 1$ to get $2x^3 + x^2 - 4x + 2$?
   (A) $-x^3 + 4x^2 - 9x + 3$
   (B) $x^3 + 4x^2 - 9x + 3$
   (C) $x^3 - 4x^2 + 9x - 3$
   (D) $-x^3 - 4x^2 + 9x - 3$

5. Divide $(-56mnp^2)$ by $(7mnp)$.
   (A) $-8p$ (B) $8mnp$
   (C) $8p$ (D) None of these

6. A factor of $x^3 - 1$ is:
   (A) $x - 1$ (B) $x^2 + x + 1$
   (C) either A or B   (D) none of these

7. The product of $\dfrac{2}{3}$ xy by $\dfrac{3}{2}$ xz is:

   (A) $\dfrac{1}{6}$ xyz   (B) x^2yz

   (C) $6 x^2yz$ (D) none of these

8. Divide $8x^2y^2 - 6xy^2 + 10x^2y^3$ by $2xy$.
   (A) $4xy - 3y + 5xy^2$ (B) $4xy + 3y - 5xy^2$
   (C) $8xy + 3y - 5xy^2$(D) $4xy - 3y - 5xy^2$

9. The product of $(x^2 + 3x + 5)$ and

   $(x^2 - 1)$ is:
   (A) $x^4 + 3x^3 - 4x^2 - 3x - 5$
   (B) $x^4 + 3x^3 + 4x^2 - 3x - 5$
   (C) $x^4 + 3x^3 + 4x^2 + 3x - 5$
   (D) none of these

10. If quotient = $3x^2 - 2x + 1$, remainder = $2x - 5$ and divisor = $x + 2$ then the dividend is:
    (A) $3x^3 - 4x^2 + x - 3$
    (B) $3x^3 - 4x^2 - x + 3$
    (C) $3x^3 + 4x^2 - x + 3$
    (D) $3x^3 + 4x^2 - x - 3$

11. If $(x - 2)$ is one factor of $x^2 + ax - 6 = 0$ and $x^2 - 9x + b = 0$ then $a + b =$ ____ .
    (A) 15   (B) 13   (C) 11   (D) 10

12. The remainder obtained when

    $t^6 + 3t^2 + 10$ is divided by $t^3 + 1$ is:
    (A) $t^2 - 11$ (B) $t^3 - 1$
    (C) $3t^2 + 11$ (D) none of these

13. The value of the product $(3x^2 - 5x + 6)$ and $(-8x^3)$ when $x = 0$ is:

    (A) $\dfrac{1}{2}$ (B) 2   (C) 1   (D) 0

14. The difference of the degrees of the polynomials $3x^2y^3 + 5xy^7 - x^6$ and $3x^5 - 4x^3 + 2$ is:
    (A) 2   (B) 3
    (C) 1   (D) none of these

15. What must be added to $x^2 + 5x - 6$ to get $x^3 - x^2 + 3x - 2$?
    (A) $x^3 - 2x^2 - 2x - 4$(B) $x^3 + 2x^2 - 2x + 4$
    (C) $x^3 - 2x^2 - 2x + 4$(D) None of these

16. What must be subtracted from

$x^4 + 2x^2 - 3x + 7$ to get $x^3 + x^2 + x - 1$?
(A) $x^4 - x^3 + x^2 - 4x + 8$
(B) $x^3 + x^2 - 4x + 8$
(C) $x^4 - x^3 + x^2 + 4x - 8$
(D) $x^4 - x^3 - x^2 + 4x - 8$

17. The product of x^2y and $\dfrac{x}{y}$ is equal to

the quotient obtained when x^2 is divided by _____ .

(A) 0   (B) 1   (C) x   (D) $\dfrac{1}{x}$

18. If $(3x - 4)(5x + 7) = 15x^2 - ax - 28$ then a = _____ .
(A) 1   (B) –1
(C) –2   (D) none of these

19. The product of two factors with unlike signs is_____ .
(A) positive
(B) negative
(C) cannot be determined
(D) none of these

20. Subtracting $x^3 - xy^2 + 5x^2y - y^3$ from

$-y^3 - 6x^2y - xy^2 + x^3$, we get:
(A) $2y^3 - 8x^2y + 3xy^2 - 2x^3$
(B) $2x^3 - 2xy^2 - x^2y - 2y^3$
(C) $-11x^2y$
(D) None of these

21. The value of $25x^2 + 16y^2 + 40xy$ at x = 1 and y = –1 is:
(A) 81   (B) –49
(C) 1   (D) none of these

22. Find the missing term in the following problem.

$\left(\dfrac{3x}{4} - \dfrac{4y}{3}\right)^2 = \dfrac{9x^2}{16} + \underline{\quad} + \dfrac{16y^2}{9}$

(A) 2xy   (B) –2xy (C) 12xy (D) –12xy

23. The value of

$\dfrac{7.83 \times 7.83 - 1.17 \times 1.17}{6.66}$ is:

(A) 9   (B) 6.66
(C) 1.176   (D) none of these

24. If $x - \dfrac{1}{x} = \sqrt{6}$ then $x^2 + \dfrac{1}{x^2} =$ ____

(A) 2   (B) 4   (C) 6   (D) 8

25. If $x^2 + \dfrac{1}{x^2} = 79$ then $x + \dfrac{1}{x} =$ ____

(A) $\sqrt{75}$ (B) 9
(C) $\sqrt{79}$ (D) none of these

26. If $3x - 7y = 10$ and $xy = -1$ then the value of $9x^2 + 49y^2$ is:
(A) 58   (B) 142 (C) 104   (D) –104

27. If $a + b + c = 10$ and $a^2 + b^2 + c^2 = 36$ then $ab + bc + ca =$ _____.
(A) 136   (B) 64   (C) 32   (D) 68

28. If $x - y = 4$ and $xy = 21$ then $x^3 - y^3 =$ _____.
(A) 361   (B) 316
(C) –188   (D) none of these

29. $(a + b)^3 - (a - b)^3 =$ ____
(A) $b^3 + 3a^2b$ (B) $2(b^3 + 3a^2b)$
(C) $2(a^3 + 3ab^2)$ (D) 0

30. The product of $(4x - 3y)$ and $(6x^2 + 12xy + 9y^2)$ is:
(A) $(4x - 3y)^3$
(B) $(16x^2 + 12xy + 9y^2)^2$
(C) $64x^3 - 27y^3$
(D) none of these

31. $(3x - 5y)^3 - (5x - 2y)^3 + (2x + 3y)^3$
(A) $(3x - 5y)(5x - 2y)(2x + 3y)$
(B) $3(3x - 5y)(5x - 2y)(2x + 3y)$
(C) $(3x - 5y)(2y - 5x)(2x + 3y)$
(D) $-3(3x - 5y)(5x - 2y)(2x + 3y)$

32. If $a + b + c = 9$ and $ab + bc + ca = 26$, then the value of $a^3 + b^3 + c^3 - 3abc$ is:
(A) 27   (B) 29   (C) 495   (D) 729

33. If $x^3 + y^3 + z^3 = 3xyz$ then the relation between x, y and z is:
(A) $x + y + z = 0$
(B) $x = y = z$
(C) either $x + y + z = 0$ (or) $x = y = z$
(D) neither $x + y + z = 0$ nor $x = y = z$

34. The inequality $b^2 + 5 > 9b + 12$ is satisfied if :
(A) $b > 9$ (or) $b < 1$
(B) $b > 9$ (or) $b < 0$
(C) $b = 10$ (or) $b = -1$
(D) $b > 8$ (or) $b < 0$

35. If $0 < a < 1$, then the value of

$a + \dfrac{1}{a}$ is:

(A) greater than 2 (B) less than 2
(C) greater than 4 (D) less than 4

36. The value of

$$\dfrac{(67.542)^2 - (32.458)^2}{75.458 - 40.374} \text{ is:}$$

(A) 1   (B) 10
(C) 100   (D) none of these

37. If

$$y = \dfrac{(0.42)^3 + (0.25)^3 + (0.33)^3 - 3 \times 0.42 \times 0.25 \times 0.33}{(0.42)^2 + (0.25)^2 + (0.33)^2 - 0.42 \times 0.25 - 0.25 \times 0.33 - 0.33 \times 0.42}$$

then the value of y is:
(A) 1   (B) 0

(C) $\dfrac{1}{2}$ (D) none of these

38. The value of

$$\dfrac{(0.31)^3 - (0.21)^3}{0.0961 + 0.0651 + 0.0441} \text{ is:}$$

(A) 0   (B) 0.1
(C) 0.2   (D) 0.04

39. If $2x + y = 5$ then $4x + 2y$ is equal to:
(A) 5   (B) 8   (C) 9   (D) 10

40. If $x + y = 6$ and $3x - y = 4$ then $x - y$ is equal to:
(A) –1   (B) 0
(C) 2   (D) 4

41. If the product of two numbers is 10 and the sum is 7, then the larger of the two numbers is:
(A) –2   (B) 2
(C) 5   (D) $4\dfrac{1}{4}$

42. The value of $(55)^3 - (75)^3 + (20)^3$ is:
(A) –247500   (B) 251750
(C) 125320   (D) none of these

43. The value of the product

$$\left(3 + \dfrac{5}{x}\right)\left(9 - \dfrac{15}{x} + \dfrac{25}{x^2}\right) \text{ at } x = 1 \text{ is:}$$

(A) 150   (B) 148
(C) 152   (D) none of these

44. $\dfrac{a^3 + b^3 + c^3 - 3abc}{a^2 + b^2 + c^2 - ab - bc - ca} = $ _____ .

(A) 0   (B) $a + b + c$
(C) 1   (D) none of these

45. The value of $(x + 3)^3 - (x - 3)^3$ is:
(A) 0   (B) $1 - x^3$
(C) $3x^2 - 5$ (D) $18x^2 + 54$

Previous Contest Questions

1. Factorise $9(p-q)^2 - 4(2p+q)^2$:

    (A) $-(7p-q)(p+5q)$

    (B) $(7p-q)(p+5q)$

    (C) $-(7p+q)(p+5q)$

    (D) $(7p+q)(p-5q)$

2. Factorise $x^2 - xy + y - x$:

    (A) $(x-1)(x+y)$ (B) $(x+1)(x+y)$

    (C) $(x-1)(x-y)$ (D) None of these

3. Factorise $a - b - a^2 + b^2$:

    (A) $(a-b)\left[1-(a+b)\right]$

    (B) $(a+b)\left[1-(a-b)\right]$

    (C) $(a-b)\left[1-(a-b)\right]$

    (D) None of these

4. What is the H.C.F $8x^2y^2, 12x^3y^2$ and $24x^4y^3z^2$?

    (A) $4xy^2z$ (B) $4x^2y^2z^2$

    (C) $4x^2y^2$ (D) None of these

5. If $2a - \dfrac{1}{2a} = 3$ then $16a^4 + \dfrac{1}{16a^4}$ is ?

    (A) 11   (B) 119   (C) 117   (D) 121

6. If $a^2 + b^2 + c^2 - ab - bc - ca = 0$ then:

    (A) $a = b = c$ (B) $a \neq b \neq c$

    (C) $a = b \neq c$ (D) None of these

7. Factorise $4x^4 + 3x^2 + 1$:

    (A) $\left(2x^2 + x + 1\right)\left(2x^2 + x - 1\right)$

    (B) $\left(2x^2 + x + 1\right)\left(2x^2 - x + 1\right)$

    (C) $\left(2x^2 + x - 1\right)\left(2x - x + 1\right)$

    (D) None of these

8. If $\dfrac{3x+5}{2x+7} = 4$ then x is:

    (A) $\dfrac{23}{5}$ (B) $\dfrac{-23}{5}$

    (C) -23 (D) None of these

9. If $\dfrac{17-3x}{5} - \dfrac{4x+2}{3} = 5 - 6x + \dfrac{7x+14}{3}$.

    then x is:

    (A) 2   (B) 4

    (C) -4 (D) None of these

10. If $\dfrac{x^2 - (x+1)(x+2)}{5x+1} = 6$ then x is:

    (A) $\dfrac{8}{33}$ (B) $\dfrac{8}{3}$ (C) $\dfrac{-8}{33}$ (D) $\dfrac{-6}{33}$

⊘ Answers ⊘

Multiple Choice Questions

1. C	2. B	3. A	4. D	5. A	6. C	7. B	8. A	9. B	10. D
11. A	12. C	13. D	14. B	15. C	16. A	17. D	18. B	19. B	20. C
21. C	22. B	23. A	24. D	25. B	26. A	27. C	28. B	29. B	30. C
31. D	32. A	33. C	34. B	35. A	36. C	37. A	38. B	39. D	40. A
41. C	42. A	43. C	44. B	45. D					

Previous Contest Questions

1. A	2. C	3. A	4. C	5. B	6. A	7. B	8. B	9. B	10. C

Explanatory Answers

1. **(C)** For polynomials, power should be non-negative integer.

2. **(B)** $\because$ highest power is $3 + 1 = 4$.

3. **(A)**
$$3x^3 + x^2 \qquad\quad + 6$$
$$(+) x^3 \qquad\quad (+)3x - 8$$
$$\underline{\quad - \qquad\qquad - \qquad + \quad}$$
$$2x^3 + x^2 - 3x + 14$$

4. **(D)**
$$x^3 - 3x^2 + 5x - 1$$
$$+2x^3 + x^2 - 4x + 2$$
$$\underline{\quad - \qquad - \quad + \qquad - \quad}$$
$$-x^3 - 4x^2 + 9x - 3$$

5. **(A)** $\dfrac{-56\ mnp^2}{7\ mnp} = -8p$

6. **(C)** $x^3 - 1 = x^3 - 1^3 = (x - 1)(x^2 + x + 1)$

7. **(B)** $\dfrac{2}{3}xy \times \dfrac{3}{2}xz = x^2yz$

8. **(A)** $\dfrac{8x^2y^2 - 6xy^2 + 10x^2y^3}{2xy}$

$$= \dfrac{8x^2y^2}{2xy} - \dfrac{6xy^2}{2xy} + \dfrac{10x^2y^3}{2xy}$$

$$= 4xy - 3y + 5xy^2$$

9. **(B)** $(x^2 + 3x + 5) \times (x^2 - 1)$

$$= x^2 \times x^2 + 3x \times x^2 + 5 \times x^2 +$$
$$\quad x^2 \times -1 + 3x \times -1 + 5 \times -1$$

$$= x^4 + 3x^3 + 5x^2 - x^2 - 3x - 5$$

$$= x^4 + 3x^3 + 4x^2 - 3x - 5$$

10. **(D)** Dividend

$$= (divisor \times quotient) + remainder$$
$$= (3x^2 - 2x + 1) \times (x + 2) + (2x - 5)$$
$$= 3x^3 + 4x^2 - x - 3$$

11. **(A)**

$x^2 + ax - 6 = 0$	$x^2 - 9x + b = 0$
$2^2 + a(2) - 6 = 0$	$2^2 - 9(2) + b = 0$
$2a = 2$	$b = 14$
$a = 1$	

$$\therefore a + b = 1 + 14 = 15$$

12. **(C)** $t^3 + 1 \,) \, t^6 + 3t^2 + 10 \, (\, t^3 - 1$

$$\frac{t^3 + t^6}{-t^3 + 3t^2 + 10}$$

$$\frac{-t^3 \qquad -1}{3t^2 + 11}$$

13. **(D)** $(3x^2 - 5x + 6) \times -8x^3$

$= -24x^5 + 40x^4 - 48x^3$

Put $x = 0$

$-24(0)^5 + 40(0)^4 - 48(0)^3 = 0$

14. **(B)** $8 - 5 = 3$

15. **(C)** $x^3 - x^2 + 3x - 2$

$(-) \quad \dfrac{x^2 + 5x - 6}{x^3 - 2x^2 - 2x + 4}$

16. **(A)** $x^4 + 0 + 2x^2 - 3x + 7$

$(-) \quad \dfrac{x^3 + \ x^2 + \ x - 1}{x^4 - x^3 + x^2 - 4x + 8}$

17. **(D)** $x^2 y \times \dfrac{x}{y} = x^3$

$x^2 \div \dfrac{1}{x} = x^3$

18. **(B)** $(3x - 4)(5x + 7) = 15x^2 - ax - 28$

$15x^2 + x - 28 = 15x^2 - ax - 28$

Comparing we get $a = -1$.

20. **(C)** $x^3 - 6x^2y - xy^2 - y^3$

$(-) \quad \dfrac{x^3 + 5x^2y - xy^2 - y^3}{-11x^2y}$

21. **(C)** $25x^2 + 16y^2 + 40xy$

at $x = 1$ and $y = -1$

$25(1)^2 + 16(-1)^2 + 40(1)(-1)$

$= 25 + 16 - 40$

$= 1$

22. **(B)** $\left(\dfrac{3x}{4} - \dfrac{4y}{3} \right)^2 =$

$$\left(\dfrac{3x}{4} \right)^2 - 2\left(\dfrac{3x}{4} \right)\left(\dfrac{4y}{3} \right) + \left(\dfrac{4y}{3} \right)^2$$

$= \dfrac{9x^2}{16} - 2xy + \dfrac{16y^2}{9}$

$= \dfrac{9x^2}{16} + (-2xy) + \dfrac{16y^2}{9}$

23. **(A)** $\dfrac{7.83 \times 7.83 - 1.17 \times 1.17}{6.66}$

$= \dfrac{(7.83 + 1.17)(7.83 - 1.17)}{6.66}$

$= \dfrac{9 \times 6.66}{6.66} = 9$

24. **(D)** $x - \dfrac{1}{x} = \sqrt{6}$

Squaring on both sides

$\left(x - \dfrac{1}{x} \right)^2 = \left(\sqrt{6} \right)^2$

$x^2 + \dfrac{1}{x^2} - 2.x.\dfrac{1}{x} = 6$

$x^2 + \dfrac{1}{x^2} = 6 + 2 = 8$

25. **(B)** $\left(x + \dfrac{1}{x} \right)^2 = x^2 + \dfrac{1}{x^2} + 2$

$= 79 + 2 = 81$

$\therefore x + \dfrac{1}{x} = \sqrt{81} = 9$

26. **(A)** $3x - 7y = 10$

Squaring on both sides

$(3x - 7y)^2 = 10^2$

$9x^2 + 49y^2 - 42xy = 100$

$9x^2 + 49y^2 = 100 - 42 = 58$

27. **(C)** $a + b + c = 10$

Squaring on both sides

$a^2 + b^2 + c^2 + 2ab + 2bc + 2ca = 100$

$36 + 2(ab + bc + ca) = 100$

$2(ab + bc + ca) = 100 - 36 = 64$

$ab + bc + ca = \dfrac{64}{2} = 32$

28. **(B)** $x - y = 4$

Cubing on both sides

$(x - y)^3 = (4)^3$

$x^3 - y^3 - 3xy(x - y) = 64$

$x^3 - y^3 - 3(21)(4) = 64$

$x^3 - y^3 = 316$

29. **(B)** $(a + b)^3 - (a - b)^3$

$= (a^3 + b^3 + 3a^2b + 3ab^2) -$

$\quad (a^3 - b^3 - 3a^2b + 3ab^2)$

$= 2(b^3 + 3a^2b)$

30. **(C)** $(4x - 3y)(16x^2 + 12xy + 9y^2)$

$= (4x - 3y)[(4x)^2 + (4x)(3y) + (3y)^2]$

$= (4x)^3 - (3y)^3$

$\left[(a - b)\left(a^2 + ab + b^2\right) = a^3 - b^3\right]$

$= 64x^3 - 27y^3$

31. **(D)** let $a = 3x - 5y$

$\qquad b = 2y - 5x$

$\qquad c = 2x + 3y$

$a + b + c = 0$

We have

If $a + b + c = 0$ then

$a^3 + b^3 + c^3 = 3abc$

So, $(3x - 5y)^3 - (5x - 2y)^3 + (2x + 3y)^3$

$= 3(3x - 5y)(2y - 5x)(2x + 3y)$

$= -3(3x - 5y)(5x - 2y)(2x + 3y)$

32. **(A)** $a + b + c = 9$

Squaring on both sides

$(a + b + c)^2 = 81$

$a^2 + b^2 + c^2 + 2ab + 2bc + 2ca = 81$

$a^2 + b^2 + c^2 + 2(ab + bc + ca) = 81$

$a^2 + b^2 + c^2 + 2(26) = 81$

$a^2 + b^2 + c^2 = 81 - 52 = 29$

$a^3 + b^3 + c^3 - 3abc$

$= (a + b + c)(a^2 + b^2 + c^2$
$\qquad\qquad - ab - bc - ca)$

$= (a + b + c)[(a^2 + b^2 + c^2)$
$\qquad\qquad -(ab + bc + ca)]$

$= (9)(29 - 26)$

$= 9 \times 3 = 27$

33. **(C)** We have

$x^3 + y^3 + z^3 - 3xyz$

$= (x + y + z)(x^2 + y^2 + z^2 - xy - yz - zx)$

$0 = (x + y + z)(x^2 + y^2 + z^2$
$\qquad\qquad - xy - yz - zx)$

So either $x + y + z = 0$ (or)

$x^2 + y^2 + z^2 - xy - yz - zx = 0$

$x^2 + y^2 + z^2 - xy - yz - zx = 0$

$2x^2 + 2y^2 + 2z^2 - 2xy - 2yz - 2zx = 0$

$(x^2 - 2xy + y^2) + (y^2 - 2yz + z^2) +$
$\qquad\qquad (z^2 - 2zx + x^2) = 0$

$(x - y)^2 + (y - z)^2 + (z - x)^2 = 0$

$\Rightarrow x = y = z$

$\therefore$ either $x + y + z = 0$ or $x = y = z$

34. **(B)** $b > 9$ (or) $b < 0$

35. **(A)** Let $a = 0.5$

$\therefore a + \dfrac{1}{a} = 0.5 + \dfrac{1}{0.5} = 2.5 > 2$

36. **(C)** $\dfrac{(67.542)^2 - (32.458)^2}{75.458 - 40.374}$

$$= \frac{100 \times 35.084}{35.084}$$

$$= 100$$

37. (A) $\dfrac{a^3 + b^3 + c^3 - 3abc}{a^2 + b^2 + c^2 - ab - bc - ca}$

$$= \frac{(a+b+c)(a^2 + b^2 + c^2 - ab - bc - ca)}{a^2 + b^2 + c^2 - ab - bc - ca}$$

$$= a + b + c$$
$$a + b + c = 0.42 + 0.25 + 0.33 = 1$$

38. (B) $\dfrac{a^3 - b^3}{a^2 + ab + b^2} = a - b$

$$a - b = 0.31 - 0.21 = 0.1$$

39. (D) $2x + y = 5$

$$\Rightarrow 4x + 2y = 10$$

40. (A) $x + y = 6$

$$\underline{3x - y = 4}$$
$$\underline{4x = 10}$$

$$x = \frac{5}{2}, \ y = \frac{15}{2} - 4 = \frac{7}{2}$$

$$x - y = \frac{5}{2} - \frac{7}{2} = -1$$

41. (C) $a + b = 7, \ ab = 10$

$$(a - b)^2 = (a + b)^2 - 4ab$$
$$= 7^2 - 4(10) = 9$$

$$a - b = 3.$$

Solving we get $a = 5, b = 2$

$\therefore$ larger number is 5

42. (A) $a = 55, b = -75, c = 20$

$$a + b + c = 0$$
$$a^3 + b^3 + c^3 = 3abc$$
So, $(55)^3 + (-75)^3 + (20)^3$

$$= 3(55)(-75)(20)$$

$$= -2,47,500$$

43. (C) $\left(3 + \dfrac{5}{x}\right)\left(9 - \dfrac{15}{x} + \dfrac{25}{x^2}\right)$

$$= 3^3 + \left(\frac{5}{x}\right)^3$$

$$= 27 + \frac{125}{x^3}$$

At $x = 1$,

$$27 + \frac{125}{x^3} = 27 + \frac{125}{1^3}$$

$$= 27 + 125 = 152$$

44. (B) $\dfrac{a^3 + b^3 + c^3 - 3abc}{a^2 + b^2 + c^2 - ab - bc - ca}$

$$= \frac{(a + b + c)(a^2 + b^2 + c^2 - ab - bc - ca)}{a^2 + b^2 + c^2 - ab - bc - ca}$$

$$= a + b + c$$

45. (D) We have,

$$(a + b)^3 - (a - b)^3 = 2(b^3 + 3a^2 b)$$
$$(x + 3)^3 - (x - 3)^3$$

$$= 2\left[3^3 + 3\left(x^2\right)(3)\right]$$

$$= 2(27 + 9x^2) = 18x^2 + 54$$

Previous Contest Questions

1. (A) $\left[3(p - q)\right]^2 - \left[2(2p + q)\right]^2$

$$= \left[3(p - q) + 2(p + q)\right]$$

$$\left[3(p - q) - 2(p + q)\right]$$

$$= [3p - 3q + 4p + 2q][3p - 3q - 4p - 2q]$$

$$= [7p - q][-p - 5q] = -(7p - q)(p + 5q)$$

2. (C) $x(x - y) + (y - x) = x(x - y) - (x - y)$

$= (x-y)(x-1)$

3.(A) $(a-b)-\left(a^2-b^2\right)$

$\qquad = (a-b)-(a+b)(a-b)$

$\qquad = (a-b)\big[1-(a+b)\big]$

4.(C) $8x^2y^2 = 2\times2\times2\times x\times x\times y\times y$

$\qquad 12x^3y^2 = 2\times2\times3\times x\times x\times x\times y\times y$

$\qquad 24x^4y^3z^2 = 2\times2\times2\times3\times x\times x\times x\times x\times$

$\qquad\qquad\qquad\qquad y\times y\times y\times z\times z$

$\qquad = 4x^2y^2$ is the H.C.F

5.(B) $\left(2a-\dfrac{1}{2a}\right)^2 = 3^2 = 4a^2+\dfrac{1}{4a^2}-2 = 9$

$\qquad = 4a^2+\dfrac{1}{4a^2} = 11 = \left(4a^2+\dfrac{1}{4a^2}\right)^2 = 11^2$

$\qquad = 16a^4+\dfrac{1}{16a^4}+2 = 121$

$\qquad\qquad = 16a^4+\dfrac{1}{16a^4} = 119$

6.(A) $a^2+b^2+c^2-ab-bc-ca = 0$

$\qquad = 2a^2+2b^2+2c^2-2ab-2bc-2ca = 0$

$\qquad = \left(a^2-2ab+b^2\right)+\left(b^2-2bc+c^2\right)$

$\qquad\qquad +\left(c^2-2ac+a^2\right) = 0$

$\qquad = (a-b)^2+(b-c)^2+(c-a)^2 = 0$

$a-b = 0,\, b-c = 0,\, c-a = 0$

$a = b,\, b = c,\, c = a\,,\ \text{a = b = c}$

7.(B) $4x^4+4x^2+1-x^2 = \left(2x^2+1\right)^2-x^2$

$\qquad = \left(2x^2+1+x\right)\left(2x^2+1-x\right)$ or

$\qquad = \left(2x^2+x+1\right)\left(2x^2-x+1\right)$

8.(B) $\dfrac{3x+5}{2x+7} = \dfrac{4}{1} \Rightarrow 3x+5 = 8x+28$

$\qquad -5x = 23 \Rightarrow x = \dfrac{-23}{5}$

9.(B) Multiplying both sides by 15. (i.e) L.C.M of 5 and 3,

$\qquad 3(17-3x)-5(4x+2)$

$\qquad\qquad = 15(5-6x)+5(7x+14)$

$\qquad 51-9x-20x-10 = 75-90x+35x+70$

$\qquad\qquad 41-29x = 145-55x$

$\qquad\qquad -29x+55x = 145-41$

$\qquad\qquad 26x = 104 \Rightarrow x = \dfrac{104}{26} \Rightarrow x = 4$

10.(C) $\qquad x^2-\left(x^2+3x+2\right) = 6(5x+1)$

$\qquad x^2-x^2-3x-2 = 30x+6$

$\qquad -3x-2 = 30x+6$

$\qquad -3x-30x = 6+2 \Rightarrow -33x = 8$

$\qquad x = \dfrac{-8}{33}$

Chapter 10 Visualising Solid Shapes

Error in finding number of edges of some geometrical shapes.

e.g. (i) How many edges does a cone have ?

✗ Incorrect

It has no edges but have only base and curved surface.

✓ Correct

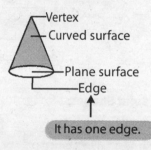

Vertex
Curved surface
Plane surface
Edge

It has one edge.

(ii) How many edges does a cylinder have ?

✗ Incorrect

It has no edges but have only two plane faces and one curved surface.

✓ Correct

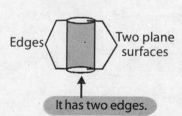

Edges
Two plane surfaces

It has two edges.

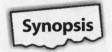

GEOMETRICAL SHAPES:

2D Shapes:

Square   Rectangle   Triangle   Circle

3D Shapes:

Cube   Cuboid   Cone   Cylinder

Sphere   Rectangular prism   Square pyramid

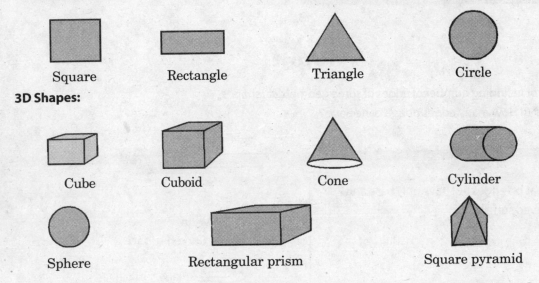

Description of Solid Shapes:

S.No	Solid Shape	Number of Vertices	Number of edges	Number of faces
1.	Cube	8	12	6
2.	Cuboid	8	12	6
3.	Cone	1	1 curved edge	1curved face, 1 flat face
4.	Cylinder	Nil	2 curved edges	2 flat faces, 1 curved face
5.	Sphere	Nil	Nil	1 curved face

Polyhedron:

A solid figure bounded by plane polygonal faces.

♦ The point at which three or more faces intersect on a polyhedron is called a vertex.

♦ A line along which two faces intersect in a polyhedron is called an edge.

Regular Polyhedron:

A polyhedron with all its faces as regular polygons is called regular polyhedron.

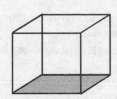

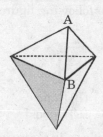

This polyhedron is regular. Its faces are congruent, regular polygons. Vertices are formed by the same number of faces.

This polyhedron is not regular. All the sides are congruent; but the vertices are not formed by the same number of faces. Here three faces meet at A but four faces meet at B.

Convex Polyhedron:

A polyhedron in which a line segment connecting any two vertices of the polyhedron contains only points that are on a face or inside the polyhedron.

Prism:

A polyhedron with two parallel opposite faces, called bases, that are congruent polygons and the lateral faces are parallelograms.

Pyramid:

A solid figure formed by connecting every point on or interior to a plane polygon to a single point, not in the plane.

Euler's formula for convex polyhedron:

$$F + V = E + 2$$

where,

F = number of faces,

V = number of vertices,

E = number of edges.

Multiple Choice Questions

1. The three-dimensional figure formed by rotating a circle is:
   (A) Cone   (B) Sphere
   (C) Cylinder   (D) None of these

2. The three-dimensional figure formed by rotating a triangle is:
   (A) Cone   (B) Quadrilateral
   (C) Prism   (D) Square

3. Which of the following is/are two dimensional figures ?
   (A) Square   (B) Circle
   (C) Cube   (D) Both A and B

4. Which is/are three dimensional figures shapes ?
   (A) Sphere   (B) Cylinder
   (C) Cone   (D) All of the above

5. How many faces a cube has ?
   (A) 4   (B) 6   (C) 8   (D) 12

6. The shape of the following figure given below is:

(A) Circle   (B) Cone
(C) Cylinder   (D) Cuboid

7. The flat surface of a solid figure is called as :
(A) Vertex   (B) face
(C) edge   (D) None of these

8. The number of flat surfaces in a cone is:
(A) 1
(B) 2
(C) 3
(D) It has no flat surface

9. The faces of a cube are:
(A) Squares   (B) Rectangles
(C) Circles   (D) None of these

10. The faces of a cuboid are:
(A) Squares   (B) Rectangles
(C) Circles   (D) None of these

11. The number of corners in a cube is:
(A) 4   (B) 6   (C) 8   (D) 12

12. The number of corners in a cone is:
(A) 1   (B) 2
(C) 3   (D) None of these

13. The number of corners in a cylinder is:
(A) 1   (B) 2   (C) 3   (D) None

14. Solid figures with line segments as their edges are called as:
(A) Polygons   (B) Squares
(C) Cylinders   (D) Polyhedrons

15. The difference between a rectange and a cube is:
(A) Rectangle is 3-dimensional and cube is 2-dimensional.
(B) Rectangle and cube are both 2-dimensional.
(C) Rectangle is 2-dimensional and cube is 3-dimensional.
(D) None of these

16. How many edges a cuboid has ?
(A) 6   (B) 8   (C) 12   (D) 16

17. Bases of a cylinder are:
(A) Squares   (B) Rectangles
(C) Circles   (D) None of these

18. Which of the following statement is false?
(A) Sphere has one flat surfact.
(B) A cone has one flat face.
(C) A cylinder has one cylinder face.
(D) A sphere has one curved face

19. The following figure represents a:

(A) Polygon
(B) Convex polyhedron
(C) Cylinder
(D) None of these

20. If F = 4 and V = 3, then the value of E is (Use Euler's formula) :
(A) 7   (B) 5   (C) 4   (D) 1

Previous Contest Questions

1. The given figure is a shape of :

(A) Rectangle   (B) Square
(C) Quadrilateral   (D) None of these

2. The difference between a cube and cuboid is:

(A) no difference between a cube and cuboid

(B) a cube has equal length, breadth and height where as cuboid has different measures for length, breadth and height.

(C) A cube has not equal length, breadth and height and a cuboid has equal length breadth and height.

(D) None of these

3. Which of the given geometric solids has the maximum number of vertices ?
   (A) Cone   (B) Cylinder
   (C) Cuboid   (D) Pyramid

4. If two cubes of dimension 3 cm by 3 cm by 3 cm are placed side by side, what would be the dimensions of the resulting cuboid be ?
   (A) 6 cm × 6 cm × 6 cm
   (B) 12 cm × 12 cm × 12 cm
   (C) 9 cm × 6 cm × 3 cm
   (D) 6 cm × 3 cm × 3 cm

5. Which of the following is not the net of a cube ?

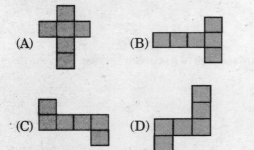

   (A)   (B)

   (C)   (D)

6. What solid do you get when you give a verticle cut of a cubical brick of dimensions 5 cm×5 cm×10 cm along 10 cm side.
   (A) Cuboid   (B) Cylinder
   (C) Cube   (D) Triangle

7. A geometrical shape with no vertices and no flat surfaces is:
   (A) Sphere
   (B) Cone
   (C) Cylinder
   (D) None of these

8. The shape formed by rotating a right triangle about its height is:
   (A) sphere   (B) Cylinder
   (C) Cone   (D) Cuboid

9. If F = n and E = n + 1, then using Eulers formula, the value of V, is:
   (A) 3   (B) 2   (C) 1   (D) 0

10. The total length of edges of the following cube is:

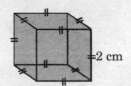

=2 cm

   (A) 24 cm
   (B) 30 cm
   (C) 32 cm
   (D) 36 cm

◎ Answers ◎

Multiple Choice Questions

1. B	2. A	3. D	4. D	5. B	6. C	7. B	8. A	9. A	10. B
11. C	12. A	13. D	14. D	15. C	16. C	17. C	18. A	19. B	20. B

Previous Contest Questions

1. C	2. B	3. C	4. D	5. D	6. C	7. A	8. C	9. A	10. A

Explanatory Answers

20. (B) ∵ F = 4 and V = 3

We have Euler formula as:
F + V = E +2

⇒ 4 + 3 = E + 2
⇒ E = 5

Get It
Right

A Error in using height of cone for finding volume of cone.

e.g. find the volume of the cone.

✗ **Incorrect**

Volume of cone $= \frac{1}{3} \times \pi \times 6^2 \times 10$

$= 120\pi\,\text{cm}^3$ ↑

Incorrect because 10 cm is the length of the slant edge.

✓ **Correct**

Volume of cone $= \frac{1}{3} \times \pi \times 6^2 \times 8$

$= 96\pi\,\text{cm}^3$ ↑

Height of cone = VO

$VO = \sqrt{10^2 - 6^2}$

$= \sqrt{64} = 8\,\text{cm}$

B. Error in using the height of the cone to find surface area of its curved surface.

e.g.

The above diagram shows a cone. Calculate the surface area of this curved surface.

✗ **Incorrect**

Area of curved surface $= \pi r s$

$= \frac{22}{7} \times 7 \times 24 = 528\,\text{cm}^2$ ↑

This is the height, not the slant height.

✓ **Correct**

Firstly, find the length of the slant heights

$s^2 = 24^2 + 7^2 = 576 + 49 = 625$

$s = \sqrt{625} = 25\,\text{cm}$

The slant height = 25 cm, Area of curved

surface $= \pi \times$ radius $\times$ slant height

$= \frac{22}{7} \times 7 \times 25 = 550\,\text{cm}^2$

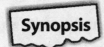

Synopsis

Perimeter:

The length of the boundary of a plane figure is called its perimeter.

Area:

The amount of surface enclosed by a plane figure is called its area.

Rectangle :

Given a rectangle of length = l units and breadth = b units. Then

(i) Perimeter of the rectangle = $2(l + b)$ units

(ii) Diagonal of the rectangle d = $\sqrt{l^2 + b^2}$ units

(iii) Area of the rectangle = $(l \times b)$ sq units

(iv) Length = $\left(\dfrac{\text{area}}{\text{breadth}}\right)$ units

(v) Breadth = $\left(\dfrac{\text{area}}{\text{length}}\right)$ units

Area of four walls of room :

Let there be a room with length = l units, breadth = b units and height =h units, then (i) Area of four walls = $2(l + b) \times$ h sq units

(ii) Diagonal of room = $\sqrt{l^2 + b^2 + h^2}$ units

Perimeter and area of a square :

Let there be a square of each side measuring 'a' units. Then:

(i) Perimeter of the square = $(4a)$units

(ii) Diagonal of the square = $\sqrt{a^2 + a^2} = \sqrt{2a^2} = a\sqrt{2}$ units

(iii) Area of the square = a^2 sq units

(iv) Area of the square = $\dfrac{1}{2} \times (\text{diagonal})^2$ sq units

(v) Side of the square = $\sqrt{\text{Area}}$ units

Perimeter and area of a triangle :

(i) Let a, b and c be the lengths of sides of a triangle. Then, perimeter of the triangle = (a + b + c) units

$S = \dfrac{1}{2}(a + b + c)$ is called semi-perimeter of the triangle.

(ii) Area of the triangle $= \sqrt{s(s-a)(s-b)(s-c)}$ sq units

(iii) Let the base of a triangle be b units and its corresponding height (or altitude) be h units. Then the

Area of the triangle $= \left(\dfrac{1}{2} \times b \times h\right)$ sq units

Note : We may take any side of the triangle as its base.

Then the corresponding height would be the length of perpendicular to this side from the opposite vertex.

(iv) Area of an equilateral triangle with each side 'a'$= \left(\dfrac{\sqrt{3}}{4} \times a^2\right)$ sq units

(v) Height of an equilateral triangle of side a $= \left(\dfrac{\sqrt{3}a}{2}\right)$ units

(vi) Area of a right triangle $= \dfrac{1}{2} \times$ (product of legs) sq units

The sides containing the right angle are known as legs of a right triangle.

Area of a parallelogram :

Let ABCD be a parallelogram with base 'b' units and height 'h' units.

Area of parallelogram

= (base × height) sq units

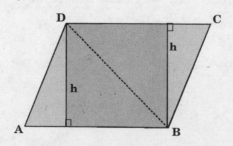

Let ABCD be a rhombus in which diagonal AC = d_1 units and diagonal BD = d_2 units.

Area of rhombus ABCD = $\left(\dfrac{1}{2} \times d_1 \times d_2\right)$ sq units

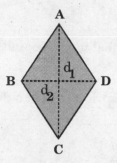

Let ABCD be a trapezium in which AB || DC. Let AB = a units, DC = b units. Area of trapezium ABCD

$= \dfrac{1}{2} \times$ (sum of parallel sides)$\times$ distance between them

$= \dfrac{1}{2} \times (a+b) \times h$ sq units

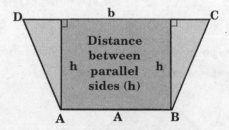

Circle:

A circle is a closed curve in a plane drawn in such a way that every point on this curve is at a constant distance (r units) from a fixed point O inside it.

The fixed point O is called the centre of the circle and the constant distance r is called the length of radius of the circle.

Circumference of a circle :

The perimeter of a circle is called its circumference. The length of the thread that winds tightly around the circle exactly once gives the circumference of the circle.

Circumference = $2\pi r = \pi d$, where r= radius and d= diameter

Here π (Pi) is a constant.

NOTE : The approximate value of π is taken as $\frac{22}{7}$ or 3.14. However π is not a rational number. It is an irrational number and is defined as the ratio of circumference of a circle to its diameter.

Area of a circle :

Area of a circle with radius r units is equal to πr^2 sq units.

Area of a ring :

The region enclosed between two concentric circles of different radii is called a ring.

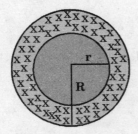

Area of path formed $= \left(\pi R^2 - \pi r^2\right)$ sq units $= \pi\left(R^2 - r^2\right)$ sq units

$$= \pi(R+r)(R-r) \text{ sq units}$$

Length of Arc of a circle :

Let A and B be any two points on a circle. The length of the thread that will wrap along this arc from A to B is the length of AB written as $\overline{AB}$.

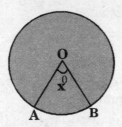

In a circle of radius r, we have

$$\frac{l\left(\overline{AB}\right)}{\text{Circumference}} = \frac{x^0}{360^0} \text{ or}$$

$$l\left(\overline{AB}\right) = \frac{2\pi r x^0}{360^0}$$

Area of a sector :

A sector of a circle is the region enclosed by an arc of a circle and two radii to its end

points. Area of sector $= \dfrac{x°}{360°} \times \pi r^2$ where x is sector angle and r is radius of circle.

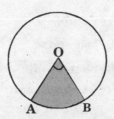

Segment of a circle :

A segment of a circle is the region enclosed by an arc of the circle and its chord.

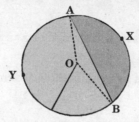

Area of minor segment A X B = area of sector OA X B – area of $\triangle$ OAB

Area of major segment A Y B = area of circle – area of minor segment A X B

The space occupied by a solid body is called its volume.

The units of volume are cubic centimetre (cm³) or cubic metres (m³) etc.

Cuboid :

A solid bounded by six rectangular plane faces is called a cuboid.

Cube :

A cuboid whose length, breadth and height are all equal is called a cube.

Cuboid :

For a cuboid of length = l units, breadth = b units and height = h units

(i) Volume of cuboid = $(l \times b \times h)$ cubic units

(ii) Diagonal of the cuboid = $\sqrt{l^2 + b^2 + h^2}$ units

(iii) Total surface area of the cuboid = $2(lb + bh + lh)$ sq units

(iv) Lateral surface area of the cuboid = $[2(l + b) \times h]$ sq units

(v) Area of 4 walls of a room = $[2(l + b) \times h]$ sq units

Cube :

For a cube of edge = a units

(i) Volume of the cube=a^3 cubic units

(ii) Diagonal of the cube = $a\sqrt{3}$ units

(iii) Total surface area of the cube = $(6a^2)$ sq units

(iv) Lateral surface area of the cube = $(4a^2)$ sq units

Relation between units	
Length units	volume units
1 cm = 10 mm	1 cm³ = 1000 mm³
100 cm = 1 m	1 m³ = 1000000 cm³
	1 litre = 1000 cm³
	1 kilolitre = 1000 litres = 1 m³

Cylinder :

A solid having a curved surface as a lateral surface and a uniform circular cross-section is known as a cylinder.

NOTE : If the axis of the cylinder is perpendicular to each cross-section then the cylinder is called a right circular cylinder.

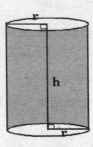

CYLINDER

Volume of a cylinder :

For a cylinder whose height is h units and the radius of whose base is r units,

Volume of cylinder = $(\pi r^2 h)$ cubic units = (base area) × height

Surface area of cylinder :

For a cylinder of height h and radius r :

(a) Area of curved surface = $(2\pi rh)$ sq units

(b) Total surface area = $(2\pi rh + 2\pi r^2)$ sq units

$$= 2\pi r(h + r)$$

Multiple Choice Questions

1. The area of a rhombus is 28 cm² and one of its diagonals is 4 cm. Its perimeter is:
   (A) $4\sqrt{53}$ cm   (B) 36 cm
   (C) $2\sqrt{53}$ cm   (D) none of these

2. The area of a trapezium is 28 cm² and one of its parallel sides 6 cm. If its altitude is 4 cm then its other parallel side is:
   (A) 8 cm   (B) 4 cm
   (C) 6 cm   (D) none of these

3. The perimeter of a trapezium is 52 cm and its non-parallel sides are each equal to 10 cm and its altitude is 8 cm. Its area is :
   (A) 128 cm²   (B) 112 cm²
   (C) 118 cm²   (D) 124 cm²

4. A man bought a rectangular plot of 144 m length and 64 m width. In exchange for this field he wanted to buy a square field of the same area. Then the side of the square field would be:
   (A) 104 m (B) 208 m (C) 96 m (D) 416 m

5. The area of a parallelogram is 120 cm² and its altitude is 10 cm. The length of the base is:
   (A) 24 cm (B) 12 cm (C) 8 cm (D) 4 cm

6. The area of an isosceles triangle having base x cm and one side y cm is :
   (A) $\dfrac{x}{2}\sqrt{y^2 + \dfrac{x^2}{4}}$ cm² (B) $\dfrac{x}{2}\sqrt{\dfrac{4y^2 - x^2}{4}}$ cm²
   (C) $\dfrac{x^2 - y^2}{4}$ cm²   (D) none of these

7. The length of diagonal of a square whose area is 16,900 m² is:
   (A) 130 m   (B) $130\sqrt{2}$ m
   (C) 169 m   (D) 144 m

8. The sides of a triangle are 3 cm, 5 cm and 4 cm. Its area is:
   (A) 6 cm²   (B) 7.5 cm²
   (C) $5\sqrt{2}$ cm²   (D) none of these

9. The base of an isosceles right triangle is 30 cm. Its area is :
   (A) 225 cm²   (B) $225\sqrt{3}$ cm²
   (C) $5\sqrt{2}$ cm²   (D) none of these

10. One side of an equilateral triangle is 30 cm. Its area is :
    (A) 225 cm²   (B) $225\sqrt{3}$ cm²
    (C) $225\sqrt{2}$ cm²   (D) 112.5 cm²

11. The sides of a triangle are 16 cm, 30 cm and 34 cm. Its area is:
    (A) 120 cm²   (B) 260 cm²
    (C) 240 cm²   (D) 272 cm²

12. The adjacent sides of a parallelogram are 8 cm and 9 cm. The diagonal joining the ends of these sides is   13 cm. Its area is:
    (A) 72 cm²   (B) $12\sqrt{35}$ cm²
    (C) $24\sqrt{35}$ cm²   (D) 150 cm²

13. A square is a special case of :
    (A) parallelogram
    (B) isosceles trapezium
    (C) rhombus
    (D) trapezium

14. Opposite angles of a rhombus are:
    (A) complementary (B) equal
    (C) supplementary (D) never equal

15. The sides of a triangle are 11 cm, 15 cm and 16 cm. The altitude to largest side is:
    (A) $30\sqrt{7}$ cm   (B) $\dfrac{15\sqrt{7}}{2}$ cm
    (C) $\dfrac{15\sqrt{7}}{4}$ cm   (D) 30 cm

16. The perimeter of a triangular field is 144 m and the ratio of the sides is 3 : 4 : 5. The area of the field is :
(A) 864 m²   (B) 468 m²
(C) 824 m²   (D) none of these

17. A rectangular field has its length and breadth in the ratio 5 : 3. Its area is 3.75 hectares. The cost of fencing it at Rs. 5 per meter is:
(A) Rs. 400   (B) Rs. 4,000
(C) Rs. 1,000   (D) Rs. 500

18. If the altitude of an equilateral triangle is $\sqrt{6}$ cm, its area is
(A) $2\sqrt{3}$ cm²   (B) $2\sqrt{2}$ cm²
(C) $3\sqrt{3}$ cm²   (D) $6\sqrt{2}$ cm²

19. The ratio between the length and the perimeter of a rectangular plot is 1 : 3 and the ratio between the breadth and perimeter of that plot is 1 : 6. What is the ratio between the length and area of that plot?
(A) 2 : 1   (B) 1 : 6
(C) 1 : 8   (D) Data inadequate

20. What change in percent is made in the area of a rectangle by decreasing its length and increasing its breadth by 5%?
(A) 2.5% increase   (B) 0.25% increase
(C) 0.25% decrease (D) 2.5% decrease

21. The radius of a circle is 14 m, then the circumference of a circle is:
(A) 616 m   (B) 88 m
(C) 154 m   (D) none of these

22. The circumference of a circle is 44 m, then the area of the circle is:
(A) 6084.5 m²   (B) 276.5 m²
(C) 154 m²   (D) 44 m²

23. The area of a circle is 2464 m², then the diameter is:
(A) 56 m   (B) 154 m
(C) 176 m   (D) none of these

24. A circular grass lawn of 35 m in radius has a path 7 m wide running around it on the outside. The area of the path is
(A) 1,496 m²   (B) 1,450 m²
(C) 1,576 m²   (D) 1,694 m²

25. The difference between circumfer-ence and radius of a circle is 37 m. The circumference of that circle is:
(A) 7 m   (B) 44 m
(C) 154 m   (D) none of these

26. The area of the sector of a circle, whose radius is 6 m when the angle at the centre is 42⁰ is:
(A) 13.2 m²   (B) 14.2 m²
(C) 13.4 m²   (D) 14.4 m²

27. If the radius of a circle is $\dfrac{7}{\sqrt{\pi}}$ cm, then the area of the circle is:
(A) 154 cm²   (B) $\dfrac{49}{\pi}$ cm²
(C) 22 cm²   (D) 49 cm²

28. If the circumference of a circle is $\dfrac{30}{\pi}$ then the diameter of the circle is:
(A) 60π   (B) $\dfrac{15}{\pi}$ (C) $\dfrac{30}{\pi^2}$ (D) 30

29. How many plants will be there in a circular bed whose outer edge measures 30 cm allowing 4 cm² for each plant?
(A) 18   (B) 750   (D) 24   (D) 120

30. When the circumference and area of a circle are numerically equal, then the diameter is numerically equal to:
(A) area   (B) circumference
(C) 2π   (D) 4

31. If the ratio of areas of two circles is 16 : 25 the ratio of their circumference is:
(A) 25 : 16 (B) 5 : 4 (C) 4 : 5 (D) 3 : 5

32. If the ratio of circumference of two circles is 4 : 9, the ratio of their area is:
(A) 9 : 4   (B) 16 : 81 (C) 4 : 9 (D) 2 : 3

33. If the area of a circle is A, radius of the circle is r and circumference of it is C, then:

(A) rC = 2A   (B) $\dfrac{C}{A} = \dfrac{r}{2}$

(C) AC = $\dfrac{r^2}{4}$ (D) $\dfrac{A}{r} = C$

34. The area of a sector of a circle of radius 16 cm cut off by an arc which is 18.5 cm long is:

(A) 168 cm²   (B) 148 cm²
(C) 154 cm²   (D) 176 cm²

35. The area of a segment of a circle of radius 21 cm if the arc of the segment has a measure of 60⁰ is:
(Take $\sqrt{3} = 1.73$)
(A) 45.27 cm²   (B) 40.27 cm²
(C) 40.8 cm²   (D) none of these

36. If the radii of two concentric circles are 15 cm and 13 cm respectively, then the area of the circulating ring in sq cm will be:
(A) 176   (B) 178   (C) 180   (D) 200

37. The area of the largest triangle that can be inscribed in a semicircle whose radius is r cm is:
(A) 2r cm²   (B) r² cm²

(C) 2r² cm²   (D) $\dfrac{r}{2}$ cm²

38. A wire bent in the form of a circle of radius 42 cm is cut and again bent in the form of a square. The ratio of the regions enclosed by the circle and the square in the two cases is given by:
(A) 11 : 12   (B) 21 : 33
(C) 22 : 33   (D) 14 : 11

39. The radius of a circle is 20 cm. Three more concentric circles are drawn inside it in such a manner that it is divided into four parts of equal area. The radius of cone of the three concentric circles is:
(A) $8\sqrt{3}$ cm   (B) $2\sqrt{3}$ cm
(C) $10\sqrt{3}$ cm   (D) $14\sqrt{3}$ cm

40. A sector of 120⁰ cut out from a circle has an area of $9\dfrac{3}{7}$ sq cm. The radius of the circle is:
(A) 3 cm   (B) 2.5 cm
(C) 3.5 cm   (D) 3.6 cm

41. The radius of the cylinder whose lateral surface area is 704 cm² and height 8 cm is:
(A) 6 cm   (B) 4 cm (C) 8 cm (D) 14 cm

42. The radius of a cylinder is doubled but its lateral surface area is unchanged. Then its height must be:
(A) doubled   (B) halved
(C) trebled   (D) constant

43. Vertical and horizontal cross-sections of a right circular cylinder are always respectively:
(A) rectangle, square
(B) rectangle, circle
(C) square, circle
(D) rectangle, ellipse

44. In the figure below, LMNO and GHJK are rectangles where GH = $\dfrac{1}{2}$ LM and

HJ = $= \dfrac{1}{2}$ MN. What fraction of the region is bounded by LMNO that is not shaded?

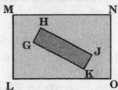

(A) $\frac{1}{4}$ (B) $\frac{1}{3}$ (C) $\frac{1}{2}$ (D) $\frac{3}{4}$

45. In the figure below, RSTV is a square inscribed in a circle with centre O and radius r. The total area of shaded region is :

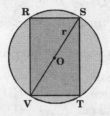

(A) $r^2(\pi-2)$ (B) $2r(2-\pi)$

(C) $\pi(r^2-2)$ (D) πr^2-8r

46. The ratio of radii of two cylinders is $1:\sqrt{3}$ and heights are in the ratio 2 : 3. The ratio of their volumes is:
(A) 1 : 9   (B) 2 : 9   (C) 4 : 9   (D) 5 : 9

47. The dimensions of a hall are 40 m, 25 m and 20 m. If each person requires 200 cubic metre, then the number of persons who can be accomodated in the hall are:
(A) 120   (B) 150   (C) 140   (D) 100

48. Correct the perimeter of the figure given below to one decimal place.
(A) 56.0 m   (B) 56.6 m
(C) 57.2 m   (D) 57.9 m

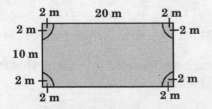

49. Each side of a cube is increased by 50%. Then the surface area of the cube increases by :
(A) 50%   (B) 100%   (C) 125%   (D) 150%

50. Three cylinders each of height 16 cm and radius of base 4 cm are placed on a plane so that each cylinder touches the other two. Then the volume of region enclosed between the three cylinders in cm³ is:

(A) $98\left(4\sqrt{3}-\pi\right)$ (B) $98\left(2\sqrt{3}-\pi\right)$

(C) $98\left(\sqrt{3}-\pi\right)$ (D) $128\left(2\sqrt{3}-\pi\right)$

51. Instead of walking along two adjacent sides of a rectangular field, a boy took a short cut along the diagonal and saved a distance equal to half the longer side. Then the ratio of the shorter side to the longer side is:

(A) $\frac{1}{2}$ (B) $\frac{2}{3}$

(C) $\frac{1}{4}$ (D) $\frac{3}{4}$

52. The number of surfaces in right circular cylinder is :
(A) 1   (B) 2   (C) 3   (D) 4

53.

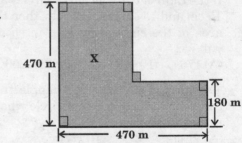

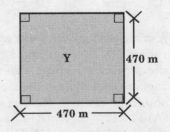

Field X and Y are to be enclosed with a fencing at the cost of Rs 40 per meter. If the cost on field X is denoted by C_x and that on field Y is denoted by C_y we have

(A) $C_x = C_y$
(B) $C_x < C_y$
(C) $C_x > C_y$
(D) cannot be determined

54. A covered wooden box has the inner measures as 115 cm, 75 cm and 35 cm and the thickness of wood is 2.5 cm. Then the volume of the wood.

(A) 80,000 cu cm   (B) 82,125 cu cm
(C) 84,000 cu cm   (D) 85,000 cu cm

55. The edge of a cube is 20 cm. How many small cubes of 5 cm edge can be formed from this cube?

(A) 4   (B) 32   (C) 64   (D) 100

56. Two cylinders of same volume have their heights in the ratio 1 : 3. Find the ratio of their radii.

(A) $\sqrt{3} : 1$ (B) $\sqrt{2} : 1$
(C) $\sqrt{5} : 2$ (D) $2 : \sqrt{5}$

Previous Contest Questions

1. In the diagram shown, ABCD is a parallelogram and CDEF is a rectangle.

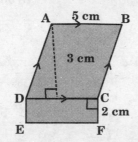

The total area of the whole figure is:

(A) $35\,cm^2$ (B) $30\,cm^2$

(C) $25\,cm^2$ (D) $20\,cm^2$

2. The area of the shaded region in the following figure is:

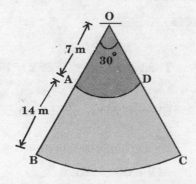

(A) $51.33\,cm^2$

(B) $102.67\,cm^2$

(C) $205.34\,cm^2$

(D) can not be determined

3. If the areas of three adjacent faces of a rectanglular block are in the ratio of $2 : 3 : 4$ and its volume is $9000\,cm^2$; then the length of the shortest side is:
(A) 10 cm (B) 15 cm (C) 20 cm (D) 30 cm

4. Two equal volumes circular cylinders have their heights in t he ratio 2 : 1. The ratio of their radii is:

(A) 2 : 1   (B) 1 : 2 (C) $\sqrt{2} : 1$ (D) $1 : \sqrt{2}$

5. A well is to be dug 20 m deep, 2.25 m inside diameter, with a brick lining of 0.35 m thickness. Then the quantities of brickwork is:

(A) $14.75\,m^3$ (B) $57.2\,m^3$

(C) $136.75\,m^3$ (D) $572\,m^3$

6. The radius of the outer circumference of a cylindrical ring is 12 cm and the diameter of the cross- section is 1.5 cm. Then, the volume of circular ring is:

(A) $22.5\,cm^2$ (B) $125\,cm^3$

(C) $12.5\,cm^3$ (D) $1250\,cm^3$

7. A rectangular sheet of paper, $36\,cm \times 22\,cm$, is rolled along its length to form a cylinder. Then the volume of cylinder so formed is:

(A) $2268\,cm^3$ (B) $226.8\,cm^3$

(C) $226\,cm^3$ (D) $23.4\,cm^3$

8. PQRS is quadrilateral formed by joining two triangles edge to edge as given in the following figure. The area of PQRS is:

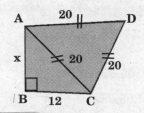

(A) 452 sq. units

(B) 269 sq.units

(C) 134.5 sq. units

(D) can't be determined

9. A wooden box (open at the top) of thickness 0.5 cm, length 21 cm, width 11 cm and height 6 cm is painted on the inside. The expenses of painting are Rs. 70. What is the rate of painting per square centimetre ?

(A) Rs. 0.7   (B) Rs. 0.5

(C) Rs.0.1   (D) Rs. 0.2

10. If each edge of a cube is increased by 25%, then the percentage increase in its surface area is:

(A) 25%   (B) 48.75%

(C) 50%   (D) 56.25%

⊘ Answers ⊘

Multiple Choice Questions

1. A	2. A	3. A	4. C	5. B	6. B	7. B	8. A	9. A	10. B
11. C	12. B	13. C	14. B	15. C	16. A	17. B	18. A	19. D	20. C
21. B	22. C	23. A	24. D	25. B	26. A	27. D	28. C	29. A	30. D
31. C	32. B	33. A	34. B	35. B	36. A	37. B	38. D	39. C	40. A
41.D	42. B	43. B	44. D	45. A	46. B	47. D	48. B	49. C	50. D
51. D	52. C	53. A	54. B	55. C	56. A				

Previous Contest Questions

1. D	2. B	3. B	4. D	5. B	6. B	7. A	8. B	9. C	10. D

Explanatory Answers

1. (A) Let AD = x and BC = 4 cm (given)

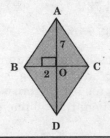

Then $\dfrac{1}{2} \times x \times 4 = 28$ or x = 14 cm.

Clearly, AO = $\dfrac{14}{2}$ = 7 cm

By Pythagorus theorem,

$AO^2 + BO^2 = AB^2$

or $7^2 + 2^2 = 53$ or $AB = \sqrt{53}$

$\therefore$ perimeter = $4AB = 4\sqrt{53}$

2. (A) Area of trapezium

$= \dfrac{1}{2}$ (sum of parallel sides) $\times$

altitude

Let other parallel side be x cm.

Then $\dfrac{1}{2}(x + 6) \times 4 = 28$

or x = 8 cm

3. (A) As shown in figure, ADE is a triangle. $\therefore DE^2 = 10^2 - 8^2 = 6^2$

or DE = 6 cm

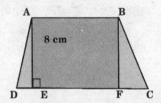

By symmetry, FC = 6 cm
Let AB = x
Then (x + 10 + 6 + x + 6 + 10)
$\qquad\qquad = 52$
or 2x + 32 = 52 or x = 10 cm
$\therefore$ Area of trapezium

$= \dfrac{1}{2}(10 + 22) \times 8 = 128 cm^2$

4. (C) Equating both areas, we have,
144 $\times$ 64 = x^2 or

$x = \sqrt{144 \times 64} = \sqrt{144} \times \sqrt{64} =$
$\qquad\qquad 12 \times 8 = 96$ m

5. (B) Area of parallelogram
= Base$\times$ Height = 120 cm^2.
$\therefore$ Base = 12 cm

6. (B) Consider the isosceles triangle as shown in the figure. Drop a perpendicular AD to base.

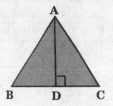

It bisects the base. $\therefore$ BD= $\dfrac{x}{2}$

Now, by Pythagorus theorem, we have $AD^2 = AB^2 - BD^2$ or

$y^2 - \dfrac{x^2}{4} = \dfrac{4y^2 - x^2}{4}$

or $AD = \sqrt{\dfrac{4y^2 - x^2}{4}}$

Area of triangle

$= \dfrac{1}{2} \times base \times height$

$\therefore$ area of ABC

$= \dfrac{1}{2} \times x \times \sqrt{\dfrac{4y^2 - x^2}{4}}$ cm^2

7. (B)

Let the side of square be x m. then
$x^2 = 16900$ m^2 or $x = \sqrt{16900}$
or x = 130 m
Diagonal BD = $\sqrt{DC^2 + BC^2}$

$= \sqrt{130^2 + 130^2}$ $= 130\sqrt{2}$

8. (A) Since $3^2 + 4^2 = 5^2$, clearly given triangle is a right angled triangle. Hence

area $= \dfrac{1}{2} \times base \times height$

$$= \frac{1}{2} \times 3 \times 4 = 6 \text{ cm}^2$$

9.   (A)   As shown in the diagram below, in the isosceles right triangle, the base is bisected by the altitude and BD = AD.

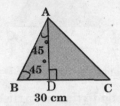

$$\therefore AD = 15 \text{ cm}$$

$$\text{Area} = \frac{1}{2} \times \text{base} \times \text{height}$$

$$= \frac{1}{2} \times 30 \times 15 = 225 \text{ cm}^2$$

10.   (B)   Area of an equilateral triangle

$$= \frac{\sqrt{3}}{4} a^2 = \frac{\sqrt{3}}{4} \times 30^2 = 225\sqrt{3} \text{ cm}^2$$

11.   (C)   Since $16^2 + 30^2 = 34^2$, clearly, given triangle is a right angled triangle. Hence

$$\text{area} = \frac{1}{2} \times \text{base} \times \text{height}$$

$$= \frac{1}{2} \times 16 \times 30 = 240 \text{ cm}^2$$

12.   (B)

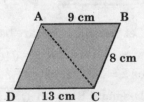

As shown in the diagram, area of triangle ABC = 1/2 area of the parallelogram ABCD. By Heron's formula, area of triangle

$$= \sqrt{S(S-a)(S-b)(S-C)}$$

Here $S = \dfrac{9 + 8 + 13}{2} = 15$

$\therefore$ Area of ABC = $\sqrt{15(6)(2)(7)}$

$\sqrt{180 \times 7} = \sqrt{1260} = \sqrt{6 \times 210}$

$\sqrt{6 \times 7 \times 30} = 6\sqrt{35}$ sq cm.

Hence, area of ABCD

$= 2 \times 6\sqrt{35} = 12\sqrt{35}$ sq cm

13.   (C)   As we can see from the Venn diagram of quadrilaterals given in the previous chapter, all squares are rhombuses and rectangles. Since 'rectangle' is not given in the choices, we choose (C).

NOTE: All squares are parallelograms, but rhombus would be the more appropriate choice in this question.

14.   (B)   It is a property of rhombus that opposite angles are equal.

15.   (C)   By Heron's formula, we have area of triangle

$$= \sqrt{S(S-a)(S-b)(S-c)}$$

Here, $S = \dfrac{11 + 15 + 16}{2} = \dfrac{42}{2}$

$$= 21 \text{ cm}$$

$\therefore$ Area = $= \sqrt{21(10)(6)(5)}$

$$= 30\sqrt{7} \text{ sq cm}$$

$$\text{height} = \frac{2 \text{ area}}{\text{base}} = \frac{30\sqrt{7}}{8}$$

$$= \frac{15\sqrt{7}}{4} \text{ cm}$$

16.   (A)   Let the sides be 3x, 4x and 5x. Then 3x + 4x + 5x = 144 or x = 12

$\therefore$ sides are 36, 48 and 60 m. Clearly, $36^2 + 48^2 = 60^2$. It is a right angled triangle.

$\therefore$ Area $=\dfrac{1}{2}\times 36\times 48 = 864$ m^2

17. (B)   Let length = 5x, breadth = 3x.

Area $= l \times$ b $= 5x \times 3x = 15x^2$

We have,

$15x^2 = 3.75$ hectares

$= 37500$ sq m

($\because$ 1 hectare = 10,000 sq m)

$x^2 = \dfrac{37500}{15} = 2500$

x = 50 m

Perimeter $= 2(l + b) = 2(250 + 150)$

$= 800$ m

Cost of fencing $= 800\times 5 =$ Rs. 4000

18. (A) $\dfrac{\sqrt{3}}{2}\times$ side $= \sqrt{6}$

Side $= 2\sqrt{2}$ cm.

area $= \dfrac{\sqrt{3}}{4}\times(\text{side})^2 = \dfrac{\sqrt{3}}{4}\times\left(2\sqrt{2}\right)^2$

$= 2\sqrt{3}$ cm^2

19. (D)   Given that,

L : P = 1 : 3, B : P = 1 : 6,

L : B : P = 2 : 1 : 6

Let length = 2x, breadth = x,

perimeter = 6x.

Area $= l \times$ b $= 2x\times x = 2x^2$.

$\therefore$ ratio between length and area

$= 2x : 2x^2$

$= 1 : x$

which cannot be determined.

20. (C) $\dfrac{5\times 5}{100} = 0.25\%$ decrease

21. (B)   r = 14 m

Circumference $= 2\pi r$

$= 2\times\dfrac{22}{7}\times 14 = 88$ m

22. (C) $2\pi r = 44$

$r = \dfrac{44}{2\times\dfrac{22}{7}} = 7$ m

Area of a circle $= \pi r^2$

$= \dfrac{22}{7}\times 7\times 7 = 154$ m^2

23. (A) $\dfrac{\pi d^2}{4} = 2464$

$d^2 = \dfrac{2464\times 4}{\dfrac{22}{7}} = 3136$

$d = \sqrt{3136} = 56$ m

24. (D)

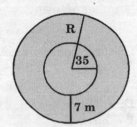

r = 35 m

R = 35 + 7 = 42 m

Area of circular path

$= \pi(R+r)(R-r)$

$= \dfrac{22}{7}(42+35)(42-35)$

$= 1694$ m^2

25. (B) $2\pi r - r = 37$

$r = \dfrac{37}{2\pi - 1} = \dfrac{37}{2\times\dfrac{22}{7}-1} = 7$ m

Circumference

$= 2\pi r = 2\times\dfrac{22}{7}\times 7 = 44$ m

26. (A) Area of sector $= \dfrac{42}{360} \times \pi r^2$

$= \dfrac{42}{360} \times \dfrac{22}{7} \times 6 \times 6 = 13.2 \text{ m}^2$

27. (D) $\pi r^2 = \dfrac{22}{7} \times \dfrac{7}{\sqrt{\pi}} \times \dfrac{7}{\sqrt{\pi}} = 49 \text{ cm}^2$

28. (C) $2\pi r = \dfrac{30}{\pi}$

$2r = \dfrac{30}{\pi^2}$

29. (A) Circumference = 30 cm

Area $= \dfrac{C^2}{4\pi} = \dfrac{30 \times 30}{4 \times \dfrac{22}{7}} = 71.6 \text{ cm}^2$

Number of plants $= \dfrac{A}{4} = \dfrac{71.6}{4}$

$= 17.9 \cong 18$

30. (D) Circumference = area

$2\pi r = \pi r^2$

$\Rightarrow r = 2$

Diameter $= 2r = 2 \times 2 = 4$

31. (C) We have,

$A_1 : A_2 = 16 : 25$

$\dfrac{C_1}{C_2} = \sqrt{\dfrac{A_1}{A_2}} = \sqrt{\dfrac{16}{25}} = \dfrac{4}{5}$

∴ The ratio of circumferences is 4 : 5

32. (B) Given that $C_1 : C_2 = 4 : 9$

We have,

$\dfrac{A_1}{A_2} = \dfrac{C_1{}^2}{C_2{}^2} = \dfrac{4^2}{9^2} = \dfrac{16}{81}$

∴ $A_1 : A_2 = 16 : 81$

33. (A) $A = \pi r^2$

$= \dfrac{r \times (2\pi r)}{2} = \dfrac{rc}{2}$

$\Rightarrow rc = 2A$

34. (B) $A = \dfrac{1}{2} lr = \dfrac{1}{2} \times 18.5 \times 16 = 148 \text{ cm}^2$

35. (B)

Area of sector OAB $= \dfrac{x}{360} \times \pi r^2$

$= \dfrac{60}{360} \times \dfrac{22}{7} \times 21 \times 21$

$= 231 \text{ cm}^2.$

Area of $\triangle OAB = \dfrac{\sqrt{3}}{4} r^2$

$= \dfrac{\sqrt{3}}{4} \times 21 \times 21$

$= 190.73 \text{ cm}^2.$

∴ Area of shaded region

$= 231 - 190.73$

$= 40.27 \text{ cm}^2$

36. (A) R = 15 cm, r = 13 cm.

Area of the circulating ring

$= \pi(R + r)(R - r)$

$= \dfrac{22}{7}(15 + 13) \times (15 - 13)$

$= \dfrac{22}{7} \times 28 \times 2$

$= 176 \text{ sq cm}$

37. (B) Angle in a semicircle is a right angle.

We have, the largest triangle is having diameter of the circle as base and radius as its height.

Area of the triangle

$= \dfrac{1}{2} \times \text{base} \times \text{height}$

$$= \frac{1}{2} \times 2r \times r$$

$$= r^2 \text{ cm}^2$$

38. **(D)** Length of wire =
$$2\pi \times 42 = 84\pi \text{ cm.}$$
Let x be the side of the square.
We have,
$$4x = 84\pi$$
$$x = 21\pi$$
Area of the circle : Area of the square
$$= \pi(42)^2 : (21\pi)^2$$
$$\pi \times 42 \times 42 : 21 \times 21 \times \pi \times \pi$$
$$= 4 : \pi$$
$$= 4 : \frac{22}{7}$$
$$= 14 : 11$$

39. **(C)** Suppose r is the radius of the largest of the three circles.
∴ area of the largest circle
$$= \frac{3}{4} \times \text{area of given circle.}$$
We have,
$$\pi r^2 = \frac{3}{4} \times \pi \times (20)^2$$
$$r^2 = \frac{3}{4} \times 20 \times 20 = 300$$
$$r = \sqrt{300} = 10\sqrt{3} \text{ cm}$$

40. **(A)** We have,
$$\frac{x}{360} \times \pi r^2 = 9\frac{3}{7}$$
$$\frac{120}{360} \times \frac{22}{7} \times r^2 = \frac{66}{7}$$
$$r^2 = \frac{66}{7} \times \frac{360}{120} \times \frac{7}{22} = 9$$
$$r = \sqrt{9} = 3 \text{ cm}$$

41. **(D)** Lateral surface area of a cylinder
$$= 2\pi rh = 704 \text{ cm}^2.$$

$$\therefore r = \frac{704}{2\pi h} = \frac{704}{2 \times \frac{22}{7} \times 8} = 14 \text{ cm}$$

42. **(B)** Lateral surface area of a cylinder $= 2\pi rh$. Let h_1 and h_2 be the heights.
Then $2 \times \frac{22}{7} \times r \times h_1$
$$= 2 \times \frac{22}{7} \times 2r \times h_2$$
Clearly $h_2 = \frac{h_1}{2}$

43. **(B)** The vertical section of a right circular cylinder is a rectangle and the horizontal section is always a circle.

44. **(D)** Area of rectangle GHKJ
$$= GH \times HJ = \frac{1}{2}LM \times \frac{1}{2}MN$$
$$= \frac{1}{4}LM \times MN = \frac{1}{4} \text{ rectangle LMNO}$$
Hence, unshaded region
= rectangle LMNO – rectangle GHKJ
$$= \frac{3}{4} \text{ rectangle LMNO}$$

45. **(A)** Clearly, area of shaded region
= area of circle – area of square RSTV
But, diameter of circle
= diagonal of square
or $2r = \sqrt{2}l$ or $r = \frac{l}{\sqrt{2}}$ or $l = r\sqrt{2}$
Area of shaded Region
$$= \pi r^2 - l^2 = \pi r^2 - (r\sqrt{2})^2$$
$$= \pi r^2 - 2r^2 = r^2(\pi - 2) \text{ sq units}$$

46. **(B)** The radii are x and $\sqrt{3}x$ and heights be 2y and 3y.
The ratio of volumes

$$\pi x^2 (2y) : \pi \left(\sqrt{3}x\right)^2 (3y)$$

$$= \pi x^2 (2y) : \pi \left(3x^2\right)(3y)$$

or 2 : 9

47. (D) The volume of the hall is
40 × 25 × 20 cu m.
Since each person needs
200 cu m, number of persons

$$= \frac{40 \times 25 \times 20}{200} = 100$$

48. (B) The corners are quadrants, i.e.,

$$\frac{1}{4} \times 2 \times \pi \times 2 = \pi$$

For 4 corners, we have peri-meter
of quadrants = 4π
Perimeter of horizontal portions
= 2(20 − 4) = 32 m
Perimeter of vertical portions
= 2(14 − 4) = 12 m.
Hence total perimeter = 44 + 4π

$$= 44 + \frac{88}{7} = \frac{154 + 88}{7}$$

$$= 56.57 \approx 56.6 \text{ m}$$

49. (C) Let each side be 1.5l (after
increase). Then % increase in
surface area

$$= \frac{6(1.5l)^2 - 6l^2}{6l^2} \times 100$$

$$= \frac{13.5l^2 - 6l^2}{6l^2} \times 100 = 125\%$$

50. (D)

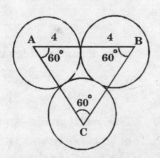

Required area is darkened.
The required area
= area of ABC − 3 × area of 60⁰
                                    sectors

$$= \frac{\sqrt{3}}{4} \times 8^2 - 3 \times \frac{60}{360} \times \pi \times 4^2$$

$$= 16\sqrt{3} - 8\pi = 8\left(2\sqrt{3} - \pi\right) \text{ cm}^2$$

Hence, required volume

$$= 16(8)\left(2\sqrt{3} - \pi\right)$$

$$= 128\left(2\sqrt{3} - \pi\right) \text{cm}^3$$

51. (D) Hint, distance saved = (l + b) −

$$\sqrt{l^2 + b^2} = \frac{l}{2}$$

or $\dfrac{l}{2} + b = \sqrt{l^2 + b^2}$ or

$$\frac{l^2}{4} + b^2 + lb = l^2 + b^2$$

or $l^2 + 4lb = 4l^2$ or $3l^2 = 4lb$

or $3l = 4b$ or $\dfrac{b}{l} = \dfrac{3}{4}$

52. (C) The number of surfaces in a right
circular cylinder = 3

53. (A) Perimetre of field X = 470 + 290
+ (470 − 180) + 180
+ (470 − 290) + 470
= 4 × 470 = 1880 m.

Perimetre of field Y
= 4 × 470 = 1880 m.
Hence C_x = 1880 × 40
and Cy = 1880 × 40
or $C_x = C_y$

54. (B) Internal volume
= 115 × 75 × 35 = 301875 cu cm
External measurements are

length = $115 + 2 \times 2.5 = 120$ cm

breadth = $75 + 2 \times 2.5 = 80$ cm

height = $35 + 2 \times 2.5 = 40$ cm

External volume

= $120 \times 80 \times 40 = 384000$ cu cm

Volume of wood

= $384000 - 301875$

= $82,125$ cu cm

55. (C)   Number of cubes = $\dfrac{(20)^3}{(5)^3}$

$= \dfrac{8000}{125} = 64$

56. (A)   Given that $h_1 : h_2 = 1 : 3$
We have,

$\pi r_1^2 h_1 = \pi r_2^2 h_2$

$\dfrac{r_1^2}{r_2^2} = \dfrac{\pi h_2}{\pi h_1} = \dfrac{h_2}{h_1} = \dfrac{3}{1}$

$\dfrac{r_1}{r_2} = \dfrac{\sqrt{3}}{1}$

$\therefore r_1 : r_2 = \sqrt{3} : 1$

Previous Contest Questions

1. (D)   Total area of the whole diagram = Area of parallelogram ABCD + Area of rectangle CDEF = $(5 \times 3)(5 \times 2) = 25\,cm^2$

2. (B)   Area of OBCD sector,

$= \dfrac{30}{360} \times \pi \times 21 \times 21$

$= \dfrac{22}{7} \times \dfrac{7}{4} \times 21 = \dfrac{231}{2} = 115.5\,cm^2$

Area of OADO sector,

$= \dfrac{30}{360} \times \pi \times 7 \times 7$

$= \dfrac{1}{126} \times \dfrac{22}{7} \times 7 \times 7 = \dfrac{77}{6} = 12.8$

So, area of shaded region

$= 11.5 - 12.8 = 102.7\,cm^2$

3. (B)   Let dimensions of rectangular block are a, b, c given
ab : bc : ca = 2 : 3 : 4 and

abc = $9000\,cm^3$

Now, $\dfrac{ab}{abc} : \dfrac{bc}{abc} : \dfrac{ca}{abc}$

$= \dfrac{2}{9000} : \dfrac{3}{9000} : \dfrac{4}{9000}$

$\therefore c : a : b = 4500 : 3000 : 2250$
= 450 : 300 : 225
c : a : b = 30 : 20 : 15
$\therefore a = 20; b = 15; c = 30$
($\because 20 \times 15 \times 30 = 9000$)
$\therefore$ shortest side is 15 cm

4. (D) $\pi r_1^2 l_1 = \pi r_2^2 l_2$

Given: $\dfrac{l_1}{l_2} = \dfrac{2}{1}$; $\left(\dfrac{r_1}{r_2}\right)^2 = \dfrac{l_2}{l_1} = \dfrac{1}{2}$

$\Rightarrow \dfrac{r_1}{r_2} = \dfrac{1}{\sqrt{2}}$

So, ratio of radii of two cylinders
$= 1 : \sqrt{2}$

5. (B)

Area of brick work = area of shaded region = $\pi(R+r)\,wh$

$$= \frac{22}{7} \times (2.6) \times 0.35 \times 20 \, \text{m}^3$$

$$= 57.2 \, \text{m}^3$$

6. **(B)** Let ABCD be a cylindrical ring whose outer radius = R = 12 cm
⇒ outer diameter = D = 24 cm
diameter of cross - section
CD = 1.5 cm

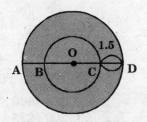

Area of cross - section

$$CD = \frac{\pi}{4}(CD)^2 = \frac{\pi}{4}(1.5)^2 \, \text{cm}^2$$

∴ Volume of circular ring = Al

where $A = = \frac{\pi}{4}(1.5)^2 \, \text{cm}^2$

$l = \pi(D - W) \, \pi(24 - 1.5)$

$\pi \times 22.5 \, \text{cm}$

∴ Volume $= \frac{\pi}{4} \times (1.5)^2 \times \pi \times 22.5$

$= 125 \, \text{cm}^3$

7. **(A)**

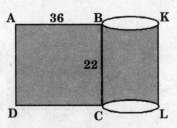

Height of cylinder = Width of sheet = BC = 22 cm
Circumference of top = 2πr = Length of sheet = AB = 36 cm

$$\Rightarrow r = \frac{36}{2\pi}$$

Now, volume = $\pi r^2 h$

$$= \pi \times \left(\frac{36}{2\pi}\right)^2 \times 22$$

$$= \frac{36 \times 36 \times 7 \times 22}{4 \times 22} = 2268 \, \text{cm}^3$$

Hence, the volume of the cylinder is 2,268 cm³.

8. **(B)** $x = \sqrt{400 - 144} = \sqrt{256} = 16$

Area of $\triangle ADC = \frac{\sqrt{3}}{4} \times 20 \times 20$

$$= 100\sqrt{3}$$

Area of $\triangle ABC = \frac{1}{2} \times 16 \times 12$

$$= 96$$

So, area of ABCD = $100\sqrt{3} + 96$
= 173 + 96 = 269 sq.units

9. **(C)**

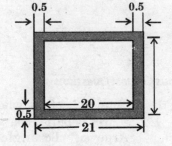

(View from top)

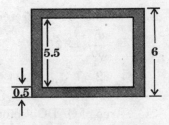

(View from front)

Length of the wall

$= (21 - 0.5 - 0.5) = 20$ cm,

Width $= 11 - 0.5 - 0.5 = 10$ cm
and height $= (6 - 0.5) = 5.5$ and
Total number of faces to be
painted = 4 walls + one base (as
its open from the top)
The dimensions of two of the
walls $= (10 \times 5.5)$
That of the remaining two walls
$= (20 \times 5.5)$ and
that of base $= 20 \times 10$
$\therefore$ Total area to be painted =
$2 \times (10 \times 5.5) + 2 \times (20 \times 5.5) +$
$(20 \times 10) = 530 \, \text{cm}^2$.

$\because$ The total expenses of painting
this area is Rs. 70,

the rate of painting $= \dfrac{70}{530} = 0.13$

$=$ Re. 0.1 per sq cm.
(approximately)

10. (D) Let original edge be 'a'

Surface are $= 6a^2$

New edge $= \dfrac{125}{100} a = \dfrac{5a}{4}$

New surface area

$= 6 \times \left(\dfrac{5a}{4}\right)^2 = \dfrac{75a^2}{8}$

Increase in surface area

$= \left(\dfrac{75a^2}{8} - 6a^2\right) = \dfrac{27a^2}{8}$

$\therefore$ increase%

$= \left(\dfrac{27a^2}{8} \times \dfrac{1}{6a^2} \times 100\right)\%$

$= 56.25\%$

Get It
Right

A Error in applying the law $\dfrac{a^m}{a^n} = a^{m-n}$

e.g. Simplify $\dfrac{x^7}{x^{-3}}$

✗ Incorrect

$$\dfrac{x^7}{x^{-3}} = x^{7-3} = x^4$$

Incorrect because

$$\dfrac{1}{x^{-3}} = x^3$$

✓ Correct

$$\dfrac{x^7}{x^{-3}} = x^{7-(-3)} = x^{10}$$

B Error in applying the low $a^m \times a^n = a^{m+n}$

e.g. Simplify $\left(y^2\right)\left(y^5\right)$

✗ Incorrect

$$\left(y^2\right)\left(y^5\right) = y^{2\times5} = y^{10}$$

Incorrect because the
indices should be added

✓ Correct

$$\left(y^2\right)\left(y^5\right) = y^{2+5} = y^7$$

Synopsis

Exponential Equation:

An equation which has an unknown quantity as an exponent is called an exponential equation.

Eg : (1) $5^x = 625$

(2) $3^{x-5} = 1$

Law of exponents :

If 'a' and 'b' are any rational numbers different from zero and if x, y are any rational numbers, then

♦ $a^x \times a^y = a^{x+y}$ ♦ $a^x \div a^y = a^{x-y}$ ♦ $\left(a^x\right)^y = a^{xy}$

♦ $(ab)^x = a^x \times b^x$ ♦ $\left(\dfrac{a}{b}\right)^x = \dfrac{a^x}{b^x}$ ♦ $a^0 = 1$

♦ $a^{-m} = \dfrac{1}{a^m}$ ♦ $\left(\dfrac{a}{b}\right)^{-m} = \left(\dfrac{b}{a}\right)^m$

Multiple Choice Questions

1. The value of $\left(3^0 - 4^0\right) \times 5^2$ is:

   (A) 25   (B) 0
   (C) –25   (D) none of these

2. The solution of $3^{3x-5} = \dfrac{1}{9^x}$ is:

   (A) $\dfrac{5}{2}$ (B) 5   (C) 1   (D) $\dfrac{7}{3}$

3. The value of $\left[(-2)^{(-2)}\right]^{(-3)}$ is:

   (A) 64
   (B) 32
   (C) cannot be determined
   (D) none of these

4. $\left(\dfrac{16}{81}\right)^{\frac{3}{4}} = $ _____

   (A) $\dfrac{9}{2}$ (B) $\dfrac{2}{9}$ (C) $\dfrac{8}{27}$ (D) $\dfrac{27}{8}$

5. The value of $(512)^{\frac{-2}{9}}$ is:

   (A) $\dfrac{1}{2}$ (B) 2   (C) 4   (D) $\dfrac{1}{4}$

6. Simplify $(32)^{\frac{-2}{5}} \div (125)^{\frac{-2}{3}}$

   (A) $\dfrac{4}{25}$ (B) $\dfrac{25}{4}$ (C) $\dfrac{2}{5}$ (D) $\dfrac{5}{2}$

(A) 545   (B) 500

(C) 630   (D) none of these

7. If $x^y = y^x$, then $\left(\dfrac{x}{y}\right)^{\frac{x}{y}}$ is equal to:

(A) $x^{\frac{x}{y}}$ (B) $x^{\frac{x}{y}-1}$ (C) $x^{\frac{y}{x}}$ (D) $x^{\frac{y}{x}-1}$

16. If x is any non-zero, $m < n$ then $\dfrac{x^m}{x^n}$ is:

(A) $\dfrac{1}{x^{m-n}}$ (B) $\dfrac{1}{x^{n-m}}$

(C) x^{n-m} (D) None of these

8. If $\dfrac{x}{y} = \dfrac{6}{5}$ then $\dfrac{x^2 + y^2}{x^2 - y^2}$ is:

(A) $\dfrac{36}{25}$ (B) $\dfrac{25}{36}$ (C) $\dfrac{61}{11}$ (D) $\dfrac{11}{61}$

17. The value of

$(-3)^0 - (-3)^3 - (-3)^{-1} + (-3)^4 - (-3)^{-2}$ is:

(A) $109\dfrac{2}{9}$ (B) $109\dfrac{9}{2}$

(C) 109 (D) None of these

9. $(64)^{\frac{-2}{3}} \times \left(\dfrac{1}{4}\right)^{-3}$ equals to:

(A) 4   (B) $\dfrac{1}{4}$ (C) 1   (D) 16

18. The value of $4\left(7^1.7^{-1}.7^{-1}.7^0\right)$ is:

(A) $3\dfrac{7}{3}$ (B) $\dfrac{6}{7}$

10. The value of $\dfrac{(5)^{0.25} \times (125)^{0.25}}{(256)^{0.10} \times (256)^{0.15}}$ is:

(A) $\dfrac{\sqrt{5}}{2}$ (B) $\dfrac{5}{4}$ (C) $\dfrac{25}{2}$ (D) $\dfrac{25}{16}$

(C) $3\dfrac{3}{7}$ (D) None of these

19. The value of

$\dfrac{(-1)^{13}}{2^3} + \dfrac{2^3 - 1^{10} + 3^2}{3^2 - 2^2} + \left(\dfrac{7}{11}\right)^3 \div \dfrac{98}{121}$ is:

11. The value of $\dfrac{(67.542)^2 - (32.458)^2}{75.458 - 40.374}$ is:

(A) 1   (B) 10

(C) 100   (D) none of these

(A) $3\dfrac{173}{440}$ (B) $3\dfrac{17}{44}$

(C) $3\dfrac{137}{440}$ (D) None of these

12. Which of the following values are equal?

I. 1^4 II. 4^0 III. 0^4 IV. 4^1

(A) I and II   (B) II and III

(C) I and III   (D) I and IV

20. If $(25)^x = (125)^y$ then $x : y = $ _____

(A) 1:1   (B) 2:3   (C) 3:2   (D) 1:3

13. The sum of the powers of the prime factors in 108×192 is:

(A) 5   (B) 7   (C) 8   (D) 12

21. If $x = 2$, $y = 3$ then $\dfrac{1}{x^y} + \dfrac{1}{y^x} = $ _____

(A) 72   (B) $\dfrac{17}{72}$

14. The value of $\sqrt{1^3 + 2^3 + 3^3}$ is:

(A) 5   (B) 6   (C) 7   (D) 8

(C) $\dfrac{31}{108}$ (D) None of these

15. The value of $3\sqrt[3]{2} \times 7\sqrt[3]{6} \times 5\sqrt[3]{18}$ is:

22. The value of

$$\frac{(64)^{-1/6} \times (216)^{-1/3} \times (81)^{1/4}}{(512)^{-1/3} \times (16)^{1/4} \times (9)^{-1/2}}$$

(A) 3   (B) 6

(C) 1   (D) None of these

23. Simplified form of $\left[\sqrt[3]{x^4 y} \times \dfrac{1}{\sqrt[4]{x^2 y^8}} \right]^{-6}$

(A) $x^5 . y^{10}$ (B) $\dfrac{y^{10}}{x^5}$ (C) $\dfrac{y^2}{x}$ (D) $\dfrac{x^5}{y^5}$

24. Simplified form of $\left\{ \sqrt[4]{\left(\dfrac{1}{2} \right)^{-12}} \right\}^{-2/3}$

(A) x^{-2} (B) $\dfrac{1}{x^{-2}}$

(C) $\dfrac{1}{x}$ (D) x^{-1}

25. The value of $\dfrac{1}{1+x^{-m}} + \dfrac{1}{1+x^{m}}$

(A) 0   (B) x^m

(C) 1   (D) None of these

26. Simplified form of $\dfrac{3^a 4^{a-2} 25^{a+1}}{9^{a-1} 2^{a+1} 5^{a-2}}$

(A) $3^{a-2} . 2^{a-5} . 5^{a+4}$ (B) $2^{a-5} . 3^{2-a} . 5^{a+4}$

(C) $2^{a+5} . 3^{-a+2} . 5^{a+4}$ (D) $2^{a-5} . 3^{-a-2} . 5^{a+4}$

27. Which is greater in $2^{12}, 3^8$?

(A) 2^{12} (B) 3^8

(C) Can't say   (D) None of these

28. Simplified form of

$$\frac{\left(x^{a+b} \right)^3 . \left(x^{b+c} \right)^3 . \left(x^{c+a} \right)^3}{\left(x^a . x^b . x^c \right)^6} \text{ is:}$$

(A) 0   (B) 1

(C) x^{a+b+c} (D) None of these

29. If $3^n = 729$ then 3^{3n+1} is:

(A) 3^{21} (B) 3^{10}

(C) 3^{19} (D) None of these

30. Simplified form of $\left(\dfrac{x^{2-3n} . x^{4+3n}}{x^3} \right)^2$

(A) x^2 (B) x^{12}

(C) x^4 (D) x^6

31. If $27^{x+1} = 9^{x+3} = 3^y$ then x and y are:

(A) 3, 12   (B) 12, 3

(C) 6,6   (D) None of these

32. The value of $\left[5 \left(8^{1/3} + 27^{1/3} \right)^3 \right]^{1/4}$ is:

(A) 5^4 (B) $5^{1/4}$

(C) 5   (D) None of these

33. The value of

$(0.000064)^{5/4} \times (0.04)^{5/4}$ is:

(A) $2^{10} . 0^{10}$

(B) $2^{10} . 10^{-10}$

(C) $2^{-10} . 10^{10}$

(D) None of these

Previous Contest Questions

1. The value of $(256)^{5/4}$ is:

   (A) 512   (B) 984   (C) 1024   (D) 1032

2. The value of $\left(\sqrt{8}\right)^{1/3}$ is:

   (A) 2   (B) 4   (C) $\sqrt{2}$ (D) 8

3. The value of $\left(\dfrac{-1}{216}\right)^{-2/3}$ is:

   (A) 36   (B) -36
   (C) 1/36   (D) -1/36

4. The value of

   $\dfrac{1}{(216)^{-2/3}} + \dfrac{1}{(256)^{-3/4}} + \dfrac{1}{(32)^{-1/5}}$ is:

   (A) 102   (B) 105   (C) 107   (D) 109

5. The value of $\left[10^{150} \div 10^{146}\right]$ is:

   (A) 1000   (B) 10000
   (C) 100000   (D) 10^6

6. The value of $5^{1/4} \times (125)^{0.25}$ is:

   (A) $\sqrt{5}$ (B) 5   (C) $5\sqrt{5}$ (D) 25

7. $(256)^{0.16} \times (256)^{0.09} = ?$

   (A) 4   (B) 16   (C) 64   (D) 256.25

8. $(0.04)^{-15} = ?$

   (A) 25   (B) 125   (C) 250   (D) 625

9. The value of $\left(8^{-25} - 8^{-26}\right)$ is:

   (A) 7×8^{-25} (B) 7×8^{-26}

   (C) 8×8^{-26} (D) None of these

10. $(25)^{7.5} \times (5)^{2.5} \div (125)^{1.5} = 5^{?}$

    (A) 8.5   (B) 13   (C) 16   (D) 17.5

⊘ Answers ⊘

Multiple Choice Questions

1. B	2. C	3. A	4. C	5. C	6. B	7. B	8. C	9. A	10. B
11. C	12. A	13. D	14. B	15. C	16. B	17. A	18. C	19. A	20. C
21. B	22. A	23. B	24. B	25. C	26. B	27. B	28. B	29. C	30. D
31. A	32. C	33. B							

Previous Contest Questions

1. C	2. C	3. A	4. A	5. B	6. B	7. A	8. B	9. B	10. B

Explanatory Answers

1. (B) $\left(3^0 - 4^0\right) \times 5^2 = (1 - 1) \times 5^2 = 0$

2. (C) $3^{3x-5} = \dfrac{1}{9^x}$

   $3^{3x-5} = 3^{-2x}$
   $3x - 5 = -2x$
   $x = 1$

3. (A) $\left[(-2)^{(-2)}\right]^{(-3)} = (-2)^6 = 64$

4. (C) $\left(\dfrac{16}{81}\right)^{\frac{3}{4}} = \left[\left(\dfrac{2}{3}\right)^4\right]^{\frac{3}{4}} = \dfrac{8}{27}$

5. (D) $(512)^{\frac{-2}{9}} = \left(2^9\right)^{\frac{-2}{9}} = 2^{-2} = \dfrac{1}{4}$

6. (B) $\dfrac{(32)^{\frac{-2}{5}}}{(125)^{\frac{-2}{3}}} = \dfrac{\frac{1}{4}}{\frac{1}{25}} = \dfrac{25}{4}$

$= \dfrac{100 \times 35.084}{35.084} = 100$

7. (B) $x^y = y^x$

$x = y^{\frac{x}{y}}$

$\left(\dfrac{x}{y}\right)^{\frac{x}{y}} = \dfrac{x^{\frac{x}{y}}}{y^{\frac{x}{y}}} = \dfrac{x^{\frac{x}{y}}}{x} = x^{\frac{x}{y}-1}$

12. (A) $4^0 = 1 = 1^4$

$\therefore$ I and II have equal value

13. (D) $108 = 2 \times 2 \times 3 \times 3 \times 3 = 2^2 \times 3^3$

$192 = 2 \times 2 \times 2 \times 2 \times 2 \times 2 \times 3$

$\qquad = 2^6 \times 3^1$

$108 \times 192 = 2^2 \times 3^3 \times 2^6 \times 3^1$

$\qquad = 2^8 \times 3^4$

Sum of the powers $= 8 + 4 = 12$

8. (C) $\dfrac{x}{y} = \dfrac{6}{5}$

Let $x = 6k$, $y = 5k$

$\dfrac{x^2 + y^2}{x^2 - y^2} = \dfrac{(6k)^2 + (5k)^2}{(6k)^2 - (5k)^2} = \dfrac{61k^2}{11k^2} = \dfrac{61}{11}$

14. (B)

$\sqrt{1^3 + 2^3 + 3^3} = \sqrt{1 + 8 + 27} = \sqrt{36} = 6$

15. (C) $3\sqrt[3]{2} \times 7\sqrt[3]{6} \times 5\sqrt[3]{18}$

$= 105 \times \sqrt[3]{216} = 105 \times 6 = 630$

9. (A) $(64)^{\frac{-2}{3}} \times \left(\dfrac{1}{4}\right)^{-3} = (4^3)^{\frac{-2}{3}} \times \left(\dfrac{1}{4}\right)^{-3}$

$= 4^{-2} \times \dfrac{1}{4^{-3}} = 4$

17. (A) $1 - (-3 \times -3 \times -3) - \dfrac{-1}{3}$

$+ (-3 \times -3 \times -3 \times -3) - \dfrac{1}{(-3)^2}$

$= 1 + 27 + \dfrac{1}{3} + 81 - \dfrac{1}{9}$

$= 109 + \dfrac{2}{9} = 109\dfrac{2}{9}$

10. (B) $\dfrac{(5)^{0.25} \times (125)^{0.25}}{(256)^{0.10} \times (256)^{0.15}}$

$= \dfrac{(5)^{0.25} \times (5^3)^{0.25}}{(4^4)^{0.10} \times (4^4)^{0.15}}$

$= \dfrac{(5)^{0.25} \times (5)^{0.75}}{(4)^{0.40} \times (4)^{0.60}}$

$= \dfrac{(5)^1}{(4)^1} = \dfrac{5}{4}$

18. (C) $4\left[7 \times \dfrac{1}{7} - \dfrac{1}{7} \times 1\right] = 4\left(1 - \dfrac{1}{7}\right) = 4 \times \dfrac{6}{7}$

$= \dfrac{24}{7} = 3\dfrac{3}{7}$

19. (A) $\dfrac{-1}{2 \times 2 \times 2} + \dfrac{2 \times 2 \times 2 - 1 + 3 \times 3}{3 \times 3 - 2 \times 2}$

$+ \dfrac{7 \times 7 \times 7}{11 \times 11 \times 11} \times \dfrac{121}{98}$

11. (C) $\dfrac{(67.542)^2 - (32.458)^2}{75.458 - 40.374}$

$= \dfrac{(67.542 + 32.458)(67.542 - 32.458)}{75.458 - 40.374}$

$= \dfrac{-1}{8} + \dfrac{8 - 1 + 9}{9 - 4} + \dfrac{7}{22} = \dfrac{-1}{8} + \dfrac{16}{6} + \dfrac{7}{22}$

$= \dfrac{-55 + 1408 + 140}{440} = \dfrac{1493}{140} = 3\dfrac{173}{440}$

20. (C) $\left(5^2\right)^x = \left(5^3\right)^y$

$\Rightarrow 5^{2x} = 5^{3y} \Rightarrow 2x = 3y$

$\dfrac{x}{y} = \dfrac{3}{2} \Rightarrow x : y = 3 : 2$

21. (B) $\dfrac{1}{2^3} + \dfrac{1}{3^2} = \dfrac{1}{8} + \dfrac{1}{9} = \dfrac{9+8}{72} = \dfrac{17}{72}$

22. (A) $\dfrac{2^{6\times\frac{-1}{6}} \times 6^{3\times\frac{-1}{3}} \times 3^{4\times\frac{1}{4}}}{8^{3\times\frac{-1}{3}} \times 2^{4\times\frac{1}{4}} \times 3^{2\times\frac{-1}{2}}} = \dfrac{2^{-1} \times 6^{-1} \times 3}{8^{-1} \times 2^{1} \times 3^{-1}}$

$= \dfrac{8 \times 3 \times 3}{2 \times 6 \times 2} = \dfrac{72}{24} = 3$

23. (B) $\left[\left(x^4 . y\right)^{1/3} . \dfrac{1}{\left(x^2 . y^3\right)^{1/4}}\right]^{-6}$

$= \left[x^{4/3} . y^{1/3} \times \dfrac{1}{\left(x^{2/4} . y^{3/4}\right)}\right]^{-6}$

$= \left[x^{\frac{4}{3}-\frac{1}{2}} \times y^{\frac{1}{3}-2}\right]^{-6} = \left[x^{\frac{8-3}{6}} . y^{\frac{1-6}{3}}\right]^{-6}$

$= \left(x^{5/6} . y^{-5/3}\right)^{-6} = x^{\frac{5}{6}\times -6} . y^{\frac{-5}{3}\times -6}$

$= x^{-5} \times y^{+10} = \dfrac{y^{10}}{x^5}$

24. (B) $\left[x^{-12\times\frac{1}{4}}\right]^{\frac{-2}{3}} = x^{-3\times\frac{-2}{3}} = x^2 = \dfrac{1}{x^{-2}}$

25. (C) $\dfrac{1}{1+\dfrac{1}{x^m}} + \dfrac{1}{1+x^m} = \dfrac{1}{\dfrac{x^m+1}{x^m}} + \dfrac{1}{1+x^m}$

$= \dfrac{x^m}{x^m+1} + \dfrac{1}{x^m+1} = \dfrac{x^m+1}{x^m+1} = 1$

26. (B) $\dfrac{3^a . \left(2^2\right)^{a-2} . \left(5^2\right)^{a+1}}{\left(3^2\right)^{a-1} . 2^{a+1} . 5^{a-2}} = \dfrac{3^a . 2^{2a-4} . 5^{2a+2}}{3^{2a-2} . 2^{a+1} . 5^{a-2}}$

$= 3^{a-2a+2} . 2^{2a-4-a-1} . 5^{2a+2-a+2}$

$= 3^{-a+2} . 2^{a-5} . 5^{a+4} = 2^{a-5} . 3^{-a+2} . 5^{a+4}$

27. (B) $2^{12} = 2^{3\times4} = \left(2^3\right)^4 = 8^4$

$3^8 = 3^{2\times4} = \left(3^2\right)^4 = 9^4$

Since the powers of $8^4, 9^4$ is same

$\Rightarrow 9^4$ is greater than 8^4

28. (B) $\dfrac{x^{3a+3b} . x^{3b+c} . x^{3c+3c}}{x^{6a+6b+6c}}$

$= \dfrac{x^{3a+3b+3b+c+3c+3c}}{x^{6a+6b+6c}}$

$= \dfrac{x^{6a+6b+6c}}{x^{6a+6b+6c}}$

$= x^{6a+6b+6c-6a-6b-6c}$

$= x^0 = 1$

29. (C) $3^n = 729 \Rightarrow 3^n = 3^6 \Rightarrow n = 6$

$3^{3n+1} = 3^{3(6)+1} = 3^{18+1} = 3^{19}$

30. (D) $\dfrac{x^{4-6n} . x^{8+6n}}{x^6} = \dfrac{x^{4-6n+8+6n}}{x^6}$

$= \dfrac{x^{12}}{x^6} = x^{12-6} = x^6$

31. (A) $27^{x+1} = 9^{x+3} \Rightarrow \left(3^3\right)^{x+1} = \left(3^2\right)^{x+3}$

$\Rightarrow 3^{3x+3} = 3^{2x+6} \Rightarrow 3x+3 = 2x+6$

$\Rightarrow 3x-2x = 6-3 \Rightarrow x = 3$

Consider $9^{x+3} = 3^y \Rightarrow \left(3^2\right)^{x+3} = 3^y$

$\Rightarrow 3^{2x+6} = 3^y \Rightarrow 2x+6 = y$

$\therefore 2(3) + 6 = y = 12$

32. (C) $\left[5\left(2^{3\times\frac{1}{3}}+3^{3\times\frac{1}{3}}\right)^3\right]^{1/4}$

$=\left[5(2+3)^3\right]^{1/4}$

$=\left(5\times5^3\right)^{1/4}=5^{4\times\frac{1}{4}}=5$

33. (B) $\left(\dfrac{64}{1000000}\right)^{5/4}\times\left(\dfrac{4}{100}\right)^{5/4}$

$=\left(\dfrac{2^6}{10^6}\right)^{5/4}\cdot\left(\dfrac{2^2}{10^2}\right)^{5/4}=\left(\dfrac{2^6\times2^2}{10^6\times10^2}\right)^{5/4}$

$=\left(\dfrac{2^8}{10^8}\right)^{5/4}=\dfrac{2^{8\times\frac{5}{4}}}{10^{8\times\frac{5}{4}}}=\dfrac{2^{10}}{10^{10}}=2^{10}.10^{-10}$

Previous Contest Questions

1. (C) $(256)^{5/4}=\left(4^4\right)^{5/4}=4^{\left(4\times\frac{5}{4}\right)}$

$=4^5=1024$

2. (C) $\left(\sqrt{8}\right)^{1/3}=\left(8^{1/2}\right)^{1/3}$

$=8^{\left(\frac{1}{2}\times\frac{1}{3}\right)}=8^{\frac{1}{6}}$

$=\left(2^3\right)^{1/6}=2^{\left(3\times\frac{1}{6}\right)}=2^{\frac{1}{2}}=\sqrt{2}$

3. (A) $\left(\dfrac{-1}{216}\right)^{-2/3}=\left[\left(\dfrac{-1}{6}\right)^3\right]^{-2/3}=\left(\dfrac{-1}{6}\right)^{3\times\frac{-2}{3}}$

$=\left(\dfrac{-1}{6}\right)^{-2}=\dfrac{1}{\left(-1/6\right)^2}=\dfrac{1}{\left(1/36\right)}=36$

4. (A) $\dfrac{1}{(216)^{-2/3}}+\dfrac{1}{(256)^{-3/4}}+\dfrac{1}{(32)^{-1/5}}$

$=\dfrac{1}{\left(6^3\right)^{-2/3}}+\dfrac{1}{\left(4^4\right)^{-3/4}}+\dfrac{1}{\left(2^5\right)^{-1/5}}$

$=\dfrac{1}{6^{3x-2/3}}+\dfrac{1}{4^{4x-3/4}}+\dfrac{1}{2^{5x-1/5}}$

$=\dfrac{1}{6^{-2}}+\dfrac{1}{4^{-3}}+\dfrac{1}{2^{-1}}=\left(6^2+4^3+2^1\right)$

$=\left(36+64+2^1\right)=102$

5. (B) $(10)^{150}\div(10)^{146}=\dfrac{(10)^{150}}{(10)^{146}}$

$=10^{(150-146)}=10^4=10000$

6. (B) $5^{1/4}\times(125)^{0.25}=5^{0.25}\times\left(5^3\right)^{0.25}$

$=5^{0.25}\times5^{(3\times0.25)}=5^{0.25}\times5^{0.75}$

$=5^{(0.25+0.75)}=5^1=5$

7. (A) $(256)^{0.16}\times(256)^{0.09}$

$=(256)^{(0.16+0.09)}$

$=(256)^{0.25}=(256)^{25/100}=(256)^{1/4}$

$=\left(4^4\right)^{1/4}=4^1=4$

8. (B) $(0.04)^{-1.5}=\left(\dfrac{4}{100}\right)^{-1.5}$

$=\left(\dfrac{1}{25}\right)^{-3/2}=(25)^{3/2}=\left(5^2\right)^{3/2}$

$=5^3=125$

9. (B) $\left(8^{-25}-8^{-26}\right)$

$=\left(8^{\frac{1}{25}}-8^{\frac{1}{26}}\right)=\dfrac{(8-1)}{8^{26}}$

$=7\times8^{-26}$

10. (B) Let $=(25)^{7.5}\times(5)^{2.5}\div(125)^{1.5}=5^x$

Then, $\dfrac{\left(5^2\right)^{7.5}\times\left(5\right)^{2.5}}{\left(5^3\right)^{1.5}}=5^x$

$\dfrac{5^{(2\times7.5)}\times5^{2.5}}{5^{(3\times1.5)}}=5^x \Rightarrow \dfrac{5^{15}\times5^{2.5}}{5^{4.5}}=5^x$

$\Rightarrow 5^x=5^{(15+2.5-4.5)}=(5)^{13}\Rightarrow x=13$

A Confusion between direct and inverse proportion.

e.g. If 2 men can complete a work in 10 days. How many days will be taken by 4 men (having same capability to do work) to complete the same work.

✗ **Incorrect**	✓ **Correct**
$2 \to 10$	$2 \to 10$
$4 \to ?$	$4 \to ?$
Number of days required	Number of days required
$= \dfrac{4 \times 10}{2} = 20 \text{ days}$	$= \dfrac{2 \times 10}{4} = 5 \text{ days}$
Here, Men and time are taken in direct proportion.	Men and time are taken in inverse proportion.

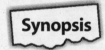

Synopsis

Unitary Method:

A method in which the value of a quantity is first obtained to find the value of any required quantity is called unitary method.

Direct Proportion:

Two quantities are said to be directly proportional if the increase (or decrease) in one quantity causes the increase (or decrease) in the other quantity by same proportion.

Examples:

1. Cost is directly proportional to the number of articles.
2. Work done is directly proportional to the number of men working on it.

Inverse Proportion:

Two quantities are said to vary inversely proportional if the increase (or decrease) in one quantity causes the decrease (or increase) in the other quantity by same proportion.

Examples:

1. The time taken to finish a work is inversely proportional to the number of persons working at it.

2. The time taken by any vehicle in covering a certain distance is inversely proportional to the speed of the car.

Multiple Choice Questions

1. If $a:b = 3:4$ and $b:c = 5:9$, then $a:b:c$ is:
   (A) $15:20:36$ (B) $20:36:15$
   (C) $3:20:9$ (D) None of these

2. If $a:b = 8:9$, $b:c = 18:40$, then $a:c$ is:
   (A) $1:5$ (B) $5:2$
   (C) $2:5$ (D) None of these

3. What number shall be added to each of the numbers 4, 7, 14, 22 to form the terms in a proportion?
   (A) 1   (B) 2   (C) 3   (D) 4

4. What is the correct order in which 4, 12, 15, 5 be written so as to form the terms in proportion?
   (A) 4, 15, 12, 5   (B) 4, 15, 5, 12
   (C) 15, 5, 4, 12   (D) 15, 12, 5, 4

5. If the cost of 48 bags of paddy is Rs. 16,800, then cost of 36 bags of paddy is:
   (A) Rs. 12,000   (B) Rs. 12,600
   (C) Rs. 16,200   (D) None of these

6. If $A:B = 5:7$ and $B:C = 6:11$, then $A:B:C$ is:
   (A) $55:77:66$ (B) $30:42:77$
   (C) $35:49:42$ (D) None of these

7. If $A:B:C = 2:3:4$, then $\dfrac{A}{B}:\dfrac{B}{C}:\dfrac{C}{A}$ is equal to:
   (A) $4:9:16$ (B) $8:9:12$
   (C) $8:9:16$ (D) $8:9:24$

8. If $A:B = \dfrac{1}{2}:\dfrac{3}{8}$, $B:C = \dfrac{1}{3}:\dfrac{5}{9}$ and $C:D = \dfrac{5}{6}:\dfrac{3}{4}$, then the ratio $A:B:C:D$ is:
   (A) $4:6:8:10$
   (B) $6:4:8:10$ (C) $6:8:9:10$
   (D) $8:6:10:9$

9. If $\dfrac{1}{5}:\dfrac{1}{x} = \dfrac{1}{x}:\dfrac{1}{1.25}$, then the value of x is:
   (A) 1.5   (B) 2   (C) 2.5   (D) 3.5

10. If $0.75:x::5:8$, then x is equal to:
    (A) 1.12   (B) 1.20   (C) 1.25   (D) 1.30

11. If 76 is divided into four parts proportional to 7, 5, 3, 4, then the smallest part is:
    (A) 12   (B) 15   (C) 16   (D) 19

12. What least number must be subtracted from each of the numbers 14, 17, 34 and 42 so that the remainders may be proportional?
    (A) 0   (B) 1   (C) 2   (D) 7

13. The ratio of third proportional to 12 and 30 and the mean proportional between 9 and 25 is:
    (A) $2:1$ (B) $5:1$ (C) $7:15$ (D) $9:14$

14. The average age of three boys is 25 years and their ages are in the ratio $3:5:7$. The age of the youngest boy is:
    (A) 21 years   (B) 18 years
    (C) 15 years   (D) 9 years

15. Three containers have their volumes in the ratio $3:4:5$. They are full of mixtures of milk and water. The mixtures contain milk and water in the ratio of $(4:1), (3:1)$ and $(5:2)$ respectively. The ratio of milk and water in the fourth continer contains all the above three mixtures is:
    (A) $4:1$ (B) $151:48$
    (C) $157:53$ (D) $5:2$

16. x varies inversely as square of y. Given that $y = 2$ for $x = 1$. The value of x for $y = 6$ will be equal to:
    (A) 3   (B) 9   (C) $\frac{1}{3}$ (D) $\frac{1}{9}$

17. If the cost of "x" metres of wire is "d" rupees, then what is the cost of "y" metres of wire at the same rate ?
    (A) Rs. $\left(\dfrac{xy}{d}\right)$ (B) Rs. (xy)
    (C) Rs. (yd) (D) Rs. $\left(\dfrac{yd}{x}\right)$

18. If the price of 6 toys is Rs. 264. 37, What will be the approximate price of 5 toys?
    (A) Rs. 140   (B) Rs. 100
    (C) Rs. 200   (D) Rs. 220

19. The price of 357 mangoes is Rs. 1517.25. What will be the approximate price of 49 dozens of such mangoes?
    (A) Rs. 3000   (B) Rs. 3500
    (C) Rs. 4000   (D) Rs. 2500

20. If a quarter kg of green chillies cost 60 paise, how many paise will 200 g cost?
    (A) 48 paise   (B) 54 paise
    (C) 56 paise   (D) 72 paise

21. If 11.25 m of a uniform iron rod weighs 42.75 kg, what will be the weight of 6 m of the same rod ?
    (A) 22.8 kg   (B) 25.6 kg
    (C) 28 kg   (D) 26.5 kg

22. On a scale of map, 0.6 cm represents 6.6 km. If the distance between the points on the map is 80.5 cm, the actual distance between these points is:
    (A) 9 km   (B) 72.5 kg
    (C) 190.75 km   (D) 885.5 km

23. A flagstaff 17.5 m high casts a shaded length of 40.25 m. The height of the building which costs a shadow of length 28.75 m under similar conditions will be:
    (A) 10 m   (B) 12.5 m
    (C) 17.5 m   (D) 21.25 m

24. 36 men can complete a piece of work in 18 days. In how many days will 27 men complete the same work?
    (A) 12   (B) 18   (C) 22   (D) 24

25. A rope makes 70 rounds of the circumference of a cylinder whose radius of the base is 14 cm. How many times can it go round a cylinder with radius 20 cm?
    (A) 40   (B) 49
    (C) 100   (D) None of these

26. A certain number of men can finish a piece of work in 100 days. If, there were 10 men less, it would take 10 days more for the work to be finished. How many men were there originally ?
    (A) 75   (B) 82   (C) 100   (D) 110

27. In a camp, 95 men had provision for 200 days. After 5 days, 30 men left the camp. For how many days will the remaining food last now ?
    (A) 180   (B) 285
    (C) $139\dfrac{16}{19}$ (D) None of these

28. A garrison of 500 men had provision for 27 days. After 3 days a reinforcement of 300 men arrived. For how many more days will the remaining food last now ?
    (A) 15   (B) 16   (C) $17\dfrac{1}{2}$ (D) 18

29. A contractor undertook to do a certain piece of work in 9 days. He employed certain number of men, but 6 of them being absent form the very first day,

the rest could finish the work in 15 days. The number of men originally employed were:

(A) 12   (B) 15   (C) 18   (D) 24

Previous Contest Questions

1. If 6 note books cost Rs. 45, how much would 8 note books cost?
   (A) Rs.57 (B) Rs.60 (C) Rs.312 (D) Rs.360

2. If 45 students can consume a stock of food in 2 months, then for how many days the same stock of food will last for 27 students ?
   (A) 100 days   (B) 144 days
   (C) 160 days   (D) 180 days

3. A man working 8 hours a day takes 5 days to complete a project. How many hours a day must he work to complete it in 4 days?
   (A) 10 hours   (B) 11 hours
   (C) 12 hours   (D) 14 hours

4. If 40 articles cost Rs. 180, the cost of 18 articles is:
   (A) Rs. 18   (B) Rs. 36
   (C) Rs. 81   (D) Rs. 40.5

5. If 20 persons can do a piece of work in 7 days, then the number of persons required to complete the work in 28 days:
   (A) 4   (B) 5   (C) 14   (D) 10

6. A rope makes 260 rounds of a cylinder with base radius 20 cm. How many

times can it go round a cylinder with base radius 26 cm?
(A) 130   (B) 300   (C) 200   (D) 150

7. In a camp, there is a meal for 120 men or 200 children. If 150 children have taken the meal, how many men will be catered to with the remaining meal ?
(A) 20   (B) 30   (C) 40   (D) 50

8. A wheel that has 6 cogs is meshed with a larger wheel of 14 cogs. When the smaller wheel has made 21 revolutions, then the number of revolutions made by the larger wheel is:
(A) 4   (B) 9   (C) 12   (D) 49

9. A fort had provision of food for 150 men for 45 days. After 10 days, 25 men left the fort, The number of days for which the remaining food will last, is:

(A) $29\dfrac{1}{5}$ (B) $37\dfrac{1}{4}$

(C) 42   (D) 54

10. A man completes $\dfrac{5}{8}$ of a job in 10 days. At this rate, how many more days will it take him to finish the job ?

(A) 5   (B) 6   (C) 7   (D) $7\dfrac{1}{2}$

◇ Answers ◇

Multiple Choice Questions

1. A	2. C	3. B	4. D	5. B	6. B	7. D	8. D	9. C	10. B
11. A	12. C	13. B	14. C	15. C	16. D	17. D	18. D	19. D	20. A
21. A	22. D	23. B	24. D	25. B	26. D	27. B	28. A	29. B	

Previous Contest Questions

1. B	2. A	3. A	4. C	5. B	6. C	7. B	8. B	9. C	10. B

Explanatory Answers

1. **(A)** To find a : b : c, b is made same in both the ratios. L.C.M fo 4 and 5 is 20

$$a:b = \frac{3}{4} = \frac{3 \times 5}{4 \times 5} = \frac{15}{20}$$

$$b:c = \frac{5}{9} = \frac{5 \times 4}{9 \times 4} = \frac{20}{36}$$

$$\therefore a:b:c = 15:20:36$$

2. **(C)** Given $a:b = 8:9$, $b:c = 18:40$

$$\frac{a}{c} = \frac{a}{c} \times \frac{b}{b} = \frac{a}{b} \times \frac{b}{c} = \frac{8}{9} \times \frac{18}{40} = \frac{2}{5}$$

$$a:c = 2:5$$

3. **(B)** Let the number to be added be 'x'

$$\therefore \quad (4+x),(7+x),(14+x),(22+x)$$
are in proportion.

$$\Rightarrow (4+x)(22+x) = (7+x)(14+x)$$

$$\Rightarrow 88 + 4x + 22x + x^2$$
$$= 98 + 7x + 14x + x^2$$

$$\Rightarrow 88 + 26x = 98 + 21x$$

$$\Rightarrow 26x - 21x = 98 - 88 \Rightarrow 5x = 10$$

$$\Rightarrow x = \frac{10}{5} \Rightarrow x = 2$$

4. **(D)** Since $\quad 15 \times 4 = 12 \times 5 \Rightarrow 60 = 60$
(Product of extremes = Product of means)

5. **(B)** Let the cost of 36 bags be Rs. x
∴ Ratio between the number of books = Ratio between their costs
$$48:36 = 16,800:x$$

$$\Rightarrow \frac{48}{36} = \frac{16800}{x} \Rightarrow x = \frac{16800 \times 36}{48}$$

$$= 12,600$$
∴ The cost of 36 bags is Rs. 12,600

6. **(B)** $A:B = 5:7, C:C = 6:11 =$

$$\left(6 \times \frac{7}{6}\right):\left(11 \times \frac{7}{6}\right) = 7:\frac{77}{6}.$$

$$\therefore A:B:C = 5:7:\frac{77}{6} = 30:42:77.$$

7. **(D)** Let A = 2x, B = 3x and C = 4x.

Then, $\dfrac{A}{B} = \dfrac{2x}{3x} = \dfrac{2}{3}$, $\dfrac{B}{C} = \dfrac{3x}{4x} = \dfrac{3}{4}$,

and $\dfrac{C}{A} = \dfrac{4x}{2x} = \dfrac{2}{1}$

$$\Rightarrow \frac{A}{B}:\frac{B}{C}:\frac{C}{A} = \frac{2}{3}:\frac{3}{4}:\frac{2}{1} = 8:9:24.$$

8. **(D)** $A:B = \dfrac{1}{2}:\dfrac{3}{8} = 4:3$,

$$B:C = \frac{1}{3}:\frac{5}{9} = 3:5,$$

$$C:D = \frac{5}{6}:\frac{3}{4} = 10:9$$

$$\Rightarrow A:B = 4:3, B:C = 3:5 \text{ and}$$

$$C:D = 5:\frac{9}{2}$$

$$\Rightarrow A:B:C:D = 4:3:5:\frac{9}{2}$$

$$= 8:6:10:9$$

9. **(C)** $\dfrac{1}{5}:\dfrac{1}{x} = \dfrac{1}{x}:\dfrac{100}{125}$

$$\Rightarrow \left(\frac{1}{x} \times \frac{1}{x}\right) = \left(\frac{1}{5} \times \frac{100}{125}\right) = \frac{4}{25}$$

$$\Rightarrow \frac{1}{x^2} = \frac{4}{25} \Rightarrow x^2 = \frac{25}{4}$$

$$\Rightarrow x = \frac{5}{2} = 2.5.$$

10. (B) $(x \times 5) = (0.75 \times 8)$

$$\Rightarrow x = \frac{6}{5} = 1.20$$

11. (A) Given ratio = 7 : 5 : 3 : 4, Sum of ratio terms = 19.

$$\therefore \text{Smallest part} = \left(76 \times \frac{3}{19}\right) = 12.$$

12. (C) Let the required number be x. Then

$(14 - x) : (17 - x) :: (34 - x) : (42 - x)$

$$\therefore \frac{14 - x}{17 - x} = \frac{34 - x}{42 - x}$$

$\Leftrightarrow (14 - x)(42 - x) = (17 - x)(34 - x)$

$\Leftrightarrow x^2 - 56x + 588 = x^2 - 51x + 578$

$\Leftrightarrow 5x = 10 \Leftrightarrow x = 2$

$\therefore$ Required number = 2.

13. (B) Let the third proportional to 12 and 30 be x.
Then, 12 : 30 :: 30 : x

$\Leftrightarrow 12x = 30 \times 30$

$$\Leftrightarrow x = \frac{(30 \times 30)}{12} = 75$$

$\therefore$ Third proportional to 12 and 30 = 75.

Mean proportional between 9 and

$25 = \sqrt{9 \times 25} = 15$.

$\therefore$ Required ratio = 75 : 15 = 5 : 1.

14. (C) Total age of 3 boys = (25×3) years
= 75 years.
Ratio of their ages = 3 : 5 : 7.

Age of the youngest = $\left(75 \times \frac{3}{15}\right)$

years = 15 years.

15. (C) Let the three containers contain 3x, 4x and 5x litres of mixtures respectively. Milk in 1st mixture

$$= \left(3x \times \frac{4}{5}\right) \text{litres} = \frac{12x}{5} \text{ litres.}$$

Water in 1st mixture

$$= \left(3x - \frac{12x}{5}\right) \text{ litres} = \frac{3x}{5} \text{ litres.}$$

Milk in 2nd mixture = $\left(4x \times \frac{3}{4}\right)$

litres = 3x litres.

Water in 2nd mixture = $(4x - 3x)$ litres = x litres.

Milk in 3rd mixture = $\left(5x \times \frac{5}{7}\right)$

litres = $\frac{25x}{7}$.

Water in 3rd mixture

$$= \left(5x - \frac{25x}{7}\right) \text{ litres} = \frac{10x}{7} \text{ litres.}$$

Total milk in final mixture =

$$\left(\frac{12x}{5} + 3x + \frac{25x}{7}\right) \text{ litres} = \frac{314x}{35}$$

litres. Total water in final mixture

$$= \left(\frac{3x}{5} + x + \frac{10x}{7}\right) \text{ litres} = \frac{106x}{35}$$

litres. Required ratio of milk and

water = $\dfrac{314x}{35} : \dfrac{106x}{35} = 157 : 53$

16. (D) Given $x = \dfrac{k}{y^2}$, where k is a constant.

Now, y = 2 and x = 1 gives k = 4.

$\therefore x = \dfrac{4}{y^2} \Rightarrow x = \dfrac{4}{6^2}$, when y = 6

$\Rightarrow x = \dfrac{4}{36} = \dfrac{1}{9}$.

17. (D)   Cost of x metres = Rs. d

Cost of 1 metre = Rs. $\left(\dfrac{d}{x}\right)$

Cost of y metres = Rs. $\left(\dfrac{d}{x}\times y\right)$

= Rs. $\left(\dfrac{yd}{x}\right)$

18. (D)   Let the required price be Rs. x.
Then, less toys, less cost
∴ $6:5::264.37:x$

$\Rightarrow 6x=(5\times264.37)$

$\Rightarrow x=\dfrac{5\times264.37}{6}\Rightarrow x=220.308$

∴ Approximate price of 5 toys = Rs. 220

19. (D)   Let the required price be Rs. x.
Then, more mangoes, more price.
∴ $357:(49\times12)::1517.25:x$

$\Rightarrow 357x=(49\times12\times1517.25)$

$\Rightarrow x=\dfrac{(49\times12\times1517.25)}{357}=2499$

Hence, the approximate price is Rs. 2,500

20. (A)   Let the required cost be x paise.
Less weight, less cost.
∴ $250:200::60:x$

$\Rightarrow 250\times x=200\times60$

$\Rightarrow x=\dfrac{200\times60}{250}=48$ paise

21. (A)   Let the required weight be x kg.
Then less length, less weight.
∴ $11.25:6::42.75:x$

$\Rightarrow 11.25\times x=6\times42.75$

$\Rightarrow x=\dfrac{(6\times42.75)}{11.25}\Rightarrow x=22.8$

22. (D)   Let the actural distance be x km.
Then, more distance on the map,
more is the actual distance.
∴ $0.6:80.5::6.6:x$

$\Rightarrow 0.6x=80.5\times6.6$

$\Rightarrow x=\dfrac{80.5\times6.6}{0.6}\Rightarrow x=885.5$

23. (B)   Let the height of the building be x
metres.
Less length shadow, less is the
height
∴ $40.25:28.75::17.5:x$

$\Rightarrow 40.25\times x=28.75\times17.5$

$\Rightarrow x=\dfrac{(28.75\times17.5)}{40.25}\Rightarrow x=12.5$

24. (D)   Let the required number of days
be x. Then, less men, more days.
∴ $27:36::18:x$

$\Rightarrow 27\times x=36\times18$

$\Rightarrow x=\dfrac{36\times18}{27}\Rightarrow x=24$

25. (B)   Let the required number of rounds
be x. More radius, Less rounds.
∴ $20:14::70:x$

$\Rightarrow x\times20=14\times70$

$\Rightarrow x=\dfrac{14\times70}{20}=49$ rounds.

26. (D)   Originally, let there be x men.
Less men, more days.
∴ $(x-10):x::100:110$

$\Rightarrow (x-10)\times110=x\times100$

$\Rightarrow 10x=1100\Rightarrow x=110$

27. (B)   Let the remaining food will last
for x days.
95 men had provisions for 195
days. 65 men had provisions for x

days. Less men, more days

$\therefore 65 : 95 :: 195 : x$

$\Rightarrow (65 \times x) = (95 \times 195)$

$\Rightarrow x = \dfrac{95 \times 195}{65} = 285$

28. **(A)** Let the remaining food will last for x days.
500 men had provisions for
$(27 - 3) = 24$ days.
$(500 + 300)$ men had provisions for x days.
More men, less days
$\therefore 800 : 500 :: 24 : x$

$\Rightarrow 800 \times x = 500 \times 24$

$\Rightarrow x = \dfrac{500 \times 24}{800} = 15$

29. **(B)** Let there be x men at the begining
less men, more days

$\therefore 15 : 9 :: x : (x - 6)$

$\Rightarrow 15(x - 6) = 9x$

$\Rightarrow 6x = 90 \Rightarrow x = 15$

Previous Contest Questions

1. **(B)** More note books more cost, less note books, less cost

Note books	Cost
6	45
1	45/6
8	$\dfrac{8 \times 45}{6} = 60$

2. **(A)** More students, less days ; less students, more days

Students	Days
45	60
1	60×45
27	$\dfrac{60 \times 45}{27} = 100$ days.

3. **(A)** More days, less hours; less days, more hours

Days	Hours
5	8
1	5×8
4	$\dfrac{5 \times 8}{4} = 10$ hours

4. **(C)** More articles, More cost; less articles, less cost.

Articles	Cost
40	180
1	$\dfrac{180}{40}$
18	$\dfrac{180}{40} \times 18 = Rs.81$

5. **(B)** More days, less persons; less days, more persons

Days	Persons
7	20
1	20×7
28	$\dfrac{20 \times 7}{28} = 5$

6. **(C)** Less Radius, More rounds; more radius, less rounds.

Radius	Rounds
20	260
1	260×20
26	$\dfrac{260 \times 20}{26} = 200$

7.　(B)　There is a meal for 200 children. 150 children have taken the meal. Remaining meal is to be catered to 50 children. Now,

Children	Men
200	120
1	$\dfrac{120}{200}$
50	$\dfrac{120}{200} \times 50 = 30$

8.　(B)　More cogs, less revolutions; Less cogs, more revolutions

Cogs	revolutions
6	21
1	6×21
14	$\dfrac{6 \times 21}{14} = 9$

9.　(C)　After 10 days : 150 men had foood for 35 days.

Suppose 125 men had food for x days. Less men, More days ; More men less days.

$\therefore$ 125 : 150 : : 35 : x

$\Rightarrow 125 \times x = 150 \times 35$

$\Rightarrow x = \dfrac{150 \times 35}{125} \Rightarrow x = 42$.

10.　(B)　Work done = $\dfrac{5}{8}$,　Balance =

$\left(1 - \dfrac{5}{8}\right) = \dfrac{3}{8}$ Less work, Less days; More work, more days

Let the required number of days be x.

Work	Days
$\dfrac{5}{8}$	10
1	$10 \div \dfrac{5}{8}$ or $10 \times \dfrac{8}{5}$
$\dfrac{3}{8}$	$10 \times \dfrac{8}{5} \times \dfrac{3}{8} = 6$ days

A Error in simplifying an algebraic fraction.

e.g. (a) Simplify $\dfrac{2m+4}{6m}$

✗ Incorrect

$$\dfrac{\overset{1}{\cancel{2m}}+4}{\underset{3}{\cancel{6m}}} = \dfrac{1+4}{3} = \dfrac{5}{3}$$

Incorrect because cancelling the individual terms of the numerator is not allowed.

✓ Correct

$$\dfrac{2m+4}{6m} = \dfrac{\overset{1}{\cancel{2}}(m+2)}{\underset{3}{\cancel{6}}m} = \dfrac{m+2}{3m}$$

(b) Simplify $\dfrac{(2p-3q)}{9q-6p}$

✗ Incorrect

$$\dfrac{(2p-3q)}{9q-6p} = \dfrac{(2p-3q)}{3(3q-2p)} = = \dfrac{1}{3}$$

Incorrect because these two factors are not the same.

✓ Correct

$$\dfrac{(2p-3q)}{3(3q-2p)} = \dfrac{\cancel{(2p-3q)}}{-3\cancel{(2p-3q)}} = -\dfrac{1}{3}$$

Synopsis

Factorization:

The process of writing an algebraic expression as the product of two or more algebraic expressions is called factorization.

Some important identities:

◆ $(a + b)^2 = a^2 + 2ab + b^2$

◆ $(a – b)^2 = a^2 – 2ab + b^2$

◆ $(a + b)(a – b) = a^2 – b^2$

◆ $(a + b + c)^2 = a^2 + b^2 + c^2 + 2ab + 2bc + 2ca$

◆ $(a + b)^3 = a^3 + b^3 + 3ab(a + b) = a^3 + b^3 + 3a^2b + 3ab^2$

◆ $(a – b)^3 = a^3 – b^3 – 3ab(a – b) = a^3 – b^3 – 3a^2b + 3ab^2$

◆ $a^3 + b^3 = (a + b)(a^2 – ab + b^2)$

◆ $a^3 – b^3 = (a – b)(a^2 + ab + b^2)$

◆ $a^3 + b^3 + c^3 – 3abc = (a + b + c)(a^2 + b^2 + c^2 – ab – bc – ca)$

◆   If $a + b + c = 0$ then $a^3 + b^3 + c^3 = 3abc$

Multiple Choice Questions

1. The real factors of $x^2 + 4$ are:
    (A) $(x^2 + 2)(x^2 – 2)$ (B) $(x + 2)(x – 2)$
    (C) does not exist   (D) none of these

2. One of the factors of $x^4 + 4$ is:
    (A) $x^2 + 2$ (B) $x^2 – 2x + 2$
    (C) $x^2 – 2$ (D) none of these

3. The factors of $x^4 + 2x^2 + 9$ is:
    (A) $(x^2 – 2x + 3)(x^2 + 2x + 3)$
    (B) $(x^2 + 3)(x^2 – 3)$
    (C) factorization is not possible
    (D) none of these

4. For $x^2 + 2x + 5$ to be a factor of $x^4 + px^2 + q$, the values of p and q must be:
    (A) –2, 5   (B) 5, 25 (C) 10, 20 (D) 6, 25

5. The factors of $x^2 + xy – 2xz – 2yz$ are:
    (A) $(x – y)(x + 2z)$ (B) $(x + y)(x – 2z)$
    (C) $(x – y)(x – 2z)$ (D) $(x + y)(x + 2z)$

6. The number of factors of $(x^9 – x)$ is :
    (A) 5
    (B) 4
    (C) 2
    (D) cannot be determined

7. The factors of $\dfrac{x^2}{4} - \dfrac{y^2}{9}$ are:

    (A) $\left(\dfrac{x}{4} + \dfrac{y}{9}\right)\left(\dfrac{x}{4} - \dfrac{y}{9}\right)$

    (B) $\left(\dfrac{x}{2} + \dfrac{y}{9}\right)\left(\dfrac{x}{2} - \dfrac{y}{9}\right)$

    (C) $\left(\dfrac{x}{2} + \dfrac{y}{3}\right)\left(\dfrac{x}{2} - \dfrac{y}{3}\right)$

    (D) none of these

8. The factors of $1 – p^3$ are:
    (A) $(1 – p)(1 + p + p^2)$
    (B) $(1 + p)(1 – p – p^2)$
    (C) $(1 + p)(1 + p^2)$
    (D) $(1 + p)(1 – p^2)$

9. The factors of $x^4 + y^4 + x^2y^2$ are:
   (A) $(x^2 + y^2)(x^2 + y^2 - xy)$
   (B) $(x^2 + y^2)(x^2 - y^2)$
   (C) $(x^2 + y^2 + xy)(x^2 + y^2 - xy)$
   (D) factorization is not possible

10. The factors of $15x^2 - 26x + 8$ are:
    (A) $(3x - 4)(5x + 2)$ (B) $(3x - 4)(5x - 2)$
    (C) $(3x + 4)(5x - 2)$ (D) $(3x + 4)(5x + 2)$

11. One of the factors of
    $a^3(b - c)^3 + b^3(c - a)^3 + c^3(a - b)^3$ is:
    (A) $a - b$ (B) $b - c$
    (C) $c - a$ (D) all the above

12. One of the factor of
    $a^3 + 8b^3 - 64c^3 + 24abc$ is:
    (A) $a + 2b - 4c$ (B) $a - 2b + 4c$
    (C) $a + 2b + 4c$ (D) $a - 2b - 4c$

13. The value of
    $\dfrac{0.76 \times 0.76 \times 0.76 + 0.24 \times 0.24 \times 0.24}{0.76 \times 0.76 - 0.76 \times 0.24 + 0.24 \times 0.24}$ is:
    (A) 0.52   (B) 1   (C) 0.01   (D) 0.1

14. The factors of $a^2 + b - ab - a$ are:
    (A) $(a - 1)(a - b)$ (B) $(a + b)(a - 1)$
    (C) $(a + 1)(a - b)$ (D) none of these

15. One of the factors of
    $x^2 + \dfrac{1}{x^2} + 2 - 2x - \dfrac{2}{x}$ is:

    (A) $x - \dfrac{1}{x}$ (B) $x + \dfrac{1}{x} - 1$

    (C) $x + \dfrac{1}{x}$ (D) $x^2 + \dfrac{1}{x^2}$

16. If the factors of $a^2 + b^2 + 2(ab + bc + ca)$
    are $(a + b + m)$ and $(a + b + nc)$, then
    the value of m + n is:
    (A) 0   (B) 2   (C) 4   (D) 6

17. If $(x^2 + 3x + 5)(x^2 - 3x + 5) = m^2 - n^2$,
    then m = _____

    (A) $x^2 - 3x$ (B) $3x$
    (C) $x^2 + 5$ (D) none of these

18. One of the factors of
    $(a^2 - b^2)(c^2 - d^2) - 4abcd$ is:
    (A) $(ac - bd + bc + ad)$
    (B) $ac - bd + bc - ad$
    (C) cannot be determined
    (D) none of these

19. The factors of
    $\sqrt{3}x^2 + 11x + 6\sqrt{3}$ are:

    (A) $\left(x - 3\sqrt{3}\right)\left(\sqrt{3}x + 2\right)$

    (B) $\left(x - 3\sqrt{3}\right)\left(\sqrt{3}x - 2\right)$

    (C) $\left(x + 3\sqrt{3}\right)\left(\sqrt{3}x - 2\right)$

    (D) $\left(x + 3\sqrt{3}\right)\left(\sqrt{3}x + 2\right)$

20. One of the factors of $x^7 + xy^6$ is:
    (A) $x^2 + y^2$ (B) x
    (C) either A or B (D) neither A nor B

21. Factors of $a^2 + 4a + 4$ are:

    (A) $(a + 2)^2$ (B) $(a + 1)^2$

    (C) $(a - 2)^2$ (D) $(a - 1)^2$

22. $x^3 + 6x^2 + 9x$ can be factorised as:

    (A) $x^2(x + 2)^2$ (B) $x(x + 3)^2$

    (C) $x(x + 3)$ (D) None of these

23. $(2x + 3y)^2 + 2(2x + 3y)(x + y)$

    $= (x + y)^2$ can be factorised as:

    (A) $(3x + 4y)(3x - 4y)$

    (B) $(3x + 4y)^2$

    (C) $(3x + 2y)(2x - 3y)$

    (D) None of these

24. Factors for $a^2b^2 + c^2d^2 - a^2c^2 - b^2d^2$
    are:

(A) $(a+d)(a-d)(b+c)(b-c)$

(B) $\left(a^2-b^2\right)$

(C) $\left(a^2-d^2\right)\left(b^2-c^2\right)$

(D) None of these

25. Factors of $8x^3+27y^3$ are:

(A) $(x+2)\left(x^2-2x+4\right)$

(B) $(3x+4)\left(ax^2-12x+16\right)$

(C) $(2x+3y)\left(4x^2-6xy+9y^2\right)$

(D) $(x-1)\left(x^2+4x+7\right)$

26. $a^{12}-1$ cab be factorised as:

(A) $(a-1)(a-2)(a-3)(a-4)$

(B) $(a-1)\left(a^2+a+1\right)(a+1)\left(a^2+a+1\right)$

(C) $\left(a^2+a+1\right)\left(a^2-a+1\right)$

(D) $(a-1)\left(a^2+a+1\right)(a+1)\left(a^2-a+1\right)$

$$\left[\left(a^2+1\right)\left(a^4-a^2+1\right)\right]$$

27. If $x+y+z=0$, then $x^3+y^3+z^3=$ ____

(A) $3xyz$ (B) x^2yz

(C) xy^2z (D) xyz^2

28. Factorization of

$(a-b)^3+(b-c)^3+(c-a)^3$ is:

(A) $(a-b)(a-c)$

(B) $(a-b)(b-c)(c-a)$

(C) $3(a-b)(b-c)(c-a)$

(D) $3^2(a-b)(b-c)(c-a)$

29. Given $x^2+7x+12=0$. Then factors of $x^2+7x+12$ are:

(A) $(x+2)(x+1)$ (B) $(x+3)(x+2)$

(C) $(x+4)(x+3)$ (D) None of these

30. Factors of $x^2-3x-18$ are:

(A) $(x-6)(x+3)$ (B) $(x=6)(x-3)$

(C) $(x-3)^2$ (D) $(x+6)^2$

31. Factors of $x^2+4x-21$ are:

(A) $(x-3)(x-7)$ (B) $(x+7)(x-3)$

(C) $(x+3)(x+7)$ (D) None of these

32. Factors of $12-x-x^2$ are:

(A) $(x+2)(x-3)$ (B) $(x+4)(3-x)$

(C) $(x-2)(x-3)$ (D) None of these

33. Factors of $27-6x-x^2$ are:

(A) $(3-x)(9+x)$ (B) $(x-3)(x+9)$

(C) $(x-2)(x+7)$ (D) None of these

34. Factors of $x^2+11xy+24y^2$ are:

(A) $(x+8y)(x+3y)$ (B) $(x+6y)(x+3y)$

(C) $(x-8y)(x+3y)$ (D) None of these

35. Factors of x^6+9x^3+8 are:

(A) $(x-2)\left(x^2+2x+4\right)$

(B) $(x+2)\left(x^2-2x+4\right)(x+1)\;\left(x^2-x+1\right)$

(C) $(x+4y)(x-4y)(x+2y)(x-2y)$

(D) None of these

36. Factorization of $3x^2+17x+20$ is:

(A) $(x+4)(3x+5)$ (B) $(x-4)(3x-5)$

(C) $(x-4)(x-5)$ (D) None of these

37. $3x^2-17x+20$ can be factorised as:

(A) $(x+4)(3x+5)$

(B) $(x-4)(3x-5)$

(C) $(x-4)(x-5)$

(D) None of these

38. Factorization of $7x^2 - 8x - 12$ is:

(A) $(x+12)(3x-20)$

(B) $(x-2)(6x+7)$

(C) $(x-4)(3x-4)$

(D) $(x-2)(7x+6)$

39. The factors of $6 - x - 2x^2$ are:

(A) $(x+2)(3-2x)$ (B) $(3-x)(3x+2)$

(C) $(x-2)(x+6)$ (D) None of these

40. Factors of $12 - 4x - 5x^2$ are:

(A) $(x+1)(5-4x)$

(B) $(x+2)(6-5x)$

(C) $(3x+4)(4-x)$

(D) None of these

41. Factors of $4x^4 - 25x^2 + 36$ are:

(A) $(x+2)(x-2)(2x+3)(2x-3)$

(B) $(x+1)(x-1)(x+3)(x-3)$

(C) $(x+3)(x-3)(4x+3)(4x-3)$

(D) None of these

42. Factors of $8x^6 - 65x^3 + 8$ are:

(A) $(2x-1)(4x^2+2x+1)$

(B) $(x=1)(2x-3)(x-1)(2x+3)$

(C) $(x+2)(2x-3)(x-1)(2x+3)$

(D) $(x-2)(x^2+2x+4)(2x-1)$ $(4x^2+2x+1)$

43. Factors of $x^2 - x - 12$ are:

(A) $(x-1)(x-2)$

(B) $(x-2)(x-3)$

(C) $(x-3)(x+4)$

(D) $(x-4)(x+3)$

44. Expansion of $(a+b+c)^2$ is:

(A) $a^2 + b^2 + c^2 + 2(ab+bc+ca)$

(B) $a^2 + b^2 + c^2$

(C) $a^2 + b^2 + c^2 + 2ab - 2bc - 2ca$

(D) None of these

45. If $a^2 + b^2 + c^2 = 44$ and $ab + bc + ca = 10$, then $a+b+c$ is:

(A) ± 9 (B) ± 8

(C) ± 7 (D) ± 6

46. If $x - \dfrac{1}{x} = 6$ then the value of $x^3 - \dfrac{1}{x^3}$ is:

(A) 144   (B) 169

(C) 234   (D) 269

47. The value of $(1002)^2$ [using expansion] is:

(A) 10004004

(B) 1044

(C) 1004400

(D) 1004004

48. Factors of $ax + by + bx + az + ay + bz$ are:

(A) $(bx+ay)(ax+by)$

(B) $(a+b)(2x+2y+2z)$

(C) $(x+y+z)(a+b)$

(D) None of these

Previous Contest Questions

1. Factors of

   $(4a-3b)^3 - (3a-b)^3 - (a-2b)^3$ are:

   (A) $3(4a-3b)(b-3a)(2b-a)$

   (B) $3(a-b)(b-c)(c-a)$

   (C) $(a-b)^2(c-a)$

   (D) None of these

2. Factors of $x^4 - 13x^2y^2 + 36y^4$ are:

   (A) $(x+4y)(x-4y)(x+2y)(x-2y)$

   (B) $(x^2+2x-8)(x^2+2x-3)$

   (C) $(x+3y)(x-3y)(x+2y)(x-2y)$

   (D) None of these

3. Factors of $3x^2 + 8xy + 4y^2$ are:

   (A) $(3x+4)(4-x)$ (B) $(3-x)(3x+2)$

   (C) $(x+2y)(3x+2y)$ (D) None of these

4. $9x^4 - 40x^2 + 16$ can be factorised as:

   (A) $(x+1)(x-1)(2x+1)(2x-1)$

   (B) $(2x-1)(4x^2+2x+1)$

   (C) $(x+2)(2x-3)(x-1)(2x+3)$

   (D) None of these

5. Factors of $8x^6 - 9x^3 + 1$ are:

   (A) $(x-1)(x^2+x+1)(2x-1)$

   $(4x^2+2x+1)$

   (B) $(x-2)(x^2+2x+4)(2x-1)$

   $(4x^2+2x+1)$

   (C) $(x+1)(x-1)(3x-3)(4x+4)$

   (D) $(x-1)(3x+2)(x+2)(2x-1)$

6. Factors of $a^4 + a^2 + 1$ are:

   (A) $(a-4)(a+2)$

   (B) $(a^2+a-1)(a^2+a+2)$

   (C) $(a^2+a+1)(a^2-a+1)$

   (D) $(a-1)(a^2-a+1)$

7. $9a^2 - \dfrac{12}{5}a + \dfrac{4}{25}$ can be written as following perfect square:

   (A) $\left(a-\dfrac{2}{5}\right)^2$ (B) $\left(3a-\dfrac{2}{5}\right)^2$

   (C) $\left(2a-\dfrac{2}{5}\right)^2$ (D) None of these

8. Factors of $a(x-y)^2 - by + bx + 3x - 3y$ are:

   (A) $(x-y)[a(x-y)+b+3]$

   (B) $(a-b)(3x-3y)$

   (C) $(x-y)(x^2+a+1)(y^2+b+1)$

   (D) None of these

9. Value of $(99.8)^2 - (0.2)^2$ is:

   (A) 9980   (B) 9960 (C) 9860 (D) 9680

10. Factors of $2a^2 + 13ab - 24b^2$ are:

    (A) $(a+8b)(2a-3b)$

    (B) $(a-8b)(2a+3b)$

    (C) $(a-3b)(2a-8b)$

    (D) None of these

11. Factorization of $x^2 + \dfrac{a^{2-1}}{a}x - 1$ is:

(A) $\left(x - \dfrac{1}{a}\right)(x+a)$

(B) $\left(x - \dfrac{1}{a^2}\right)(x+a)$

(C) $\left(x - \dfrac{1}{a^2}\right)(x-a)$

(D) None of these

12. Factors from of $\left(p^2 + q^2 - r^2\right) - 4p^2q^2$ is:

(A) $(p+q+r)(p+q-r)$

$(p-q+r)(p-q-r)$

(B) $(p-q-r)\left(p^2 - q^2 - r^2\right)$

(C) $(p-q-r)(2p+2q+2r)$

(D) None of these

⊘ Answers ⊘

Multiple Choice Questions

1. C	2. B	3. A	4. D	5. B	6. A	7. C	8. A	9. C	10. B
11. D	12. A	13. B	14. A	15. C	16. B	17. C	18. A	19. D	20. C
21. A	22. B	23. B	24. A	25. C	26. D	27. A	28. C	29. C	30. A
31. B	32. B	33. A	34. A	35. B	36. A	37. B	38. D	39. A	40. B
41. A	42. D	43. D	44. A	45. B	46. C	47. D	48. C		

Previous Contest Questions

1. A	2. C	3. C	4. D	5.A	6. C	7. B	8. A	9. B	10. A
11. A	12. A								

Explanatory Answers

1. (C) Real factors do not exist for $x^2 + 4$.

2. (B) $x^4 + 4 = (x^4 + 4x^2 + 4) - 4x^2$

   $= (x^2 + 2)^2 - (2x)^2$

   $= (x^2 + 2x + 2)(x^2 - 2x + 2)$

3. (A) $x^4 + 2x^2 + 9 =$

   $(x^4 + 6x^2 + 9) - 4x^2$

   $= (x^2 + 3)^2 - (2x)^2$

   $= (x^2 + 2x + 3)(x^2 - 2x + 3)$

4. (D) Let the other factor be $x^2 + ax + b$.

   We have

   $(x^2 + 2x + 5)(x^2 + ax + b)$

   $= x^4 + px^2 + q$

   $x^4 + (2 + a)x^3 + (2a + b + 5)x^2 +$

   $(5a + 2b)x + 5b = x^4 + px^2 + q$

   Comparing the coefficients

   $2a + b + 5 = p$ —— (1)

   $5b = q$ —— (2)

   $2 + a = 0 \Rightarrow a = -2$

   $5a + 2b = 0 \Rightarrow b = 5$

   $\therefore p = 2a + b + 5 = 2(-2) + 5 + 5 = 6$

   $q = 5b = 5(5) = 25$

5. (B) $x^2 + xy - 2xz - 2yz$

   $= x(x + y) - 2z(x + y)$

   $= (x + y)(x - 2z)$

6. (A) $x^9 - x = x(x^8 - 1)$

$$x\left[\left(x^4\right)^2 - \left(1\right)^2\right] = x\left(x^4 + 1\right)\left(x^4 - 1\right)$$

$$= x\left(x^4 + 1\right)\left(x^2 + 1\right)\left(x + 1\right)\left(x - 1\right)$$

7. (C) $\dfrac{x^2}{4} - \dfrac{y^2}{9} = \left(\dfrac{x}{2}\right)^2 - \left(\dfrac{y}{3}\right)^2$

$$= \left(\dfrac{x}{2} + \dfrac{y}{3}\right)\left(\dfrac{x}{2} - \dfrac{y}{3}\right)$$

8. (A) $1 - p^3 = 1^3 - p^3$

$$= (1 - p)(1 + p + p^2)$$

9. (C) $x^4 + y^4 + x^2y^2$

$$= (x^4 + y^4 + 2x^2y^2) - x^2y^2$$

$$= (x^2 + y^2)^2 - (xy)^2$$

$$= (x^2 + y^2 + xy)(x^2 + y^2 - xy)$$

10. (B) $15x^2 - 26x + 8 = 15x^2 - 20x - 6x + 8$

$$= 5x(3x - 4) - 2(3x - 4)$$

$$= (3x - 4)(5x - 2)$$

11. (D) $\left[a(b - c)\right]^3 + \left[b(c - a)\right]^3 + \left[c(a - b)\right]^3$

$$= 3a(b - c)\,b(c - a)\,c(a - b)$$

$$= 3abc(a - b)(b - c)(c - a)$$

12. (A) $a^3 + 8b^3 - 64c^3 + 24abc$

$$= (a)^3 + (2b)^3 + (-4c)^3 - 3(a)(2b)(-4c)$$

$$= (a + 2b - 4c)(a^2 + 4b^2 + 16c^2 -$$
$$2ab + 8bc - 4ac)$$

13. (B) $\dfrac{0.76 \times 0.76 \times 0.76 + 0.24 \times 0.24 \times 0.24}{0.76 \times 0.76 - 0.76 \times 0.24 + 0.24 \times 0.24}$

$$= \dfrac{(0.76)^3 + (0.24)^3}{(0.76)^2 - 0.76 \times 0.24 + (0.24)^2}$$

$$= 0.76 + 0.24 = 1$$

14. (A) $a^2 + b - ab - a$

$$= a^2 - ab + b - a$$

$$= a(a - b) - 1(a - b)$$

$$= (a - 1)(a - b)$$

15. (C) $x^2 + \dfrac{1}{x^2} + 2 - 2x - \dfrac{2}{x}$

$$= \left(x^2 + \dfrac{1}{x^2} + 2\right) - 2\left(x + \dfrac{1}{x}\right)$$

$$= \left(x + \dfrac{1}{x}\right)^2 - 2\left(x + \dfrac{1}{x}\right)$$

$$= \left(x + \dfrac{1}{x}\right)\left(x + \dfrac{1}{x} - 2\right)$$

16. (B) $a^2 + b^2 + 2ab + 2bc + 2ca + c^2 - c^2$

$$= (a + b + c)^2 - c^2$$

$$= (a + b)(a + b + 2c)$$

On comparision we get,

m = 0, n = 2

m + n = 0 + 2 = 2

17. (C) $(x^2 + 3x + 5)(x^2 - 3x + 5)$

$$= (x^2 + 5 + 3x)(x^2 + 5 - 3x)$$

$$= (x^2 + 5)^2 - (3x)^2$$

$$\therefore \ m = x^2 + 5$$

18. (A) $(a^2 - b^2)(c^2 - d^2) - 4abcd$

$$= (ac - bd)^2 - (bc + ad)^2$$

$$= (ac - bd + bc + ad)(ac - bd - bc - ad)$$

19. (D) $\sqrt{3}x^2 + 11x + 6\sqrt{3}$

$$= \sqrt{3}x^2 + 9x + 2x + 6\sqrt{3}$$

$$= \sqrt{3}x\left(x + 3\sqrt{3}\right) + 2\left(x + 3\sqrt{3}\right)$$

$$= \left(x + 3\sqrt{3}\right)\left(\sqrt{3}x + 2\right)$$

20. (C) $x^7 + xy^6 = x(x^6 + y^6)$

$$= x\left[\left(x^2\right)^3 + \left(y^2\right)^3\right]$$

$$= x\left(x^2 + y^2\right)\left(x^4 - x^2 y^2 + y^4\right)$$

21. (A) $\quad a^2 + 4a + 4 = a^2 + 2(a)(2) + (2)^2$

$$= (a+2)^2$$

22. (B) $\quad x^3 + 6x^2 + 9x = x\left(x^2 + 6x + 9\right)$

$$= x\left[x^2 + 2(x)(3) + (3)^2\right] = x(x+3)^2$$

23. (B) $\quad$ Let $2x + 3y = A$; $x + y = B$

$\quad\quad \therefore$ Given expression $= A^2 + 2AB + B^2$

$$= (A+B)^2$$

$$= (2x + 3y + x + y)^2 = (3x + 4y)^2$$

24. (A) $\quad a^2b^2 + c^2d^2 - a^2c^2 - b^2d^2$

$$= a^2b^2 - a^2c^2 - b^2d^2 + c^2d^2$$

$$= a^2\left(b^2 - c^2\right) - d^2\left(b^2 - c^2\right)$$

$$= \left(a^2 - d^2\right)\left(b^2 - c^2\right)$$

$$= (a+d)(a-d)(b+c)(b-c)$$

25. (C) $\quad 8x^3 + 27y^3 = (2x)^3 + (3y)^3$

$$= (2x + 3y)\left(4x^2 - 6xy + 9y^2\right)$$

26. (D) $\quad a^{12} - 1 = \left(a^6\right)^2 - (1)^2$

$$= \left(a^6 - 1\right)\left(a^6 + 1\right)$$

$$= \left[\left(a^3\right)^2 - (1)^2\right]\left(a^6 + 1\right)$$

$$= \left(a^3 - 1\right)\left(a^3 + 1\right)\left(a^6 + 1\right)$$

$$= (a-1)\left(a^2 + a + 1\right)(a+1)$$

$$\left(a^2 - a + 1\right)\left(a^6 + 1\right)$$

$$= (a-1)\left(a^2 + a + 1\right)\left(a^2 - a + 1\right)$$

$$\left[\left(a^2 + 1\right)\left(a^4 - a^2 + 1\right)\right]$$

27. (A) $\quad x + y + z = 0 \Rightarrow x + y = -z$

$\quad\quad$ cubing on both sides,

$$(x + y)^3 = (-z)^3$$

$$\Rightarrow x^3 + y^3 + 3xy(x + y) = z^3$$

$$\Rightarrow x^3 + y^3 + 3xy(-z) = -z^3$$

$$\Rightarrow x^3 + y^3 - 3xyz + z^3 = 0$$

$$\therefore \; x^3 + y^3 + z^3 = 3xyz$$

28. (C) $\quad$ Let $x = a - b; y = b - c; z = c - a$

$\quad\quad$ On adding $x + y + z = 0$

$$\therefore \; x^3 + y^3 + z^3 = 3xyz$$

$\quad\quad$ Substituting

$$x = (a - b); y = (b - c)$$

$$\text{and } z = (c - a)$$

$$(a - b)^3 + (b - c)^3 + (c - a)^3$$

$$= 3(a - b)(b - c)(c - a)$$

29. (C) $\quad x^2 + 7x + 12 = x^2 + 4x + 3x + 12$

$$= x(x + 4) + 3x(x + 4) = (x + 4)(x + 3)$$

30. (A) $\quad x^2 - 3x + 18 = x^2 - 6x + 3x + 18$

$$= x(x - 6) + 3(x - 6) = (x - 6)(x + 3)$$

31. (B) $\quad x^2 + 4x - 21 = x^2 + 7x - 3x - 21$

$$= x(x + 7) - 3(x + 7) = (x + 7)(x - 3)$$

32. (B) $\quad 12 - x - x^2 = -\left(x^2 + x - 12\right)$

$$= -\left(x^2 + 4x - 3x - 12\right)$$

$$= -\left[x(x + 4) - 3(x + 4)\right]$$

$$= -\left[(x + 4)(x - 3)\right] = (x + 4)(3 - x)$$

33. (A) $\quad 27 - 6x - x^2 = 27 - 9x + 3x - x^2$

$$= 9(3 - x) + x(3 - x) = (3 - x)(9 + x)$$

34. (A) $x^2 + 11xy + 24y^2$

$$= x^2 + 8xy + 3xy + 24y^2$$

$$= x(x + 8y) + 3y(x + 8y)$$

$$= (x + 8y)(x + 3y)$$

35. (B) $x^6 + 9x^3 + 8 = x^6 + 8x^3 + x^3 + 8$

$$= x^3(x^3 + 8) + 1(x^3 + 8)$$

$$= (x^3 + 8)(x^3 + 1)$$

$$= (x^3 + 2^3)(x^3 + 1^3)$$

$$= (x + 2)(x^2 - 2x + 4)(x + 1)$$

$$(x^2 - x + 1)$$

36. (A) $3x^2 + 17x + 20 = 3x^2 + 12x + 5x + 20$

$$= 3x(x + 4) + 5(x + 4) = (x + 4)(3x + 5)$$

37. (B) $3x^2 - 17x + 20 = 3x^2 - 12x - 5x + 20$

$$= 3x(x - 4) - 5(x - 4) = (x - 4)(3x - 5)$$

38. (D) $7x^2 - 8x - 12 = 7x^2 - 14x + 6x - 12$

$$= 7x(x - 2) + 6(x - 2) = (x - 2)(7x + 6)$$

39. (A) $6 - x - 2x^2 = -(2x^2 + x - 6)$

$$= -\left[2x^2 + 4x - 3x - 6\right]$$

$$= -\left[2x(x + 2) - 3(x + 2)\right]$$

$$= -\left[(x + 2)(2x - 3)\right]$$

$$= (x + 2)(3 - 2x)$$

40. (B) $12 - 4x - 5x^2 = -(5x^2 + 4x - 12)$

$$= -(5x^2 + 10x - 6x - 12)$$

$$= -\left[5x(x + 2) - 6(x + 2)\right]$$

$$= -\left[(x + 2)(5x - 6)\right] = (x + 2)(6 - 5x)$$

41. (A) $4x^4 - 25x^2 + 36$

$$= 4x^4 - 16x^2 - 9x^2 + 36$$

$$= 4x^2(x^2 - 4) - 9(x^2 - 4)$$

$$= (x^2 - 4)(4x^2 - 9)$$

$$= (x + 2)(x - 2)(2x + 3)(2x - 3)$$

42. (D) $8x^6 - 65x^3 + 8 = 8x^6 - 64x^3 - x^3 + 8$

$$= 8x^3(x^3 - 8) - 1(x^3 - 8)$$

$$= (8x^3 - 1)(x^3 - 8)$$

$$= (2x - 1)(4x^2 + 2x + 1)(x - 2)$$

$$(x^2 + 2x + 4)$$

43. (D) $x^2 - x - 12 = x^2 - 4x + 3x - 12$

$$= x(x - 4) + 3(x - 4)$$

$$= (x - 4)(x + 3)$$

44. (A) $(a + b + c)^2 = \left[(a + b) + c\right]^2$

$$= (a + b)^2 + 2(a + b)(c) + c^2$$

$$= (a^2 + 2ab + b^2) + 2(ca + bc) + c^2$$

$$= a^2 + b^2 + c^2 + 2(ab + bc + ca)$$

45. (B) $(a + b + c)^2$

$$= a^2 + b^2 + c^2 + 2(ab + bc + ca)$$

$$= 44 + 2 \times 10 = 44 + 20 = 64$$

Now $(a + b + c)^2 = 64$

$\therefore (a + b + c) = \sqrt{64} = \pm 8$

46. (C)   Given $x - \dfrac{1}{x} = 6$

$$\Rightarrow \left(x - \frac{1}{x}\right)^3 = 6^3$$

$\Rightarrow x^3 - \left(\dfrac{1}{x}\right)^3 - 3 \times x \times \dfrac{1}{x} \times \left(x - \dfrac{1}{x}\right)$

$= 216$

$\Rightarrow x^3 - \dfrac{1}{x^3} - 3\left(x - \dfrac{1}{x}\right) = 216$

$\Rightarrow x^3 - \dfrac{1}{x^3} - 3 \times 6 = 216$

$\Rightarrow x^3 - \dfrac{1}{x^3} = 216 + 18 = 234$

47. (D) $(1002)^2 = (1000 + 2)^2$

$= (1000)^2 + 2 \times 1000 \times 2 + (2)^2$

$= 1000000 + 4000 + 4 = 1004004$

48. (C) $ax + by + bx + az + ay + bz$

$= (ax + ay + az) + (bx + by + bz)$

$= a(x + y + z) + b(x + y + z)$

$= (x + y + z)(a + b)$

Previous Contest Questions

1. (A) $(4a - 3b)^3 - (3a - b)^3 - (a - 2b)^3$

$= (4a - 3b)^3 + (b - 3a)^3 + (2b - a)^3$

Let,

$x = 4a - 3b; y = b - 3a; z = 2b - a$

On adding, $x + y + z = 0$

$\therefore \ x^3 + y^3 + z^3 = 3xyz$

Substituting x, y, z values, we get

$(4a - 3b)^3 + (b - 3a)^3 + (2b - a)^3$

$= 3(4a - 3b)(b - 3a)(2b - a)$

2. (C) $x^4 - 13x^2 y^2 + 36 y^4$

$= x^4 - 9x^2 y^2 - 4x^2 y^2 + 36 y^4$

$= x^2\left(x^2 - 9y^2\right) - 4y^2\left(x^2 - 9y^2\right)$

$= \left(x^2 - 9y^2\right)\left(x^2 - 4y^2\right)$

$= (x + 3y)(x - 3y)(x + 2y)(x - 2y)$

3. (C) $3x^2 + 8xy + 4y^2 = 3x^2 + 6xy + 2xy + 4y^2$

$= 3x(x + 2y) + 2y(x + 2y)$

$= (x + 2y)(3x + 2y)$

4. (D) $9x^4 - 40x^2 + 16 = 9x^4 - 36x^2 - 4x^2 + 16$

$= 9x^2\left(x^2 - 4\right) - 4\left(x^2 - 4\right)$

$= \left(x^2 - 4\right)\left(9x^2 - 4\right)$

$= (x + 2)(x - 2)(3x + 2)(3x - 2)$

5. (A) $8x^6 - 9x^3 + 1 = 8x^6 - 8x^3 - x^3 + 1$

$= 8x^3\left(x^3 - 1\right) - 1\left(x^3 - 1\right)$

$= \left(x^3 - 1\right)\left(8x^3 - 1\right)$

$= (x - 1)\left(x^2 + x + 1\right)(2x - 1)$

$\left(4x^2 + 2x + 1\right)$

6. (C) $a^4 + a^2 + 1 = \left(a^2 + 1\right)^2 - a^2$

$= \left(a^2 + 1\right)^2 - (a)^2$

$= \left(a^2 + a + 1\right)\left(a^2 - a + 1\right)$

7. (B) $9a^2 - \dfrac{12}{5}a + \dfrac{4}{25}$

$= (3a)^2 - 2 \times 3a \times \dfrac{2}{5} + \left(\dfrac{2}{5}\right)^2$

$= \left(3a - \dfrac{2}{5}\right)^2$

8. (A) $a(x - y)^2 - by + bx + 3x - 3y$

$= a(x - y)^2 + (bx - by) + (3x - 3y)$

$= a(x - y)^2 + b(x - y) + 3(x - y)$

$$= (x-y)\big[a(x-y)+b+3\big]$$

9. (B) $(99.8)^2 - (0.2)^2$

$$= (99.8+0.2)(99.8-0.2)$$

$$= 100 \times 99.6 = 9960$$

10. (A) $2a^2 + 13ab - 24b^2$

$$= 2a^2 + 16ab - 3ab - 24b^2$$

$$= 2a(a+8b) - 3b(a+8b)$$

$$= (a+8b)(2a-3b)$$

11. (A) $x^2 + \dfrac{a^2-1}{a}x - 1 = x^2 + \left(\dfrac{a^2}{a} - \dfrac{1}{a}\right)x - 1$

$$= x^2 + ax - \dfrac{x}{a} - 1$$

$$= \left(x^2 - \dfrac{x}{a}\right) + (ax - 1)$$

$$= x\left(x - \dfrac{1}{a}\right) + a\left(x - \dfrac{1}{a}\right)$$

$$= \left(x - \dfrac{1}{a}\right)(x + a)$$

12. (A) $\left(p^2 + q^2 - r^2\right)^2 - (2pq)^2$

$$= \left(p^2 + q^2 - r^2 + 2pq\right)\left(p^2 + q^2 - r^2 - 2pq\right)$$

$$= \left(p^2 + q^2 + 2pq - r^2\right)\left(p^2 + q^2 - 2pq - r^2\right)$$

$$= \left[(p+q)^2 - r^2\right]\left[(p-q)^2 - r^2\right]$$

$$= (p+q+r)(p+q-r)(p-q+r)(p-q-r)$$

Chapter 15 Introduction to graphs

Error in plotting points on a graph sheet.

e.g. Plot the point (4,3) on a graph sheet.

X Incorrect

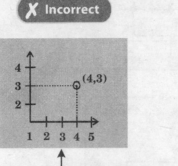

Incorrect because X and Y axes meet at '0' not '1'.

✓ Correct

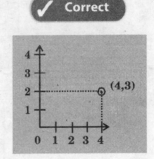

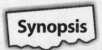

Bar Graph:

A bar graph is used to show comparison among categories.

Pie Graph:

A pie graph is used to compare parts of whole.

Histogram:

Represention that shows data in intervals.

Line Graph:

It shows data that changes continuously over periods of time.

Linear Graph:

A straight line graph is called as linear graph.

The cartesian system

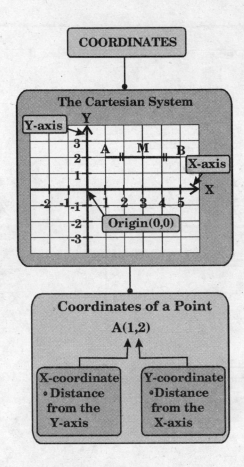

Advantages and disadvantages of various graphs:

Representation of data	Advantages	Disadvantages
Pictogram **Sales of fruits** Stall A Stall B Stall C Represents 50 durians	Data is represented in an attractive manner.	Not accurate. Difficult and time consuming to draw the figures.

Bar Chart

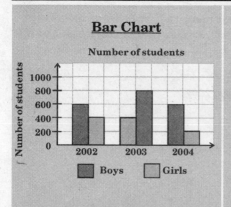

Number of students

| Boys | Girls |

- Easy to construct shows the exact quantities of each data category.

- Two or more types of data can be displayed simultaneously.

- Does not show comparisons between the catagories of data.

Pie chart
Nationality of tourists

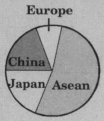

- Shows clearly the difference in magnitude between the categories.

- Long calculations are needed.

- Not suitable if too many categories of data are involved.

- Actual quantities are not displayed.

Multiple Choice Questions

1. Which of the following statements is true?

   (A) The x-axis is a vertical line.

   (B) The y-axis is a horizontal line.

   (C) The scale on both axes must be the same in a cartesian plane.

   (D) The point of intersection between the x-axis and y-axis is called the origin

2. Which of the points below is a point on the x-axis?
   (A) (5,0)　　　　　(B) (0,5)
   (C) (5,3)　　　　　(D) (3,5)

3. Which of the points A, B, C and D below has the coordinates of the origin?
   (A) (3,1)　　　　　(B) (0,0)
   (C) (1,2)　　　　　(D) (9,0)

4. Which of the points below is a point on the y-axis?
   (A) (5,0)　　　　　(B) (6,5)
   (C) (3,12)　　　　(D) (0,11)

5–9 The bar-graph provided gives the sales of books (in thousand numbers) from six branches of a publishing company during two consecutive years 2000 and 2001. Answer the questions based on this bar-graph.

Sales of books (in thousands numbers) from Six branches –

B1, B2, B3, B4, B5 and B6 of a publishing company in 2006 and 2007.

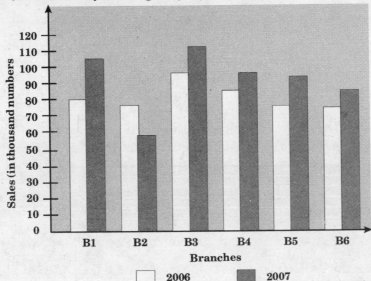

□ 2006   ■ 2007

5.   Total sales of branches B_1, B_3 and B_5 together for both the years (in thousand numbers) is:
(A) 250   (B) 310   (C) 435   (D) 560

6.   Total sales of branch B_6 for both the years is what percent of the total sales of branch B_3 for both the years?
(A) 68.54%   (B) 71.11%
(C) 73.17%   (D) 75.55%

7.   What is the average sale of all the branches (in thousand numbers) for the year 2006 ?
(A) 73   (B) 80   (C) 83   (D) 88

8.   What is the ratio of the total sales of branch B_2 for both years to the total sales of branch B_4 for both years?
(A) 2 : 3   (B) 3 : 5
(C) 4 : 5   (D) 7 : 9

9.   What percent to the average sales of branches B_1, B_2 and B_3 in 2007 is the average sales of branches B_1, B_3 and B_6 in 2006 ?
(A) 75%   (B) 77.5%
(C) 87.5%   (D) 90%

10-14 The following pie-charts show the distribution of students of graduate and post graduate levels in seven different institutes M, N, P, Q, R, S and T in a town.

DISTRIBUTION OF STUDENTS AT GRADUATE AND POST GRADUATE LEVELS IN SEVEN INSTITUTES M, N, P, Q, R, S, and T
Total number of students of graduate level = 27,300

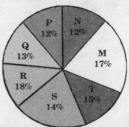

Total number of students of postgraduate level = 24,700

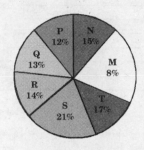

Note : Figure (pie-charts) are not drawn according to scale.

10. How many students of institutes M and S are studying at graduate level?
(A) 7516 (B) 8463 (C) 9127 (D) 9409

11. Total number of students studying at post-graduate level from institute N and P is:
(A) 5601 (B) 5944 (C) 6669 (D) 7004

12. What is the total number of graduate and post-graduate level students in institute R ?
(A) 8320 (B) 7916 (C) 9116 (D) 8372

13. What is the ratio between the number of students studying at post-graduate and graduate levels respectively from institute S?
(A) 14 : 19   (B) 19 : 21
(C) 17 : 21   (D) 19 : 14

14. What is the ratio between the number of students at post graduate level from institute S and the number of students studying at graduate level from instiue Q ?
(A) 13 : 19   (B) 21 : 13
(C) 13 : 8   (D) 19 : 13

15. The bar chart shows the number of 'Maruti' and 'Benz' cars sold by three dealers, A, B and C. Which of the following statements is true ?

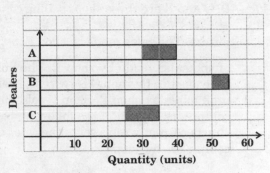

(A) Dealer A sold 40 Maruti cars less than dealer B
(B) Dealer B sold 50 Maruti cars more than dealer C
(C) Dealer B sold the most number of Benz cars
(D) The total number of Benz cars by dealers B and C is 15

16. The bar chart shows the number of workers employed by a trading company in three years. Calculate the difference between the total number of male and female workers employed over those three years.

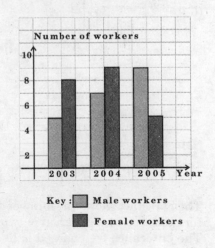

(A) 1   (B) 2   (C) 4   (D) 6

17. P, Q and R are three shops selling computers. The sales made by shop P is $\frac{2}{3}$ of the sales made by shop R. The volume of sales by shop Q is twice the volume made by shop P. Shop R sold 600 computers. Which of the following bar charts correctly represents the sales of computers by shops P, Q and R ?

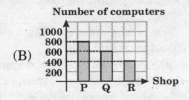

(A)

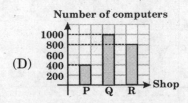

(B)

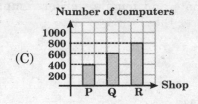

(C)

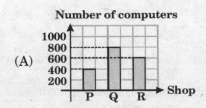

(D)

18. The bar chart shows the number of visitors to a zoo over a period of two days. The enterance fee charged is Rs. 3 for an adult and Re. 1 for a child. Calcutlate the total amount (In Rs.) collected over the two days.

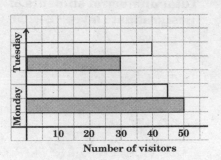

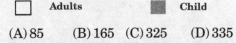

(A) 85   (B) 165   (C) 325   (D) 335

19. The line graph shows the sale of dolls by Suhas from Monday to Saturday on a particular week. Given that cost of one doll is Rs. 35, how much did Suhas receive from the sale of dolls on Saturday ?

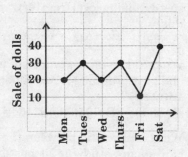

(A) Rs. 200   (B) Rs. 700
(C) Rs. 1050   (D) Rs. 1400

20. The line graph shows the price of chickens in towns M and N. On which days are the price of chickens the same in bothe the towns?

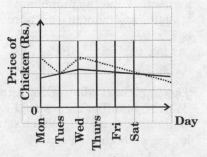

Key: ···· Town M ——Town N

(A) Tuesday only
(B) Friday only
(C) Wednesday and Friday only
(D) Tuesday and Friday only

21. The line graph shows the sale of watches in a company. How many watches were sold in those 5 months?

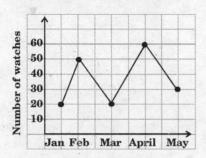

(A) 160   (B) 170   (C) 175   (D) 180

22. The line graph shows the monthly expenditure of Vasu family. The total expenditure over the first 3 months is:

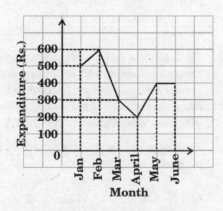

(A) Rs. 320   (B) Rs. 600
(C) Rs. 1100   (D) Rs. 1400

23. The line graph shows the monthly expenditure of the Vasu family. The difference between their highest and lowest monthly expenditure is:

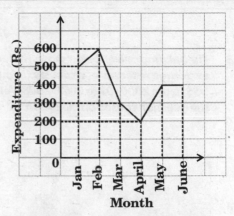

(A) Rs. 100   (B) Rs. 200
(C) Rs. 300   (D) Rs. 400

24. The line graph shows the number of road accidents over the first four months of a certain year. Which of the following statements is false?

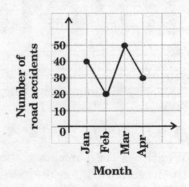

(A) The number of accidents is the highest in March

(B) The number of accidents fell by 50% in February compared to the number in January

(C) The total number of accidents over the four months is 140

(D) The number of accidents increased by 3 times in March as compared to the number in February

Previous Contest Questions

1–3 *The bar graph given below shows the foreign exchange reserves of a country (in million US$) from 2000–01 to 2007–2008. Answer the questions based on this graph*

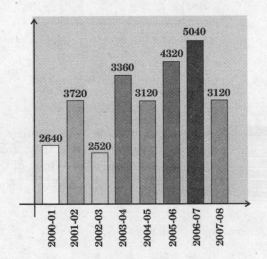

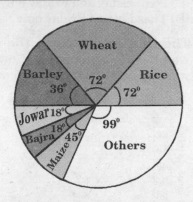

1. The foreign exchange reserves in 2006-2007 was how many times that in 2003-2004.

   (A) 0.7   (B) 1.2   (C) 1.4   (D) 1.5

2. What was the percentage increase in the foreign exchange reserves in 2006-2007 over 2002-2003 ?
   (A) 100   (B) 150   (C) 200   (D) 620

3. The ratio of the number of years, in which the foreign exchange reserves are above the average reserves, to those in which the reserves are below the average reserves, is:
   (A) 2 : 6   (B) 3 : 4 (C) 3 : 5 (D) 5 : 3

4–5 *The pie-chart provided below gives the distribution of land (in a village) under various food crops. Study the pie-chart and answer the questions that are given below.*

4. Which combination of three crops contribute to 50% of the total area under the food crops ?
   (A) Wheat, Barley and Jowar
   (B) Rice, Wheat and Jowar
   (C) Rice, Wheat and Barley
   (D) Bajra, Maize and Rice

5. If the total area under jowar was 1.5 million acres, then what was the area (in millions acres) under rice ?
   (A) 6   (B) 7.5   (C) 9   (D) 4.5

6–8 *The following line graphs gives the ratio of the amounts of imports by a company to the amount of exports from that company ever the period from 2002 to 2008. The questions given below are based on this graph.*

Ratio of value of imports to exports by a company ever the years.

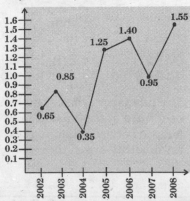

6. In how many of the given years were the exports more than the imports?
    (A) 1   (B) 2
    (C) 3   (D) 4

7. The imports of the company in 2003 was Rs. 272 crores, the exports from the company in 2003 was:
    (A) Rs. 370 crores
    (B) Rs. 320 crores
    (C) Rs. 280 crores
    (D) Rs. 275 crores

8. The imports were minimum proportionate to the exports of th company in the year:
    (A) 2002   (B) 2003
    (C) 2004   (D) 2005

9.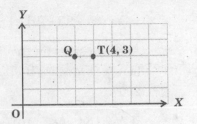

    What are the coordinates of Q ?
    (A) (6,6)   (B) (3,3)
    (C) (10,6)   (D) (12,9)

10. Which of the points below is a point on the y-axis ?
    (A) (7,0)   (B) (6,5)
    (C) (5,3)   (D) (0,5)

⊘ **Answers** ⊘

Multiple Choice Questions

1. D	2. A	3. B	4. D	5. D	6. C	7. B	8. D	9. C	10. B
11. C	12. D	13. D	14. D	15. D	16. A	17. A	18. C	19. D	20. D
21. C	22. D	23. D	24. D						

Previous Contest Questions

1. D	2. A	3. C	4. C	5. A	6. D	7. B	8. C	9. B	10. D

Explanatory Answers

5. (D)   Total sales of branches B_1, B_3 and B_5 together for both the years (in thousand numbers)
    $= (80 + 105) + (95 + 110) + (75 + 95) = 560$

6. (C)   Required Percentage
    $= \left[\dfrac{(70+80)}{(95+110)} \times 100 \right] \%$
    $= \left(\dfrac{150}{205} \times 100 \right) \% = 73.17 \%$

7. (B)   Average sales of all the six branches (in thousand numbers)

for the year 2006
$= \dfrac{1}{6} \times [80 + 75 + 95 + 85 + 75 + 70]$
$= 80$

8. (D)   Required ratio $= \dfrac{(75+65)}{(85+95)}$
    $= \dfrac{140}{180} = \dfrac{7}{9}$

9. (C)   Average sales (in thousand numbers) of branches B_1, B_3 and B_6 in 2006.

$$= \frac{1}{3} \times (80 + 95 + 70) = \left(\frac{245}{3}\right)$$

Average sales (in thousand numbers) of branches B_1, B_2 and B_3 in 2007.

$$= \frac{1}{3} \times (105 + 65 + 110) = \left(\frac{280}{3}\right)$$

∴ Required percentage

$$= \left[\frac{\left(\frac{245}{3}\right)}{\left(\frac{280}{3}\right)} \times 100\right]\% = \left(\frac{245}{280} \times 100\right)\%$$

$$= 87.5\%$$

10. **(B)** Students of institute M at graduate level 17% of 27,300 = 4,641
Students of institute S at graduate level = 14 % of 27,300 = 3,822
∴ Total number of students at graduate level in institute M and S = 4,641 + 3,822 = 8,463

11. **(C)** Required number = (15% of 24700) + (12% of 24700) = 3705 + 2964 = 6669

12. **(D)** Required number = (18% of 27300) + (14% of 24700)
4914 + 3458 = 8372

13. **(D)** Required ratio = $\dfrac{(21\% \text{ of } 24700)}{(14\% \text{ of } 27300)}$

$$= \frac{21 \times 24700}{14 \times 27300} = \frac{19}{14}$$

14. **(D)** Required ratio = $\dfrac{(21\% \text{ of } 24700)}{(13\% \text{ of } 27300)}$

$$\frac{21 \times 24700}{13 \times 27300} = \frac{19}{13}$$

Previous Contest Questions

1. **(D)** Required ratio = 5040/3360 = 1.5

2. **(A)** Foreign exchange reserves in 2006 – 2007 = 5040 millions
foreign exchange reserves in 2002 – 2003 = 2520 millions
∴ Increase = (5040 – 2520) = 2520 millions
∴ Percentage increase =

$$\left(\frac{2520}{2520} \times 100\right)\% = 100\%$$

3. **(C)** Average foreign exchange reserves over the given period = 3480 millions.
The country had reserves above 3480 millions during the years 2001 – 2002, 2005 – 2006, 2006 – 07 i.e., for 3 years and below 3480 millions during the years 2000 – 2001, 2002 – 2003, 2003 – 2004, 2004-2005 and 2007 – 2008 i.e. for 5 years.
Hence, required ratio = 3 : 5.

4. **(C)** The total of the central angles corresponding to the threee crops which cover 50% of the total area, should be $180°$. Now, the total of the central angles for the given combinations are:
(A) Wheat, Barley and Jowar =
$$\left(72° + 36° + 18°\right) = 126°$$
(B) Rice, Wheat and Jowar =
$$\left(72° + 72° + 18°\right) = 162°$$
(C) Rice, Wheat and Barley =
$$\left(72° + 72° + 36°\right) = 180°$$
(D) Bajra, Maize and Barley =
$$\left(18° + 45° + 72°\right) = 135°$$
Clearly 'C' is the required combination.

5. **(A)** The area under any of the food crops is proportional to the central angle corresponding to that crop. Let, the area under rice production be x million acres.
Then, $18 : 72 = 1 : 5 : x$

$$\Rightarrow x = \left(\frac{72 \times 1.5}{18}\right) = 6$$

6. **(D)** The exports are more than the imports implies that the ratio of value of imports to exports is less than 1.
Now, this ratio is less than 1 in the years 2002, 2003, 2004 and 2008.
Thus, there are 4 such years.

7. **(B)** Ratio of imports to exports in the year 2003 = 0.85.
Let the exports in 2003 = Rs. x crores
Then,

$$\frac{272}{x} = 0.85 \Rightarrow x = \frac{272}{0.85} = 320$$

∴ Exports in 2003 = Rs. 320 crores.

8. **(C)** The imports are minimum proportionate to the exports implies that the ratio of the value of imports to exports has the minimum value
Now, this ratio has a minimum value of 0.35 in 2004, i.e., the imports are minimum proportionate to the exports in 2004.

16 Playing with Numbers

Get It Right

Error in applying divisibility tests.

e.g. Is 49,036 divisible by 9 ?

✗ Incorrect

49,036

Number formed by last two digits is divisible by 9, ∴ 49036 is also divisible by 9.

✓ Correct

49,036

4 + 9 + 0 + 3 + 6 = 22

∵ the sum of the digits of 49,036 is 22 and 22 is not divisible by 9.

Hence 49,036 is also not divisible by 3.

Synopsis

General form of a number :

The general form of a number abc can be written as: $abc = a \times 100 + b \times 10 + c$

Divisibility Rules:

The number is divisible by	Conditions	Example	
2.	The last digit is 0 or an even number.	9 340 3 456	0 (Last digit 0) 6 (Last digit is an even numbers) ∴ 9 340 & 3 456 are multiples of 2.
3	The sum of all the digits of the number is divisible by 3.	4 746	(4 + 7 + 4 + 6) ÷ 3 = 21 ÷ 3 = 7 ∴ 4 746 is a multiple of 3.
4.	The last two digits of the number is divisible by 4 or are 00.	6 16 8 900	16 ÷ 4 = 4 00 (Last two digits are 00) ∴ 616 and 8 900 are multiples of 4.

5.	The last digit of the number is 0 or 5.	60 41**5** 76 29**0**	5 (Last digit is 5) 0 (Last digit is 0) ∴ 60 415 and 76 290 are multiples of 5.
6.	The last digit is 0 or an even number, and the sum of all the digits of the number is divisible by 3.	7 596	$(7 + 5 + 9 + 6) \div 3$ $= 27 \div 3 = 9$ ∴ 7 596 is a multiple of 6.
7.	The difference between the digit/digits in front and the doubled value of the last digit is 0 (or) is divisible by 7.	406 672 815	406 is divisible by 7 because $40 - (6 \times 2) = 28$ 28 is divisible by 7. ∴ 406 is the multiple of 7. 672 is divisible by 7 because $67 - (2 \times 2) = 63$ 63 is divisible by 7. ∴ 672 is the multiple of 7. 815 is not divisible by 7 because $81 - (5 \times 2) = 71$ 71 is not divisible by 7. ∴ 815 is not the multiple of 7.
8.	The last three digits of the number is divisible by 8.	3 **568**	$568 \div 8 = 71$ ∴ 3 568 is a multiple of 8.
9.	The sum of all the digits of the number is divisible by 9.	6 048	$(6 + 0 + 4 + 8) \div 9 = 18 \div 9 = 2$ ∴ 6 048 is a multiple of 9.
10.	The last digit is 0.	9 31**0**	0 (Last digit is 0) ∴ 9 310 is a multiple of 10.
11.	If you sum every second digit and then subtract the sum of all other digits and the answer is: 0, or divisible by 11	1364 3729 25176	$((3 + 4) - (1 + 6)) = 0$ YES $((7 + 9) - (3 + 2)) = 11$ YES $((5 + 7) - (2 + 1 + 6)) = 3$ NO
12.	The number is divisible by both 3 and 4.	648 916	$(6 + 4 + 8 = 18$ and also $48 \div 4 = 12)$ Yes $(9 + 1 + 6 = 16, 16,$ No

Multiple Choice Questions

1. The number 3,116,365 is divisible by:
   (A) 5   (B) 7
   (C) both 5 & 7   (D) none of these

2. Which of the following number is divisible by 11?
   (A) 3,116,365   (B) 901,351
   (C) 8,790,322   (D) None of these

3. Which of the following statement is false?

   (A) If a number is divisible by 8, it must be divisible by 4.
   (B) If a number is divisible by both 9 and 10, it must be divisible by 90
   (C) The sum of two consecutive odd numbers is always divisible by 4
   (D) None of these

4. What value should be given to * so that the number 653*47 is divisible by 11?
(A) 9   (B) 6   (C) 2   (D) 1

5. The least number of 4 digits which is exactly divisible by 13 is:
(A) 1,052   (B) 1,039
(C) 1,032   (D) 1,001

6. A number is always divisible by 90 if:
(A) it is divisible by both 2 and 45
(B) it is divisible by both 5 and 18
(C) it is divisible by both 9 and 10
(D) all the above

7. Find a number which is a multiple of all the numbers from 1 to 10?
(A) 5,040   (B) 1,260
(C) 720   (D) 1,440

8. The number 477 is divisible by each of the following numbers except_____

(A) 3   (B) 9
(C) 6   (D) None of these

9. The number 348 is divisible by each of the following numbers except_____
(A) 6   (B) 5
(C) 4   (D) 2

10. If a number is divisible by 9, then it is also divisible by which number?
(A) 3   (B) 6
(C) 2   (D) None of these

11. Which number is divisible by 8 ?
(A) 23, 624   (B) 39, 126
(C) 1, 20, 458   (D) None of these

12. Which number is divisible by 6 ?
(A) 213   (B) 468
(C) 621   (D) None of these

Previous Contest Questions

1. The sum of the digits of a 3 digit number is subtracted from the number. The resulting number is always.
(A) Divisible by 6
(B) Not divisible by 6
(C) Divisible by 9
(D) Not divisible by 9

2. How many five-digit multiples of 11 are there, if the five digits are 3, 4, 5, 6 and 7 same order?
(A) 12   (B) 13
(C) 10   (D) None of these

3. The number of positive integers less than or equal to 100, which are not divisible by 2, 3 or 5, is:
(A) 24   (B) 26   (C) 29   (D) 32

4. The number of natural number divisible by 5 between 1 and 1000 is:
(A) 197   (B) 199   (C) 198   (D) 200

5. Which of the following integers has the most divisors?
(A) 88   (B) 91   (C) 99   (D) 101

6. Which of the following integers has most numer of divisors?
(A) 176   (B) 182   (C) 99   (D) 101

7. Which of the following numbers is exactly divisible by 99?
(A) 114345   (B) 135792
(C) 3572404   (D) 913464

8. $4^{16} + 4^{62} + 4^{63} + 4^{64}$ is divisible by:
(A) 3   (B) 10   (C) 11   (D) 13

9.   There is one number which is formed by writing one digit 6 times (e.g. 111111, 444444 etc.) . Such a number is always divisible by:

(A) 7 only   (B) 11 only

(C) 13 only   (D) All of these

10. In which of the following pairs of numbers it is true that their sum is 11 times their product?

(A) 1, 1/11   (B) 1, 1/10

(C) 1, 1/12   (D) 1, 10

⊘ Answers ⊘

Multiple Choice Questions

1. C	2. B	3. D	4. D	5. D	6. D	7. A	8. C	9. B	10. A
11. A	12. B								

Previous Contest Questions

1. C	2. A	3. B	4. D	5. A	6. A	7. A	8. B	9. D	10. B

Explanatory Answers

1.   (C)   Since, last digit is 5, the number is divisible by 5.

∵ 3116–365 = 2751 ÷ 7 = 393

So, it is divisible by 7 also.

2.   (B)   In 901,351

sum of the digits in odd positions = 9 + 1 + 5 = 15.

Sum of the digits in even positions = 0 + 3 + 1 = 4

Difference = 15 – 4 = 11

∵ Difference is a multiple of 11, so 901,351 is divisible by 11.

3.   (D)   Since, all the given statements are true.

4.   (D)   Adding digits at even places of

given number 653 * 47, we get 13

Now if the number is divisible by 11, then the sum of digits at odd places should also be 13, so that 13 – 13 = 0 is divisible by 11.

⇒ 7 + * + 5 = 12

∴ 13 – 12 = 1 is the required value.

5.   (D)   ∵ 1001 is divisible by 13.

6.   (D)   ∵ If a number is divisible by 'a' and 'b', where 'a' & 'b' are co–primes, then that number is divisible by 'ab'.

Here 2, 45; 5, 18; 9, 10 are co–primes.

In each case, the product as also equal to 90.

7.   (A)   Required number

$= 7 \times 8 \times 9 \times 10 = 5040$

CROSSWORD – I (MATHEMATICS)

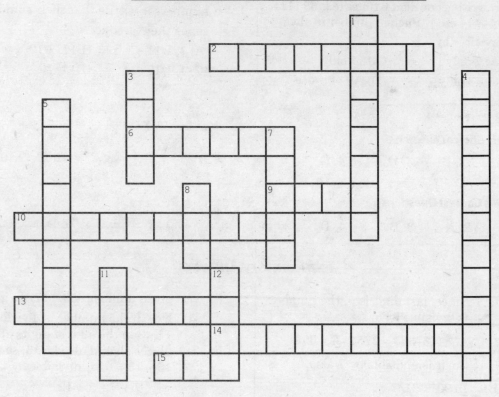

ACROSS

2   An equality which is true for all values of the variables in it is called as an _____

6   Amount of region occupied by a solid is called its _____

9   Every number that is divisible by two is also _____

10   A solid formed by polygonal regions meeting at edges which are line segments is called a _____

13   The unknown quantity in an equation is called as _____

14   The multiplicative inverse of a rational number is its _____

15   The number of integral square roots of a perfect square number is _____

DOWN

1   A certain reduction given on marked price of an article by a shopkeeper is called _____

3   The number of measurements required to construct a quadrilateral is _____

4   A factor which cannot be expressed further as a product of factors is termed as _____

5   A bar graph that shows data in intervals is called a _____

7   One or more outcomes of an experiment make an _____

8   The cube of an odd number is _____

11   A quadrilateral with exactly two pairs of equal consecutive sides is _____

12   The number added to its additive inverse gives _____

NOTE: Answer to this crossword puzzle is given at the end of this book.

1. The average of the middle two rational numbers if $\frac{4}{7}, \frac{1}{3}, \frac{2}{5}, \frac{5}{9}$ are arranged in ascending order is:

   (A) $\frac{86}{90}$ (B) $\frac{86}{45}$

   (C) $\frac{43}{45}$ (D) $\frac{43}{90}$

2. By what rational number should $\frac{-8}{39}$ be multiplied to obtain 26 ?

   (A) $\frac{507}{4}$ (B) $\frac{-507}{4}$

   (C) $\frac{407}{4}$ (D) None of these

3. The product of two rational numbers is $\frac{-9}{16}$. If one of the numbers is $\frac{-4}{3}$, then the other number is:

   (A) $\frac{36}{48}$ (B) $\frac{25}{64}$

   (C) $\frac{27}{49}$ (D) $\frac{27}{64}$

4. $\frac{2}{3}$ rd of a number when multiplied by $\frac{3}{4}$ th of the same number make 338. The number is:

   (A) 18   (B) 24
   (C) 36   (D) 26

5. There were only two candidates in an election. One got 62% votes and was elected by a margin of 144 votes. The total number of voters were:

   (A) 500   (B) 600
   (C) 700   (D) 800

6. The ratio of two numbers is 3 : 8 and their difference is 115. The largest number is:

   (A) 69   (B) 115   (C) 184   (D) 230

7. How much pure alcohol should be added to 400 ml of strength 15% to make its strength 32%?

   (A) 50 ml   (B) 75 ml
   (C) 100 ml   (D) 150 ml

8. Given that $\frac{-6p-9}{3} = \frac{2p+9}{5}$, find the value of p.

   (A) –4   (B) –2
   (C) 3   (D) 5

9. ABCD is a parallelogram as shown in figure. If AB = 2AD and P is mid-point of AB, then $\angle CPD$ is equal to:

   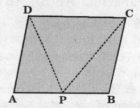

   (A) 90°   (B) 60°
   (C) 45°   (D) 135°

10. The following figure shows a polygon with all its exterior angles.

   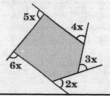

The value of x is:
(A) 10^0 (B) 18^0 (C) 20^0 (D) 36^0

11. In the figure given below, PTU is a straight line.

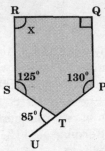

What is the value of x ?
(A) 100^0 (B) 110^0 (C) 120^0 (D) 130^0

12. The minimum number of dimensions needed to construct a rectangle is:
(A) 1   (B) 2   (C) 3   (D) 4

13. The diagram shows the construction of:

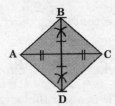

(A) a trapezium   (B) a rhombus
(C) a rectangle   (D) a kite

14. In a trapezium ABCD, AB||CD. If $\angle A = 60^0$ then $\angle D = ?$
(A) 110^0 (B) 120^0 (C) 70^0 (D) 300^0

15. The bar chart shows the number of television sets sold by a shop in 5 months. The sales in May, as a percentage of the total sales in the 5 months is:

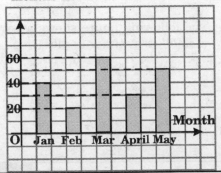

(A) 25%   (B) $33\frac{1}{3}\%$

(C) 50%   (D) $66\frac{2}{3}\%$

16. The pie chart shows the number of participants from four countries P, Q, R and S taking part in a tennis tournament. Given that there are 18 participants from country S, find the number of participants from country R.

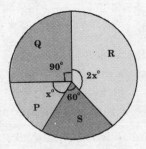

(A) 18   (B) 21   (C) 27   (D) 42

17. The least perfect square exactly divisible by each of the numbers 6, 9, 15 and 20 is:
(A) 3,600 (B) 900   (C) 400   (D) 225

18. The value of
$1 + 3 + 5 + 7 + 9 + \ldots\ldots + 25$ is:
(A) 196   (B) 625   (C) 225   (D) 169

19. $\sqrt{1 + \sqrt{1 + \sqrt{1 + \ldots\ldots}}}$ = _____
(A) equals 1
(B) lies between 0 and 1
(C) lies between 1 and 2
(D) is greater than 2

20. If $\sqrt{6} = 2.55$, then the value of

$\sqrt{\dfrac{2}{3}} + 3\sqrt{\dfrac{3}{2}}$ is:

(A) 4.48   (B) 4.49
(C) 4.50   (D) none of these

21. If $\sqrt{3} = 1.732$, then the approximate

value of $\dfrac{1}{\sqrt{3}}$ is:

(A) 0.617   (B) 0.313

(C) 0.577   (D) 0.173

22. The smallest number by which 2560 must be multiplied so that the product is a perfect cube is:

(A) 5   (B) 25   (C) 10   (D) 15

23. The square of a natural number subtracted from its cube is 48. The number is:

(A) 6   (B) 5   (C) 4   (D) 8

24. In what time will Rs. 1000 amount to Rs. 1331 at 10% p.a. in CI?

(A) 4 years   (B) 3 years

(C) 2 years   (D) 1 year

25. A merchant buys a 50 litre cask of wine for Rs. 6250 and sells it at Rs. 130 per litre. His loss or gain percent is:

(A) $3\dfrac{11}{50}\%$ loss   (B) 4% profit

(C) 25% profit   (D) 8% gain

26. A cask containing 425 litres lost 8% by leakage and evaporation. The number of litres left in the case were:

(A) $\dfrac{425 \times 8}{100}$ (B) $425 - \dfrac{425 \times 8}{100}$

(C) $425 + \dfrac{425 \times 8}{100}$ (D) $425 \times \dfrac{425 \times 8}{100}$

27. A bag marked at Rs. 80 is sold for Rs. 68. The rate of discount is:

(A) 12%   (B) 15%   (C) $17\dfrac{11}{17}\%$ (D) 20%

28. What is the difference between the compound interests on Rs. 5,000 for $1\dfrac{1}{2}$ years at 4% per annum compounded yearly and half-yearly?

(A) Rs. 2.04   (B) Rs. 3.06

(C) Rs. 4.80   (D) Rs. 8.30

29. If quotient = $3x^2 - 2x + 1$, remainder = $2x - 5$ and divisor = $x + 2$ then the dividend is:

(A) $3x^3 - 4x^2 + x - 3$

(B) $3x^3 - 4x^2 - x + 3$

(C) $3x^3 + 4x^2 - x + 3$

(D) $3x^3 + 4x^2 - x - 3$

30. Find the missing term in the following problem.

$$\left(\dfrac{3x}{4} - \dfrac{4y}{3}\right)^2 = \dfrac{9x^2}{16} + \underline{\quad} + \dfrac{16y^2}{9}$$

(A) 2xy   (B) –2xy (C) 12xy (D) –12xy

31. $\dfrac{a^3 + b^3 + c^3 - 3abc}{a^2 + b^2 + c^2 - ab - bc - ca} = \underline{\quad}$.

(A) 0   (B) a + b + c

(C) 1   (D) none of these

32. The number of flat surfaces in a cone is:

(A) 1   (B) 2

(C) 3   (D) It has no flat surface

33. The number of corners in a cylinder is:

(A) 1   (B) 2   (C) 3   (D) None

34. If F = 4 and V = 3, then the value of E is (Use Euler's formula) :

(A) 7   (B) 5   (C) 4   (D) 1

35. The ratio between the length and the perimeter of a rectangular plot is 1 : 3 and the ratio between the breadth and perimeter of that plot is 1 : 6. What is the ratio between the length and area of that plot?

(A) 2 : 1   (B) 1 : 6

(C) 1 : 8   (D) Data inadequate

36. If the ratio of areas of two circles is 16 : 25 the ratio of their circumference is:

(A) 25 : 16 (B) 5 : 4 (C) 4 : 5 (D) 3 : 5

37. A sector of 120° cut out from a circle has an area of $9\dfrac{3}{7}$ sq cm. The radius of the circle is:

(A) 3 cm   (B) 2.5 cm

(C) 3.5 cm   (D) 3.6 cm

38. The value of $\dfrac{(5)^{0.25} \times (125)^{0.25}}{(256)^{0.10} \times (256)^{0.15}}$ is:

(A) $\dfrac{\sqrt{5}}{2}$ (B) $\dfrac{5}{4}$ (C) $\dfrac{25}{2}$ (D) $\dfrac{25}{16}$

39. The value of $(0.000064)^{5/4} \times (0.04)^{5/4}$ is:

   (A) $2^{10}.0^{10}$

   (B) $2^{10}.10^{-10}$

   (C) $2^{-10}.10^{10}$

   (D) None of these

40. $(256)^{0.16} \times (256)^{0.09} = ?$

   (A) 4   (B) 16   (C) 64   (D) 256.25

41. A certain number of men can finish a piece of work in 100 days. If, there were 10 men less, it would take 10 days more for the work to be finished. How many men were there originally ?

   (A) 75   (B) 82   (C) 100   (D) 110

42. If 45 students can consume a stock of food in 2 months, then for how many days the same stock of food will last for 27 students ?

   (A) 100 days   (B) 144 days

   (C) 160 days   (D) 180 days

43. A wheel that has 6 cogs is meshed with a larger wheel of 14 cogs. When the smaller wheel has made 21 revolutions, then the number of revolutions made by the larger wheel is:

   (A) 4   (B) 9   (C) 12   (D) 49

44. The real factors of $x^2 + 4$ are:

   (A) $(x^2 + 2)(x^2 - 2)$ (B) $(x + 2)(x - 2)$

   (C) does not exist   (D) none of these

45. If the factors of $a^2 + b^2 + 2(ab + bc + ca)$ are $(a + b + m)$ and $(a + b + nc)$, then the value of m + n is:

   (A) 0   (B) 2   (C) 4   (D) 6

46. The factors of

   $\sqrt{3}x^2 + 11x + 6\sqrt{3}$ are:

(A) $\left(x - 3\sqrt{3}\right)\left(\sqrt{3}x + 2\right)$

(B) $\left(x - 3\sqrt{3}\right)\left(\sqrt{3}x - 2\right)$

(C) $\left(x + 3\sqrt{3}\right)\left(\sqrt{3}x - 2\right)$

(D) $\left(x + 3\sqrt{3}\right)\left(\sqrt{3}x + 2\right)$

47. The line graph shows the monthly expenditure of Vasu family. The total expenditure over the first 3 months is:

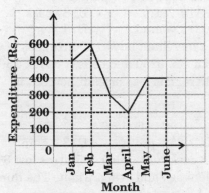

   (A) Rs. 320   (B) Rs. 600

   (C) Rs. 1100   (D) Rs. 1400

48. The number of positive integers less than or equal to 100, which are not divisible by 2, 3 or 5, is:

   (A) 24   (B) 26   (C) 29   (D) 32

49. The number of natural number divisible by 5 between 1 and 1000 is:

   (A) 197   (B) 199   (C) 198   (D) 200

50. Which of the following numbers is exactly divisible by 99?

   (A) 114345   (B) 135792

   (C) 3572404   (D) 913464

◎ **Answers** ◎

1. D	2. B	3. D	4. D	5. B	6. C	7. C	8. B	9. A	10. B
11. A	12. B	13. B	14. B	15. A	16. D	17. B	18. D	19. C	20. D
21. C	22. B	23. C	24. B	25. B	26. B	27. B	28. A	29. D	30. B
31. B	32. A	33. D	34. B	35. D	36. C	37. A	38. B	39. B	40. A
41. D	42. A	43. B	44. C	45. B	46. D	47. D	48. B	49. D	50. A

PHYSICS

Common misconception	Fact
1. Force and pressure are same. (Reason apparently both appears to produce same result whom applied to a body.	1. Force and pressure are different. Force is defined as a push or a pull, while pressure is equal to force per unit area.
2. Pressure can be applied on a body.	2. Force is applied on a body. Pressure is an out come of application of force and depends upon area of contact.
3. Bodies must be in physical contact for application of force.	3. Magnetic, electrostatic and gravitational forces are non-contact forces.

Synopsis

1. A force is a push or a pull. It can cause any or all of the following when applied to a body.

   (a) movement or stop motion of an object.

   (b) changes speed / direction of a body.

   (c) change in shape & size of a body.

2.   Types of forces

   Contact forces   **Non contact forces**
   - Muscular force   - Magnetic force
   - Friction force   - Electrostatic force
   - Elastic spring force   - Gravitational force

3. Force is due to interaction between two or more bodies.

4. The strength of a force is expressed by its magnitude and is a vector quantity.

5. Net force on an object can be zero if two (or more) forces acting on it in opposite directions are equal in magnitude.

6. The force, responsible for change of speed of an object is the friction force. It tends to stop/slow down a moving object in the absence of external forces.

7. Friction force can be due to surface, wind (drag) or due to water (ex. : moving boat stops in water if you stop rowing).

8. Non contact forces like magnetic, electrostatic and gravitational forces act between bodies even if they are not in contact.

9. Force acting on a unit area of a surface is called pressure.

    Pressure = Force / Area on which it acts

    Note: S.I. unit of force = Newton

               S.I. unit of pressure = Newton / (Metre)^2

10. Pressure depends upon the area of contact.

    Ex. : A sharp needle causes more pain in the body as compared to a blunt object.

11. Pressure exerted by water at the bottom of a container depends upon the height of the water column.

12. A liquid exerts pressure on the walls of a container. Gases also exert pressure on walls of a container.

13. Liquids exert equal pressure at the same depth.

14. Pressure exerted by the air mass sorrounding the earth is called the atmospheric pressure. The reason we donot feel this pressue is due to the fact that the pressure inside our bodies (Our blood contains dissolved oxygen at a pressure, equal to or slightly more than the atmospheric pressure blood vessels) is equal to the atmospheric pressure and hence cancels the pressure from outside.

    Atmospheric pressure is measured in pascals or kilopascals.

    1 atmosphere => 1 atm = $10 N/m^2$ = 100,000 pa = 100 kpa

15. Pressure decreases with height (high attitude / mountains) and increases with depth. (deep sea).

Multiple Choice Questions

1. Which of the following action describes pushing by a body?
   (A) kicking   (B) lifting
   (C) picking   (D) opening

2. Which of the following is NOT a type of force?
   (A) muscular
   (B) magnetic
   (C) chemical
   (D) pulling a bucket of water from a well

3. A force is applied to an object in the direction of its motion. The speed of object will _____.
   (A) increase
   (B) decrease
   (C) can't say
   (D) remain unchanged

4. If no force acts on a body it will _____.
   (A) change shape
   (B) move with increased speed
   (C) either remain in rest or move in a straight line
   (D) break up

5. In football, a goal keeper stops a ball. This is due to:
   (A) friction between the ball and hand of goal keeper
   (B) decrease in speed of ball due to air resistance
   (C) application of force by goal keeper
   (D) all of the above

6. Which of the following example describes change of shape by applying force?
   (A) kicking a ball to move faster
   (B) switching on a fan to rotate
   (C) jumping from a height
   (D) tearing a paper into two pieces

7. Friction force is responsible for changing:
   (A) shape of an object
   (B) direction of an object
   (C) speed of an object
   (D) all of the above

8. The force of friction between two bodies is:
   (A) parallel to contact surface
   (B) perpendicular to contact surface
   (C) inclined to contact surface
   (D) a non contact force

9. Which of the following is a non contact force?
   (A) muscular
   (B) electrostatic attraction
   (C) elastic spring force
   (D) friction force

10. A force of 16 N is distributed uniformly on one surface of a cube of edge '8' cm. The pressure on this surface is:

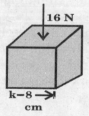

   (A) 3500 pa   (B) 2500 pa
   (C) 4500 pa   (D) 2000 pa

11. The atmospheric pressure is due to the:
    (A) sky above our head
    (B) air mass surrounding earth
    (C) gravitational force of sun and other planets
    (D) mass of the earth

12. The pressure exerted by a liquid:
    (A) increases with depth
    (B) decreases with depth
    (C) is constant
    (D) first increases then decreases

13. Which of the following statement is NOT true.
   (A) A freely falling body is acted upon by gravitational force
   (B) pressure on top of mount everest is much more than 1 atm
   (C) S.I. unit of pressure is pascal
   (D) the blood vessels in our body maintains the internal pressure equal to the atmospheric pressure

14. Thrust is:
   (A) Force X area   (B) Force / Area
   (C) Pressure   (D) Pressure X Area

15. A body floats in water because:
   (A) no force is acting on it
   (B) the net force acting on this body is zero
   (C) of gravitational pull
   (D) friction between body and the water

16. In which of the following cases the net force is not equal to zero?
   (A) A kite skillfully held stationary in the sky
   (B) A ball falling feeely from a height
   (C) A helicopter hovering above the ground
   (D) A cork floating on the surface of water

17. A car accelerates on a horizontal road due to the force exerted by:
   (A) the engine of the ear
   (B) the driver of the car
   (C) the earth
   (D) the road

18. While walking on ice, one should take small steps to avoid slipping. This is because smaller steps ensure:
   (A) larger friction
   (B) smaller friction
   (C) larger normal force
   (D) smaller normal force

19. In which of the following activity, friction is useful?

   (A) driving a car
   (B) hitting a ball with bat
   (C) rowing a boat
   (D) sitting on a chair

20. Friction can be increased by:
   (A) making the surfaces rough
   (B) using dry surfaces
   (C) increasing the weight
   (D) all of the above

21. If the roughness of a surface is increased to a large extent, then the friction of the surface would:
   (A) increase and then decrease
   (B) increase continuously
   (C) decrease continuously
   (D) decrease and then increase

22. The given figure shows the cross section of a dam and its reservoir. The widening of the wall, towards the bottom is because of _____.

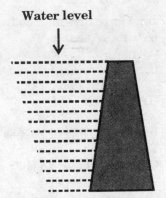

Thickness of wall

   (A) increase in pressure with depth of water
   (B) decrease pressure with depth of water
   (C) change in density of water
   (D) increase in mass of the wall

23. Which of the following statements is NOT true for friction force?

(A) Friction force is produced when two objects rub against each other

(B) A lighter object will experience a smaller frictional force

(C) friction produces more wear and tear

(D) friction is harmful

24. We use a straw (narrow pipe) to drink juice from a glass. This is possible due to presence of:
(A) liquid pressure
(B) atmospheric pressure
(C) gravitational pull
(D) all of the above

25. The magnetic force between a magnet and a magnetic substance can cause:
(A) change of state
(B) change of shape
(C) change of size
(D) change of property

26. Two magnets A & B are placed with like poles having one above another. What will happen?

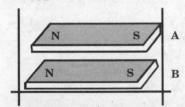

(A) A will stuck to B
(B) A will remain as shown in the figure
(C) A will move side ways
(D) Can't say

27. In cities water supply from an overhead tank to the houses is done due to:
(A) difference in pressure
(B) gravitational force
(C) decrease of friction in pipes
(D) flow of liquid

28. A mountain climber experiences a nose bleed due to:
(A) decrease in atm pressure
(B) increase in atm pressure
(C) more gravitational pull
(D) effect of high altitude

29. A deep sea diver may hurt his ear drum during diving because of:

(A) lack of oxygen
(B) more atm pressure
(C) more water pressure
(D) all of the above

30. Which of the following is NOT true?
(A) A sharp knife can easily cut due to its small cutting surface
(B) It is easier to walk in sand than on road
(C) A battle tank can move easily on soft ground because its tracks have bigger surface
(D) The pressure exerted by a needle is much more than the foot of an elephant

31. What is wrong in this figure?

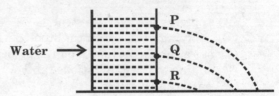

(A) water flowing through hole 'P' will move a smaller distance as compared to Q and R
(B) water flowing through hole 'Q' will be maximum
(C) water flowing through 'R' will be more than 'Q' but les than 'p'
(D) water flowing through all holes will travel same distance as pressure exerted by a liquid is equal in all direction

32. Barometer is used for measuring:
(A) Liquid pressure
(B) Thrust
(C) Atmospheric pressure
(D) Air temp.

33. The force used by an archer to pull a bow is:
(A) muscular force
(B) friction force
(C) gravitational force
(D) elsatic spring force

Previous Contest Questions

1. Which of the following is NOT attributable to application of force?
   (A) rowing of a boat
   (B) bursting of a balloon while blowing
   (C) pedaling a cycle
   (D) catching a moving cricket ball

2. In the picture shown below, the man is:

   (A) applying force on the stool
   (B) applying pressure on the stool
   (C) not applying any force on the stool
   (D) adding to the gravitational pull of earth on the stool

3. The speed of a falling body increases continuously. This is because:
   (A) no force acts on it
   (B) it is very light
   (C) air exerts a frictional force along the direction of motion
   (D) the earth attracts it

4. A book remains at rest on a table. It is so because of:
   (A) no force acts on it
   (B) friction between the book and the surface of table
   (C) force exerted by book on the table, is same as the force exerted by the table on the book
   (D) all of the above

5. Deep sea divers put on special suit to:
   (A) maintain their body temperature in cold sea water
   (B) protect against sea animals
   (C) maintain pressure
   (D) keep them dry

6. A coin flicked across a table will stop, because:
   (A) it is heavy
   (B) no force is acting on it
   (C) earth attracts the coin
   (D) table exerts a frictional force

7. The magnitude of non-contact force depends upon:
   (A) distance between two bodies
   (B) mass of the two bodies
   (C) chemical properties of the two bodies
   (D) all of the above

8. A ball placed on a table starts rolling when table is tilted. Which is the force which causes this motion?
   (A) friction
   (B) push by table
   (C) rolling force
   (D) gravitational pull by earth

9. A rubber sucker sticks to a surface because of:
   (A) property of rubber
   (B) gravitational force
   (C) elastic spring force
   (D) atmospheric pressure

10. A body submerged in the sea is brought upto its surface. Which of the following graphs represents correctly the variation of the pressure on the body with decrease in the depth?

   (A)

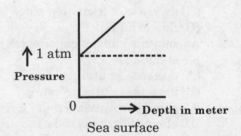

(B)

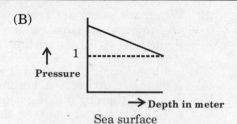

Sea surface

(D)

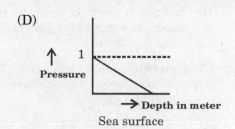

Sea surface

(C)

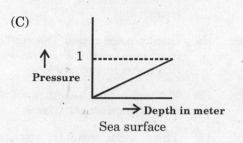

Sea surface

11. Four forces are acting on a body. If the body doesn't change its position or shape, the forces:

(A) must be of equal magnitude

(B) must be parallel & opposite

(C) must add up to zero when taken as vectors

(D) must be in a single line

⊘ Answers ⊘

Multiple Choice Answers

1. A	2. C	3. A	4. C	5. C	6. D	7. C	8. A	9. B	10. B
11. B	12. A	13. B	14. D	15. B	16. B	17. D	18. D	19. D	20. D
21. B	22. A	23. D	24. B	25. A	26. B	27. B	28. A	29. C	30. B
31. A	32. C	33. A							

Previous Contest Answers

1. B	2. A	3. D	4. D	5. C	6. D	7. A	8. D	9. D	10. B
11. C									

Explanatory Answers

1. (A) Kicking is a pushing action while all others are pulling action.

2. (C) Chemical is a type of energy not a force.

3. (A) Since the force is in the direction of motion, the speed of object will increase.

4. (C) Force is required for a, b & d. In absence of a force an object will either remain at rest (static object) or move in a straight line (moving object).

5. (C) The force applied by the goal keeper can either stop or deflect the ball.

6.   (D)   We apply certain force to fear paper. The shape of paper changes after it is form.

7.   (C)   Friction force between two surfaces tends to decrease the speed of a moving object.

8.   (A)   A force of friction is parallel to the contact surfaces and acts in a direction to opposite of the motion.

9.   (B)   The electrostatic attraction between two bodies (ex.: silk & glass rod when robbed) is a non contact force since the bodies need not touch each other.

10.   (B)   Pressure force / area
            $$= \frac{16}{8 \times 8 \times 10^{-4}}$$
            $$= 2500 \, pa$$

12.   (A)   Pressure of a liquid is directly proportional to the height of the liquid column.

13.   (B)   Atmospheric pressure decreases with high altitude. Hence the pressure on top of mount everest will be less than 1 atm.

14.   (D)   Thrust is the total force applied on a given area. It is given as pressure X area.

15.   (B)   The weight of the body is balanced by the upthrust of water. Hence net force acting on the body is zero.

19.   (D)   It will be difficult to sit on a chair without friction. In all other cases of above friction is harmful.

22.   (A)   The wall at bottom has to withstand higher pressure as compared to the top.

23.   (D)   Friction is useful for braking moving vehicles; for walking in smooth / slippery surfaces like snow and sand.

24.   (B)   When we suck air from pipe, atmospheric pressure pushes the liquid juice to fill the vacuum and it comes up.

25.   (A)   A magnet attracts a magnetic material thereby making it move from rest. Any change in shape or size due to a magnet is temporary.

26.   (B)   Unlike poles repel. The repulsive magnetic force will not allow the like poles to get stuck

27.   (B)   The water at a height flows down due to gravitational force.

28.   (A)   The atmospheric pressure decreases with height due to thinning of atmosphere. Thus the internal body pressure becomes higher than atmospheric pressure causing a nose bleed.

29.   (C)   Water pressure increases with depth of sea.

30.   (B)   It is difficult to walk in sand due to lack of friction.

31.   (A)   Pressure of liquid increases with depth. The height of water column for 'R' is maximum and for 'P' is minimum.

33.   (A)   An archer uses his strength (muscular force) to pull a bow.

Previous Contest Questions

1.   (B)   a, b & d are due to application of a force. Bursting of a balloon is due to expansion beyond the elastic limit of the balloon material.

2.   (A)   The weight of the man is the force applied by him on the stool.

3.   (D)   The gravitational force for a falling object is along the direction of motion. Hence, its speed increases continuously till it touches the ground.

5. (C) The suit (known as scuba suit) is pressurized to counter balance the heavy pressure in deep sea.

6. (D) The coin will stop because of friction exerted by the surface of the table on the coin.

7. (A) It decreases with increase of separation between the bodies.

8. (D) As long as the table is horizontal, the weight (force) of the ball is balanced by the reaction force exerted by the table. When tilled the weight component reduces and

hence the gravitatio-nal forces causes the motion.

9. (D) When you press the sticker on any surface, most of the air between its cup and the surface escapes out. The sucker sticks to the surface because the atmospheric pressure acts on it.

10. (B) Pressures decreases with decrease of depth. It is equal to atmospheric pressure at sea level.

11. (C) For a body to be in equilibrium or in rest, vector sum of all forces must be zero.

Common misconception	Fact
1. Friction is not a type of force as it is neither push nor pull.	1. Friction is a force. It can change speed of a moving object.
2. Friction force is not useful.	2. Friction is useful while braking a moving object. It also helps in walking.
3. Friction depends on the area of two surfaces on contact.	3. Friction is independent of the area of the two surfaces in contact. It depends on the roughness of the surfaces and materials of the body.

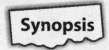

Synopsis

1. Friction opposes the relative motion between two surfaces in contact. It acts on both the surface.

2. Friction depends on the following factors.
    (a) materials of the bodies in contact.
    (b) roughness of the two surfaces in contact. More rough the surfaces, greater is the friction

3. The force of friction is independent of the area of the two surfaces in contact.

4. The force of friction between two bodies is parallel to the contact surface and always opposite in direction to that of the motion.

5. Although friction is undesirable, it is important for activities like sitting, walking, braking etc.

6. Friction in machines is reduced by using lubricants & smoothening of surfaces (polishing)

7. Harmful effects of friction:

    (a) increases wear and tear

    (b) produces heat

    (c) decreases efficiency

8. The static friction (or limiting friction) is the friction between any two bodies when one of the bodies just tends to move or slip over the surface of another body. There is no actual movement of the body in static friction.

9. Sliding friction (or dynamic friction) comes into play when one of the body slides over another.

10. When a body (like a roller or a wheel) rolls over the surface of another body (ex. road surface), the friction is called rolling friction.

11. Rolling friction is much less than sliding friction.

12. Liquids and gases (fluids) exert much less friction as compared to solids.

13. The frictional force exerted by fluids (including air) is called drag.

14. The special shape of a body (object) to reduce drag is called streamlined shape. ex.: shape of a bird, an aeroplane are streamlined shape.

15. Air also exerts friction on a moving body, but it is much smaller as compared to solid and liquid.

Multiple Choice Questions

1. Friction is a type of:
    (A) contact force
    (B) non contact force
    (C) resistance force
    (D) motion

2. A force of 5 N is required to move an object from rest. The value of static friction (f) is:

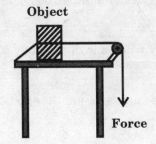

Object

Force

    (A) 5 N   (B) f > 5 N
    (C) f < 5 N   (D) 10 N

3. The value of sliding friction for the object shown in figure 2 is:
    (A) f = 5 N   (B) f > 5 N
    (C) f < 5 N   (D) 10 N

4. The surface of a table is smoother as compared to that of a road. This is due to:
    (A) irregularities in the surface of road
    (B) polishing of the table
    (C) a road surface may have more dust as compared to a table
    (D) all of the above

5. Which of the following material is likely to have least friction?
    (A) wood   (B) plastic
    (C) glass   (D) paper

6. Which of the following is used to reduce friction in a rotating machine?
    (A) wheels   (B) roolers
    (C) ball bearing   (D) polishing

7. In which of the following cases more friction is desirable?
    (A) movement of piston in a cylinder
    (B) braking of a vehicle
    (C) running on a track
    (D) all of the above

8. Powder is used in carrom board for:
    (A) increasing friction
    (B) decreasing friction
    (C) decoration
    (D) fragrance

9. Which of the following statement is CORRECT?
    (A) rolling a body is easier than sliding
    (B) sliding body is easier than rolling
    (C) dragging body is easier than sliding
    (D) dragging body is easier than rolling

10. The frictional force exerted by fluids is called:
    (A) lift   (B) drag
    (C) rolling friction   (D) dynamic friction

11. A streamlined body:
    (A) increases friction
    (B) reduces friction
    (C) decreases weight
    (D) increases weight

12. In decreasing order of magnitude which of the following is CORRECT?
    (A) rolling, static, sliding friction
    (B) static, sliding, rolling
    (C) static, rolling, sliding
    (D) sliding, static, rolling

13. In which of the following cases, the speed of the ball will be more?

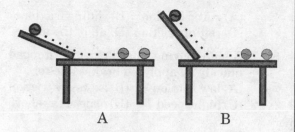

A   B

(A) A > B
(B) B > A
(C) In both cases speed will be same
(D) None of the above

14. Which of the following activities is easier to perform?
(A) dragging a box
(B) lifting a box
(C) rolling a drum of same weight
(D) all of the above need same effort

15. A meteor burns up on entering earth's atmosphere due to:
(A) atmospheric pressure
(B) heat of the earth
(C) solar radiation
(D) excessive friction

16. The surface of the head of a match stick and sides of a match box are deliberately made rough to:
(A) increase friction
(B) decrease friction

(C) increase amount
(D) decrease amount of heat

17. Spikes are provided in the shoes of athlete:
(A) for decoration
(B) to increase friction
(C) to decrease friction
(D) none of the above

18. Which of the following statements is NOT true?
(A) Friction can be reduced by converting sliding friction into roling friction.
(B) Friction in air and water can be reduced by streamlining the shape of the object.
(C) A polished surface will have less friction.
(D) Friction can be reduced to zero

19. Friction reduces efficiency of machines due to:
(A) production of heat
(B) wearing out of moving parts
(C) increase in energy consumption
(D) all of the above

20. The force which prevents us from slipping while walking on the road is:
(A) muscular force of our body
(B) gravitational pull by earth
(C) friction force
(D) balanced forces of nature

Previous Contest Questions

1. Which of the following statement is TRUE?
(A) static friction is more than dynamic friction
(E) static friction is less than dynamic friction
(C) static friction is equal to dynamic friction
(D) there is no relationship between static and dynamic friction

2. The force required to keep an object moving with the same speed is a measure of:
(A) static friction   (B) sliding friction
(C) rolling friction (D) limiting friction

3. Which of the following activity would not be possible in the absence of friciton?
(A) holding a glass
(B) writing on a paper

(C) sitting on a chair

(D) all of the above

4. The force required to overcome friction at the instant when an object starts moving from rest is a measure of its:
    (A) static friction
    (B) dynamic friction
    (C) sliding friction
    (D) rolling friction

5. What would happen to a moving object if there would be no friction?
    (A) the object will stop
    (B) the object will keep moving
    (C) the object will change speed
    (D) the object will change direciton

6. Which of the following has a stream lined body?
    (A) bird   (B) aeroplane
    (C) whale   (D) all of the above

7. Correct air pressure in our vehicle tyres help to reduce?

(A) static friction   (B) sliding friction
(C) rolling friction   (D) all of the above

8. A ship moving in sea can't be stopped quickly by applying brakes due to:
    (A) low friction   (B) excessive friction
    (C) high speed   (D) none of the above

9. When a coin and a feather are dropped simultaneously from the same height, the coin strikes the ground first. This is because of:
    (A) gravitational force
    (B) mass of coin
    (C) friction
    (D) none of these

10. The soles of our shoes wears out because:
    (A) soles are made of poor material
    (B) of poor design
    (C) of friction
    (D) none of the above

⊘ Answers ⊘

Multiple Choice Answers

1. A	2. A	3. C	4. D	5. C	6. C	7. B	8. B	9. A	10. B
11. B	12. B	13. B	14. C	15. D	16. A	17. B	18. D	19. D	20. C

Previous Contest Answers

1. A	2. B	3. D	4. A	5. B	6. D	7. C	8. A	9. C	10. C

Explanatory Answers

1. (A) Friction force is always between two surfaces in contact with each other.

2. (A) The force required to just move the body in rest is equal to its static or limiting friction.

3. (A) Static friction is the maximum (limiting) friction between two bodies.

4. (D) Friction can be reduced by reducing irregularities in a surface, cleaning and polishing it.

5. (C) Glass has comparatively a better polished and regular surface.

6. (C) Use of ball bearing brings rolling friction which is much less than sliding friction.

7.   (B)   Braking in a vehicle depends on friction between the tyre (wheel) and road surface. Hence the tyres are treaded with grooves to provide better grip (friction) with the ground.

8.   (B)   Powder is a lubricant and reduces friction.

9.   (A)   Rolling reduces friction. Rolling friction is the least amongst rolling, sliding and static friction.

11.   (B)   A stream lined body reduces drag during motion.

14.   (C)   Rolling friction is much less than sliding friction.

15.   (D)   Due to very high speed of meteor through earth's atmosphere, the heat produced by the friction of air is very large to cause the meter burn.

16.   (A)   Due to increased friction, greater frictional heat is produced in the match stick which thus lights up easily.

17.   (B)   Spikes increase friction and prevent slipping.

18.   (D)   Friction can never be made zero.

20.   (C)   When we push the ground with our feet, the friction provides a forward reaction to our push and sends us forward. Walking on slipping ground is difficult because the frictional force is not great enough to prevent slipping

Previous Contest Questions

1.   (C)   Once the body starts sliding, the force needs less than 5 N to move it. Hence sliding friction is less than 5 N.

2.   (B)   Once the applied force overcomes the static friction, the object starts moving and the force applied is a measure of the sliding friction.

3.   (D)   None of the above activity is possible without friction.

5.   (B)   Friction opposes relative motion. In its absence, a moving object will not stop.

6.   (D)   All types of fishes (including whale) and marine animals have stream-lined body to reduce friction during motion in water. Aeroplane is made streamlined to reduce drag in air.

7.   (C)   Correct air pressure helps in reducing deformation of the tyre and also provide an air cushion to reduce rolling friciton.

8.   (A)   Friction exerted by water is much less than a solid. Hence it takes more time to stop a ship in water.

9.   (C)   Due to larger surface area the feather faces more air resistance (friction by air) and hence slows down. Hence the coin moves faster.

10.   (C)   When we walk on road, the friction between the soles of our shoes and the road wears out the soles.

Get It Right

Common misconception	Fact
1. Sound is produced when one objecet collides with another.	1. Sound is produced by a vibrating body.
2. Sound travels in straight line.	2. Sound is a wave motion and travels in all directions.
3. During propogation of sound wave the material of the medium also gets transfered.	3. A wave doesnot transfer material from one place to another. It only transfers energy.

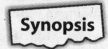

Synopsis

1. Sound is a form of energy the produces sensation of hearing in our ears.
2. Sound is produced when a body vibrates.
3. Sound needs a medium to travel (propagate). It cannot travel in vacuum.
4. Sound travels faster in solid medium (like wood) as compared to water and air.
5. All musical instruments have vibrating parts, which produce sound.
6. In human beings, sound is produced by the voice box or the larynx.
7. We hear though the vibration of our eardrum, whenever sound reaches our ears.
8. The number of oscillations per second is called the frequency of oscillation (f) and is expressed in Hertz (Hz). A ferquency of 1Hz is one oscillation per second.
9. The time needed to complete one oscillation is called time period (T). Hence the number of oscillations per unit time is the frquency of wave

    $f = 1/T$

10. The maximum displacement of the wave crest from the central position on either side is called its amplitude.

11. We differentiate sounds on the basis of their amplitudes and frequencies.

12. A human being can hear sound waves within a range of 20 Hz to 20,000 Hz. Some animals like dog can hear sound higher than 20,000 Hz.

13. Larger the amplitude of vibration, louder is the sound.

14. Loudness of sound is proportional to the square of the amplitude of the vibration producing the sound. The loudness is expressed in a unit called decibel (dB).

15. Shrillness or pitch of a sound depends upon its frequency. Higher the frequency, higher is the pitch and vice-versa.

16. Unwanted sound is noise. These are unpleasant. Loud noise produces noise pollution, which is harmful and may cause hearing impairment.

17. The velocity of sound is approx. 330 m/sec under standard temperature and pressure condition. It varies with temp, pressure, humidity and density of medium.

Multiple Choice Questions

1. When we say 'sound travels in a medium' we mean _____.
   (A) the particles of the medium travel
   (B) the source travels
   (C) the disturbance travels
   (D) the medium travels

2. The speed of sound in solid, liquid and gas can be correctly compared as:
   (A) solid > liquid > gas
   (B) liquid > gas > solid
   (C) liquid > solid > gas
   (D) gas > liquid > gas

3. A person, pressing his ear on the railway tracks can hear an approaching train. This is possible due to:
   (A) vibration of railway tracks
   (B) vibration of air
   (C) more speed of sound in solid medium
   (D) hearing ability of the man

4. A person can be identified by the quality of sound produced by him. The characteristic of a sound can be determined by:

   (A) amplitude   (B) frequency
   (C) loudness   (D) all of the above

5. In humans, the sound is produced by:
   (A) larynx   (B) wind pipe
   (C) vocal cords   (D) lungs

6. The voices of men, women and children are different due to difference in:
   (A) larynx   (B) lungs
   (C) vocal coards   (D) wind pipe

7. An object moving at a speed greater than that of sound is said to be moving at:
   (A) ultrasonic speed
   (B) sonic speed
   (C) infrasonic speed
   (D) supersonic speed

8. In which of three media; air, water and steel, does sound travel the fastest?
   (A) Air   (B) Water
   (C) Steel   (D) none of these

9. The velocity of sound in vacuum is:
   (A) 332 ms–1   (B) 330 ms–1
   (C) 288 ms–1   (D) 0

10. Flash and thunder are produced simultaneously. But thunder is heard a few seconds after the flash is seen. This is because:
    (A) speed of sound is greater than speed of light
    (B) speed of sound is equal to the speed of light
    (C) speed of light is much greater than the speed of sound
    (D) none of these

11. A to and fro motion by an object is also called _____
    (A) periodic motion
    (B) oscillatory motion
    (C) cyclic motion
    (D) none of these

12. An object oscillates 50 times in one second. What would be its frequency?
    (A) 0.2 hz   (B) 0.02 hz
    (C) 0.002 hz   (D) 50 Hz

13. The time period of a simple pendulum is 0.2 sec. What is its frequency of oscillation?
    (A) 0.5 hz   (B) 5 Hz
    (C) 50 Hz   (D) 1 Hz

14. Hertz stands for:
    (A) second   (B) second^{-1}
    (C) meter   (D) meter^{-1}

15. An aeroplane travelling at the speed of sound will have a velocity of:
    (A) 1000 km/hr
    (B) 1180 km/hr
    (C) 1540 k/hr
    (D) 1620 k/hr

16. Sound is produced in a bamboo flute because:
    (A) air starts vibrating
    (B) bamboo starts vibrating
    (C) air hits the bamboo
    (D) direction of air is changed

17. Loudness or intensity of sound depends upon:
    (A) amplitude of sound wave
    (B) area of vibrating body
    (C) distance from the source of sound
    (D) all of above

18. Pitch of sound depends upon:
    (A) frequency
    (B) amplitude
    (C) loudness
    (D) distance of source

19. Vibration of air column produces sound in which of the following instruments?
    (A) Jaltaranga   (B) Flute
    (C) Siren   (D) All of the above

20. Which of the following statement is NOT correct?
    (A) loudness of sound is determined by the amount of energy received by the ear per unit time
    (B) pitch doesn't depend upon the amount of energy
    (C) loudness changes with change of frequency
    (D) pitch changes with change in frequency

21. Birds produce sound by using:
    (A) vocal chord   (B) larynx
    (C) glottis   (D) syrix

22. A source is producing 15 oscillations (waves) in 3 seconds. Find its frequency?
    (A) 15 Hz   (B) 5 Hz
    (C) 0.2 Hz   (D) 0.66 Hz

23. Which of the following is NOT correct?
    (A) more oscillation per second, higher time period
    (B) greater amplitude greater loudness
    (C) higher pitch, higher frequency of vibration
    (D) more the value of decibel, higher is the noise

24. The difference between a muscial sound and noise is:

(A) amplitude   (B) loudness
(C) vibration   (D) all of the above

25. Which of the following sound is NOT a cause of noise pollution?
(A) loud speaker   (B) horn of vehicle
(C) explosion   (D) television

26. Noise pollution can cause:
(A) insmonia
(B) hypertension
(C) hearing impairment
(D) any or all of the above

27. The buzzing sound produced by a mosquito is produced by:

(A) its mouth
(B) vibration of sorrunding air
(C) vibration of wings
(D) none of these

28. Which of the following statement is TRUE?
(A) human ear drum senses the vibration of sound
(B) larger the amplitude of vibration, louder is the sound
(C) higher is the frequency of vibration, lower is the pitch
(D) plantations can reduce noise pollution

Previous Contest Questions

1. The membrane of a drum vibrates to produce sound. Similarly the string of a sitar vibrates to produce sound. Based on these two examples answer the following question. Which part of a whistle vibrates to produce sound?
(A) body of whistle
(B) air
(C) mouth of the person
(D) all of the above

2. When a tuning fork was struck and brought near a bucket of water, a wave as shown in figure was formed on its surface. It the fork is struck much harder and brought near the surface, what will increase?

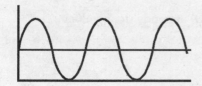

(A) frequency   (B) wavelength
(C) velocity   (D) amplitude

3. By changing length of the scale protruding out of table and vibrating it we can produce sounds of different frequencies. This is possible due to:

(A) change in frequency
(B) change in velocity
(C) change in amplitude
(D) all of the above

4. If you go on increasing the stretching force on a wire in a guitar, its frequency.
(A) increases
(B) decreases
(C) remains unchanged
(D) none of the above

5. A bomb explodes on the moon. How long will it take for the sound to reach the earth?

(A) 10 seconds   (B) 1000 seconds

(C) 1 day   (D) none of these

6. A vibrating body:
   (A) will always produce sound
   (B) may or may not produce sound if the amplitude of vibration is low
   (C) will produce sound which depends upon frequency
   (D) none of the above

7. The graph given here shows the frequency of sounds emitted by a source for 30 seconds. How many seconds of sound a normal human being be able to hear?

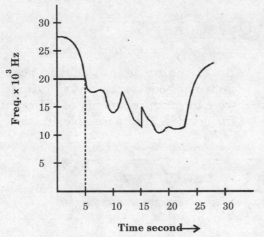

Time second⟶

(A) 10 sec   (B) 20 sec

(C) 30 sec   (D) 05 sec

8. Quality of sound is used to distinguish between:

   (A) Noise and Music

   (B) Two different vibrating bodies

(C) Two notes produced by same vibrating body

(D) all of the above

9. The amplitude of vibration and its frequency can change suddenly in a:

   (A) pitch   (B) musical sound

   (C) noise   (D) all of the above

10. Match the following and choose the

A	String vibration	1. Tabla
B	Membrane vibration	2. Bicycle bell
C	Vibration of air	3. Sitar
D	Vibration of plate	4. Flute

(A) A-1, B-2, C-3, D-4

(B) A-2, B-1, C-4, D-3

(C) A-3, B-1, C-4, D-2

(D) A-4, B-3, C-2, D-1

11. The frequency of a source is 20 kHz. The frequencies of sound wave produced by it in water and air will be:

(A) same as that of source $\sim$ 20 kHz

(B) > 20 kHz

(C) < 20 kHz

(D) depends upon velocity

⊘ Answers ⊘

Multiple Choice Answers

1. C	2. A	3. C	4. D	5. A	6. C	7. D	8. C	9. D	10. C
11. B	12. D	13. B	14. B	15. B	16. A	17. D	18. A	19. D	20. C
21. D	22. B	23. A	24. C	25. D	26. D	27. C	28. C		

Previous Contest Answers

1. B	2. D	3. A	4. A	5. D	6. C	7. B	8. B	9. C	10. C
11. A									

Explanatory Answers

1. (C) In a wave motion (like sound wave), the particles of the medium donot travel. It is the disturbance (energy) which travels along the path.

2. (A) Speed of sound is more in solids, less in liquids and least in gases.

3. (C) Velocity of sound in solid (railway track) is faster than that of air.

4. (D) A sound is characterised by its amplitude, frequency (pitch) and loudness.

5. (A) Sound is produced by larynx or voice box.

6. (C) Two vocal chords, stretched across the larynx in such a way that it leaves a narrow slit between them for passage of air. The length of vocal cords and width of the slit is different in men, women, children thus producing different sounds.

7. (D) Supersonic speed is the speed that is greater than the speed of sound.

8. (C) Sound travels the fastest in solids, then in liquids and the least in gases.

9. (D) Sound cannot travel in vacuum. It needs a medium to travel.

10. (C) This is because the speed of light (flash) is much greater $(3 \times 10^8 \text{ m/sec})$ than the speed of sound (330 m/sec).

12. (D) No. of oscillation per second is called frequency of oscillation.

13. (B) frequency = 1/time period

    = 1/0.2 = 5 Hz

14. (B) Frequency = 1/time period

    = 1/unit of time = second^{-1}

16. (B) Speed of sound

    = 330 m/sec = 330 × 3600

    = 1180 km/hr

17. (A) Sound is produced by vibration of air inside bamboo.

18. (D) Loudness is the characteristic of a sound which distinguishes a feeble sound from a loud sound of same frequency and it depends upon a number of factors.

19. (A) Pitch is the effect produced in the ear due to the sound of some particular frequency.

20. (D) These instruments produce sound based on the vibrations of air columns of different length.

21. (C) Loudness doesn't change with frequency.

22. (D) Birds produce sound by means of a ring of cartilege called syrix, fixed at the begining of their wind pipe.

23. (B) Number of waves produced in 3 seconds = 15

Number of waves produced in 1 second = 15/3 = 5

Hence, frequency of this wave is 5 Hz

24. (A) more oscillations per second, less will be the time period.

25. (C) Musical sound is produced by regular vibration where as noise is produced by irregular vibration.

26. (D) Television in a moderate volume doesn'tproduce noise pollution.

27. (D) Noise pollution is hazardous to health in many ways.

28. (C) A mosquito vibrates its wing at a rate of 500 (approx.). vibrations per second.

29. (C) Hihger is the frequency of vibration, higher is the pitch, and shriller the sound.

Previous Contest Questions

1. (B) The vibrations produced in the air while blowing a whistle, produces sound.

2. (D) The fork will vibrate with a greater amplitude when hit hard. Transfer of this high energy will create higher amplitude on the surface of water.

3. (A) The longer the vibrating material, slower is the oscillation of scale and hence low sound is produced. Shortening the scale causes it to move up and down quickly producing a higher pitched (frequency) sound.

4. (A) $f \alpha \sqrt{\text{tension}}$

5. (D) As there is no atmosphere on the moon, sound does not travel through vacuum.

6. (C) A vibrating body produces sound only if its frequency of vibration is between 10 Hz to 20,000 Hz.

7. (B) Human ear can perceive frequency of vibration between 20 to 20,000 Hz

9. (C) A noise which is produced by irregular vibration can have its vibration and frequency change suddenly.

10. (C) Vibration can be provided by various methods to produce sound.

Chapter 4

Chemical Effects of Electric Current

Common misconception	Fact
1. Electricity is flow of current	1. Electricity is flow of charges.
2. Electricity produced by a battery (cell) is different than the electricity used at home.	2. Both are the same form of electricity.
3. Liquids donot conduct electricity.	3. Most liquid which are solutions of acids, bases and salts are good conductors of electricity
4. Electric current doesn't react chemically with a conducting solution.	4. Passage of electrical current through a conducting solution causes chemical reactions.

Synopsis

1. Materials, which allow electric current to pass through them are good conductors of electricity. Ex.: Metals.

2. Materials which don't allow electric current to pass through them are bad conductors of electricity. Ex.: Wood, Plastic etc.,

3. Human body is a good conductor of electricity. Thus we should take precautions while handling electrical appliances.

4. A bulb glows due to passage of electric current since the filament of the bulb heated to a very high temperature. However, if the current through a circuit is too weak, the filament doesn't get heated sufficiently and it doesn't glow.

5. An LED (Light Emitting Diode) glows even when a weak (small) electric current flows through it.

6. Electric current produces a magnetic effect. It causes a compass needle to deflect.

7. Pure water (distilled water) is a poor conductor of electricity.

8. Most liquids that conduct electricity are solutions of acids, bases and salts.

9. Passage of an electric current through a conducting solution causes chemical reactions. As a result any of the following activities can be observed.

    (a) formation of gas bubbles

    (b) deposit of metals on electrodes

    (c) change in colour of the solution.

10. When electricity is passed through some substances they decompose. Such reactions are called electrodytic reactions. This chemical effect is used to extract elements in metallurgy and for electroplating.

11. The process of depositing a layer of any desired metal on another metal by means of electricity is called electroplating.

12. Chromium plating is done to make the object scratch proof and appear shiny.

13. Tin cans, used to preserve food items / soft drinks are made by electroplating tin onto iron.

14. A coating of zinc is deposited on iron to protect it from corrosion and formation of rust.

15. CFLs (Compact Flourscent Light) consume less electricity as compared to electric bulb and LEDs but contain mercury which is toxic and poses a disposal problem.

Multiple Choice Questions

1. Current is the flow of:
    (A) matter   (B) electrons
    (C) protons   (D) charge

2. In electrolytic solutions, carrier of charge is:
    (A) proton   (B) electron
    (C) neutron   (D) ion

3. Insulators:
    (A) conduct electricity
    (B) do not conduct electricity
    (C) conduct electricity only at low temperatures
    (D) conduct electricity at room temperature

4. Which of the following is an insulator?
    (A) Wood   (B) Iron
    (C) Carbon   (D) Silver

5. In a cell, electrons move from:
    (A) positive electrode to negative electrode
    (B) negative electrode to positive electrode
    (C) both A and B
    (D) electrons do not move and only negative charge moves from one place to another place

6. When an electron moves from negative electrode to positive electrode:
    (A) negative charge moves from negative electrode to positive electrode
    (B) positive charge moves from positive electrode to negative electrode
    (C) no charge flows from either electrode to other electrode
    (D) both A and B

7. When the ends of metal wire are not connected to a battery:

    (A) electrons move from positive electrode to negative electrode

    (B) electrons move from negative electrode to positive electrode

    (C) electrons move in random directions

    (D) protons move in random direction in such a way that their net movement in a unit volume is zero

8. Which of the following statements are true?

    (A) During electrolysis, charge flows through electrolyte solution via electrons

    (B) The randomly moving electrons in a metal wire will start moving in a particular direction when a potential difference is applied across it

    (C) A negatively charged particle has higher electric potential than a positively charged particle

    (D) Charge flows only through negative charge carriers like electrons

9. A cell converts:

    (A) electrical energy into chemical energy

    (B) chemical energy into electrical energy

    (C) magnetic energy into electrical energy

    (D) electrical energy into mechanical energy

10. An electrolyte:
    (A) has positive charge
    (B) has negative charge
    (C) should be able to conduct charge without dissociating
    (D) should able to form positive and negative ions

11. _____ present in the lemon juice acts as electrolyte.
    (A) Sulphuric acid   (B) Nitric acid
    (C) Hydrochloric acid   (D) Citric acid

12. Anode is:
    (A) positively charged electrode
    (B) negatively charged electrode
    (C) wire used to connect the electrodes
    (D) electrolyte which conducts electricity

13. Cathode is:
    (A) positively charged electrode
    (B) negatively charged electrode
    (C) a positively charged ion formed in the electrolyte
    (D) a negatively charged ion formed in the electrolyte

14. Copper electrode:
    (A) donates electrons to hydrogen ions
    (B) accepts electrons from hydrogen ions
    (C) donates electrons to sulphate ions
    (D) accepts electrons from sulphate ions

15. When copper rod donates electrons to hydrogen ions, it gains _____ charge.
    (A) positive   (B) negative
    (C) no charge   (D) can't say

16. The electrolyte in dry cell is:
    (A) copper sulphate
    (B) zinc sulphate
    (C) sulphuric acid
    (D) ammonium chloride

17. In dry cell _____ acts as positive terminal.
    (A) carbon rod
    (B) manganese dioxide
    (C) manganese dioxide and powdered carbon
    (D) metal cap on the carbon rod

18. The common dry cell produces a voltage of:
    (A) 1.5 V   (B) 30 V
    (C) 60 V   (D) 3 V

19. When electric current is flown through a conductor, some amount of:

(A) electrical energy is converted into heat energy

(B) electrical energy is converted into mechanical energy

(C) mechanical energy is converted into electrical energy

(D) heat energy is converted into electrical energy

20. Nichrome is an alloy made of:
(A) nickel and chromium
(B) nitrogen and chromium
(C) nitrogen, chlorine and chromium
(D) nickel, chromium and manganese

21. When current is passed through molten sodium chloride:
(A) sodium is deposited at the positive electrode and chlorine gas is formed at the negative electrode
(B) sodium is evaporated and chloride ions are formed at the negative electrode
(C) sodium is deposited at the positive electrode and chlorine is deposited at the negative electrode
(D) sodium is deposited at the negative electrode and the chlorine gas is formed at the positive electrode

22. Splitting a compound using electricity is called:
(A) electrolysis
(B) electrolyte
(C) electrokinesis
(D) none of the above

23. A bulb in an electric circuit glows due to:
(A) magnetic effect of current
(B) heating effect of current
(C) chemical effect
(D) conduction of current

24. LEDs are extensively used to replace bulbs because:

(A) it consumes less electricity
(B) have longer life
(C) has more power
(D) all of the above

25. Which of the following is a good conductor of electricity?
(A) tap water   (B) distilled water
(C) sea water   (D) rain water

26. A compass placed in an electric field will be deflected due to:
(A) heating effect of current
(B) magnetic effect of current
(C) conducting effect
(D) resistance of the needle to the electric field

27. The most common industrial application of chemical effects of electric current is:
(A) electroplating (B) galvanising
(C) anodising   (D) electrolysis

28. The process of depositing a layer of any desired metal on another material by passing electric current is called:
(A) electrolysis
(B) electroplating
(C) chromium plating
(D) galvanising

29. Tin cans, used for storing food are made by electroplating:
(A) chrome onto tin
(B) iron on to tin
(C) tin onto iron
(D) chrome onto iron

30. To protect iron from corrosion and rust, it is coated by:
(A) Tin   (B) Copper
(C) Zinc   (D) Mercury

Previous Contest Questions

1. In a cell, by convention, charge is taken to be flowing from :
    (A) positive electrode to negative electrode
    (B) negative electrode to positive electrode
    (C) both A and B
    (D) none of the above

2. Metals are good conductors because:
    (A) outer electrons are strongly bound to the atom
    (B) outer electrons are loosely bound to the atom
    (C) inner electrons are loosely bound to the atom
    (D) protons can detach from the nucleus and conduct electricity

3. On electrolysis, water splits into:
    (A) positively charged hydrogen ions and negatively charged oxygen ions
    (B) negatively charged hydrogen ions and positively charged oxygen ions
    (C) hydrogen and oxygen atoms having positive and negative charges respectively
    (D) hydrogen and oxygen atoms having negative and positive charges respectively

4. In electrolysis:
    (A) positive ions move toward the positive electrode and negative ions toward the negative electrode
    (B) positive ions move toward the negative electrode and negative ions toward the positive electrode
    (C) both ions move toward both the electrodes in equal amounts until they are balanced
    (D) none of the above

5. Dilute sulphuric acid splits into:
    (A) oxygen ions and hydrogen ions
    (B) oxygen ions, hydrogen ions and sulphur ions
    (C) hydrogen ions, oxygen ions and sulphate ions
    (D) hydrogen ions and sulphate ions

6. Sulphate ions move toward:
    (A) copper electrode
    (B) battery
    (C) electrolyte
    (D) zinc electrode

7. Ammonium chloride in dry cell is:
    (A) a paste
    (B) in liquid state
    (C) in solid state
    (D) in gaseous state

8. Bulb does not glow when the probs are hanged in air. The reason is:
    (A) air absorbs the electricity
    (B) air is a bad conductor of electricity
    (C) electricity is discharged into air
    (D) air disperses the electricity

9. Iron vessels are coated with tin to:
    (A) give better shining
    (B) increase the strength
    (C) increase weight
    (D) prevent rusting

10. The chemical reaction due to passage of electric current depends on:
    (A) electrodes
    (B) magnitude of current
    (C) density of liquid
    (D) all of the above

⊘ Answers ⊘

Multiple Choice Answers

1. D	2. D	3. B	4. A	5. B	6. D	7. C	8. B	9. B	10. D
11. D	12. A	13. B	14 A	15. A	16. D	17. D	18. A	19. A	20. A
21. D	22. A	23. B	24. D	25. C	26. B	27. A	28. B	29. C	30. C

Previous Contest Answers

1. A	2. B	3. A	4. B	5. D	6. D	7. A	8. B	9. D	10. A

Explanatory Answers

2. (D) In electrolytic solutions, electrolyte splits into positive and negative ions. The charge is moved via ions.

5. (B) In cells, electrons move from negative electrode to positive electrode. And an electron has negative charge. So, we can say that negative charge flows from negative electrode to positive electrode. But, by convention flow of charges are measured only through positive charges. When an electron moves from point A to point B, an equal amount of positive charge moves from point B to point A. So, the direction of charge is from positive electrode to negative electrode.

23. (B) Due to the heating effect of current, the filament of the bulb gets heated to a high temp and it starts glowing.

25. (C) Sea water is saline which is a good conductor.

29. (C) Tine being less reactive than iron is used for containerisation of food items.

Previous Contest Questions

10. (A) The reaction depend on the solution (constituent chemicals) and electrodes.

Chapter 5 — Some Natural Phenomena

Get It Right

Common misconception	Fact
1. High speed winds are accompanied by increased air pressure.	1. High speed winds are accompanied by decreased air pressure.
2. Thunderstorms are same as cyclones.	2. A thunderstorm becomes a cyclone when a very low pressure is accompanied by high speed winds revolving around it.
3. Thunderstorm are always accompanied by lightning	3. Not always. Thunderstorm causes lightning due to vigorous air movement which causes charge separation and then accumulation. When the accumulated charges become very large, electric discharge takes place. This is called lightning.
4. Earthquake are rare and only affects the land mass.	4. Earthquakes occur all the time, all over the earth. Only major earthquakes which cause extensive damage are noticed. It also affects water bodies like oceans / seas. (Ex.: Tsunami).

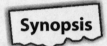
Synopsis

1.   High speed winds are accompanied by reduced air pressure.

2.   Air moves from the region of high pressure to low pressure.

3.   A thunderstorm occurs due to strong upward rising winds along with swift movement of the falling water droplets carried with lightning and sound.

4.   A thunderstorm may develop into a cyclone or a hurricane with wind speed going as high as 200 km / hr.

5.   A tornado is a dark funnel shaped cloud that reaches from the sky to the ground. A tornado may form within cyclones and can reach speed upto 300 km / hr.

6.   Electroscape is an instrument to detect presence of a charge.

7.   An electrical charge can be transferred from a charged object to another through a metal conductor.

8.   The process of transferring of charge from a charged body to the earth is called earthing.

9.   Lightning takes place when large amount of accumulated charges in the clouds passes onto the earth through atmosphere.

10.   Lightning conductors are used to protect tall buildings from the effect of lightning.

11.   An earthquake takes place due to disturbance inside earth's crust.

12.   The weak zones on earth's crust prone to earth quake are known as seismic or fault zones.

13.   The power of an earthquake is expressed in terms of a magnitude on a scale called the Richter scale. Higher the magnitude, more is the damage.

14.   Seismographs are instrument which record tremors produced by the earth.

15.   Lightning, cyclones and earthquake can cause extensive damage to mankind and properties. We should take necessary steps to protect ourselves during such natural calamities.

Multiple Choice Questions

1. The force present between two charged bodies is:
    (A) electrostatic force
    (B) electromagnetic force
    (C) gravitational force
    (D) frictional force

2. When two bodies are rubbed against each other:
    (A) they acquire equal and similar charges
    (B) they acquire equal and opposite charges
    (C) they acquire different charges but in different amounts depending upon their masses
    (D) they do not acquire any charge

3. Suppose you are in a car and it is raining heavily with thunderstorms. Then what is the best way to protect yourself from a possible thunder storm fall?
    (A) Remain in the car
    (B) Get out of the car and take cover under the car
    (C) Run to a nearby tree
    (D) Get out and stand under an electric pole

4. Electric charge is measured in:
    (A) coulombs   (B) amperes
    (C) volts   (D) watts

5. An ebonite rod rubbed with fur and a glass rod rubbed with silk cloth are brought nearer to each other. Then:
    (A) they will attract each other
    (B) they will repel each other
    (C) nothing will happen to them
    (D) they will get heated up

6. When a glass rod is rubbed with silk cloth, it acquires positive charge because:

    (A) electrons are added to it
    (B) electrons are removed from it
    (C) protons are added to it
    (D) protons are removed from it

7. Electroscope is used:
    (A) to detect and test small electric charges
    (B) to calculate the amount of electric charge flowing through the conductor in the given interval of time
    (C) to find out the presence of antimatter
    (D) to test the presence of magnetic field

8. A lightning conductor installed in a building:
    (A) does not allow the lightning to fall on the building
    (B) repels the lightning
    (C) forces the lightning to fall in an area where there are no buildings
    (D) conducts electric charge to the ground when lightning strikes the building

9. Lightning rods are made of :
    (A) copper   (B) plastic
    (C) bakelite   (D) sand paper

10. When you touch a charged body, the charge flows through you into the earth. This is called
    (A) induction   (B) conduction
    (C) capacitance   (D) earthing

11. How do cyclones decrease the fertility of the soil in the coastal areas?
    (A) By flooding the land with saline water
    (B) By dissolving soil and rocks
    (C) By increasing the water table of the place
    (D) By decreasing the water table of the place

12. Which of the following is the first sign of an aproaching cyclone?
    (A) Rains accompanied by lighting
    (B) High temperature and humidity
    (C) Cool breeze and rains
    (D) Powerful water waves

13. Which of the following plays an important role in the early-warning systems for cyclones?
    (A) Helicopters   (B) Submarines
    (C) Satellites   (D) Stars

14. Which of the following is the best thing to do during heavy lightning?
    (A) Lying on the ground in an open place
    (B) Going into the nearest water body
    (C) Staying indoors away from metalic doors or windows
    (D) Standing under a tall tree

15. When we remove polyester or woollen cloth in dark, we can see spark and hear a cracking sound. These are due to:
    (A) static electricity
    (B) current electricity
    (C) reflection of light
    (D) refraction of light

16. Electrical charge can be transferred from a charged object to another through:
    (A) vacuum   (B) air
    (C) insulator   (D) conductor

17. The streaks of bright light seen during lightning is essentially the path followed by:
    (A) UV rays from sun
    (B) cosmic rays
    (C) accumulated electric charges
    (D) none of the above

18. Which of the following is safest way to protect yourself from lightning?
    (A) run to an open field
    (B) open an umbrella for cover
    (C) take shelter under a tree
    (D) squat low on ground

19. A thunderstorm is accompanied by:
    (A) lightning   (B) cyclone
    (C) hurricane   (D) tornado

20. High speed winds are accompanied by:
    (A) increased pressure
    (B) reduced pressure
    (C) water vapour
    (D) static electricity

21. During a cyclone air moves from:
    (A) region of high pressure to low pressure
    (B) region of high pressure to high pressure
    (C) region of low velocity to high velocity
    (D) region of high pressure to low velocity

22. A typhoon is essentially:
    (A) a flood   (B) a cyclone
    (C) earthquake   (D) none of these

23. The natural calamity that cann't be predicted accurately in advance:
    (A) flood   (B) cyclone
    (C) earthquake   (D) famine

24. Earthquakes can cause:
    (A) flood
    (B) land slide
    (C) tsunami
    (D) all of the above

25. Which of the following event can cause earthquake?
    (A) volcanic eruption
    (B) meteor hitting earth
    (C) underground nuclear explosion
    (D) all of the above

26. The weak zones around the boundaries of plates underneath earth, which are prone to slide and cause earthquake are commonly known as:
    (A) fault zone
    (B) eruption zone
    (C) explosive zone
    (D) sliding zone

27. A student named the various layers of earth as shown in the figure wrongly. What is the correct sequence starting from the uppermost layer.

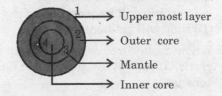

(A) 1. crust   2. outer core
    3. mantle   4. inner core
(B) 1. outer core 2. crust
    3. mantle   4. inner core
(C) 1. crust   2. mantle
    3. outer core 4. inner core
(D) 1. outer core 2. mantle
    3. crust   4. inner core

28. Magnitude of earthquake is measured by:

(A) electroscope   (B) richter scale
(C) seismograph   (D) coubmb

29. In which of the following state earthquake is most likely to occur:
(A) Gujrat   (B) Chhatisgarh
(C) Chennai   (D) Kerala

30. Which of the following country in the world is most prone to earthquake?
(A) India   (B) America
(C) China   (D) Japan

Previous Contest Questions

1.   A negatively charged rod is brought close to two metal spheres which are in contact with each other, and the spheres are separated in the presence of the rod. Then
(A) the sphere close to the rod acquires a negative charge and the other sphere acquires a positive charge
(B) the sphere close to the rod acquires a positive charge and the other sphere acquires a negative charge
(C) both the spheres will acquire positive charge
(D) both the spheres will acquire negative charge

2.   According to law of electrostatics
(A) a charged body attracts similar charged bodies but repels uncharged bodies
(B) a charged body attracts the bodies carrying similar charge and repels the bodies possessing opposite charge
(C) a charged body repels the bodies possessing similar charge and attracts the bodies with opposite charge
(D) a charged body attracts all types of other charged bodies

3.   Which of the following will rise the highest?

(A) Air at 10°C   (B) Air at 40°C
(C) Air at 20°C   (D) Air at –5°C

4.   Which of the following is most likely to be in the 'eye' of a cyclone?
(A) It is an area of high pressure
(B) It is an area of a low pressure
(C) It has lots of clouds and rains
(D) It has high speed winds

5.   During the formation of rain, when water varpour changes back to liquid in the form of rain drops:
(A) heat is absrobed
(B) heat is released
(C) heat is first absorbed and then released
(D) there is no exchange of heat

6.   Which of the following statement is NOT true?
(A) lightning and spark from wollen clothing are essentially the same phenomena.
(B) when you rub a plastic scale on your dry hair, it acquires a charge.
(C) charge acquired by a glass rod when it is rubbed with silk is called as negative charge.
(D) static charges are called so, because they donot move by themselves.

7. Earthing is provided in buildings to protect it from:
    (A) lightning
    (B) leakage of electric current
    (C) cyclone
    (D) thandorstorm

8. Wind currents are generated due to:
    (A) shape of earth
    (B) change in atmospheric pressure
    (C) thunderstorm
    (D) cyclone

9. The fragmented outermost layers of earth are known as:
    (A) crusts   (B) plates
    (C) cores   (D) zones

10. Earthquake at two places A and B were measured by a seismograph which recorded the magnitude as 2 and 4. The magnitude of tremors and its destructive energy at A and B can be compared as under:
    (A) Tremor at B are two times that at place 'A'
    (B) Tremor at B are four times that at place 'A'
    (C) Tremor at B are 100 times that at place 'A'
    (D) Tremor at B are 1000 times that at place 'A'

⊘ Answers ⊘

Multiple Choice Answers

1. A	2. B	3. A	4. A	5. A	6. B	7. A	8. D	9. A	10. D
11. A	12. D	13. C	14. C	15. A	16. D	17. C	18. D	19. A	20. B
21. A	22. B	23. C	24. D	25. D	26. A	27. C	28. B	29. A	30. D

Previous Contest Answers

1. B	2. C	3. B	4. B	5. B	6. C	7. B	8. A	9. B	10. C

Explanatory Answers

11. (A) Salinity is harmful to the plants. During cyclones, the sea waves rise high and flood the land making the soil saline (infertile).

12. (D) Even when the cyclone is very far, strong wings push water towards the shore causing huge water waves.

15. (A) Discharge of static electricity produces spark.

16. (D) Electrical charge passes through a conductor.

17. (C) The accumulated charges on clouds pass through air which is a poor conductor of electricity. When negative and positive charges meet, they produce streaks of bright light and sound.

18. (D) Squatting low on ground will make you the smallest target to be struck. In all other cases you are exposed to the atmosphere.

19. (A) A thunderstorm can be accompanied by lightning and cyclone.

22. (B) A cyclone is known by different names in different parts of the world. In America it is called a "hurricane" and a "typhoon" in Japan.

23. (C) An earthquake is a sudden shaking or trembling of earth. It is so sudden that it can't be predicted well in advance.

24. (D) The disturbance deep in earth's crust can cause flood, land slide or even tsunami (in the sea / ocean)

25. (D) All the above event can cause tremors or earthquake which may or may not be major.

26. (A) The seismic or fault zones are most prone to earthquake.

29. (A) In India, the seismic or fault zores lie below Kashmir, Western and Central Himalays, North-east, Runn of Kutch and Indo-gangetic plane.

30. (D) Japan is most prone to earthquake. People of Japan construct their buildings in a way so that these can withstand major tremors.

Previous Contest Questions

3. (B) Warmer air rises higher. This is beacuse gases expand when they are heated.

5. (B) The energy contained in the gaseous form (vapour) is more than the energy contained in the liquid form (water). Therefore when vapour changes to water it loses some heat.

6. (C) The glass rod acquires negative charge.

7. (B) Earthing is provided in the building to protect us from electrical shocks due to any leakage of electrical current.

8. (A) Uneven heating between the equator and poles (due to shape of earth) causes wind currents. It also occurs due to uneven heating of land and water.

10. (C) Richter scale is not a linear scale. It is a logarithmic scale. A difference in magnitude of '2' implies a multiplication factor of 100.

Chapter 6 Light

Common misconception	Fact
1. We can see light.	1. We can see an object which reflects light that falls on our eyes.
2. Reflection of light takes place only from regular surfaces.	2. Reflection of light takes place both from regular as well as irregular surfaces. However sharp images are formed by regular reflections only.
3. Light can't be split.	3. White light when split through a prism produces seven colours. This is known as dispersion.
4. Image formed inside our eyes is erect.	4. Image formed inside our eyes is inverted.

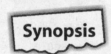

1. White light is composed of seven colours.

2. Light is a form of energy. It is an electromagnetic radiation which can travel through the vacuum with a speed of 3×10^8 m/s.

3. We can see an object only when it reflects or scatters the light falling on it.

4. Light travels along straight lines. This property is known as the rectilinear propagation of light.

5. Any polished or shining surface acts as a mirror and regular reflection takes place.

6. When there is no regular reflection, sharp images are not obtained and cannot be seen by us. This happens because of scattering of light due to irregular reflection.

7. An image which can be obtained on a screen is called a real image.

8. An image which cannot be obtained on a screen is called a virtual image.

9. The image formed by a plane mirror is erect. It is virtual and is of the same size as the object. The image is at the same distance behind the mirror as the object is in front of it.

10. In an image formed by a plane mirror, the left side of the object is seen on the right side in the image, and right side of the object appears to be on the left side in the image. This is known as lateral inversion.

11. The three laws of reflection:

    (a) The incident ray, the normal at the point of incidence and the reflected ray lie in the same plane.

    (b) The incident ray and the reflected ray lie on either side of the normal.

    (c) The angle of incidence is equal to the angle of reflection.

12. If two plane mirrors are placed at an angle between them, a number of images are formed. If the angle between the mirrors is θ, then the number of images formed "n" is given by the formula,

$$n = \left[\frac{360}{\theta} - 1 \right], \text{ if } \frac{360}{\theta} \text{ is even and } n = \frac{360}{\theta}, \text{ if it is odd.}$$

13. Persistence of eye is a phenomenon where the brain continues to sense the image, even after the object has been removed. This illusion plays for a very short time (appr. $\frac{1}{16}$ second).

14. Power of accommodation of the eye

    (i) Our eye consists of a natural lens fixed in its place with the help of ciliary muscles. This lens has a natural power of adjusting its focal length according to requirements. This is the reason why we can distinctly observe the nearer as well as distant objects.

    (ii) When the eye is focussed on a distant object the ciliary muscles are relaxed so that the focal length of the eye lens has its maximum value, which is equal to its distance from the retina. The parallel rays of light falling on our eye are then focussed onto the retina and we can see the object distinctly.

(iii)   When the eye is focussed on a closer object the ciliary muscles contract to decrease the curvature of the lens and the focal length of the lens. The ciliary muscles adjust the focal length in such a way that the image is again formed on the retina and we see the object clearly. This power of adjusting the focal length of the eye is called power of accommodation.

(iv)   As we see more and more closer objects, more and more power of accommodation is to be applied. But there is a limit of applying the power of accommodation because the muscles can not be strained beyond a limit. The nearest point up to which eye can see the objects distinctly is called 'near point of eye' and the distance of the near point from the eye is called 'least distance of distinct vision'.

(v)   The angle subtended by an extended object to our eye is known as visual angle.

15.   Splitting of light into seven colours is known as dispersion of light. Rainbow is a natural phenomenon showing dispersion.

16.   Human eye consists of structures like cornea, iris & pupil.

17.   The iris controls the amount of light entering into the eye.

18.   The retina, on which, the image is formed contains several nerve cells.

19.   Visually challenged persons (blind) can read and write using the braille code.

20.   Visually challenged persons can develop their other senses using non optical aids auditory aids (using sense of hearing) and electronic aids.

Multiple Choice Questions

1.   The surfaces which cannot produce clear images are called:
(A) rough surfaces
(B) ideal surfaces
(C) smooth surfaces
(D) curved surfaces

2.   In order to be used as mirrors, glasses are coated with:
(A) silver   (B) copper
(C) aluminium   (D) platinum

3.   We are able to see objects because:
(A) they absorb light
(B) they reflect light
(C) total internal reflection takes place in them
(D) all the light is refracted through them

4.   The image formed by a plane mirror is:
(A) at the same distance behind the mirror as the object is in front of it
(B) laterally inverted
(C) of the same size as that of the object
(D) all of the above

5.   The phenomenon of light passing through the object is called:
(A) reflection
(B) refraction
(C) dispersion
(D) total internal reflection

6.   The phenomenon of light coming back after hitting a smooth plane surface is called:
(A) reflection
(B) refraction
(C) dispersion
(D) total internal reflection

7. The image formed by a plane mirror is:
    (A) virtual and smaller
    (B) real and laterally inverted
    (C) real and the same size as that of the
        object
    (D) virtual and same size

8. Plane mirrors are arranged parallel to
    each other to get:
    (A) a single image
    (B) two images
    (C) a large number of reflected images
    (D) no image

9. If the angle of incidence is 80^0, what will
    be the angle of reflection with respect
    to the normal drawn perpendicular at
    the point of reflection?
    (A) 80^0
    (B) 100^0
    (C) 160^0
    (D) 20^0

10. The E.N.T. doctor uses a:
    (A) convex mirror
    (B) convex lens
    (C) plane mirror
    (D) concave mirror

11. When the angle between two plane
    mirrors is 60^0, how many multiple
    images will be formed by the mirrors?
    (A) 5   (B) 6
    (C) 7   (D) 8

12. If the angle of incidence is 50^0, then
    calculate the angle between the
    incidence ray and the reflected ray.
    (A) 50^0 (B) 100^0
    (C) 130^0 (D) 80^0

13. In our houses, we use a _____ to
    look at ourselves.
    (A) convex mirror
    (B) concave mirror
    (C) convex lens
    (D) plane mirror

14. The angle of incidence in a plane mirror
    is _____ angle of reflection:

(A) equal to   (B) greater than
(C) less than   (D) none of these

15. ____ are used in telescopes to reflect
    light.
    (A) Concave mirrors
    (B) Convex mirrors
    (C) Plane mirrors
    (D) Convex lenses

16. When a light ray is reflected repeatedly
    by a set of parallel plane mirrors, the
    intensity of light rays decreases after
    some reflections. This is because of:
    (A) poor reflection from mirrors
    (B) absorption of some amount of light
        by mirrors
    (C) dispersion of light when the rays
        travel through the atmosphere
    (D) scattering of light by the mirrors

17. The perpendicular drawn at any point
    on a mirror is called:
    (A) incident ray
    (B) reflected ray
    (C) normal
    (D) image

18. Which of the following statements is
    true?
    (A) The angle of incidence is twice the
        angle of reflection
    (B) The incident ray, the reflected ray
        and the normal drawn at the point
        of incidence lie in the same plane
    (C) Some types of virtual images can be
        caught on the screens.
    (D) A convex mirror forms real image

19. When the distance between the object
    and the plane mirror increases:
    (A) the image remains same
    (B) the size of the image will become
        less than the size of the object
    (C) the distance between the image and
        the plane mirror increases
    (D) the distance between the image and
        the plane mirror decreases

20. In lateral inversion:
     (A) right of the object will be right side
         of the image
     (B) left side of the object will be left side
         of the image
     (C) upside of the object will be down side
         of the object
     (D) right side of the object will be left
         side of the image

21. In a periscope, the reflecting mirrors
     will be:
     (A) perpendicular to each other
     (B) parallel to each other
     (C) at an angle of 45⁰
     (D) at an angle of 60⁰

21. In a periscope, the reflecting mirrors
     will be:
     (A) perpendicular to each other
     (B) parallel to each other
     (C) at an angle of 45^0
     (D) at an angle of 60^0

22. The nature of image formed on the
     retina of human eye is:
     (A) virtual and erect
     (B) virtual and inverted
     (C) real and erect
     (D) real and inverted

23. The presistence of the eye is only for:
     (A) 1/10th of a second
     (B) 1/12th of a second
     (C) 1/16th of a second
     (D) 1/20th of a second

24. The outer layer of the eye is called:
     (A) cornea   (B) sclerotic
     (C) choroid   (D) retina

25. The part which protects the human eye
     is called:
     (A) cornea   (B) chroid
     (C) retina   (D) blind spot

26. The 'pupil' in human eye can be dilated
     by:
     (A) retina   (B) choroid
     (C) optic nerve   (D) iris

27. Which of the following statements about
     human eye is NOT true?
     (A) the iris gives a distinct colour to the
         eye
     (B) the yellow spot is extremely
         sensitive to light
     (C) the space between lens and cornea
         is filled with celiary muscles
     (D) the optic nerves enters the eye near
         the blind spot

28. Cataract is a condition of eye when:

     (A) eye sight becomes fogsy
     (B) eye lens becomes cloudy
     (C) there is a loss of vision
     (D) all of the above

29. Nocturnal animals like owl & bat have:
     (A) large cornea
     (B) large pupil
     (C) retina with large number of rods
     (D) all of the above

30. Night blindness occurs due to deficiency
     of which vitamin?
     (A) A,   (B) B,
     (C) C,   (D) D,

31. The Braille code used by blind people
     use dot patterns for words. How many
     dot patterns or characters are used for
     this code?
     (A) 52,   (B) 63,
     (C) 48,   (D) 26,

Previous Contest Questions

1. Which of the following letters will be seen without any change in a plane mirror?
   (A) S   (B) T
   (C) L   (D) P

2. An ideal mirror:
   (A) absorbs all the amount of light incident on it
   (B) refracts all the light
   (C) reflects all the light
   (D) none of the above

3. Plane mirrors are arranged at an angle to get a number of coloured images in:
   (A) periscope   (B) kaleidoscope
   (C) telescope   (D) thermoscope

4. A series of fast moving still pictures can create an illusion of movement because:
   (A) the eye can focus on very rapidly changing pictures
   (B) eye is quicker than the brain
   (C) eye can separate two images only when the interval of separation between them is one–tenth of a second
   (D) the optical cortex can see through the rapidly moving images.

5. Internal reflections of light is prevented in human eye by:
   (A) iris   (B) pupil
   (C) choroid   (D) blind spot

6. For a normal eye, in case of an adult, the least distance of distinct vision is:
   (A) 5 to 8 cm   (B) 10 to 15 cm
   (C) 20 to 25 cm   (D) 30 to 35 cm

7. The human eye part which can be used again and again for forming different images is called:
   (A) iris   (B) pupil
   (C) cornea   (D) retina

8. The image formed by the eye lens on the retina is:
   (A) real, upright and enlarged
   (B) real, upright and diminished
   (C) real, inverted and diminished
   (D) virtual, inverted and diminished

9. Power of accomodation of eye implies:
   (A) control intensity
   (B) prevent internal reflection of light
   (C) change of focal length of eye lens
   (D) all of the above

⊘ Answers ⊘

Multiple Choice Answers

1. A	2. A	3. B	4. D	5. B	6. A	7. D	8. C	9. A	10. D
11. A	12. B	13. D	14. A	15. C	16. B	17. C	18. B	19. C	20. D
21. B	22. D	23. C	24. B	25. A	26. D	27. C	28. D	29. D	30. A
31. B									

Previous Contest Answers

1. B	2. C	3. B	4. C	5. C	6. C	7. D	8. C	9. C

Explanatory Answers

23. (C) It is a phenomenon where the brain continues to sense the image even after the object has been removed. This lasts for 1/16th of a second.

24. (B) The front of eye forms a transparent curved part called cornea.

25. (A) The front of eye forms a transparent curved part called cornea.

26. (D) Iris contains muscles which dilate the pupil.

27. (C) This space is filled with aqueous humour, a kind of transparent liquid.

28. (D) Cataract occurs at old age and can be cured by introducing a new artificial lens.

29. (D) The nocturnal animals need more light to see at night. The large cornea and pupil allow more light into their eyes.

30. (A) Food components like carrots, green vegetable, spinach, eggs, papaya, mango etc. are rich in vitamin 'A' and must be taken in adequate quantity to prevent night blindness.

31. (B) The dots are arranged in cells of two vertical rows of three dots each for letters.

Previous Contest Questions

1. (B) T is a laterally symmetrical object and hence its image in a plane mirror would be the same as itself.

4. (C) This happens due to a phenomenon called persistence of vision.

5. (C) The inner layer of eye, called the choroid, is black to prevent internal reflections of light inside eye.

6. (C) The point nearest to the eye at which an object is distinctly visible is called the near point of the eye. The distance of the near point of the eye is called the least distance of distinct vision. It varies with age. For an infant it is 5 to 8 cm, for an adult it is 20 to 25 cm.

7. (D) The image formed on retina is not permanent. It persists only for 1/16th of a second. The retina thus can be used again and again to form images.

8. (C) Although the image formed on the retina is inverted and diminished, the optic nerve transmits this message to the brain which reads it as an erect image.

9. (C) The image of the object at different distance from the eye is brought to focus on the retina by changing the focal length of eye lens. This is called the power of accomodation of the eye.

Common misconception	Fact
1. A constellation consists of 5-10 stars which is visible during a night sky.	1. A constellation consists of a large number of stars. However we can only see the brighter ones with our naked eye.
2. A satellite is a man-made object.	2. Any celestial body revolving around another celestial body is called its satelite. Ex.: Moon is satellite of earth. Man-made satellites like intelsat, Edusat have been sent into space for scientific studies / other purposes.

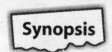

Synopsis

1. Universe is a vast collection of stars, planets, nebulae, galaxies, intergalactic matter and everything that exists in them. It is believed to be formed 15 billion years ago from a huge explosion called 'Big Bang'.

2. To measure distances on astronomical scale, the unit 'light year' is used. It is the distance travelled by light in one year.: $1 \text{ ly} = 9.46 \times 10^{12} \text{ km}$

3. Stars are self–luminous astronomical bodies which produce energy from nuclear fusion reactions. They form from a large collection of gases, called a nebula.

4. A galaxy is a group of billions of stars and other celestial bodies. Galaxies exist in different shapes such as circular, elliptical, ring and irregular. They usually revolve around themselves and move away from each other at tremendous speeds.

5. A group of stars which seem to form a pattern is called a constellation. Ex: Big bear, Orion etc.

6. Sun along with its nine planets, their satellites, asteroids and comets are together named as solar system.

7. Because of earthlike internal structure Mercury, Venus, Earth and Mars are called terrestrial planets. And since Jupiter, Uranus, Saturn and Neptune are made up of mainly gases, they are called gas planets.

8. Asteroids are irregular rocky bodies that revolve around the sun between the orbits of Mars and Jupiter.

9. A comet is a small body of rocks, ice and gases that revolves around the sun in a highly eccentric elliptical orbit.

10. A man–made spacecraft orbiting around an astronomical body is called a satellite. If the orbit of a satellite is synchronised with the earth's rotation it is called geostationary satellite. If a satellite seems to be stationary from the point of view of sun, it is called sun synchronous or polar satellite.

11. Satellites are used for communications, weather forecasting, remote sensing, conducting scientific experiments and for various other military uses.

12. The various shapes of the bright part of the moon as seen during a month are called phases of moon.

13. A planet has a definite path in which it revolves around the sun. This path is called an orbit.

14. Axis of earth is inclined to its orbital plane at an angle of 66.5°. This inclination helps in change of seasons on earth.

15. The time taken by a planet to complete one revolution around the sun is called period of revolution while, the time taken to complete one round around its own axis is called rotation.

Multiple Choice Questions

1. Light year is a unit of:
   (A) time
   (B) intensity of light
   (C) illuminance
   (D) distance

2. The speed of light in vacuum is:
   (A) 330 m/s
   (B) 300,000 m/s
   (C) 300,000 km/s
   (D) 1759 m/s

3. Stars produce energy by:
   (A) burning coal
   (B) burning petroleum
   (C) nuclear reactions
   (D) both A and B

4. Name the closest star to our solar system other than the sun.
   (A) Proxima centauri
   (B) Sirius
   (C) Swati
   (D) Ashwini

5. A group of stars which seem to form a pattern is called:
   (A) nebula   (B) galaxy
   (C) asteroid   (D) constellation

6. A meteoroid that falls on the earth is called:
   (A) asteroid   (B) comet
   (C) meteor   (D) meteorite

7. Which of the following has a highly elongated elliptical orbit?
   (A) Asteroid   (B) Meteor
   (C) Comet   (D) Meteorite

8. The approximate height of a geostationary satellite is:
   (A) 6400 km   (B) 12,800 km
   (C) 7200 km   (D) 36,000 km

9. The first Indian satellite is:
   (A) INSAT   (B) Aryabhatta
   (C) Bhaskara   (D) APPLE

10. Expand ISS:
    (A) International Space Station
    (B) International Space Society
    (C) Indian Space Station
    (D) Internet Society for Semantics

11. Jupiter is a/an:
    (A) terrestrial planet
    (B) gas planet
    (C) asteroid
    (D) hottest planet

12. All stars appear to move from:
    (A) East to west
    (B) West to east
    (C) North to south
    (D) South to north

13. Stars appear to move from east to west because:
    (A) stars actually move from east to west
    (B) stars actually move from west to east
    (C) earth rotates in west to east direction
    (D) earth rotates in east to west direction

14. Orion is a name of:

    (A) star
    (B) planet
    (C) galaxy
    (D) constellation

15. The force that is responsible for the rotation of the earth around the sun is
    (A) electric force:
    (B) magnetic force
    (C) electromagnetic force
    (D) gravitational force

16. Polar satellite orbits around:
    (A) poles
    (B) north pole
    (C) south pole
    (D) equator

17. Satellites revolve in:
    (A) circular and hyperbolic orbits
    (B) elliptical and parabolic orbits
    (C) circular and elliptical orbits
    (D) only in elliptical orbits

18. A spy satellite is deployed in:
    (A) low–earth orbit
    (B) geostationary orbit
    (C) both A and B
    (D) none of the above

19. Ceres is:
    (A) satellite of the Mars
    (B) satellite of the Jupiter
    (C) an asteroid
    (D) a meteorite that fell over Siberia in 1908

20. Name the biggest planet.
    (A) Uranus   (B) Jupiter
    (C) Neptune   (D) Mars

21. The orbits of which two planets intersect with each other?
    (A) Mercury and Venus
    (B) Mars and Jupiter
    (C) Uranus and Neptune
    (D) Neptune and Pluto

22. Name the brightest non–star visible to human eye.
    (A) Moon   (B) Venus
    (C) Mars   (D) Jupiter

23. Brightest planet visible to naked eye is:
    (A) Venus
    (B) Mars
    (C) Jupiter
    (D) Mercury

24. The only moon in the solar system with active volcanoes is:
    (A) Moon   (B) Io
    (C) Titan   (D) Ganymede

25. The largest satellite in the solar system is:
    (A) Moon   (B) Io
    (C) Eros   (D) Ganymede

26. The planet also known as red planet is:
    (A) Mars   (B) Venus
    (C) Earth   (D) Jupiter

27. Geocentric theory, proposed by Ptolemy, states that:

    (A) Sun is the centre of the universe
    (B) Earth is the centre of the universe
    (C) Moon is the centre of the universe
    (D) there is no centre for the universe

28. Heliocentric theory was proposed by:
    (A) Ptolemy   (B) Copernicus
    (C) Newton   (D) Galileo

29. Other than the earth, which other planet has the thick atmospheric layer to absorb harmful ultraviolet rays?
    (A) Mars   (B) Jupiter
    (C) Venus   (D) Mercury

30. The planet also known as "morning star" is:
    (A) Mars   (B) Mercury
    (C) Jupiter   (D) Venus

31. Name the space telescope which was put into orbit in 1990.
    (A) INSAT   (B) Aryabhatta
    (C) Sputnik   (D) Hubble

32. Which of the following planets can be seen with naked eye?
    (A) Mercury, Venus, Uranus, Jupiter
    (B) Mars, Jupiter, Uranus, Neptune
    (C) Mercury, Venus, Uranus, Pluto
    (D) Mercury, Mars, Venus, Jupiter

33. Which planet has "the great red spot"?
    (A) Mars   (B) Venus
    (C) Jupiter   (D) Mercury

34. Name the hottest planet in the solar system.
    (A) Mercury   (B) Venus
    (C) Earth   (D) Mars

35. The biggest of all constellations is:
    (A) Sirius   (B) Hydra
    (C) Andromeda   (D) Ursa minor

36. The space vehicle used to send men on to the moon is:
    (A) Gemini   (B) Apollo
    (C) Sputnik   (D) Discovery

37. Ozone is a compound containing:

(A) oxygen
(B) nitrogen
(C) carbon
(D) carbon and oxygen

38. Ozone is present in:
(A) troposphere   (B) stratosphere
(C) ionosphere   (D) ozonosphere

39. The first man to land on the moon is:
(A) Rakesh sharma
(B) Kalpana Chawla
(C) Yuri Gagarin
(D) Neil Armstrong

40. The number of satellites of Venus is:
(A) one   (B) two
(C) three   (D) zero

41. Expand ISRO.
(A) International Society for Research on Optometry
(B) Indian Satellite and Radar Organisation
(C) Indian Space Research Orga-nisation
(D) Indian Stratosphere Resourcing Organisation

42. Lunar eclipse occurs on:
(A) full moon day
(B) new moon day
(C) both the above
(D) none of the above

43. Solar eclipse occurs on:
(A) full moon day
(B) new moon day
(C) both the above
(D) none of the above

44. Lunar eclipse occurs when the:
(A) sun comes between the earth and the sun
(B) moon comes between the earth and the sun
(C) earth comes between the moon and the sun
(D) when the earth and moon collide with each other

45. Solar eclipse occurs when the:

(A) sun comes between the earth and the moon
(B) moon comes between the earth and the sun
(C) earth comes between the moon and the sun
(D) none of the above

46. Who mathematically proved that the planets revolve around the sun in elliptical orbits?
(A) Isaac Newton
(B) Albert Einstein
(C) Johannes Kepler
(D) Galilei Galileo

47. One cosmic year is equal to:
(A) 365 days   (B) 24 days
(C) 2.25×10^6 days (D) 225×10^6 years

48. Between 1979 and 1999, the farthest planet from the sun is:
(A) Jupiter   (B) Neptune
(C) Uranus   (D) Planet

49. The nearest galaxy to our galaxy is:
(A) Andromeda
(B) X 31
(C) Large magellanic cloud
(D) Small magellanic cloud

50. The planet which takes the maximum time to revolve around itself is:
(A) Mercury
(B) Pluto
(C) Venus
(D) Neptune

51. Halley is the name of a/an:
(A) comet
(B) asteroid
(C) satellite of Jupiter
(D) meteorite

52. The tail of a comet usually extends to:
(A) 10 kilometres
(B) 2 light years
(C) 25 million kilometres
(D) 1.5 billion kilometres

53. Sphere of microscopic dust surrounding the nucleus of a comet is called:
(A) coma   (B) tail
(C) tail   (D) nucleon

54. The height of low–earth satellites ranges between:
(A) 300 – 800 km   (B) 20 – 80 km
(C) 36,000 km   (D) 200 – 7200 km

55. GPS means:
(A) Global Positioning System
(B) Geometrical Processing Satellite
(C) Gestalt Psychological Synchro-nisation
(D) none of the above

56. GSLV means:

(A) Geostationary Satellite Launch Vehicle
(B) German Satellite Launching Vehicle
(C) Global Satellite Locus Verifi-cation System
(D) none of the above

57. In the sun:
(A) hydrogen is converted to helium
(B) helium is converted to hydrogen
(C) hydrogen is converted to uranium
(D) all the above

58. Solar system was formed:
(A) 15 billion years ago
(B) 4.5 billion years ago
(C) 10 billion years ago
(D) 11.5 billion years ago

Previous Contest Questions

1. Stars are mainly made up of:
(A) oxygen and hydrogen
(B) oxygen and nitrogen
(C) hydrogen and helium
(D) water and helium

2. Galaxies:
(A) move toward each other
(B) move away from each other
(C) do not move at all
(D) none of the above

3. Pole star appears to be stationary in all seasons because:
(A) pole star does not rotate on its axis
(B) pole star happens to lie on the axis of equator
(C) pole star happens to lie above the axis of north pole of the earth
(D) pole star is most distant of all the stars

4. Live telecast of a cricket match is possible due to:
(A) geostationary satellite
(B) polar satellite
(C) low–earth orbiting satellite
(D) sun–synchronous satellite

5. Where do you find the "sea of tranquility"?
(A) Moon   (B) Earth
(C) Mercury   (D) Mars

6. Mercury is closer to the sun than the Venus. But Venus is hotter than Mercury. Give reason.
(A) Venus has no atmosphere and Mercury has a thick atmosphere which can retain the heat
(B) Mercury is mostly made up of sedimentary rocks while Venus contains igneous rocks
(C) Mercury being closer to the sun, sun absorbs the heat of the Mercury
(D) All the above

7. Cosmic year is:
(A) the time taken by the earth to revolve around the sun
(B) the time taken by the sun to revolve around itself
(C) the time taken by the earth to revolve around itself
(D) the time taken by our milky way galaxy to revolve around itself

8. The closely packed part of the comet which contains solid particles, stones and frozen water is called:
    (A) coma

    (B) nucleus

    (C) tail

    (D) orbit

(A)

9. The fastest planet of the solar system is:
    (A) Mercury   (B) Uranus
    (C) Jupiter   (D) Neptune

(B)

10. Anurag recorded two observations of the Great Bear and Pole Star in a night as shown here.

(C)

Which of the following will be his recording at 3 A.M. ?

(D)

Answers

Multiple Choice Answers

1. D	2. C	3. C	4. A	5. D	6. D	7. C	8. D	9. B	10. A
11. B	12. A	13. C	14. D	15. D	16. A	17. C	18. A	19. C	20. B
21. D	22. A	23. A	24. B	25. D	26. A	27. B	28. C	29. D	30. D
31. D	32. A	33.C	34. B	35. B	36. B	37. A	38. B	39. D	40. D
41. C	42. A	43. B	44. C	45. B	46. C	47. D	48. B	49. A	50. C
51. A	52. C	53. A	54. A	55. A	56. A	57. A	58. A		

Previous Contest Answers

1. C	2. B	3. C	4. A	5. A	6. A	7. D	8. B	9. D	10. C

Explanatory Answers

Previous Contest Questions

9. (A) Mercury has the shortest period of revolution.

CROSSWORD – II (PHYSICS)

ACROSS

4   Earthquake may cuase this

7   Definite path revolved by a planet around the sun

8   Force opposing motion

9   Frictional force by fluids

14   Toxic substance inside CFL

15   Kicking action as a force

16   Eye muscle which controls pupil

17   Force per unit area

18   Unit of loudness

19   Human body part which produces sound

DOWN

1   Name of a constellation

2   Electroplating is done to prevent

3   A string instrument

5   The red planet

6   A fault zone in earth's layer

9   Splitting of light

10   Shaking of the earth

11   Evening star

12   Script for blind persons

13   Electroscope is used to detect this

NOTE: Answer to this crossword puzzle is given at the end of this book.

Model Test Paper

1. Which of the following property of a substance cannot be changed by application of force?
   (A) Shape
   (B) Size
   (C) elasticity
   (D) reactivity with water

2. A horse tied to a cart is standing stationary on road. Which of the following statement is CORRECT?
   (A) Horse is applying force on the cart
   (B) Cart is applying force on the horse
   (C) Force applied by the horse is balanced by the force applied by the cart
   (D) No force is being applied by the horse or the cart

3. A force is a result of:
   (A) interaction between two bodies
   (B) interaction of one body with itself
   (C) friction
   (D) all of the above

4. You can increase the amount of force applied on a body by repeatedly:
   (A) pushing it
   (B) pulling it
   (C) dragging it
   (D) any or all of the above

5. Which of the following statement is NOT true?
   (A) State of rest of a body is same as state of zero speed
   (B) Human body converts chemical energy into muscular force

   (C) Water in river flows down due to its kinetic energy
   (D) Liquids exert pressure on the walls of the container

6. Take a glass full of water (fig. A) put a piece of thick card on it. Now turn the glass upside down as shown in fig. B

   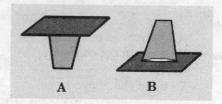

   A   B

   What will happen?
   (A) The card will not fall
   (B) The card will fall down
   (C) Water will leak through the sides
   (D) None of the above

7. You tend to slip when step on a banana peel lying on a smooth surface. This is due to:
   (A) increased friction
   (B) reduced friction
   (C) gravity
   (D) Characteristics of the banana peel

8. Which of the following is easier to hold with a greasy palm?
   (A) a glass tumbler
   (B) a polished crockery piece
   (C) a metal container
   (D) an earthen pot

9.   Our palms get warmed up when rubbed together. This is because of:
(A) kinetic energy
(B) friction
(C) electrostatic force
(D) all of the above

10.   Treading of tyre is done to:
(A) increase friction
(B) reduce friction
(C) get more mileage
(D) drive comfortably

11.   Which of the following cannot be used as a lubricant?
(A) grease   (B) powder
(C) air   (D) paper

12.   Wheels reduce friction due to:
(A) more area of contact
(B) less area of contact
(C) size
(D) all of the above

13.   A pendulum vibrates with a frequency of 1 Hz. The sound produced by it is:
(A) supersonic   (B) audible
(C) infrasonic   (D) ultrasonic

14.   Match the following and choose the correct answer.

Table A	Table B
a. Microphone	1. Wind energy to mechanical energy
b. Speaker	2. Mechanical to sound energy
c. Harmonium	3. Electrical to sound energy
d. Sails of a ship	4. Sound to electrical energy

(A) a-4, b-3, c-1, d-2   (B) a-1, b-2, c-3, d-4

(C) a-4, b-2, c-3, d-1   (D) a-4, b-3, c-2, d-1

15.   The nerve that carries the signals from the ear to the brains is called:

(A) auditory nerve
(B) optic nerve
(C) motor nerve
(D) spinal cord

16.   Which of the following is a percussion instrument?
(A) Violin   (B) Mridangam
(C) Flute   (D) Clarinet

17.   A wind instrument:
(A) Jazz   (B) Tabla
(C) Saxophone   (D) Sitar

18.   One can be recognised by his voice due to the uniqueness of:
(A) quality   (B) amplitude
(C) pitch   (D) all of the above

19.   Thermocol is a:
(A) good reflector of sound
(B) good absorber of sound
(C) bad absorber of sound
(D) good conductor of sound

20.   The equipment based on properties of sound used for medical purposes is based on:
(A) audio frquency
(B) infrasonic
(C) ultrasonic
(D) frequency ranging from 20 Hz to 20 KH$_z$

21.   Overhead electrical wires are not insulated because:
(A) air is a good conductor
(B) air is a bad conductor
(C) air offers friction
(D) to prevent theft

22.   Which of the following statements is NOT true?

(A) Vegetables conduct electricity

(B) Passage of electric current will not change the colour of a solution

(C) An electrode conducts electricity

(D) Electroplating is one of the applications of chemical effects of electrical current

23. If a body acquires electric charge temporarily under the influence of charged body, then the process is called:
   (A) conduction   (B) induction
   (C) radiation   (D) dispersion

24. A brass rod is rubbed with fur cloth. The rod acquires:
   (A) positive charge
   (B) negative charge
   (C) doesn't acquire any charge
   (D) acquires both positive and negative charge

25. Match the following and choose the correct answer.

Table A	Table B
a. conductor	1. plastic
b. charge at rest	2. current electricity
c. moving charge	3. electrostatics
d. insulator	4. copper

(A) c-1 d-2, b-3, a-4   (B) d-1, c-2, a-3, b-4

(C) c-4, d-2, b-3, a-1   (D) d-1, c-2, b-3, a-4

26. The word "earthing" also implies:
   (A) charging of a body
   (B) discharging of a body
   (C) putting a body on the surface of earth
   (D) putting a body under the surface of earth

27. A lightning conductor is a:
   (A) good conductor
   (B) bad conductor
   (C) detection device
   (D) device to block static electricity

28. Match the following and choose the correct answer.

Table A	Table B
a. Earthquake	1. Prevent leakage
b. Lightning	2. Fault zone
c. Insulation	3. Detection of charge
d. Electroscope	4. Earthing

(A) a-2 b-4, c-1, d-3   (B) a-3, b-4, c-2, d-1

(C) a-4, b-3, c-2, d-1   (D) a-1, b-2, c-3, d-4

29. What is wrong in this figure.

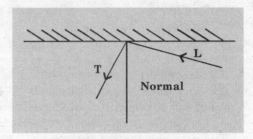

(A) angle of incidence is equal to angle of reflection
(B) angle of incidence is greater than to angle of reflection
(C) Normal is not perpendicular to incident ray
(D) Normal is not perpendicular to reflected ray

30. Phases of mmon occur due to:
   (A) rotation of moon
   (B) revolution of moon
   (C) rotation of earth
   (D) revelution of earth

31. The given figure shows the cross section of a dam and its reservoir. The widening of the wall, towards the bottom is because of _____

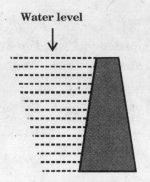

Water level

Thickness of wall

(A) increase in pressure with depth of water
(B) decrease pressure with depth of water
(C) change in density of water
(D) increase in mass of the wall

32. A force of 16 N is distributed uniformly on one surface of a cube of edge '8' cm. The pressure on this surface is:

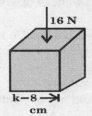

16 N

k–8→
cm

(A) 3500 pa   (B) 2500 pa
(C) 4500 pa   (D) 2000 pa

33. A force of 5 N is required to move an object from rest. The value of static friction (f) is:

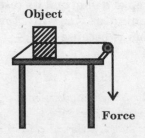

Object

Force

(A) 5 N   (B) f > 5 N
(C) f < 5 N   (D) 10 N

34. In which of the following cases, the speed of the ball will be more?

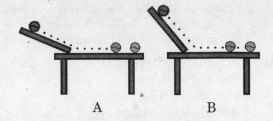

A   B

(A) A > B
(B) B > A
(C) In both cases speed will be same
(D) None of the above

35. Correct air pressure in our vehicle tyres help to reduce.
(A) static friction
(B) sliding friction
(C) rolling friction
(D) all of the above

36. A person, pressing his ear on the railway tracks can hear an approaching train. This is possible due to:
(A) vibration of railway tracks
(B) vibration of air
(C) more speed of sound in solid medium
(D) hearing ability of the man

37. Vibration of air column produces sound in which of the following instruments?
(A) Jaltaranga   (B) Flute
(C) Siren   (D) All of the above

38. By changing length of the scale protruding out of table and vibrating it we can produce sounds of different frequencies. This is possible due to:

(A) change in frequency
(B) change in velocity
(C) change in amplitude
(D) all of the above

39. Which of the following statements are true?

(A) During electrolysis, charge flows through electrolyte solution via electrons

(B) The randomly moving electrons in a metal wire will start moving in a particular direction when a potential difference is applied across it

(C) A negatively charged particle has higher electric potential than a positively charged particle

(D) Charge flows only through negative charge carriers like electrons

40. An electrolyte:
(A) has positive charge
(B) has negative charge
(C) should be able to conduct charge without dissociating
(D) should able to form positive and negative ions

41. LEDs are extensively used to replace bulbs because:
(A) it consumes less electricity
(B) have longer life
(C) has more power
(D) all of the above

42. In electrolysis
(A) positive ions move toward the positive electrode and negative ions toward the negative electrode
(B) positive ions move toward the negative electrode and negative ions toward the positive electrode

(C) both ions move toward both the electrodes in equal amounts until they are balanced
(D) none of the above

43. When we remove polyester or woollen cloth in dark, we can see spark and hear a cracking sound. These are due to:
(A) static electricity
(B) current electricity
(C) reflection of light
(D) refraction of light

44. The weak zones around the boundaries of plates underneath earth, which are prone to slide and cause earthquakeare commonly known as:
(A) fault zone
(B) eruption zone
(C) explosive zone
(D) sliding zone

45. Wind currents are generated due to:
(A) shape of earth
(B) change in atmospheric pressure
(C) thunderstorm
(D) cyclone

46. When the distance between the object and the plane mirror increases:
(A) the image remains same
(B) the size of the image will become less than the size of the object
(C) the distance between the image and the plane mirror increases
(D) the distance between the image and the plane mirror decreases

47. Which of the following letters will be seen without any change in a plane mirror?
(A) S   (B) T
(C) L   (D) P

48. Power of accomodation of eye implies:
(A) control intensity
(B) prevent internal reflection of light

(C) change of focal length of eye lens

(D) all of the above

49. Lunar eclipse occurs when the:

   (A) sun comes between the earth and the sun

   (B) moon comes between the earth and the sun

   (C) earth comes between the moon and the sun

   (D) when the earth and moon collide with each other

50. Mercury is closer to the sun than the Venus. But Venus is hotter than Mercury. Give reason.

   (A) Venus has no atmosphere and Mercury has a thick atmosphere which can retain the heat

   (B) Mercury is mostly made up of sedimentary rocks while Venus contains igneous rocks

   (C) Mercury being closer to the sun, sun absorbs the heat of the Mercury

   (D) All the above

⊘ Answers ⊘

Model Test Paper

1. D	2. D	3. A	4. D	5. C	6. A	7. B	8. D	9. B	10. A
11. D	12. B	13. C	14. D	15. A	16. B	17. C	18. C	19. B	20. C
21. B	22. B	23. B	24. C	25. D	26. B	27. A	28. A	29. B	30. B
31. A	32. B	33. A	34. C	35. C	36. C	37. D	38. A	39. B	40. D
41. D	42. B	43. A	44. A	45. A	46. C	47. B	48. C	49. C	50. A

CHEMISTRY

Chapter 1

Synthetic Fibres & Plastics

Get It Right

Common misconception	Fact
1. Fibres are synthetic.	Fibres are synthetic as well as natural. Cotton, wool, silk etc., are natural fibres, while rayon, nylon etc., are synthetic fibre.
2. All forms of plastic are remouldable.	Thermosetting plastics (e.g.: bakelite and melamine) can be moulded only once. These can't be softened by heating.

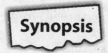

Synopsis

1. Natural fibres like cotton is obtained from plant, while wool and silk fibres are obtained from animals.

2. The rearing of silkworms for obtaining silk is called sericulture.

3. Silk fibres are made up of a protein.

4. Rayon is made from wood pulp while nylon is made from coal, air and water.

5. Nylon by far the most used synthetic fibre is prepared from coal, water and air.

6. Many articles like socks, ropes, tents, parachute etc., are made from nylon. A nylon thread is stronger than a steel wire.

7. Polyester is made up of esters. Polycot, polywool, terry cot etc., are products prepared by mixing two kinds of fibres.

8. Synthetic fibres are durable, less expensive and dry up fast.

9. Plastic because of mouldability finds versatile use. Thermoplastics like PVC and polythene can be remoulded, while thermosetting plastics (like bakelite and melamine) can't be remoulded.

10. Thermosetting plastics are used as kitchen ware and also for electrical switches and handles.

11. Plastic is non-reactive and doesn't corrode easily, hence suitable as containers of food, but are non-biodegradable.

12. Waste created by plastics is not ecofriendly. Burning of plastic releases poisonous gases. Hence these shouldn't be disposed by burning.

13. We should reduce use of plastic.

14. Polybags carelessly thrown are responsible for clogging the drains and also health problems for animals since cows and other stray animals sometimes swallow plastic bags and choke their respiratory system.

15. Use the 4R principle for use of plastic. Reduce, reuse, recycle and recover.

Multiple Choice Questions

1. Wool is obtained from _____ of sheep.
    (A) Skin   (B) Toes
    (C) Fleece   (D) All of the above

2. The process of obtaining wool is:
    (A) shearing, sorting, scouring and dyeing
    (B) shearing, scouring, sorting and dyeing
    (C) scouring, sorting, shearing and dyeing
    (D) sorting, scouring, shearing and dyeing

3. The sorter's disease is caused by a bacteria:
    (A) anthrax   (B) bacillus
    (B) virus   (D) aedes

4. The rearing of silk worms for obtaining silk is called:
    (A) pisciculture
    (B) sericulture
    (C) polyculture
    (D) arboriculture

5. Silk is obtained from _____ of the silk moth.
    (A) pupa   (B) larva
    (C) cocoon   (D) caterpillar

6. The process of taking out threads from the cocoon is known as:
    (A) rearing   (B) sorting
    (C) scouring   (D) reeling

7. Silk fibres are made up of:
    (A) vitamin
    (B) carbohydrates
    (C) protein
    (D) none of the above

8. Nylon is obtained from:
    (A) coal
    (B) air
    (C) water
    (D) all of the above

9. Nylon is useful because of following properties:
    (A) soft, strong and light
    (B) transparent, light and easy to wash
    (C) strong, elastic and light
    (D) hard, inexpensive and strong

10. Which of the following statement is TRUE?
    (A) A nylon thread is stronger than a steel wire
    (B) Rayon is a natural fibre made from wood pulp
    (C) Cotton is not a polymer
    (D) Fabric made from polyester can get wrinkles easily

11. Which of the following statements is NOT true?
    (A) Polymer occur in nature
    (B) Cellulose is made up of glucose units
    (C) Nylon is used to make parachute
    (D) Cotton thread is stronger than nylon thread

12. PET is a familiar form of:
    (A) plastic   (B) polyester
    (C) acrylic   (D) rayon

13. Fruits have their characteristic smell because of a chemical known as:
    (A) yeast   (B) aedes
    (C) cellulose   (D) esters

14. Which part of the cotton plant yields cotton balls?
    (A) Leaf   (B) Fruit
    (C) Seed   (D) Flower

15. Jute fibre is obtained from the _____ of jute plant.
    (A) leaves   (B) seeds
    (C) roots   (D) stem

16. Which of the following articles is made by using only man-made substances?

    (A)   (B)
    (C)   (D)

17. Which of the following is made from coconut fibres?

    (A) Sweaters   (B) Shoes
    (C) Mattresses   (D) Sarees

18. The two main processes of making fabrics are:
    (A) ginning and weaving
    (B) weaving and knitting
    (C) weaving and spinning
    (D) none of these

19. Which of the following statements is not true?
    (A) Fabric is made of yarn
    (B) Jute is the outer covering of coconut
    (C) Polyester is a synthetic fibre
    (D) Silk fibre is obtained from silk worms

20. Plastics find extensive use because:
    (A) plastic is a polymer
    (B) plastic has a linear arrangement of units
    (C) it is easily mouldable
    (D) it is synthetic

21. PVC is an example of:
    (A) polyethene
    (B) thermoplastic
    (C) thermosetting plastic
    (D) acrylic

22. Which of the following properties of plastic make it most convenient to use?
    (A) It is non-reactive
    (B) Light, strong and durable
    (C) Easily remouldable
    (D) All of the above

23. During long distance travel you would like to take drinking water in a bottle made up of:
    (A) glass   (B) plastic
    (C) leather   (D) steel

24. The raw materials used to prepare synthetic fibres like polyester and acrylic is:
    (A) wood pulp   (B) coconut jute
    (C) petrochemicals (D) paper pulp

25. Match column 'A' with column 'B'.

A. Fibre	B. Use
1. Silk	a. Rope
2. Nylon	b. Sweater
3. Acrylic	c. Bottle
4. Plastic	d. Saree

(A) a_1, b_2, c_3, d_4 (B) a_2, b_1, c_3, d_4
(C) a_3, b_2, c_4, d_1 (D) a_2, b_3, c_4, d_1

26. Which of the following is non-biodegradable:
(A) plastic
(B) cotton
(C) paper
(D) left over food stuff

27. Polyethene is produced by:
(A) isomerization (B) polymerisation
(C) hydrogenation (D) all of the above

28. The plastic product which can be remoulded:

(A) bakelite   (B) melamine
(C) polyethene   (D) polycot

29. Which of the following products can't be decomposed easily?
(A) Acrylic   (B) Polyethene
(C) Plastic   (D) All of the above

30. Coating of melamine plastic is used as:
(A) good conductor of heat
(B) strong and durable
(C) fire proof plastic
(D) plastic cook ware

31. Terrycot fibre is made using:
(A) wood pulp   (B) esters
(C) acrylic   (D) paper pulp

32. When you visit a hill station, which of the following you should use for shopping?
(A) bags made of cotton
(B) bags made of polyethene
(C) bags made of paper
(D) bags made of nylon

Previous Contest Questions

1. Rayon or artificial silk is obtained from:
(A) cocoon   (B) petroleum
(C) silk fibre   (D) wood pulp

2. Artificial (man made) wool is known by the name:
(A) rayon   (B) acrylic
(C) polycot   (D) none of these

3. Which type of cloth dries faster in rainy season?
(A) Cotton   (B) Wool
(C) Polyester   (D) Silk

4. What cloth should you wear while cooking in the kitchen?
(A) Rayon   (B) Cotton
(C) Polyester   (D) Polycot

5. Which of the following is NOT true?

(A) Thermosetting plastic are bad conductors of heat and electricity
(B) Thermoplastics are good conductor of heat and electricity
(C) Plastic do not get corroded easily
(D) Plastic is also a polymer

6. Which of the following is a property of plastic:
(A) flame resistant (B) noncorrosive
(C) mouldable   (D) all of the above

7. To which of the following 4R principle apply most?
(A) Synthetic fibre (B) Natural fibre
(C) Metals   (D) Plastic

8. Which of the following material take the longest to degenerate:
(A) paper   (B) cotton cloth
(C) tin can   (D) plastic bags

⊘ Answers ⊘

Multiple Choice Answers

1. C	2. B	3. A	4. B	5. C	6. D	7. C	8. D	9. C	10. A
11. D	12. B	13. D	14. B	15. D	16. B	17. C	18. C	19. B	20. C
21. B	22. D	23. B	24. C	25. D	26. A	27. B	28. C	29. D	30. C
31. B	32. A								

Previous Contest Answers

1. D	2. B	3. C	4. B	5. B	6. D	7. D	8. C

Explanatory Answers

Multiple Choice Questions:

1. (C) Wool is obtained from fleece (hair) of sheep or yak.

3. (A) Anthrax causes a fatal blood disease known as sorter's disease.

5. (C) The caterpillar covers itself by silk fibres known as cocoons.

6. (D) Reeling the silk is done in special machines.

7. (C) The caterpillar secretes fibres made of a protein which hardens on exposure to air and become silk fibre.

8. (D) Nylon was the first fully synthetic fibre obtained from coal, water and air.

9. (C) Nylon is very popular for these properties.

11. (D) Nylon thread is stronger than cotton thread.

12. (B) PET is used for making bottles (Pearl PET).

23. (B) Plastic is light, durable and doesn't react chemically with water.

24. (C) Most of the synthetic fibres are prepared from petrochemicals.

27. (B) In polymerisation, molecules of same compounds are joined together to form a polymer.

29. (D) All synthetic product/chemicals are non-biodegradable and do not get decomposed easily.

30. (C) Coating of melamine plastic makes a cloth flame resistant, used by firemen.

32. (A) Hill stations are crowded and have waste disposal problem. Thus plastic use should be minimum. Some hill stations like Nainital, have banned use of polyethene bags.

Previous Questions:

1. (D) Although rayon is obtained from a natural source wood pulp, yet it is a man made fibre.

2. (B) Acrylic used for sweaters, shawls and blankets. These synthetic fibres are cheap and comes in variety of colours.

3. (C) Synthetic fibres like polyesters dry up quickly.

4. (B) Synthetic fibres melt on heating. Therefore it is not safe while cooking. It the clothes catch fire it can be disastrous. Cotton cloth is best and safe.

5. (B) All types of plastics are bad conductor of heat and electricity.

6. (D) Plastic as such is not flame resistant but thermosetting plastic resist fire and can be used as kitchen ware.

7. (D) The 4R principle i.e., reduce, reuse, recycle and recover is most suited for use of plastic.

8. (C) Tin, aluminium and other metal cans may take 100 to 500 years to degenerate.

Common misconception	Fact
1. All metals are solid and hard.	Metals like sodium and potassium are soft and can be cut with a knife. Mercury is the only metal which is liquid.
2. Non-metals are bad conductors of heat and electricity.	Graphite is a good conductor of electricity.
3. All metals and non-metals have different, distinctive properties and hence can be differentiated easily.	Elements like antimony and arsenic have properties of both metals and non-metals Such substances are called metalloids.

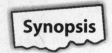

Synopsis

(A) METALS:

(1) Metals occur in combined state or in the form of compounds.

(2) Most metals are solids at room temperature except mercury which is liquid.

(3) Most metals have high densities because their atoms form close clusters.

(4) Most metals shine and can be easily polished.

(5) Metals are malleable or can be hammered into thin sheets. They are also ductile or can be drawn into thin wires.

(6) Metals are sonorous because they produce sound when struck.

(7) Most metals are good conductors of heat and electricity.

(8) Metals combine with oxygen to produce basic oxides.

$$4Na + O_2 \rightarrow 2Na_2O$$

(9) Metals react with water to form oxides and hydroxides.

$$Na + 2H_2O \rightarrow 2NaOH + H_2$$

$$Mg + H_2O \rightarrow MgO + H_2$$

(10) Metals react with dilute hydrochloric and sulphuric acids to produce salt and hydrogen.

$$2Na + 2HCl \rightarrow 2NaCl + H_2$$

$$2Na + H_2SO_4 \rightarrow Na_2SO_4 + H_2$$

(11) Metals displace one another from their salts in the order shown in electrochemical series.

$$Mg + 2HCl \rightarrow MgCl_2 + H_2$$

(12) Metals react with chlorine to form chlorides.

$$Ca + Cl_2 \rightarrow CaCl_2$$

(B) NONMETALS:

(1) Nonmetals occur in free state as well as in combined state.

(2) Many nonmetals are liquids or gases at room temperature.

(3) Nonmetals look dull. Many of them are coloured.

(4) Nonmetals are neither malleable nor ductile.

(5) They do not produce sound when struck.

(6) They are bad conductors of heat and electricity.

(7) Nonmetals combine with oxygen to produce acidic or neutral oxides.

$$2N_2 + O_2 \rightarrow 2N_2O$$

$$S + O_2 \rightarrow SO_2$$

(8) Nonmetals cannot displace hydrogen from dilute acids and water. Thus they do not react with them.

(9) Nonmetals react with hydrogen to form covalent compounds.

$$H_2 + S \rightarrow H_2S$$

(10) Nonmetals react with chlorine to form covalent chlorides.

$$P_4 + 6Cl_2 \rightarrow 4PCl_3$$

(C)   USES OF METALS:

(1)   Iron:

It is used in making pipes, tanks, cylinders, agricultural tools, mails, etc. Steel is used to make bridges, ships, buildings, utensils and machine parts. Steel is formed by mixing iron with other elements.

(2)   Copper:

It is a good conductor of heat and electricity. It is used in making electric wires, cables and utensils.

(3)   Aluminium

It is light, strong and has high tensile strength. It is used to make bodies of aircraft, automobiles, machine tools and parts.

(4)   Zinc

Zinc does not rust easily and is used to coat iron sheets by a process known as galvanising.

(5)   Mercury

Its property of not wetting glass and expanding a lot when heated makes it ideal for use in thermometers.

(6)   Silver

The lustre of this metal has made it popular for making jewellery. Things made of other metals are often coated with a protective layer of silver called electroplating.

(7)   Gold

Gold is used for making jewellery, plating metals and in medicines. The purity of gold is measured in carats. Pure gold is 24 carat.

(D)   USE OF NONMETALS:

(1)   Carbon

Both graphite and diamond are allotropic forms of carbon. Graphite is used to make the lead of pencil and crucibles. Diamond is used to make tools for cutting and grinding glass and rocks. It is also used in jewellery.

(2)   Sulphur

Sulphur is used in the manufacture of sulphuric acid, gunpowder, dyes, matches and fireworks. It is also used to treat rubber in a process called vulcanisation.

(3)   Phosphorus

Match–heads and fertilisers contain phosphorus.

(4) Hydrogen

It is used to manufacture ammonia and hydrogen chloride. Vegetable oil is treated with hydrogen, it becomes solid like butter. This process is known as hydrogenation of vegetable oils. It is used for cooking.

(5) Silicon

It is a semiconductor. It is used to make water proof materials, polishes and as an insulator in the electrical appliances.

Alloys:

Alloys are homogenous mixtures of two or more metals. Some of them may contain traces of nonmetals.

(a) Brass

It contains 60% copper and 40% zinc. It is used to make electronic equipment and parts of telescopes and microscopes.

(b) Bronze

It contains 90% copper and 10% tin. It is used to make statues, coins, bells and parts of some machines.

(c) Solder

This alloy is made of lead and tin. It is used for joining electric wires.

(d) Stainless steel

It consists of iron, carbon, chromium and nickel. It is used to make ships, bridges, railway lines, machinery, buildings, etc.

(e) Duralumin

It consists of aluminium, copper, magnesium and manganese. It is used to make bodies of aeroplanes, automobiles, spacecraft, ships and pressure cookers.

Corrosion of metals:

The slow destruction of material by chemical reaction is called corrosion.

Preventing corrosion:

The methods are:

1. Use paint or grease to prevent the contact with air,

2. Coating with another metal

3. Alloying.

Multiple Choice Questions

1. Metals generally have _____ number of electrons in their valence shell.
    (A) 1, 2 or 3   (B) 7, 8 or 9
    (C) 10, 11 or 12   (D) 20, 30 or 40

2. Nonmetals contain _____ number of electrons in their outmost shell.
    (A) 1, 2 or 3   (B) 8, 9 or 10
    (C) 10, 20 or 30   (D) 5, 6 or 7

3. Nonmetals form:
    (A) cations
    (B) anions
    (C) anions and cations
    (D) do not form ions

4. To become stable, metals:
    (A) lose or gain electrons
    (B) neither lose nor gain electrons
    (C) lose electrons
    (D) gain electrons

5. Metals tends to form:
    (A) cations
    (B) anions
    (C) cations and anions
    (D) do not form ions

6. Antimony and arsenic belong to the category of:
    (A) metals   (B) metalloids
    (C) nonmetals   (D) minerals

7. Noble gases do not react because they have _____ electrons in their valence shell.
    (A) 3   (B) 6
    (C) 1   (D) 8

8. The element present below hydrogen in electrochemical series is:
    (A) Mg   (B) Hg
    (C) Pb   (D) Sn

9. The metal which can replace magnesium from its salt is:
    (A) Ca   (B) Al
    (C) Zn   (D) Fe

10. The most reactive of the following metals is:
    (A) Ca   (B) Al
    (C) Ni   (D) Pb

11. Metals can be hammered into thin sheets. This property is called:
    (A) density   (B) malleability
    (C) ductility   (D) strength

12. Metal which is the best conductor of electricity:
    (A) nickel   (B) silver
    (C) gold   (D) sodium

13. The colour of iodine is:
    (A) violet   (B) green
    (C) white   (D) brown

14. The nonmetal which exhibits yellow colour is:
    (A) silicon   (B) phosphorus
    (C) sulphur   (D) carbon

15. Which of the following is a property of nonmetals?
    (A) Low densities
    (B) Low melting points
    (C) Poor conductor of electricity
    (D) All the three

16. The nonmetal which is a liquid at room temperature is:
    (A) chlorine   (B) nitrogen
    (C) bromine   (D) hydrogen

17. Metal which does not react with HCl is:
    (A) Ag   (B) Mg
    (C) Al   (D) Fe

18. Metal which reacts vigorously with HCl to produce salt and hydrogen is:
    (A) Na   (B) Zn
    (C) Sn   (D) Pb

19. $Cu + HCl \rightarrow$ _____.
    (A) react vigorously
    (B) no reaction
    (C) react modestly
    (D) react slowly

20. The metal with which hydrogen reacts to form metal hydride is:
    (A) Hg   (B) Ca
    (C) Ag   (D) H

21. Nonmetals combine with oxygen to produce:
    (A) acidic oxides
    (B) basic oxide
    (C) amphoteric oxide
    (D) none of these

22. The oxides of nonmetal which is neutral is:
    (A) SO_2 (B) NO_2
    (C) P_2O_3 (D) CO

23. Phosphorus combine with oxygen to form _____ types of oxides.
    (A) three   (B) two
    (C) one   (D) four

24. _____ dissolves in water to produce sulphuric acid.
    (A) SO_2 (B) S
    (C) SO_3 (D) $2S$

25. Nonmetals + acids $\rightarrow$?
    (A) react slow
    (B) react violently
    (C) react moderately
    (D) no reaction

26. Nonmetals react with hydrogen to form:
    (A) covalent compounds
    (B) ionic compounds
    (C) electrovalent compounds
    (D) coordinate compounds

27. $P_4 + 6Cl_2 \rightarrow$
    (A) $2P_2Cl_6$ (B) $4PCl_3$
    (C) PCl_6 (D) P_2Cl_5

28. Mercury is used in thermometers because:
    (A) it does not wet the glass
    (B) it expands on heating
    (C) it is a liquid
    (D) all of these

29. _____ is used to make photographic films.
    (A) sodium chloride
    (B) silver bromide
    (C) potassium iodide
    (D) copper chloride

30. A crucible used in lab to heat solid at high temperature is made of:
    (A) sulphur
    (B) silicon
    (C) graphite
    (D) phosphorus

31. The nonmetal used to treat rubber in the process of vulcanisation is:
    (A) sulphur   (B) phosphorus
    (C) carbon   (D) chloride

32. Match–head contains:
    (A) N_2 (B) I_2
    (C) P (D) C

33. _____ is used in the hydrogenation of vegetable oils.
    (A) Cl_2 (B) N_2
    (C) O_2 (D) H_2

34. Due to its semiconductor properties, the nonmetal used in computers, TV, etc. is:
    (A) carbon   (B) silicon
    (C) bromine   (D) fluorine

35. In the native state of metal, it is present:
    (A) as a mixture with a metal
    (B) in free state
    (C) as a mixture with a nonmetal
    (D) as a mixture with a compound

36. Which of the following metal is present in native state?
    (A) Platinum   (B) Iron
    (C) Potassium   (D) Copper

37. Which of the following is called as noble metal?
    (A) Mercury   (B) Gold
    (C) Lithium   (D) Cesium

38. Haematite is an ore of:
    (A) Fe   (B) Zn
    (C) Cu   (D) Al

39. Fe_3O_4 is the chemical formula of:
    (A) monazite   (B) magnetite
    (C) haematite   (D) bauxite

40. Copper, which is extracted from cuprite, is a/an:
    (A) sulphide ore   (B) carbonate ore
    (C) oxide ore   (D) halide ore

41. Which of the following is a carbonate ore of copper?
    (A) Cuprite
    (B) Pyrite
    (C) Copper glance
    (D) Malachite

42. Which of the following are the ores of zinc?
    (A) Calamine and zinc blend
    (B) Zinc blend and cerussite
    (C) Calomine and siderite
    (D) Zinc blend and carnallite

43. The metal extracted from limestone, marble and chalk is:
    (A) sodium   (B) Calcium
    (C) Aluminium   (D) iron

44. The chemical formula of bauxite is:
    (A) $CaFeS_2$ (B) $MgCO_3$
    (C) $Al_2O_3.2H_2O$ (D) $PbCO_3$

45. Rocksalt is:
    (A) KCl   (B) $CaCl_2$
    (C) $MgCl_2$ (D) NaCl

46. A homogenous solid solution of two or more metals is:
    (A) alloy   (B) allotrope
    (C) isotope   (D) isobar

47. Stainless steel is an alloy of:
    (A) Fe, Cr, C, Ni   (B) Fe, Ni, C
    (C) Cu, Al   (D) Fe, Al, Ni

48. Brass is an alloy of:
    (A) Cu, Sn   (B) Cu, Zn
    (C) Cu, Al   (D) Sn, Pb

49. The chemical formula of cuprite is:
    (A) Cu_2S (B) $CuFeS_2$
    (C) $CuCO_3$ (D) Cu_2O

50. An ore of Cu_2S is:
    (A) copper glance   (B) malachite
    (C) cuprite   (D) pyrites

51. Extraction of copper is done from copper pyrites which contain small quantity of:
    (A) zinc   (B) iron
    (C) sodium   (D) carbon

52. The alloy in which copper is a component is:
    (A) bronze   (B) steel
    (C) solder   (D) nichrome

53. Copper and tin are components of:
    (A) brass   (B) invar
    (C) bell metal   (D) alnico

54. Chemical formula of bauxite is:
    (A) $Al_2O_3.2H_2O$ (B) $Al_2SiO_2.2H_2O$
    (C) Al_2O_3 (D) Na_3AlF_6

55. Al_2O_3 is chemical formula of:
    (A) cryolite   (B) corundum
    (C) kaolin   (D) bauxite

56. What is alumina?
    (A) Al_2O_3 (B) $Al(OH)_3$
    (C) $NaAlO_2$ (D) Al

57. The alloy which contains aluminium is:
    (A) nichrome   (B) type metal
    (C) duralium   (D) gunmetal

58. Aluminium bronze is made up of:
    (A) Al, Cu, Mn   (B) Fe, Al, Ni
    (C) Al, Cu, Ni   (D) Al, Cu

59. An alloy of Al and Mg is:
    (A) duralumin   (B) t–metal
    (C) alnico   (D) magnalium

60. Which of the following is not a property of aluminium?
    (A) Good conductor of heat and electricity
    (B) It is malleable
    (C) It is heavy
    (D) It is ductile

61. The metal which is soft?
    (A) Na   (B) Pb
    (C) Al   (D) Cu

62. The metal with the lowest density from the following is:
    (A) Mg   (B) Li
    (C) Ag   (D) Au

63. The metal which is liquid at room temperature is:
    (A) Hg   (B) Mg
    (C) Ag   (D) Mn

64. Tungsten is used in electric bulbs because:
    (A) it is sonorous
    (B) it is metallic
    (C) it has high tensile strength
    (D) it has high density

65. The nonmetal which is a good conductor of electricity is:
    (A) silicon
    (B) sulphur
    (C) graphite
    (D) phosphorus

66. Metals combine with oxygen to form _____ oxides.
    (A) acidic   (B) basic
    (C) amphoteric   (D) none

67. Metals react with water to form oxides or hydroxides and _____.
    (A) hydrogen
    (B) oxygen
    (C) carbon dioxide
    (D) carbon monoxide

68. Metal which does not react even with steam:
    (A) potassium   (B) iron
    (C) magnesium   (D) silver

69. Metals displace _____ from HCl and H_2SO_4.
    (A) SO_2 (B) O_2
    (C) Cl_2 (D) H_2

70. Which of the following is not a heavy metal?
    (A) Cu   (B) Hg
    (C) Pb   (D) K

71. Metal surface reacts with oxygen and the moisture present in air and get coated with:
    (A) oxide
    (B) carbonate
    (C) hydroxide
    (D) any of these

72. Eating away of metals by water, oxygen and other chemicals is called:
    (A) carbonisation
    (B) amalgamation
    (C) oxidation
    (D) corrosion

73. Rusting of iron requires the presence of:
    (A) air and water
    (B) CO_2 and water
    (C) O_2 and H_2
    (D) O_2 and N_2

74. Total world production of iron destroyed by rusting is about:
    (A) 10%   (B) 50%
    (C) 15%   (D) 40%

75. Corrosion of metals can be prevented when contact between metal and _____ is cut off.
    (A) nitrogen
    (B) hydrogen
    (C) oxygen
    (D) carbon

76. Iron is galvanised when it is dipped in:
    (A) molten zinc
    (B) molten copper
    (C) molten carbon
    (D) molten gold

Previous Contest Questions

1. As we go down in the electro-chemical series of metals, the reactivity:
   (A) decreases and then increases
   (B) increases and then decreases
   (C) decreases
   (D) increases

2. Metals are malleable and ductile because:
   (A) metals can shine
   (B) metals produce sound
   (C) layers of metal atoms can slip over each other
   (D) atoms form close clusters

3. The nonmetal which is hard is:
   (A) sulphur
   (B) chlorine
   (C) graphite
   (D) diamond

4. The nonmetal capable of gaining as well as losing an electron is:
   (A) Hg   (B) Ca
   (C) Ag   (D) Au

5. Which of the following statement is true?
   (A) All minerals are ores
   (B) All minerals are not ores
   (C) All ores are not minerals
   (D) Some ores are minerals

6. $ZnO + C \rightarrow Zn + CO$

   $2Fe_2O + 3C \rightarrow 4Fe + 2CO_2$

   In the above reactions:
   (A) carbon is reduced
   (B) carbon is oxidised
   (C) metal oxide is reduced to metal
   (D) metal oxide is oxidised

7. Gold is mixed with copper to:
   (A) make gold soft
   (B) make gold hard
   (C) make gold more yellowish
   (D) give gold lustre

8. The process of giving a coating of _____ to copper or brass is called tinning.
   (A) zinc
   (B) copper
   (C) tin
   (D) iron

9. Which of the following statement is CORRECT?
   (A) All metals are ductile
   (B) All non-metals are ductile
   (C) Generally, metals are ductile
   (D) Some non-metals are ductile

10. The metals which are soft and can be cut by a knife:
    (A) sodium and magnesium
    (B) strontium and sodium
    (C) sodium and potassium
    (D) magnesium and strontium

⊘ Answers ⊘

Multiple Choice Answers

1. A	2. D	3. B	4. C	5. A	6. B	7. D	8. B	9. A	10. A
11. B	12. B	13. A	14. C	15. D	16. C	17. A	18. A	19. B	20. B
21. A	22. D	23. B	24. C	25. D	26. A	27. B	28. D	29. B	30. C
31. A	32. C	33. D	34. B	35. B	36. A	37. B	38. A	39. B	40. C
41. D	42. A	43. B	44. C	45. D	46. A	47. A	48. B	49. D	50. A
51. B	52. A	53. C	54. A	55. B	56. A	57. C	58. D	59. D	60. C
61. A	62. B	63. A	64. B	65. C	66. B	67. A	68. D	69. D	70. D
71. D	72. D	73. A	74. C	75. C	76. A				

Previous Contest Answers

1. C	2. C	3. D	4. D	5. B	6. C	7. B	8. C	9. C	10. C

Chapter 3 — Coal and Petroleum

Common misconception	Fact
1. Coal and coke are same.	Coal is processed in industry to get coke. Coke is an almost pure form of carbon which is used in manufacture of steel.
2. Petroleum implies only petrol and diesel.	Constituents of petroleum are not only petrol and diesel but LPG, kerosene, paraffin wax, bitumen and lubricating oil.

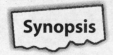

Sources of energy:

All sources of energy can be divided into two categories:

(1) renewable sources of energy and

(2) nonrenewable sources of energy.

The sources of energy which are produced continuously in nature and are inexhaustible are called renewable sources of energy. Some renewable sources of energy are given below:

(a) Solar energy:

The energy obtained from sun is called solar energy. Plants store solar energy which is used by man and other living organisms in the form of food. Energy of sun is responsible for water cycle and for change of weather and seasons. Solar cookers, heaters, watches and calculators work on solar energy.

(b) Hydral energy:

Energy obtained from flowing water is called hydral energy. It is used to produce electricity. Some important hydel power stations in India are located at Bhakra Nangal, Chibru, Sundar Nagar and Chamba.

(c) Geothermal energy:

The energy obtained from the heat of the convection currents of the earth is called geothermal energy. USA, Italy and New Zealand are using this energy as a source of power.

(d) Wind energy:

Energy obtained from the fast moving wind is called wind energy. Netherlands uses wind mills to generate electricity. Sail boats, ships and winnowing of crops are done by the use of wind energy.

(e) Tidal energy:

Energy obtained from the rising tides on the coastal areas is called tidal energy. A tidal power station has been set up at Rauce in France to generate electricity from tidal waves. India has good potential to build tidal power stations in Gujarat and West Bengal.

(f) Bio-energy:

Energy obtained by the decomposition of plants and animals in the absence of air is called biogas. Biogas is a mixture of methane and CO_2. Biogas is an excellent fuel for cooking. The slurry residue after obtaining biogas is used as manure for plants.

(g) Wood, agricultural waste and animal dung cake are used as fuels in villages. These fuels are burnt in open chullahs, where most of the heat generated is lost to the environment.

Non-renewable Source of Energy:

The sources of energy which have accumulated in nature over a period of long time and cannot be quickly replaced once exhausted are called nonrenewable sources of energy. Some of the nonrenewable sources of energy are

(a) Fossil fuels:

These are formed in nature by the decomposition of plants and animals over a long period of time. They are obtained from the earth by digging.

Eg : Coal, Petroleum, Natural gas.

(b) Nuclear power:

Nuclear energy is the energy stored in the nuclei of atoms. When radioactive elements like uranium and thorium are split, they give out large quantities of energy. For obtaining electricity, fission reaction is carried out in specially designed nuclear reactors. The heat produced in the reactor is used to generate electricity. In India nuclear power stations are at Tarapur, Kota, Kalpakkam and Narora.

In sun, nuclear fusion reactions take place. Each time a fusion occurs energy is released in the form of heat and light. It is this energy which makes the sun shine.

(c)   Electricity:

Electricity generated by using fossil fuels like coal is called thermal electricity which is a nonrenewable source. Thermal power stations have been established in India at several places.

Energy needs:

With rising population and growth of cities and industries, the requirement of energy has increased manifold. We require a lot of energy for transport, agriculture, for processing foods, in all modern electrical gadgets, etc. The demand for energy is ever on the increase and in no way it is going to decline because the activities of men are bound to expand with time.

Development of alternative sources of energy:

Most of the energy comes from the two nonrenewable sources: coal and petroleum. These resources are being used up at a very rapid rate and cannot last forever. Thus we should develop some alternate renewable sources of energy and decrease our dependence on fossil fuels. The future source of energy are solar energy, wind energy and tidal energy.

Judicious use of energy:

We must use the available energy with utmost care and not waste it. Judicious use of the available energy can help in overcoming the energy crisis. Energy must be conserved to meet our future needs.

Petroleum and its products:

Economy of a nation depends, to a great extent, on its petroleum wealth. That is why petroleum is called 'Black Gold'. Coal and petroleum are fossil fuels. The crude oil is a complex mixture of solid, liquid and gaseous hydrocarbons mixed with water, salt and other particles. Petroleum is lighter than water and insoluble in it. Petroleum is a dark coloured, viscous, strong smelling liquid.

Occurrence of petroleum:

Oil fields in India are located in Ankleshwar and Kalol in Gujarat, Rudrasagar and Lakwa in Assam and Bombay-High.

Oil production in India:

It is done under the supervision of Oil and National Gas Corporation Ltd. (ONGC) throughout the country.

Production of petroleum:

Petroleum is extracted by drilling holes in the earth's crust, sinking pipes and pumping out the oil. Petroleum is then refined by fractional distillation. Important fractions of petroleum are gasoline, kerosene, diesel, lubricating oil, petrol, etc.

Petrochemicals:

The chemicals which are prepared from the fraction of petroleum are called petrochemicals. Examples – Ethyl alcohol, Ethylene, Benzene, Acetone, DDT and BHC.

Coal and its products:

Coal is a complex mixture of compounds like carbon, hydrogen and oxygen. Coal is formed by the process of carbonisation. Coal is one of the cheapest and widely used fuels. Anthracite, bituminous, lignite and peat are different varieties of coal. Destructive distillation of coal gives the following products: coal gas, ammoniacal liquor, coal tar and coke.

(i)   The most important variety of coal which is used as a fuel is bituminous coal.

(ii)   The process of heating coal in absence of air is called destructive distillation of coal.

(iii) Coke obtained from coal is used to make fuel gases like water gas and producer gas.

(iv)   Coal gas is a mixture of hydrogen, methane and carbon monoxide.

Natural gas:

Natural gas is stored under high pressure as CNG used for power generation and fuel.

It is a cleaner fuel and less polluting.

It consists mainly of methane (85%), ethane (10%), propane (3%) and others.

Multiple Choice Questions

1. Which of the following is a fossil fuel?
    (A) Petroleum   (B) Wood
    (C) Cow dung   (D) Dry leaves

2. Which among the following is a dark coloured, viscous, strong smelling liquid?
    (A) Kerosene   (B) Petrol
    (C) Petroleum   (D) Alcohol

3. Natural gas occurs:
    (A) above the petroleum oil
    (B) below the petroleum oil
    (C) along with the petroleum oil
    (D) none of these

4. Crude oil is a complex mixture of:
    (A) solid hydrocarbons
    (B) liquid hydrocarbons
    (C) gaseous hydrocarbons
    (D) all of these

5. Petroleum is commonly called as:
    (A) Black gold
    (B) Yellow gold
    (C) Green gold
    (D) Blue gold

6. The most common sources of energy are:
    (A) wood and coal
    (B) petroleum and coal
    (C) LPG and cow dung
    (D) natural gas and coal

7. When an oil well is drilled through rocks _?_ comes out first.
    (A) coal gas
    (B) marsh gas
    (C) natural gas
    (D) gas carbon

8. Petroleum is refined by:
    (A) fractional distillation
    (B) destructive distillation
    (C) distillation
    (D) all of these

9. During fractional distillation the crude petroleum is heated to a temperature of about:
    (A) 600^{0}C   (B) 400 – 500^{0}C
    (C) 200^{0}C   (D) 100^{0}C

10. Fractional distillation is based on the property that:
    (A) density of each fraction is different
    (B) molecular weight of each fraction is different
    (C) boiling point of each fraction is different
    (D) melting point of each fraction is different

11. Which fraction of petroleum has highest boiling point?
    (A) Kerosene   (B) Gasoline
    (C) Ether   (D) Gas oil

12. Which of the following is used as fuel?
    (A) Gasoline   (B) Ether
    (C) Pitch tar   (D) Grease

13. Coal is formed by the process of:
    (A) carbonisation (B) distillation
    (C) vaporisation   (D) evaporation

14. _____ has the lowest percentage of carbon.
    (A) Lignite   (B) Bituminous
    (C) Anthracite   (D) Peat

15. _____ has the highest percentage of carbon.
    (A) Anthracite   (B) Bituminous
    (C) Peat   (D) Lignite

16. _____ is the common variety of coal used in household.
    (A) Anthracite   (B) Bituminous
    (C) Peat   (D) Lignite

17. Fuels burn to produce heat, light and _____.
    (A) CO_2 + water vapour
    (B) $CO + O_2$
    (C) $CO_2 + H_2$
    (D) $CO + H_2$

18. Fuels combine with ____ to produce heat and light.
    (A) CO_2 (B) CO
    (C) H_2 (D) O_2

19. Fuels are present in which of the following forms?
    (A) Solids   (B) Liquids
    (C) Gases   (D) All of these

20. The fuels which leave smoke and ash on burning are:
    (A) solid fuels
    (B) liquid fuels
    (C) gaseous fuels
    (D) none of these

21. Natural gas mainly consists of:
    (A) C_2H_6 (B) CH_4
    (C) C_3H_8 (D) C_4H_{10}

22. Gobar gas produced from animal and plant waste contains:
    (A) ethane   (B) methane
    (C) propane   (D) acetylene

23. $2C + O_2 + 4N_2 \rightarrow$?
    (A) $2CO + 2N_2$ (B) $CO + H_2$
    (C) $CO + CH_4$ (D) $CO + NO_2$

24. $C + H_2O$ (steam) is passed over red hot coke to produce:
    (A) $CO_2 + H_2$
    (B) $CO + O_2$
    (C) $CO + H_2$
    (D) $O_2 + H_2 + C$

25. Destructive distillation of coal produces coal gas which is a mixture of:
    (A) $CH_4 + H_2 + CO$
    (B) $C_4H_{10} + H_2$
    (C) $C_4H_{10} + H_2O$
    (D) $C_2H_6 + H_2 + O_2$

26. In LPG cylinder, the gas is liquefied by:
    (A) increasing volume
    (B) applying pressure
    (C) increasing temperature
    (D) replacing pressure

27. The product obtained by the dry distillation of coal is:
    (A) natural gas   (B) water gas
    (C) producer gas   (D) coal gas

28. Which of the following is not a solid fuel?
    (A) Paraffin   (B) Coal
    (C) Tallow   (D) Benzene

29. In fractional distillation of petroleum, the vapours with highest boiling point:
    (A) condense in upper most portion
    (B) condense in lower most portion
    (C) condense in middle portion
    (D) none of these

30. Calorific value is expressed as:
    (A) calories per gram
    (B) kilojoules per gram
    (C) kilocalories per gram
    (D) calories per kilogram

31. Which of the following is not a renewable source of energy?
    (A) Coal
    (B) Wood
    (C) Cow dung
    (D) Agriculture waste

32. The main source of energy for all living beings on earth is:
    (A) Bio energy   (B) Hydral energy
    (C) Wind energy   (D) Solar energy

33. _____energy in plants is used by man in the form of food.
    (A) Chemical   (B) Electrical
    (C) Bio   (D) Physical

34. The earth gives up ____ energy into atmosphere.
    (A) light   (B) heat
    (C) chemical   (D) wind

35. Decomposition of animal and plant waste in the absence of air produces
    (A) gas carbon   (B) coal gas
    (C) biogas   (D) marsh gas

36. The slurry residue after obtaining biogas is used as:
(A) pesticide   (B) manure
(C) insecticide   (D) none

37. Renewable sources of energy are produced in nature:
(A) biennial   (B) annually
(C) continuously   (D) quarterly

38. Match column 'A' with 'B':

'A' Process	'B' Product
a. Carbonisation	1. Coke
b. Destructive distillation	2. Coal
c. Cracking	3. Petroleum
d. Refining	4. Hydrocarbons

(A) a-1, b-2, c-3, d-4
(B) a-2, b-1, c-4, d-3
(C) a-3, b-2, c-4, d-1
(D) a-4, b-3, c-2, d-1

39. The main constituents of petroleum gas is:
(A) butane   (B) propane
(C) methane   (D) ethane

40. Fly ash is produced by:
(A) petroleum   (B) natural gas
(C) coal   (D) all of the above

41. When sand is poured over some burning material, the fire goes off. It is because:
(A) the ignition temperature is brought down by sand
(B) supply of air is cut off
(C) sand is a bad conductor of heat
(D) all of the above

42. The three essential requirements for producing a fire:
(A) fuel   (B) air
(C) heat   (D) all of the above

Previous Contest Questions

1. Petroleum is:
(A) lighter than water and soluble in it
(B) heavier than water and insoluble in it
(C) lighter than water and insoluble in it
(D) heavier than water and soluble in it

2. The residue left behind after the dry distillation of coal :
(A) coal tar
(B) coal gas
(C) coke
(D) ammonical liquor

3. Which of the following property is not a characteristic of a good fuel?
(A) High ignition temperature
(B) Low cost

(C) Causes minimum pollution
(D) Readily available

4. Producer gas is not a good fuel because:
(A) it contains CO which is poisonous
(B) it contains CO_2
(C) it contains CO_2 which does not burn
(D) it contains N_2 which does not burn

5. Plants store solar energy in the form of:
(A) electric energy   (B) thermal energy
(C) chemical energy   (D) bio energy

6. Biogas is a mixture of:
(A) methane + CO_2
(B) methane + CO
(C) ethane + CO_2
(D) ethane + CO

7. Water gas is a mixture of:
(A) H_2 and N_2 (B) H_2 and CO_2
(C) CO_2 and N_2 (D) CO and H_2

8. An aerobic fermentation is a process which helps in formation of:
    (A) Coal gas   (B) Natural gas
    (C) Water gas   (D) Petroleum

9. Which of the following is most harmful for human body?
    (A) CO
    (B) CO_2
    (C) Oxides of nitrogen
    (D) Lead compounds

10. What should be the characteristic for a rocket fuel:
    (A) light and compact
    (B) high calorific value
    (C) should burn rapidly
    (D) all of the above

11. The combustion in a match stick is started by this chemical:
    (A) antimony sulphide
    (B) potassium chlorate
    (C) phosphorous
    (D) starch and wool

⊘ Answers ⊘

Multiple Choice Answers

1. A   2. C   3. A   4. D   5. A   6. B   7. C   8. A   9. B   10. C
11. D   12. A   13. A   14. D   15. A   16. B   17. A   18. D   19. D   20. A
21. B   22. B   23. A   24. C   25. A   26. B   27. D   28. D   29. B   30. A
31. A   32. D   33. A   34. B   35. C   36. B   37. C   38. B   39. A   40. C
41. B   42. D

Previous Contest Answers

1. C   2. C   3. A   4. D   5. C   6. A   7. D   8. B   9. D   10. D
11. C

Explanatory Answers

Multiple Choice Questions:

39. The petroleum gas contains 95% of butane.

40. When coal is burnt in sufficient quantity in big factories, it leaves 10% to 20% of ash. This ash is carried upward due to air and causes pollution problems.

41. Supply of air, which supports combustion is cut off.

Previous Questions:

8. Natural gas is formed from the decomposition of organic matter buried under sea beds millions of years ago by a process called Anaerobic fermentations.

9. Lead compounds are highly toxic in nature and can cause numerous ailments in human beings and animals. They are absorbed by soil and find their way in food chain.

10. Liquid hydrogen, liquid ammonia and alcohol are suitable as rocket fuels.

11. Phosphorous which is applied on head of a metal stick has a very low ignition temperature of 35°C. During rubbing, the heat produced due to friction is sufficient to attain this temperature and combustion takes place.

Chapter 4 Combustion and Flame

Common misconception	Fact
1. Burning is same as combustion.	Combustion is a chemical process in which a substance reacts with oxygen to give heat. It is burning without flame. e.g.: Burning of a candle produces a flame. Whereas a coal doesn't produce flame while burning.
2. Fuel implies wood, petrol, diesel etc.	Any substance which undergoes combustion is a fuel. The food we eat is also a fuel for our body.
3. Explosion is different from combustion.	A combustion where large amount of gases are evolved with the production of large amount of heat, light and sound is called explosion. e.g.: Burning of crackers.

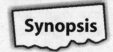

Fuels:

The substance which is burnt to produce heat energy is known as fuel. Fuels can be in the form of solid, liquid or gas. Gaseous fuels are better than liquid fuels which in turn have more calorific value than solid fuels. The main gaseous fuels are natural gas and producer gas. Water gas, LPG and biogas. LPG is a mixture of two hydrocarbons – butane and isobutane. The advantages of LPG are

(i)   high calorific value

(ii) burns with a smokeless flame

(iii) does not produce any poisonous gases on burning

Calorific value of fuel:

The amount of heat produced by burning 1 gm of fuel completely is known as its calorific value.

Characteristics of a good fuel:

Good fuel should be cheap, readily available, easy to transport and store, safe and should have a high calorific value.

Combustion:

It is an oxidation reaction which is accompanied by the evolution of heat and light. Paper, kerosene, petrol, straw, etc. are combustible substances. Iron, glass and diamond are noncombustible. The lowest temperature at which a substance starts burning is called its ignition temperature.

Conditions necessary for combustion are:

(i)   presence of combustible substance

(ii) presence of supporter of combustion (oxygen)

(iii) attainment of ignition temperature

Types of combustion:

(i)   If a combustion takes place with high speed, it is known as rapid combustion. e.g., candle starts burning when a burning match stick is brought near its wick.

(ii)   A combustion in which no external heat is given is known as spontaneous combustion. e.g., burning of white phosphorous in air.

(iii) A combustion where large amount of gases are evolved with the production of large amount of heat, light and sound is called explosion. e.g., burning of crackers.

Flame:

A flame is the zone of combustion of gaseous substances with the evolution of heat and light. The outermost zone of flame is non-luminous zone. This is the hottest zone. The pale yellow zone surrounding the zone of no combustion is known as luminous zone. Around the wick there is a zone which is black in colour. It is called the dark zone where there is no combustion. Near the bottom of the flame there is a zone in blue colour. This is called blue zone.

Fire extinguisher:

A device used to extinguish fire is called a fire extinguisher. Fire can be put out by eliminating any one of the three conditions necessary for combustion.

1. Cut off supply of air

2. Cut off supply of fuel

3. Bring down the temperature

The fire extinguisher commonly used in our contry are:

(i)   Water as a extinguisher

Water cools the combustible substance and water vapour surrounds the combustible material. Thus the fire is put out.

(ii) Soda–Acid extinguisher

It uses sodium bicarbonate and sulphuric acid. It cools burning substance below its ignition temperature and cuts the supply of air.

(iii) Foam type extinguisher

It cuts the supply of air to the burning substance. It puts out fires caused by burning oil and petrol at places like petrol pumps, airports, oil tanks etc.

(iv) Carbon tetra chloride extinguisher

It cuts off air supply to burning substance. It is used to extinguish fire caused by electricity.

Difference between combustible substance and fuel:

1. Any substance which on heating catches fire in air or oxygen with release of heat energy is a combustible substance.

Fuel, on the other hand is a readily available substance, which burns in air or oxygen at moderate rate, but doesn't produce any harmful gas or residues.

2. Combustion of most fuels releases carbon dioxide (CO_2) in the environment. Increased concentration of CO_2 in air causes global warming.

3. Oxides of sulphur and nitrogen released during burning of coal and petroleum products may cause acid rain which is harmful for crops and soil.

4. Unburnt carbon particles in air are dangerous. Air pollution causes respiratory problems.

Multiple Choice Questions

1. LPG is mainly a mixture of two hydrocarbons:
   (A) butane + ethane
   (B) butane + isobutane
   (C) propane + ethane
   (D) methane + ethane

2. The heat produced by burning 1 g of fuel completely is known as:
   (A) heat capacity
   (B) calorific value
   (C) vapour density
   (D) boiling point

3. Which among the following is the best fuel?
   (A) Wood 4000 Cal/g
   (B) Coke 8000 Cal/g
   (C) Coal 7000 Cal/g
   (D) Kerosene 11,200 Cal/g

4. Which of the following has the highest calorific value?
   (A) Petrol   (B) Coke
   (C) Natural gas   (D) Kerosene

5. Which of the following has the characteristics of a good fuel?
   (A) Coke   (B) Butane
   (C) Coal   (D) Kerosene

6. The process of burning a substance in the presence of air with the evolution of heat is called:
   (A) distillation   (B) carbonisation
   (C) combustion   (D) refining

7. Methane burns in air to form:
   (A) $CO_2 + H_2O$ (B) $CO_2 + H_2$
   (C) $CO + O_2$ (D) $CO_2 + O_2 +$ heat

8. Combustion is a _____ reaction accompanied by heat and light.
   (A) reduction   (B) redox
   (C) substitution (D) oxidation

9. Which of the following is a noncombustible substance?
   (A) Coke   (B) Diamond
   (C) Coal   (D) Wood

10. The lowest temperature at which a substance starts burning is called:
    (A) minimum temperature
    (B) maximum temperature
    (C) boiling temperature
    (D) ignition temperature

11. A burning substance will be _____ if the temperature falls below its ignition temperature.
    (A) extinguished
    (B) burning brightly
    (C) burning dimly
    (D) burning with smoke

12. The conditions necessary for combustion are:
    (A) presence of combustible substance
    (B) presence of supporter of combustion
    (C) attainment of ignition temperature
    (D) all of these

13. Types of combustion are:
    (A) rapid
    (B) spontaneous, rapid and explosive:
    (C) explosive
    (D) spontaneous

14. Which of the following is an example of rapid combustion?
    (A) Candle
    (B) Cracker
    (C) White phosphorous
    (D) None

15. Fire is extinguished by:
    (A) removing all combustible substance
    (B) cutting off supply of air
    (C) cooling the burning substance
    (D) all of these

16. Water cannot be used as fire extinguisher to put out:
   (A) burning wood
   (B) burning oil
   (C) burning cloth
   (D) burning charcoal

17. In soda-acid fire extinguisher

   $$2NaHCO_3 + H_2SO_4 \rightarrow ?$$

   (A) $Na_2SO_4 + 2H_2O + 2CO_2$
   (B) $Na_2SO_4 + CO_2 + O_2$
   (C) $Na_2SO_4 + H_2O + O_2$
   (D) $Na_2SO_4 + H_2O_2$

18. In soda–acid fire extinguisher_____ helps in putting out the fire.
   (A) CO_2
   (B) $CO_2 + H_2O$
   (C) H_2O
   (D) $H_2O + H_2$

19. In foam type fire extinguisher, which of the following products are formed?

   $$Al_2(SO_4)_3 + 6NaHCO_3 \rightarrow ?$$

   (A) $2Al(OH)_3 + 6H_2O + 3NaSO_4$
   (B) $2Al(OH)_3 + 6CO + 3NaSO_4$
   (C) $2Al(OH)_3 + 6O_2 + 3NaSO_4$
   (D) $2Al(OH)_3 + 6CO_2 + 3Na_2SO_4$

20. In foam type fire extinguisher _____ is responsible to put off fire.
   (A) H_2O
   (B) $CO_2 + H_2O$
   (C) CO_2
   (D) CO

21. Which type of fire extinguisher is used to extinguish fire caused by burning oil and petrol?
   (A) Foam type
   (B) Water type
   (C) Soda acid type
   (D) CCl_4 type

22. In foam type extinguisher_____ is present in bottle.
   (A) $NaHCO_3$
   (B) $Al_2(SO_4)_3$
   (C) $Al(OH)_3$
   (D) Na_2SO_4

23. In foam type extinguisher _____ is present in the cylinder.
   (A) $Al_2(SO_4)_3$
   (B) $NaHCO_3$
   (C) Na_2SO_4
   (D) $Al(OH)_3$

24. In soda - acid extinguisher, the bottle contains:
   (A) H_2SO_4
   (B) $NaHCO_3$
   (C) $NaOH$
   (D) HCl

25. The metallic cylinder in soda-acid extinguisher contains:
   (A) $NaOH$
   (B) $NaHCO_3$
   (C) $Al(OH)_3$
   (D) KOH

26. The type of combustion in which heat, light and sound are produced is:
   (A) rapid
   (B) explosive
   (C) spontaneous
   (D) none of these

27. Which of the following is an ideal fuel?
   (A) Coal
   (B) LPG
   (C) Petrol
   (D) None of these

28. Match column 'A' with column 'B' as regard to characteristics of a flame and its zones.

'A'	'B'
a. Dark inner zone	1. Hottest part (No carbon)
b. Blue zone	2. Partial decomposition
c. Luminous zone	3. Unburnt vapours of wax
d. Non-luminous zone	4. Complete combustion

   (A) a-1, b-2, c-3, d-4
   (B) a-2, b-3, c-4, d-1
   (C) a-3, b-4, c-2, d-1
   (D) a-4, b-1, c-2, d-3

29. The blue zone in a LPG flame indicates:
    (A) unburnt vapours
    (B) partial decomposition
    (C) moderately hot
    (D) hottest and complete combustion

30. Which of the following is an example of rapid combustion?
    (A) burning of wood
    (B) burning of LPG
    (C) burning of cracker
    (D) burning of a candle

31. Acid rain is caused by:
    (A) deforestation
    (B) CO_2
    (C) CO
    (D) oxides of sulphur and nitrogen

32. Natural gas consists of:
    (A) methane, ethane, propane and ethylene.
    (B) butane, propane and ethane.
    (C) pantene, methane and ethylene.
    (D) hexane, butane and ethane.

33. Synthetic petroleum is artificially produced from:
    (A) petroleum   (B) wood
    (C) coal   (D) L.P.G

34. Arrange the following fuels in increasing order of their calorific value:

    1. Petrol

    2. Diesel

    3. Kerosene

    4. Natural gas

    (A) 1, 2, 3, 4   (B) 2, 3, 4, 1
    (C) 2, 1, 3, 4   (D) 2, 3, 1, 4

35. Incomplete combustion of a fuel gives:
    (A) CO
    (B) CO_2
    (C) SO_2
    (D) oxides of nitrogen

36. Total amount of heat produced by a fuel having calorific value of 20 kJ/kg was found to be 50,000 Joules. How much fuel was burnt?
    (A) 2500 kg   (B) 250 kg
    (C) 25 kg   (D) 2.5 kg

37. Combustion is an:
    (A) exothermic reaction
    (B) endothermic reaction
    (C) displacement reaction
    (D) reduction reaction

38. Inspite of danger involved with hydrogen, it is used as fuel for some applications. What are these?
    (A) Rocket fuel
    (B) Oxyhydrogen flame
    (C) Car fuel
    (D) all of the above

39. A family consumes 12 kg of LPG in 30 days. Calculate the average energy consumed per day if the calorific value of LPG is 50 kJ/kg.
    (A) 10,000 J/day
    (B) 15,000 J/day
    (C) 20,000 J/day
    (D) 25,000 J/day

40. Inflammable substances have an ignition temperature:
    (A) more then 100ºC
    (B) less than 100ºC
    (C) more than 200ºC
    (D) between 200ºC to 350ºC

41. The disadvantages of incomplete combustion is/are:
    (A) unburnt carbon gets released
    (B) air is polluted
    (C) may cause respiratory problems
    (D) all of the above

Previous Contest Questions

1. Type of flame produced by a fuel depends upon:
    (A) calorific value
    (B) amount of oxygen
    (C) type of fuel and its chemical composition
    (D) all of the above

2. Which of the following statements is NOT true?
    (A) CO_2 is the best fire extinguisher
    (B) Global warming can cause acid rain
    (C) Burning of coal and diesel releases sulphur dioxide gas
    (D) LPG has higher calorific value than biogas

3. L.P.G used as domestic fuel is mixed with a strong smelling volatile liquid for:
    (A) better combustion
    (B) good smell/fragrance
    (C) detection of gas leakage
    (D) higher calorific value

4. Hydrogen gas has the highest calorific value i.e., 150 kJ/kg. yet it is not used as a fuel. The reasons are:
    (A) it is explosive in nature
    (B) it causes storage problem
    (C) it causes transportation problem
    (D) all of the above

5. When wood is used as fuel in chullahs, gaps are left in between the logs of wood. This is done for:
    (A) movement of air
    (B) less consumption of wood
    (C) to control temp
    (D) none of the above

6. For a spontaneous combustion to take place:
    (A) flame is required
    (B) spark is replied
    (C) rise in temp to ignition temp is required
    (D) nothing is required

7. An electric spark is struck between two electrodes placed near each other, inside a closed tank full of petrol. What'll happen?
    (A) Spontaneous combustion of petrol
    (B) Explosion
    (C) Slow combustion of petrol
    (D) Nothing will happen

8. Which of the following statement is NOT true?
    (A) Flame can be seen over burning solids and liquids
    (B) Type of flame depends upon the amount of oxygen available
    (C) Invisible zone of a flame is the least hot zone
    (D) Blue zone indicates complete combustion of fuel

9. When water is poured over burning wood, the fire goes off. This is because:
    (A) temperature of wood decreases
    (B) temperature of water goes up
    (C) molecules of water reacts with oxygen present in the flame
    (D) the flame vapourises

Answers

Multiple Choice Answers

1. B	2. B	3. D	4. C	5. B	6. C	7. A	8. D	9. B	10. D
11. A	12. D	13. B	14. A	15. D	16. B	17. A	18. B	19. D	20. C
21. A	22. B	23. B	24. A	25. C	26. B	27. D	28. C	29. D	30. B
31. D	32. A	33. C	34. B	35. A	36. D	37. A	38. D	39. C	40. B
41. D									

Previous Contest Answers

1. B	2. B	3. C	4. D	5. A	6. C	7. D	8. C	9. A

Explanatory Answers

Multiple Choice Questions

27. (D) There is no probability of finding an ideal fuel, since all fuels leave some residue.

30. (B) In rapid combustion, the combustion of combustible material is complete.

31. (D) The sulphur dioxide gas released during burning of coal and oxides of nitrogen released during combustion of petrol dissolve in rain water and form acids.

33. (C) Synthetic petroleum is prepared from coal in factories.

35. (A) Carbon monoxide is a poisonous gas and is dangerous if inhuled.

36. (D) $\dfrac{50,000\,J}{20,000\,J/kg} = 2.5$ kg.

37. (A) Combustion releases heat. It is therefore an exothermic reaction.

38. (D) Because of its high calorific value, it is used as rocket fuel. It is also used for cutting and welding as oxy-hydrogen flame. Some latest car manufactures have started experimenting hydrogen as a car fuel under stringent safety conditions.

39. (C) Energy released by 12 kg of LPG

$$= 12 \times 50\ kJ = 600\ kJ$$

∴ energy consumed per day

$$= \frac{600\,kJ}{30} = 20,000 \text{ Joules/day.}$$

40. (B) Inflammable substances catch fire easily since their ingition temperature is low.

Previous Questions

1. (B) Type of flame depends upon the amount of oxygen available for burning of the fuel. In the form of vapours.

2. (B) Global warming may cause glaciers to melt, which may lead to rise in sea level and submerge low lying areas.

3. (C) If the gas leaks in air, it can be easily detected due to smell and preventive measures can be taken.

4. (D) Hydrogen forms an explosive mixture with air or oxygen and can cause serious problems.

5. (A) The gaps allow air (supporter of combustion) to freely come in contact with wood and hence combustion continues.

6. (C) No flame or spark is required to start spontaneous combustion. It is only the rise in temperature to the ignition temperature which starts oxidation of material producing heat and light energy.

7. (D) The petrol will not catch fire because there is no supporter of combustion, i.e., air. Hence combustion will not take place.

8. (C) The invisible zone or non-luminous flame is the hottest part of the flame.

9. (A) Water, when poured over fire absorbs large amount of heat and hence the temperature of wood falls below the ignition temperature. Thus the fire goes off.

Common misconception	Fact
1. Sulphur dioxide is also a greenhouse gas.	Sulphur dioxide is not a greenhouse gas and does not contribute to an increase in the Earth's temperature. It causes the formation of acid rain.
2. Global warming is due to heat released by industries.	Global warming is due to a layer of carbon dioxide in the atmosphere, which reflects heat radiated from the Earth back to the Earth.

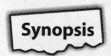

1. Pollution is the introduction into the environment of substances which can harm the health, survival or activities of living organisms. Pollutants may be biodegradable or non-biodegradable. Biodegradable pollutants can be broken down by biological agents, whereas nonbiodegradable pollutants cannot.

2. The major sources of air pollution are industries and automobiles. The burning of fossil fuels releases carbon dioxide, carbon monoxide, sulphur dioxide, oxides of nitrogen, hydrocarbons and particulate matter. Industrial processes release polluting gases and particulate matter.

3. Oxides of nitrogen and sulphur combine with rainwater to form acid rain, which affects soil fertility, vegetation, buildings and monuments.

4. Carbon dioxide and some other gases, like methane, are called greenhouse gases. They trap radiation from the earth and are considered to be the cause of global warming.

5.   Air pollution is reduced by :

(i) modifying automobile engines

(ii) using CNG in preference to petrol or diesel

(iii) using unleaded petrol

(iv) removing pollutants from industrial waste gases

(v) using cleaner sources of energy.

6.   Water pollution can be classified into two types - chemical and biological.

7.   Chemical pollution of water is caused by the discharge of unwanted chemicals into water bodies.

8.   Biological pollution of water bodies is caused by oxygen-demanding wastes and disease-causing microorganisms.

9.   The major sources of water pollution are industrial effluents and urban sewage. Disease-causing organisms, agricultural and industrial chemicals, oxygen-demanding organic waste and hot water are some of the major categories of pollutants.

10.   The accumulation of plant nutrients in water bodies and the rapid growth of algae that results from this is called eutrophication. The algae cut off the supply of light to other organisms, and their decomposition by bacteria uses up dissolved oxygen.

11.   Water pollution can be prevented or reduced by the:

(i) treatment of sewage

(ii) treatment of industrial wastes

(iii) limited use of pesticides and fertilisers

(iv) burning of hospital wastes

(v) proper disposal of dead bodies.

12.   Water fit for drinking is called potable water.

13.   Alum facilitates the removal of suspended particles from water by sedimentation.

14.   Water can be disinfected by boiling, chlorination, ozonisation or irradiation with ultraviolet rays.

15.   Sustainable development implies a change in all aspects of life. The public must be educated on the 3Rs concept, that is recycle, reuse and reduce to conserve and preserve resources.

Multiple Choice Questions

1.

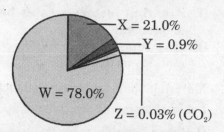

X = 21.0%
Y = 0.9%
W = 78.0%
Z = 0.03% (CO$_2$)

The pie chart shows the composition of air. Identify the gases W, X, Y and Z.

	W	X	Y
(A)	Nitrogen	Rare gases	Oxygen
(B)	Carbon	Oxygen	Rare gases
(C)	Nitrogen	Oxygen	Rare gases
(D)	Rare gases	Hydrogen	Oxygen

2. Which air pollutant is wrongly matched with the effect?
   (A) Dust - reduces photosynthesis in green plants
   (B) Carbon monoxide - reduces oxygen in the blood
   (C) Chlorofluorocarbon - damages nerves and tissues
   (D) Nicotine - hardens and narrows blood vessels

3. Which of the following does NOT cause air pollution?
   (A) Establishing forest reserves
   (B) Using pesticides in farms
   (C) Developing housing estates
   (D) Quarrying for limestone

4. The following diseases are related to smoking except:
   (A) emphysema
   (B) measles
   (C) high blood pressure
   (D) cancer of the lungs

5. Which of the following is NOT due to air pollution?
   (A) Thinning of the ozone layer
   (B) Increase in the number of diabetic patients
   (C) Destruction of habitats
   (D) Global warming

6. Ozone consists of:
   (A) three carbon atoms
   (B) three oxygen atoms
   (C) one carbon atom and two oxygen atoms
   (D) one oxygen atom and two hydrogen atoms

7. The gas associated with the greenhouse effect is:
   (A) carbon dioxide
   (B) oxygen
   (C) nitrogen dioxide
   (D) sulphur dioxide

8. Which of the following is a fossil fuel?

   I Tar

   II Coal

   III Petroleum

   (A) I only
   (B) I and II only
   (C) II and III only
   (D) I, II and III

9. Carbon particles and smoke from factories:
   (A) increase the rate of respiration in plants
   (B) decrease the rate of photosynthesis in plants
   (C) increase the absorption of carbon dioxide by plants
   (D) decrease the rate of transpiration in plants

10. The ozone layer is important because it:
    (A) is used by living organisms for respiration.
    (B) increases the temperature of the earth.
    (C) reduces the amount of ultraviolet rays reaching the earth.
    (D) reflects the heat from the earth back into the atmosphere.

11. The gases released from vehicle exhausts are:

    I carbon monoxide

    II sulphur dioxide

    III oxides of nitrogen

    (A) I and II only   (B) I and III only
    (C) II and III only (D) I, II and III

12. Which of the following gases can result in the formation of acid rain?
    (A) Ozone
    (B) Carbon monoxide
    (C) Sulphur dioxide
    (D) Chlorofluorocarbon

13. Exposure to too much ultraviolet rays can affect the:
    (A) skeletal system
    (B) immune system
    (C) nervous system
    (D) digestive system

14. When heat is reflected from the Earth's surface and trapped in the atmosphere, this phenomenon is referred to as:
    (A) global warming
    (B) ozone depletion
    (C) the greenhouse effect
    (D) thermal pollution

15. The leaching of chemical fertilizers into rivers and ponds cause:
    (A) the rapid growth of algae
    (B) air pollution
    (C) an increase in the oxygen concentration of the water
    (D) an increase in number of aquatic organisms

16. Environmental pollution can be controlled by:
    (A) spraying insecticides and pesticides
    (B) the open burning of tree stumps
    (C) treating factory wastes before disposing them
    (D) disposing hot water from power stations into the sea

17. Materials that can be recycled include:

    I old newspapers

    II aluminium tin cans

    III plastic pails

    (A) I only
    (B) I and II only
    (C) I and III only
    (D) I, II and III

18. Which method of water purification does NOT kill microorganisms?
    (A) Boiling
    (B) Filtration
    (C) Chlorination
    (D) Distillation

19. Which water pollutant is incorrectly paired with the source?
    (A) Oil spill - ship
    (B) Pesticide - oil palm plantation
    (C) Sewage - large factory
    (D) Nitrate - farm

20. Sulphur dioxide in air:
    (A) harms the skin and the lungs
    (B) mixes with the blood and prevents it from carrying oxygen
    (C) affects the heart and the liver
    (D) makes the air temperature rise

21. Lead particles are released into the air by the burning of:
    (A) coal in thermal power stations
    (B) petrol in automobiles
    (C) biomass in chullahs
    (D) LPG for cooking

22. The ozone layer in our atmosphere protects us from the bad effects of:
    (A) carbon dioxide
    (B) CFC's
    (C) the sun's ultraviolet rays
    (D) all of these

23. Which of the following gases is regarded as an atmospheric pollutant?
    (A) O_2 (B) O_3
    (C) SO_2 (D) N_2

24. Monuments of marble can be destroyed by:
    (A) sulphur dioxide pollution
    (B) carbon monoxide pollution
    (C) pesticide pollution
    (D) dust particles

25. The pollutants chlorofluorocarbons are major source of air pollution contributed by:
    (A) industrial effluents
    (B) aerosols
    (C) sewage pollutants
    (D) all of the above

26. Which of these is the major air pollutant in cities like Delhi and Kolkata?
    (A) Carbon monoxide
    (B) Hydrocarbons
    (C) Suspended particulate matter
    (D) Oxides of nitrogen

27. Which of the following is NOT a general pollutant of atmosphere?
    (A) CO_2 (B) SO_2
    (C) SO_3 (D) NO_2

28. Catalytic converters are used in:
    (A) automobiles   (B) wind mills
    (C) poultry farms   (D) diary farms

29. Smog is a combination of:
    (A) fire and water
    (B) smoke and fog
    (C) water and smoke
    (D) air and water

30. Carbon monoxide emitted by automobiles prevents oxygen transport to body tissues by:
    (A) changing O_2 to CO_2
    (B) destroying haemoglobin
    (C) forming a stable compound with haemoglobin
    (D) obstructing the reaction of oxygen with haemoglobin

31. If there was no CO_2 in the atmosphere, the earth's temperature would be:
    (A) less than the present
    (B) same as present
    (C) higher than the present
    (D) dependent on O_2 content of air

32. One of the causes of water pollution is that the farmers use excessive:
    (A) manure and water
    (B) fertilizers and pesticides
    (C) fertilizers and seeds
    (D) pesticides and seeds

33. Which of the following is NOT a feature of potable water?
    (A) It must be clean, colourless and odourless
    (B) It must be free from bacteria
    (C) It must have excessive sodium, calcium and magnesium as they give special taste
    (D) It must contain dissolved oxygen and carbon dioxide

34. Which of the following pollutants is NOT present in the vehicular exhaust emissions?
    (A) Lead
    (B) Ammonia
    (C) Carbon monoxide
    (D) Particulate matter

35. What is the main source of water pollution in India?
    (A) Discharge of untreated sewage
    (B) Bathing
    (C) Discharge of industrial waste
    (D) Both A and C

36. What is the source of sulphur dioxide emissions?
(A) Agricultural forms
(B) Petroleum refineries
(C) Hydroelectric power stations
(D) None of the above

37. Which of the following steps must be adopted by us to contribute towards better waste management?
(A) Reduce the amount of waste formed
(B) Reuse the waste
(C) Recycle the waste
(D) All of the above

38. In which part of atmosphere, ozone layer is present?
(A) Stratosphere
(B) Troposphere
(C) Mesosphere
(D) Thermosphere

39. There is a possibility of melting of polar ice caps and increase in the level of sea water due to:
(A) depletion of ozone layer
(B) green house effect
(C) acid rain
(D) all of the above

40. Modes of controlling pollution in large cities include:
(A) less use of insecticides
(B) proper disposal of organic wastes, sewage and industrial effluents
(C) shifting of factories out of the residential area
(D) all the above

Previous Contest Questions

1. Among the following, which will NOT help to reduce air pollution?
(A) Burn household rubbish in incinerators
(B) Use catalytic converters on motor vehicles
(C) Fix electric precipitators to factory chimneys
(D) Ban smoking in public places such as in offices

2. Global warming causes:

I an increase in the sea level

II the melting of ice at mountain peaks

III a decrease in food production by plants

(A) I only
(B) I and II only
(C) II and III only
(D) I, II and III

3. Conserving the environment means:
(A) not destroying natural resources
(B) not lowering the quality of the environment
(C) changing natural resources from its original state
(D) preserving the condition of the nature that has been destroyed

4. Pollution from the burning of fossil fuels can be reduced by:

I using an incinerator

II using renewable energy

III fixing catalytic converters in vehicles

(A) I only   (B) II and III only
(C) I and III only (D) I, II and III

5. The release of carbon dioxide into the air causes:
(A) acid rain
(B) eutrophication
(C) global warming
(D) respiratory problems

6. Sewage water is purified for recycling
    by the action of:
    (A) fish
    (B) microorganisms
    (C) fuels
    (D) non-biodegradable chemicals

7. The bioindicators of air pollution are:
    (A) algae   (B) ferns
    (C) mushrooms   (D) lichens

8. What are the effects of discharging
    excess heat from electrical power
    stations into rivers and lakes?

    I The biological oxygen demand value
      of the water decreases.

    II Instant death of certain organisms.

    III The population of algae increases.

    IV. The concentration of dissolved
        oxygen increases.

(A) I and IV only
(B) II and III only
(C) I, II and III only
(D) II, III and IV only

9. Which of the following dissolves more
    rapidly in blood haemoglobin than
    oxygen?
    (A) Ozone
    (B) Nitrous oxide
    (C) Sulphur dioxide
    (D) Carbon monoxide

10. Which of the following is NOT an air
    pollutant?
    (A) N_2 (B) N_2O
    (C) NO   (D) CO

⊘ Answers ⊘

Multiple Choice Answers

1. C	2. C	3. A	4. B	5. B	6. B	7. A	8. C	9. B	10. C
11. D	12. C	13. B	14. C	15. A	16. C	17. D	18. B	19. C	20. A
21. B	22. C	23. C	24. A	25. B	26. C	27. A	28. A	29. B	30. C
31. A	32. B	33. C	34. B	35. D	36. B	37. D	38. B	39. B	40. D

Previous Contest Answers

1. A	2. D	3. A	4. B	5. C	6. B	7. D	8. B	9. D	10. A

CROSSWORD – III (CHEMISTRY)

ACROSS

4 Synthetic petroleum is produced from

6 A soft metal that can be cut by knife

7 Smell of LPG indicates

9 Residual of coal in factory

11 Process to obtain fuels from petroleum

12 Property of metals

13 Synthetic unit of polyester

14 Artificial wool

16 Main constituent of CNG

18 Type of flame depends upon

19 Fire proof plastic has a coating of

DOWN

1 Example of a thermoplastic

2 The only non-metal which is a good conductor

3 The colour of flame when complete combustion takes place

4 Main constituent of petroleum

8 Oxides of sulphur and nitrogen reacts with the atmospheric rain water vapour to form

10 Fuel with highest calorific value

14 Supporter of combustion

15 A synthetic fibre from wood pulp

17 Destructive distillation of coal produces

NOTE: Answer to this crossword puzzle is given at the end of this book.

Class VIII

1. Which of the following house hold articles is not made up of fibre:
   (A) cloth   (B) table
   (C) rope   (D) carpet

2. The polymer, which is the constituent of cotton.
   (A) Cellulose   (B) Ester
   (C) Rayon   (D) Nylon

3. Dress material terylene is essentially:
   (A) a nylon product
   (B) acrylic product
   (C) polyester product
            (D) rayon product

4. Synthetic fibres:
   (A) burn slowly
   (B) burn vigorously
   (C) donot catch fire
   (D) melt on heating

5. A silk saree and a nylon saree, both of same length are put to dry under sun. Which one will dry faster?
   (A) Silk saree
   (B) Nylon saree
   (C) Both will take same time
   (D) Depends on weather condition

6. Teflon is:
   (A) a natural fibre
   (B) a synthetic fibre
   (C) a polymer
   (D) a cellulose

7. A blacksmith beats up a piece of iron to change its:
   (A) physical properties
   (B) chemical properties
   (C) both A and B
   (D) none of the above

8. The property due to which aluminium foils are prepared from aluminium metal is known as _____ of metal.
   (A) ductility   (B) malleability
   (C) conductivity   (D) sonorus

9. The property due to which a metal pan can be heated quicker than an earthen pot is:
   (A) ductility   (B) malleability
   (C) agility   (D) conductivity

10. Which of the following statement is NOT true?
    (A) Metals produce a ringing sound when struck hard
    (B) Copper doesn't get rusted
    (C) Coal and sulphur are soft and dull in appearance
    (D) Magnesium and phosphorous burn vigorously in air

11. Sulphurous acid turns:
    (A) blue litmus into red
    (B) red litmus into blue
    (C) no change to any of the litmus paper
    (D) can't say

12. Sodium can be stored safely:
    (A) in a fridge
    (B) inside water
    (C) wrapped in a moist cloth
    (D) in kerosene

13. Which of the following metal/non metal is stored in water?
    (A) Sodium
    (B) Mercury
    (C) Oxygen
    (D) Phosphorous

14. In which of the following use of non-metals is more as compared to metals:
(A) human body
(B) fertilisers
(C) crackers
(D) all of the above

15. Fossils are essentially:
(A) dead remains of living organism
(B) petroleum products
(C) chemicals
(D) man made objects

16. Main constituent of coal is:
(A) dead remains of living organism
(B) dead vegetation
(C) both A and B
(D) none of the above

17. Which of the following statement is NOT true?
(A) A refinery is used for fractional distillation
(B) Coke is a pure form of carbon
(C) Coal gas was used earlier for lighting street lights
(D) Petroleum can be created in laboratory

18. Apurva covered a burning candle with a glass. What'll happen to the burning candle?

— Glass

(A) It will extinguish immediately
(B) It will burn for some time before being cut off
(C) It will continue burning
(D) Candle will melt

19. Fire caused by an electrical equipment can be extinguished by using:

(A) water
(B) CO_2
(C) by a blanket
(D) any or all of the above

20. A material when burnt gives out flame because of:
(A) vapourisation   (B) melting
(C) combustibility (D) conductivity

21. Silk fibres are made up of:
(A) vitamin
(B) carbohydrates
(C) protein
(D) none of the above

22. Which of the following is made from coconut fibres?
(A) Sweaters   (B) Shoes
(C) Mattresses   (D) Sarees

23. Match column 'A' with column 'B'.

A. Fibre	B. Use
1. Silk	a. Rope
2. Nylon	b. Sweater
3. Acrylic	c. Bottle
4. Plastic	d. Saree

(A) a_1, b_2, c_3, d_4 (B) a_2, b_1, c_3, d_4
(C) a_3, b_2, c_4, d_1 (D) a_2, b_3, c_4, d_1

24. Which of the following is a property of plastic:
(A) flame resistant
(B) noncorrosive
(C) mouldable
(D) all of the above

25. Which of the following material take the longest to degenerate:
(A) paper   (B) cotton cloth
(C) tin can   (D) plastic bags

26. The most reactive of the following metals is:
(A) Ca   (B) Al
(C) Ni   (D) Pb

27. Which of the following is a property of nonmetals?
(A) Low densities
(B) Low melting points
(C) Poor conductor of electricity
(D) All the three

28. Cu + HCl →
(A) react vigorously
(B) no reaction
(C) react modestly
(D) react slowly

29. Nonmetals + acids → ?
(A) react slow
(B) react violently
(C) react moderately
(D) no reaction

30. Corrosion of metals can be prevented when contact between metal and _____ is cut off.
(A) nitrogen
(B) hydrogen
(C) oxygen
(D) carbon

31. Metals are malleable and ductile because:
(A) metals can shine
(B) metals produce sound
(C) layers of metal atoms can slip over each other
(D) atoms form close clusters

32. The nonmetal which is hard is:
(A) sulphur
(B) chlorine
(C) graphite
(D) diamond

33. Which of the following statement is CORRECT?
(A) All metals are ductile
(B) All non-metals are ductile
(C) Generally, metals are ductile
(D) Some non-metals are ductile

34. During fractional distillation the crude petroleum is heated to a temperature of about:
(A) 600^0C (B) $400 - 500^0C$
(C) 200^0C (D) 100^0C

35. _____ is the common variety of coal used in household.
(A) Anthracite
(B) Bituminous
(C) Peat
(D) Lignite

36. Fuels burn to produce heat, light and _____.
(A) CO_2 + water vapour
(B) $CO + O_2$
(C) $CO_2 + H_2$
(D) $CO + H_2$

37. The product obtained by the dry distillation of coal is:
(A) natural gas   (B) water gas
(C) producer gas   (D) coal gas

38. Decomposition of animal and plant waste in the absence of air produces
(A) gas carbon   (B) coal gas
(C) biogas   (D) marsh gas

39. Petroleum is:
(A) lighter than water and soluble in it
(B) heavier than water and insoluble in it
(C) lighter than water and insoluble in it
(D) heavier than water and soluble in it

40. An aerobic fermentation is a process which helps in formation of:
(A) Coal gas   (B) Natural gas
(C) Water gas   (D) Petroleum

41. Which of the following has the highest calorific value?
(A) Petrol   (B) Coke
(C) Natural gas   (D) Kerosene

42. The process of burning a substance in the presence of air with the evolution of heat is called:
    (A) distillation   (B) carbonisation
    (C) combustion   (D) refining

43. Fire is extinguished by:
    (A) removing all combustible substance
    (B) cutting off supply of air
    (C) cooling the burning substance
    (D) all of these

44. The blue zone in a LPG flame indicates:
    (A) unburnt vapours
    (B) partial decomposition
    (C) moderately hot
    (D) hottest and complete combustion

45. L.P.G used as domestic fuel is mixed with a strong smelling volatile liquid for:
    (A) better combustion
    (B) good smell/fragrance
    (C) detection of gas leakage
    (D) higher calorific value

46. The gases released from vehicle exhausts are:

    I carbon monoxide

    II sulphur dioxide

    III oxides of nitrogen

    (A) I and II only
    (B) I and III only
    (C) II and III only
    (D) I, II and III

47. The pollutants chlorofluorocarbons are major source of air pollution contributed by:
    (A) industrial effluents
    (B) aerosols
    (C) sewage pollutants
    (D) all of the above

48. Which of these is the major air pollutant in cities like Delhi and Kolkata?
    (A) Carbon monoxide
    (B) Hydrocarbons
    (C) Suspended particulate matter
    (D) Oxides of nitrogen

49. In which part of atmosphere, ozone layer is present?
    (A) Stratosphere   (B) Troposphere
    (C) Mesosphere   (D) Thermosphere

50. There is a possibility of melting of polar ice caps and increase in the level of sea water due to:
    (A) depletion of ozone layer
    (B) green house effect
    (C) acid rain
    (D) all of the above

⊘ Answers ⊘

Model Test Paper

1. B	2. A	3. C	4. D	5. B	6. C	7. A	8. B	9. D	10. B
11. A	12. D	13. D	14. D	15. A	16. B	17. D	18. B	19. B	20. A
21. C	22. C	23. D	24. D	25. C	26. A	27. D	28. B	29. D	30. C
31. C	32. D	33. C	34. B	35. B	36. A	37. D	38. C	39. C	40. B
41. C	42. C	43. D	44. D	45. C	46. D	47. B	48. C	49. B	50. B

BIOLOGY

Chapter 1

Food Production and Management

Get It Right

	Common misconception	Fact
1.	The world's major food crops are all grown from seeds.	Many crops such as corn, wheat and rice are produced from seeds, but most of the top ten crops such as sugar, potatoes, bananas, sweet potatoes and yams are produced using vegetative reproduction techniques.
2.	Pest control can be made only by using pesticides, which are prepared from chemicals.	Biological control is a form of pest control that uses living things including microorganisms, to control or kill pests. For e.g., bacteria of a certain type are used to stop the reproduction in beetles and produce poison to kill aphids.

Scientists have used genetic engineering technique to insert the genes of certain microorganisms into the cells of plants so that these plants will produce poisons to kill certain pests.

Synopsis

1. Agriculture is the science or practice of growing crops.
2. Plants of the same kind are grown and cultivated at one place on a large scale is called a crop.
3. There are three main crop seasons - kharif (June-September), e.g., rice, jute, maize, groundnut and cotton, rabi (October-March), e.g., wheat mustard, potato, barley and cotton and summer crops.

4.   The steps involved in cultivating a crop are as follows.

(a)   Ploughing, levelling and manuring the soil.

(b)   Sowing seeds at the correct depth and with right spaces between them. Some seeds are sown in nurseries and the seedlings are then transplanted to the main field.

(c)   Improving soil fertility by adding manure and chemical fertilizers and also by adopting methods like crop rotation and leaving the field fallow.

(d)   Ensuring irrigation at right time.

(e)   Protecting crops from weeds, pests and diseases either by using chemicals or by using natural methods.

(f)   Harvesting, threshing and winnowing.

5.   Legumes are often used in crop rotation, because the nitrogen fixing bacteria live in their roots improve soil fertility.

6.   Nitrogen fixation is a part of the nitrogen cycle, which is continued cycling of nitrogen from the air to the soil and to living organisms.

7.   Grains are stored in silos or godowns that have been fumigated. Buffer stock is maintained for emergencies.

8.   Scientists have developed hybridisation processes to grow disease resistant varieties of plants. The earliest success is the production of high–yielding varieties of plants which led to increase in the production of food crops. This is often referred as the green revolution.

9.   The branch of agriculture dealing with the rearing of farm animal is called animal husbandry.

10.   Animals give us milk, meat and eggs. Animal products are an excellent source of protein. Animal proteins are superior to plant proteins. Egg white contains the protein albumen.

Multiple Choice Questions

1. What do you call the place where crops such as rice and wheat are grown?
   (A) Garden
   (B) Ground
   (C) Field
   (D) Lane

2. Which of the following is explained in the given information?

   I It is the science or practice of growing crops

   II It covers all the activities connected with cultivation

   III It covers all the activities of animals for food and for doing useful work

   (A) Animal husbandry
   (B) Horticulture
   (C) Agriculture
   (D) Nurseries

3. Which of the following should come in the box 'X' in the given sequence?

   Ploughing → Levelling → X →

   Sowing seeds → Irrigation

   (A) Broadcasting
   (B) Transplanting
   (C) Manuring
   (D) Drilling

4. The use of machinery in agriculture helps to:

   I increase the quantity of crop yield

   II get the job done faster

   III reduce the dependency on human and animal labour

   (A) I and II only
   (B) I and III only
   (C) II and III only
   (D) I, II and III

5. Which of these is the correct sequence of steps to develop a new plant variety?

   P - Evaluation

   Q - Multiplication of improved seeds

   R - Selection

   S - Distribution of improved seeds

   T - Development of gene variation

   (A) T, R, P, Q, S
   (B) R, T, P, Q, S
   (C) S, Q, P, R, T
   (D) P, Q, R, T, S

6. What will improve the quantity of food production?
   (A) Pesticides
   (B) Synthetic hormones
   (C) Education and guidance for consumers
   (D) Optimum use of land for agriculture

7. Which of the following parts have bacteria in the figure given below?

   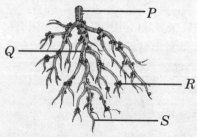

   (A) P
   (B) Q
   (C) R
   (D) S

8. Which practices are examples of an integrated cultivation system?

   I Breeding livestock on oil palm plantations

   II Breeding small fishes in paddy fields

   III Planting many types of crops on a small area

   (A) I and II only
   (B) I and III only
   (C) II and III only
   (D) I, II and III

9. Food production can be increased to meet the demand of an increasing population by:

I practising efficient land management and development

II continuous research to ensure sustainable development

III using more pesticides to control pests

(A) I and II only   (B) I and III only
(C) II and III only (D) I, II and III

10. What is considered modern technology in agriculture?

I   Genetic engineering to produce high quality traits in livestock and poultry

II Application of synthetic chemicals to improve soil fertility

III Using agromachinery for planting, harvesting and collecting agriculture produce

(A) I and II only   (B) I and III only
(C) II and III only (D) I, II and III

11. Which methods of cultivation will result in loss of soil fertility?

I Crop rotation

II Shifting cultivation

II Excessive use of chemical fertilizers

(A) I and II   (B) I and III
(C) II and III   (D) I, II and III

12. Transferring and combination of desirable characteristic features into plants and multiplying them is called:
(A) eugenics
(B) plant breeding
(C) genetic engineering
(D) crop improvement

13. Which of the following methods of cultivation causes salinisation of soil?
(A) Transplantation
(B) Crop rotation
(C) Excessive irrigation
(D) Broadcasting

14. Which of the following classes of microorganisms play an important role in the nitrogen-cycle?

I Bacteria

II Algae

III Fungi

(A) I only   (B) I and II only
(C) II and III only (D) I, II and III

15. The nitrogen cycle is important because it:

I maintains the concentration of nitrogen in the air

II ensures a continous source of protein

III increases water pollution

(A) I only   (B) I and III only
(C) I and II only   (D) I, II and III

16. Grain stocked for emergencies is called:
(A) surplus stock   (B) storage
(C) buffer stock   (D) regular

17. Sprinkler system of irrigation is very advantageous because it:
(A) helps the fields to get water logged
(B) controls the water supply
(C) increases the evaporation of water
(D) decrease the fertility of soil

18. Arrange the following agricultural practices in the correct order.

Sowing, manuring, irrigation, harvesting, ploughing and levelling.

(A) Ploughing, sowing, levelling, harvesting, manuring and irrigation
(B) Ploughing, levelling, irrigation, sowing, manuring and harvesting
(C) Ploughing, irrigation, sowing, manuring, harvesting and levelling
(D) Ploughing, levelling, manuring, sowing, irrigation and harvesting

19. The advantage of ploughing is:
    (A) it allows the penetration of roots of plants
    (B) it helps in proper aeration and eradicates weeds
    (C) it promotes the growth of useful soil bacteria
    (D) all of the above

20. The practice which does NOT improve the fertility of soil from the following is:
    (A) keeping the land fallow
    (B) practicing crop rotation
    (C) practicing monocropping
    (D) practicing multiple cropping

21. The practice of keeping the fields free for a season to replenish the lost nutrients is:
    (A) monocropping
    (B) crop rotation
    (C) multiple cropping
    (D) field fallow

22. A farmer sows beans in his fields after harvesting a crop of wheat. The agricultural practice he is following is:
    (A) crop rotation
    (B) multiple cropping
    (C) fallow field
    (D) mixed cropping

23. Which of the following crops would enrich the soil with nitrogen?
    (A) Apple   (B) Pea
    (C) Paddy   (D) Potato

24. Which of the following statements is NOT true?
    (A) Rotation of crops improves the fertility of soil
    (B) Rotation of crops saves a lot of nitrogenous fertilisers
    (C) Rotation of crops helps in the weed control and pest control
    (D) Rotation of crops helps mixing of nutrients uniformly

25. The method which enables us to select better and healthy seedlings for cultivation of rice is:
    (A) transplantation
    (B) broadcasting
    (C) spacing
    (D) all of the above

26. Which of the following is NOT true for chemical fertilizers?
    (A) They are nutrient specific
    (B) They are readily soluble in water
    (C) They provide organic matter (humus) to the soil
    (D) Overuse of chemical fertilisers pollute the soil

27. Eutrophication means:
    (A) toxication of water by fertilisers
    (B) decrease the growth of algae
    (C) increase in the fertility of the soil
    (D) all of the above

28. The crop that requires more irrigation is:
    (A) wheat   (B) rice
    (C) maize   (D) jowar

29. Removing chaff from the grains is:
    (A) weeding
    (B) threshing
    (C) harvesting
    (D) winnowing

30. Gundhi bug is a small insect that attacks:
    (A) wheat
    (B) sorghum
    (C) paddy
    (D) cotton

31. The disadvantage of high yielding varieties of crops is:
    (A) they give less fodder
    (B) they require frequent weeding
    (C) they require higher inputs
    (D) all of the above

32. The ill effect of green revolution is:
    (A) improvement in economic condition of farmers
    (B) development of agriculture as an industry
    (C) dependence on fertilisers, weedicides and pesticides
    (D) wiping out of hunger and starvation

33. Animal husbandry deals with:
    (A) increase in milk production
    (B) proper utilisation of animal wastes
    (C) protection of animals against diseases
    (D) all of the above

34. Which of the following is used as roughage?
    (A) Napier grass   (B) Cotton seeds
    (C) Oil cakes   (D) Rice polish

35. The milch cattle are given more of _____ diet to get useful food products.
    (A) carbohydrate   (B) protein
    (C) fat   (D) water

36. Operation flood is otherwise called:
    (A) green revolution
    (B) white revolution
    (C) black revolution
    (D) yellow revolution

37. Which of the following has been recently used for increasing productivity of super milk cows?
    (A) Artificial insemination by a pedigree bull only
    (B) Super ovulation of a high production cow only
    (C) Embryo transplantation only
    (D) A combination of all the above into a carrier cow

38. Which of the following is NOT a rabi crop?
    (A) Rice   (B) Wheat
    (C) Mustard   (D) Potato

39. Match the following with correct answers.

a. Kharif crops	I Wheat
b. Rabi crops	II Ploughing
c. Tilling	III Harvesting
d. Combine	IV Paddy

    (A) a-I, b-II, c-III, d-IV
    (B) a-IV, b-I, c-II, d-III
    (C) a-IV, b-III, c-II, d-I
    (D) a-III, b-IV, c-I, d-II

40. The agricultural tool used to level the field is:
    (A) harrow   (B) leveller
    (C) seed drill   (D) plough

41. A harrow is used to remove:
    (A) weeds   (B) crop plants
    (C) stones   (D) rocks

42. Ploughing helps in:
    (A) loosening of soil
    (B) distribution of nutrients
    (C) removal of microorganisms
    (D) removal of pests

43. The common weed which grows along with every crop is:
    (A) chenopodium
    (B) amaranthus
    (C) convolvulus
    (D) wild oat

44. To prevent seed-borne diseases the seeds must be:
    (A) sown at right depth
    (B) spaced at right intervals
    (C) sown in highly wet soil
    (D) treated with fungicide solutions

45. The crop cultivated by sowing seeds directly into the soil from the following is:
    (A) paddy   (B) sorghum
    (C) tomatoes   (D) chillies

Previous Contest Questions

1. The agricultural tool used to sow seeds is:
    (A) wooden plank (B) drill
    (C) leveller   (D) plough

2. Besides carbon, hydrogen and oxygen, the synthesis of proteins by plants require:

    I Magnesium

    II Nitrogen

    III Potassium

    (A) I only   (B) III only
    (C) II only   (D) II and III only

3. Nitrogen-fixing bacteria can be found in:

    I the soil

    II root nodules

    III leaves

    (A) I only   (B) I and II only
    (C) II and III only (D) I, II and III

4. The figure given below shows a part of nitrogen cycle.

    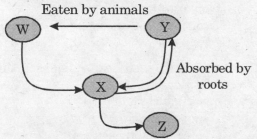

    Which of the following represents nitrates?
    (A) W   (B) X
    (C) Y   (D) Z

5. Which of the following crops seedlings need to be transplanted?

    (A) Wheat   (B) Potato
    (C) Mustard   (D) Rice

6. The practice of keeping the fields free for a season to replenish the lost nutrients is called:
    (A) monocropping
    (B) crop rotation
    (C) multiple cropping
    (D) field fallow

7. Some farmers were seen adding a type of algae to barren field to support crop growth. Which algae could they be using?
    (A) Blue algae
    (B) Green algae
    (C) Blue green algae
    (D) Brown algae

8. Identify the correct sequence in farming.
    (A) Sowing → tilling → irrigation → manuring
    (B) Sowing → tilling → manuring → irrigation
    (C) Tilling → sowing → irrigation → manuring
    (D) Tilling → sowing → manuring → irrigation

9. Fallowing is the process of:
    (A) ploughing
    (B) irrigating
    (C) sowing
    (D) leaving the field uncultivated

10. Which of the following is a 'rabi' crop?
    (A) Groundnut
    (B) Maize
    (C) Wheat
    (D) Sugarcane

⊘ Answers ⊘

Multiple Choice Answers

1. C	2. C	3. C	4. C	5. A	6. D	7. C	8. B	9. A	10. D
11. C	12. C	13. C	14. B	15. C	16. C	17. B	18. D	19. D	20. C
21. D	22. A	23. B	24. C	25. A	26. C	27. A	28. B	29. D	30. C
31. D	32. C	33. D	34. A	35. B	36. B	37. D	38. A	39. B	40. B
41. A	42. A	43. B	44. D	45. B					

Previous Contest Answers

1. B	2. C	3. B	4. B	5. D	6. D	7. C	8. D	9. D	10. C

Chapter 2 Cell

Get It Right

Common misconception	Fact
1. Muscles are organs.	Muscles are formed from muscle cells. They are tissues which are found in most organs and helps in movement.
2. Protoplasm and cytoplasm is one and the same or synonymous.	Protoplasm is the living matter. It contains the total substance of a living cell, i.e., the cytoplasm and the nucleus, cytoplasm contains everything within the cell, except the nucleus.

Giardia lamblia is considered one of the deepest branching or most primitive eukaryotes in existence and some scientists have called Giardia a 'missing link' in the evolution of eukaryotic cells from prokaryotic cells. Giardia lamblia was the first eukaryotic cell to ever be seen using one of the first good quality microscopes developed by Antonie van Leeuwenhoek, a Dutchman, back in the late 1600's. Although Giardia is a single cell organism, van Leeuwenhoek called it an 'animacule' because he thought it had an amazing similarity with the general appearance of animals.

Synopsis

1. The structural and functional unit of living organisms is cell. Organisms that consist of only one cell are called unicellular. A tissue is made of cells. Tissues organise to form organs which in turn form organ systems and the organism.

2. The cell is enclosed by a cell membrane enclosing the cytoplasm, nucleus and cell organelles.

3. The cell membrane is selectively permeable, i.e., it lets the passage of certain substances only.

4. The cytoplasm contains organelles, water and many dissolved substances such as proteins, carbohydrates, inorganic substances, fats, etc.

5. The nucleus is bound by the nuclear membrane. Inside it, nucleoplasm and a dense network of chromatin are present. Chromatin condenses during cell division and separates into chromosomes which bear genes.

6. Mitochondria are the power houses of the cell. They release energy by oxidising food using oxygen.

7. Endoplasmic reticulum helps in the transport of substances within the cell. It is a network of tubelike structures.

8. Golgi body is a stack of tubes and vesicles. It helps in the synthesis and storage of many substances. Some vesicles form lysosomes that digest and destroy cells. Hence they are called suicidal bags.

9. Centrioles are present in animal cells. These help in cell division for the formation of astral fibres.

10. Plastids are exclusively present in plants. They are of three types. Chloroplasts are photosynthetic in function. Leucoplasts are for storage and chromoplasts are coloured.

11. Vacuoles are present in plant cells. It is covered by a tonoplast and has vacuolar sap which stores food, wastes and water.

12. Plant cells have a cell wall. It is thick, rigid and is made of cellulose. It gives support, shape and protection to the cell.

13. Cells without well organised nucleus, i.e., lacking nuclear membrane, are called prokaryotic cells and cells with definite nucleus are called eukaryotic cells.

14. The outermost region of the stem of a plant is called the epidermis. Ground tissue occupies most of the inner region. It consists of different types of tissue. The central core is called the pith, while the region inside the epidermis and extending up to the vascular bundles is called the cortex.

15. The vascular bundles are distinct groups of cells arranged in a ring inside the stem. They consist of xylem and phloem tissues. Xylem cells transport water and minerals, while phloem cells transport food.

16. There are four types of animal tissue epithelial, muscular, connective and nervous. Epithelial tissue is protective. Connective tissue has cells embedded in a matrix. Muscular tissue helps in movement. Nervous tissue consists of nerve cells. It makes up the brain and spinal cord.

Multiple Choice Questions

1. Some cells of our body can be over a foot long. These are:
   (A) nerve cells   (B) muscle cells
   (C) bone cells   (D) gland cells

2. Blood is:
   (A) epithelial tissue
   (B) muscle tissue
   (C) connective tissue
   (D) nervous tissue

3.

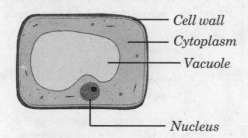

   Cell wall
   Cytoplasm
   Vacuole
   Nucleus

   The cell shown above cannot be an animal cell because it has:

   I cytoplasm

   II a nucleus

   III a cell wall

   IV a large vacuole

   (A) I and II only   (B) I and III only
   (C) II and IV only   (D) III and IV only

4. Some plants have chloroplasts. What is the function of the chloroplasts?
   (A) To absorb carbon dioxide during photosynthesis
   (B) To break up water into hydrogen and oxygen during photosynthesis
   (C) It has chlorophyll for absorbing light energy
   (D) To form starch and glucose in sunlight

5. Which one of the following sentences is false?

(A) The cells of a whale are much larger than that of an ant
(B) The cells in our body continue to grow and divide to replace the old and damaged ones
(C) The nucleus controls most of the cellular activities within the cell
(D) The cell wall gives plant cells a regular shape

6. Which of the following is an example of an organ that contains a smooth muscle?
   (A) Iris of eye only   (B) Uterus only
   (C) Bronchi only   (D) All of these

7. Nervous system consists of:
   (A) brain
   (B) spinal cord
   (C) cranial and spinal nerves
   (D) all of these

8. Which type of tissues support, defend and store food in animals?
   (A) Epithelial   (B) Connective
   (C) Nervous   (D) Muscular

9. Which type of tissue lines body cavities and covers body surface?
   (A) Nervous tissue
   (B) Muscle tissue
   (C) Epithelial tissue
   (D) Connective tissue

10. Which type of tissue is responsible for receiving, interpreting and producing a response to stimuli?
    (A) Muscle tissue
    (B) Nervous tissue
    (C) Epithelial tissue
    (D) Connective tissue

11. Golgi apparatus are involved in:
    (A) transporting proteins that are to be released from the cell only
    (B) packaging proteins into vesicles only
    (C) altering or modifying proteins only
    (D) all of these

12. Carbohydrates of plasma membrane help in:
    (A) passive transport
    (B) active transport
    (C) cell adhesion
    (D) cellular recognition

13. Cell is best defined as:
    (A) the smallest part of a living being
    (B) the part that can be seen only under microscope
    (C) the starting point in the life of all organisms
    (D) the structural and functional unit of life

14. Which of the following gives the cell its shape, maintains its size, protects the structures inside and is selectively permeable?
    (A) Cell wall
    (B) Nuclear membrane
    (C) Cell membrane
    (D) Tonoplast

15. The jellylike substance inside the plasma membrane in which all the cell organelles are floating is called:
    (A) cytoplasm
    (B) tonoplasm
    (C) karyoplasm
    (D) cellsap

16. The largest organelle in the cell is:
    (A) nucleus   (B) mitochondria
    (C) Golgi complex (D) lysosomes

17. Arrange the following in the ascending order of the number of nuclei present in each of them. Brain cell, paramoecium, RBC of mammals.
    (A) Paramoecium, brain cell, RBC of mammals
    (B) RBC of mammals, brain cell, paramoecium
    (C) Brain cell, RBC of mammals, paramoecium
    (D) All of these have same number of nuclei, i.e., one

18. The dense threadlike and rodlike structures present in the nucleus are respectively:
    (A) genes and chromatin
    (B) chromosomes and centrosomes
    (C) centrosome and chromatin
    (D) chromatin and chromosome

19. Control room of the cell is:
    (A) nucleus with its chromatin network
    (B) nucleoplasm
    (C) chromosomes only
    (D) nucleoid

20. The small rod shaped structure bound by a double membrane which helps in the oxidation of food to release energy is:
    (A) mitochondrion
    (B) Golgi complex
    (C) nucleus
    (D) vacuole

21. Energy currency of the cell is:
    (A) ADP   (B) FTP
    (C) ATP   (D) all of these

22. The intracellular transport structure which helps in the protein and lipid synthesis is:
    (A) ribosomes
    (B) microtubules & microfilaments
    (C) Golgi complex
    (D) endoplasmic reticulum

23. Saclike structures which help in the synthesis and storage of many substances is:
    (A) endoplasmic reticulum
    (B) nucleus
    (C) mitochondria
    (D) Golgi bodies

24. Which of the following organelle acts as digestive system within the cell?
    (A) Golgi bodies   (B) Centrosomes
    (C) Lysosomes   (D) Mitochondria

25. Suicidal bags and power houses of the cell are respectively:
    (A) mitochondria and lysosomes
    (B) lysosomes and mitochondria
    (C) lysosomes and Golgi complex
    (D) Golgi complex and lysosomes

26. The structure found only in animal cells, which regulate cell division is:
    (A) chromosomes
    (B) chromatin
    (C) centrosome
    (D) spindle fibrils

27. The colourless plastids are called _____ and their main function is _____.
    (A) chloroplasts, photosynthesis
    (B) leucoplasts, respiration
    (C) chromoplasts, protection from sunlight
    (D) leucoplasts, storage of food

28. The green plastids contain:
    (A) carotenoids   (B) xanthophyll
    (C) chlorophyll   (D) all the above

29. The membrane-bound, saclike structures which store food, wastes and water are called:
    (A) lysosomes   (B) centrosomes
    (C) chromosomes   (D) vacuoles

30. The extra protection in a plant cell which is made up of cellulose is:
    (A) cell membrane
    (B) plasma membrane
    (C) cell wall
    (D) all of these

31. Cheek cells are made up of:
    (A) muscle cells   (B) epithelial cells
    (C) nerve cells   (D) brain cells

32. Cell membrane is:
    (A) selectively permeable
    (B) impermeable
    (C) both A & B
    (D) differentially permeable

33. Holozoic unicellular organisms are:
    (A) amoeba   (B) paramoecium
    (C) both A & B   (D) fish

34. The component of the cell with heriditary material is.
    (A) nucleus in the cell
    (B) protoplasm
    (C) cytoplasm
    (D) plastid

35. Non-living part of the plant cell is:
    (A) nucleus
    (B) cytoplasm
    (C) mitochondrion
    (D) cell wall

36. Mitochondria help in the process of:
    (A) protein synthesis
    (B) respiration
    (C) photosynthesis
    (D) transpiration

37. DNA and RNA are found in the:
    (A) nucleus   (B) cell wall
    (C) cell sap   (D) vacuole

38. Protein synthesis is associated with:
    (A) ribosomes   (B) mitochondria
    (C) Golgi bodies   (D) centrosomes

39. The vacuoles in the cells are filled up with:
    (A) water   (B) cell sap
    (C) protoplasm   (D) gases

40. Nucleus is concerned with:
    (A) respiration
    (B) secretion
    (C) control of cellular activities
    (D) protein synthesis

41. Bacteria are considered more as plants than animals because of the presence of:
    (A) DNA
    (B) plasma membrane
    (C) cell wall
    (D) mitochondria

42. The yellow and orange colour of petals and fruits are due to:
    (A) chloroplasts   (B) chromoplasts
    (C) leucoplasts   (D) anthocyanin

43. One of the following does not possess nuclear membrane in its cells.
    (A) Chlamydomonas
    (B) Blue-green algae
    (C) Riccia
    (D) Cycas

44. Mitochondria are absent in:
    (A) fungi
    (B) bacteria & blue-green algae
    (C) animal cells
    (D) plant cells

45. Cell organelle that is responsible for the autolysis of a cell is:
    (A) dictyosome   (B) lysosome
    (C) peroxisome   (D) glyoxysome

46. Sugars are manufactured in:
    (A) mitochondria   (B) ribosomes
    (C) chloroplasts   (D) Golgi apparatus

47. Which of the following has highest resolving power?
    (A) UV microscope
    (B) Polarising microscope
    (C) Electron microscope
    (D) Fluorescent microscope

48. A membranous network of channels which transport materials in a cell is:
    (A) mitochondria
    (B) lysosomes
    (C) endoplasmic reticulum
    (D) chromatin reticulum

49. Organisms in which nuclear material is not bound by a definite nuclear membrane are called:
    (A) prokaryotes
    (B) mesokaryotes
    (C) eukaryotes
    (D) both B & C

50. The similarity between blue-green algae and bacteria in their nuclear organization is that both are:
    (A) mesokaryotes
    (B) prokaryotes
    (C) eukaryotes
    (D) enucleates

51. The study related to the structure and functioning of cells is known as:
    (A) palynology   (B) karyology
    (C) cytology   (D) embryology

52. Which of the following is permeable?
    (A) Plasma membrane
    (B) Tonoplast
    (C) Nuclear membrane
    (D) Cell wall

53. Which of the following cell organelle is not membrane bound?
    (A) Mitochondria
    (B) Lysosomes
    (C) Spherosomes
    (D) Ribosomes

54. Besides leucoplasts starch grains are developed in:
    (A) chromoplasts   (B) chloroplasts
    (C) mitochondria   (D) lysosomes

55. Structure for storage of starch and pigments is:
    (A) ribosomes   (B) plastids
    (C) nucleus   (D) Golgi bodies

56. If the contents of a leaf tissue are carefully fractioned, which of the fraction could be called alive?
    (A) Mitochondria
    (B) ER
    (C) Cell wall
    (D) Ribosomes

57. Plastids are absent in:
    (A) bacteria   (B) nostoc
    (C) animal cells   (D) all the above

58. The region of chromosomes to which spindle fibres are attached is:
    (A) centriole   (B) chromomeres
    (C) centromere   (D) chromocentre

59. Process of uncoiling of DNA in high temperature is:
    (A) replication   (B) melting
    (C) transcription   (D) reannealing

60. All organelles have double membranes except:
    (A) nucleus   (B) lysosomes
    (C) chloroplast   (D) mitochondria

61. Which of the following plants does not contain chloroplasts?
    (A) Green leaf   (B) Moss plant
    (C) Mushroom   (D) Green algae

62. Which of the following is a storage organelle?
    (A) Mitochondria
    (B) Leucoplast
    (C) Chloroplast
    (D) Ribosome

63. Match the following and select the correct answer.

1. Mitochondria	a. Helps in synthesis of food
2. Chloroplast	b. Controls all the activities of the cell
3. Nucleus	c. Gives shape to the cell
4. Cell wall	d. Provides energy

    (A) 1 - d, 2 - a, 3 - c, 4 - b
    (B) 1 - d, 2 - c, 3 - a, 4 - b
    (C) 1 - d, 2 - a, 3 - b, 4 - c
    (D) 1 - d, 2 - c, 3 - b, 4 - a

64. The structure(s) found in chlamydomonas but not in amoeba is/are:
    (A) cell wall   (B) pyrenoid
    (C) plastids   (D) all the above

65. The diagrams given below are the organelles of a cell. Which of the following organelles is responsible for mechanical support and enzyme transport?

(A)   (B)

(C)   (D)

Previous Contest Questions

1. The cell organelle which receives the substances synthesized and released by the ER, condenses, modifies, packs and releases them in the form of secretory vesicles is:
   (A) Golgi complex
   (B) mitochondrion
   (C) lysosome
   (D) ribosome

2. DNA is NOT a component of:
   (A) mitochondria
   (B) chloroplast
   (C) nucleus
   (D) lysosome

3. Mitochondria will be more in:
   (A) germinating seeds
   (B) dry seeds
   (C) dormant seeds
   (D) none of these

4. Compartmentalisation of cells is useful in:
   (A) making organelles separate
   (B) avoiding mix up of cytoplasm
   (C) retention of shape
   (D) individual metabolism

5. Cell membrane is composed of:
    (A) lipids and starch
    (B) lipids and proteins
    (C) lipids and sugars
    (D) sugars and proteins

6. Which one of the following is a liquid connective tissue?
    (A) Bone   (B) Blood
    (C) Pancreas   (D) Liver

7. Arrange the cell organelles useful for intracellular digestion, intracellular respiration, intracellular movements and cell secretion in a sequence.

P	Golgi complex
Q	Lysosomes
R	Mitochondria
S	Microtubules

    (A) Q - R - S - P   (B) R - Q - P - S
    (C) S - P - Q - R   (D) P - S - R - Q

8. The stomach is made up of:

    I muscle tissues

    II reproductive tissues

    III epithelial tissues

    IV connective tissues

    (A) I and II only
    (B) III and IV only
    (C) I, II and IV only
    (D) I, III and IV only

9. Identify the cells having branched structure.
    (A) Muscle cells   (B) Nerve cells
    (C) Blood cells   (D) Cuboidal cells

10. Which of the following is the main difference between onion peel cells and human cheek cells?

    (A) Presence of mitochondria in onion peel cells only
    (B) Presence of cell wall in onion peel cells only
    (C) Absence of plasma membrane in cheek cells
    (D) Absence of endoplasmic reticulum

Answers

Multiple Choice Answers

1. A	2. C	3. D	4. C	5. A	6. D	7. D	8. B	9. C	10. B
11. D	12. D	13. D	14. C	15. A	16. A	17. B	18. D	19. A	20. A
21. C	22. D	23. D	24. C	25. B	26. C	27. D	28. C	29. D	30. C
31. B	32. A	33. C	34. A	35. D	36. B	37. A	38. A	39. B	40. C
41. C	42. B	43. B	44. B	45. B	46. C	47. C	48. C	49. A	50. B
51. C	52. D	53. C	54. B	55. B	56. A	57. C	58. C	59. A	60. B
61. C	62. B	63. C	64. D	65. B					

Previous Contest Answers

1. A	2. D	3. A	4. A	5. B	6. B	7. A	8. D	9. B	10. B

Explanatory Answers

17. (B)   RBC of mammals do not contain nucleus, brain cells contain single nucleus and paramoecium contains two nuclei.

23. (D)   Golgi body helps in the secretion of substances, e.g., enzymes, which help in the proper metabolic functioning of the cell.

24. (C)   Lysosomes are called digestive organs of the cell which are capable of engulfing of food materials and other substances. These are hydrolysed inside lysosomes by certain enzymes.

33. (C)   Holozoic unicellular organisms are those which can engulf the whole organism.

41. (C)   Bacteria comes under the kingdom Monera as it contains cell wall which is a typical character of a plant cell. Bacteria is said to be more like plant cell than animal cell.

46. (C)   Sugars are same as starch which are manufactured in the chloroplasts with the help of chlorophyll.

56. (A)   Mitochondria contains DNA. Thus it is called semiautonomous organelle and it can survive the fractionation process.

✧ ✧ ✧

Chapter 3 Microorganisms

Common misconception	Fact
1. A bacteriophage is a bacterium.	A bacteriophage is a virus which multiplies inside a bacterium.
2. All microorganisms are harmful and cause diseases in humans, animals and plants.	Not all microorganisms are harmful. Certain microbes such as fungi and bacteria are beneficial. For example, the E.coli bacteria which live inside the large intestine of humans produce vitamins B_{12} and K. The Rhizobium bacteria fixes atmospheric nitrogen in the root nodules of leguminous plant. Yeast, a fungus is used to produce alcohol and in making bread. Penicillin, an antibiotic is obtained from a fungus called Penicillium notatum.

The use of microorganisms to clean up the environment or to remove pollutants from the environment is called bioremediation.

Synopsis

1. Microorganisms are tiny organisms that can be seen only under a microscope.

2. Microorganisms are classified into : bacteria, fungi, protozoa, viruses and algae.

3. Bacterial cells are prokaryotic cells possessing a relatively simple nucleus without any nucleolus and nuclear membrane and are surrounded by a rigid cell wall.

4. On the basis of their structure bacteria can be classified into four types: coccus (spherical), bacillus (rod shaped), spirullum (spiral shaped) and vibrio (comma shaped).

5. Fungi are a group of non-green plants. They are heterotrophs and they obtain their nutrients through saprophytism and parasitism.

6. Protozoa are the biggest unicellular microorganisms. They show the characteristics of animals. The size of a protozoan ranges from 5 μm to 250 μm. Most protozoans are aquatic and exists in various shapes.

7. Protozoa obtain their nutrients by parasitism or as autotrophs. Protozoa multiply through binary fission (asexual reproduction) or conjugation (sexual reproduction).

8. Viruses are a group of ultramicroscopic forms which do not have a cellular organisation like other organisms. They always occur as parasites in the cells of bacteria, plants and animals. They cannot live or reproduce outside the cell.

9. Algae are simple plants which do not have real roots, stems and leaves. Algae may be unicellular (chlamydomonas) or multicellular (spirogyra).

10. Algae are autotrophs. They breed through asexual and sexual reproduction.

11. Factors which affect the growth of microorganisms are nutrients, humidity, light, temperature and pH.

12. Some microorganisms are useful for commercial production of medicines and alcohol.

13. Some microorganisms decompose the organic waste and dead plants and animals into simple substances and clean up the environment.

14. Some of the microorganisms grow on our food and cause food poisoning.

15. Some microorganisms reside in the root nodules of leguminous plants. They can fix nitrogen from air into soil and increase the soil fertility.

16. Some bacteria and blue green algae present in the soil fix nitrogen from the atmosphere and convert into nitrogenous compounds.

Useful mocroorganisms :

E.coli bacteria produce vitamins B_{12} and K. In herbivores and some insects bacteria and protozoa digest cellulose.

Decomposition and recycling of materials :

Microorganisms such as bacteria, protozoa and fungi break down the harmful organic portion of raw sewage to less harmful sludge.

Medicine and health supplements :

Antibiotic penicillin is produced by a type of fungus Pencillium notatum. Insulin used for treating diabetics is produced by genetically modified bacteria, a vaccine, consisting of dead or weakened harmful microorganisms.

Agriculture :

Nitrogen fixation by Rhizobium bacteria, decomposition of organic wastes by saprophytic bacteria and fungi.

Industries :

In food industry lactic bacteria is used in the preparation of curd and cheese. In making bread and in brewing alcoholic drinks, yeast is used.

Harmful Microorganisms :

Diseases caused by bacteria in humans.

Name of the disease	Name of the Pathogen	Symptoms of the disease
1. Cholera	Vibrio cholerae	Severe diarrhoea
2. Leprosy	Mycobacterium leprae	Deformities of limbs
3. Gonorrhoea	Coccus bacteria	Pain in reproductive organs
4. Pneumonia	Diplococcus pneumoniae	Fluid in the lungs
5. Tetanus (lockjaw)	Clostridium tetani	Muscular spasms
6. Tuberculosis	Mycobacterium bacteria	Persistent cough, weight loss
7. Typhoid	Salmonella typhi	Fever

Diseases caused by bacteria in plants: Blackrot in cabbage, fire blight in paddy.

Diseases caused by protozoans.

Name of the disease	Name of the Pathogen	Symptoms of the disease
Dysentry	Amoeba histolytica	Diarrhoea
Malaria	Plasmodium sps	High fever
Sleeping sickness	Trypanosoma gambiense	Fever

Diseases caused by virus.

Name of the disease	Symptoms of the disease
Common cold and influenza	Running nose, fever.
Dengue fever	Running nose, fever, headache.
Mumps	Fever, headache swelling below the ear.
Measles	Fever and red rashes
Poliomyelitis	Weak muscles, paralysis of the limbs.
Rubella	Cough, fever.
Chicken pox	Fever, headache, appearance of blisters.
AIDS	Intermittent fever, diarrhoea,
(Acquired Immune Deficiency Syndrome)	loss of appetite, weight loss.
Rabies	Hydrophobia attacks central nervous system.

Diseases caused by virus in plants: Corn stunt, little leaf of brinjal

Diseases caused by Fungi.

Name of the disease	Symptoms of the disease
Ringworm	Scaly patches, itchy skin.
Athlete's foot	Itchy rash between the toes

Diseases caused by fungi in plants: Rust, smut, wilt and blight.

Multiple Choice Questions

1. Which of the following is the smallest microorganism?
   (A) Alga   (B) Bacterium
   (C) Protozoan   (D) Virus

2. The figures given below shows microorganisms W, X and Y. Identify them.

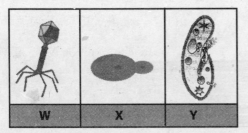

	W	X	Y
(A)	virus	protozoan	fungus
(B)	alga	bacterium	virus
(C)	virus	fungus	protozoan
(D)	fungus	alga	bacterium

3. Bacteria are classified according to their
   I nutrition
   II respiration
   III reproduction
   (A) I only   (B) I and II only
   (C) II and III only (D) I, II and III

4. Which of the following statements describe bacteriophage correctly?
   (A) It is a bacterium which causes diseases in plants
   (B) It is a type of virus which attacks bacteria
   (C) It is a bacterium which kills viruses
   (D) It can multiply inside both living and non-living cells

5. At 37°C and in damp conditions, bacteria reproduce easily through:
   (A) budding
   (B) binary fission
   (C) conjugation
   (D) spore formation

6. The figure given below shows the method of reproduction of a microorganism.

Which of the following combination is correct?

Microorganisms	Method of reproduction
(A) Viruses	Binary fission
(B) Fungi	Budding
(C) Algae	Conjugation
(D) Fungi	Spore formation

7. Which of the following characteristics is true of a virus?
   I It has a nucleus
   II It reproduces only in living cells
   III It contains either DNA or RNA
   (A) I only
   (B) I and III only
   (C) II and III only
   (D) I, II and III

8. Algae are autotrophs because they:
   (A) carry out anaerobic respiration
   (B) can manufacture their own food
   (C) feed on dead organisms
   (D) feed on other living organisms

9. When fungal spores land on a piece of bread left on a table after a few days, the bread becomes mouldy. What conditions favour the growth of the fungus?

I The presence of food

II The moist temperature

III The absence of water

(A) I only   (B) I and II only
(C) II and III only   (D) I, II and III

10. Which of the following microorganisms play important roles in maintaining the balance of nitrogen gas in the atmosphere?
(A) Viruses   (B) Bacteria
(C) Algae   (D) Protozoa

11. What causes dough to rise when yeast is added to it?
(A) An increase in temperature
(B) An increase in the amount of substance
(C) An increase in the number of yeast cells
(D) the release of carbon dioxide gas

12. What process takes place when yeast is added to grape juice and left for a week?
(A) Decomposition (B) Fermentation
(C) Distillation   (D) Oxidation

13. Cellulose found in plants can be digested by herbivores because of the presence of certain bacteria which secrete:
(A) amylase   (B) cellulase
(C) lipase   (D) protease

14. Microorganisms are used in biotechnology for:

I the production of bioplastic

II the production of hormones

III gene therapy

(A) II only   (B) II and III only
(C) I and III only   (D) I, II and III

15. Bacteria are used in the production of:

I alcohol

II cheese

III yoghurt

(A) I only
(B) II and III only
(C) I and III only
(D) I, II and III

16. Hepatitis is caused by:
(A) viruses   (B) bacteria
(C) fungi   (D) protozoa

17. Microorganisms which cause diseases are called:
(A) antigens   (B) antibodies
(C) pathogens   (D) vectors

18. Mosquitoes are vectors for:

I dengue fever

II malaria

III cholera

(A) I only
(B) I and II only
(C) II and III only
(D) I, II and III

19. Which of the following acts as a host for the virus which cause dengue fever?
(A) Mosquitoes   (B) Houseflies
(C) Rats   (D) Humans

20. It is caused by a protozoan

It causes fever

It can cause anaemia

The above information describes the disease:
(A) cholera
(B) malaria
(C) filiriasis
(D) hepatitis B

21. Among the diseases given below, which is true about the microorganisms which cause them and the symptoms of the diseases?

	Diseases	Microorganisms	Symptoms
I	Malaria	Protozoan	Fever and chills
II	Hepatitis B	Virus	Swollen liver
III	Cholera	Virus	Vomiting, diarrhoea

   (A) I only   (B) I and II only
   (C) II and III only (D) I, II and III

22. Ringworm can be prevented by:
(A) vaccination
(B) vector control
(C) improving personal hygiene
(D) using antibiotics

23. Tuberculosis is spread by:
(A) mosquitoes
(B) houseflies
(C) contaminated water
(D) droplets

24. A bacterial cell divides once in every minute. It takes one hour to fill a cup. How much time will it take to fill half the cup?
(A) 32 minutes   (B) 60 minutes
(C) 59 minutes   (D) 29 minutes

25. Which of the following bacteria can live symbiotically?
(A) Rhizobium   (B) Nitrosomonas
(C) Azotobacter   (D) Clostridium

26. Cholera is caused by:
(A) Streptococcus (B) Clostridium
(C) Pasteurella   (D) Vibrio

27. Bacteria living in the intestines of herbivorous animals help in the digestion of:
(A) cellulose   (B) proteins
(C) fats   (D) vitamins

28. Fungi can be distinguished by:
(A) absence of chlorophyll
(B) presence of chitin in cell wall
(C) presence of plastids
(D) Both A and B

29. Bread mould is the common name of:
(A) Batrachospermum
(B) Rhizopus
(C) Agaricus
(D) Fusarium

30. Which one of the following produces antibiotic?
(A) Mucor   (B) Rhizopus
(C) Penicillium   (D) Agaricus

31. The fungus that altered the course of history by reducing the population of Ireland from eight million in 1845 to six million a decade later was:
(A) Penicillium glucum
(B) Phytophthora
(C) Synchytrium
(D) Olpidium

32. The fungus which gave one of the greatest drugs to the world of medicine is:
(A) Penicillium notatum
(B) Ustilago maydis
(C) Colletorichum falcatum
(D) Alternaria solani

33. If a bell jar is immediately placed over a slice of moist bread and observed after a few days:
(A) the bread swells
(B) fungal mycelium is developed
(C) fungus does not develop
(D) water drops accumulate as the bread respires

34. Which of the following is an unbranched filament?
(A) Spirogyra   (B) Vaucheria
(C) Volvox   (D) Cladophora

35. A unicellular algae is:
(A) Volvox
(B) Spirogyra
(C) Chlamydomonas
(D) Vaucheria

36. Which one of the following is called pond silk?
    (A) Spirogyra
    (B) Volvox
    (C) Chlamydomonas
    (D) Euglena

37. Algae differ from fungi in being:
    (A) heterotrophic
    (B) autotrophic
    (C) parasitic
    (D) sporophytic

38. Which of the following is a closely related character of euglena with higher plants?
    (A) Presence of a flexible pellicle made of protein
    (B) They have an eye spot astaxanthin bearing pigment
    (C) Euglenoids bear one or two flagella
    (D) Chlorophyll is localised in chloroplasts

39. The transmission and infection of Entamoeba histolytica is through:
    (A) mosquito bite
    (B) bird droppings
    (C) contaminated food and water
    (D) sweat

40. Spraying of oil on stagnant water controls malaria because the:
    (A) oil kills malarial parasites in mosquitoes
    (B) water becomes too dirty for mosquitoes
    (C) mosquito larvae cannot breathe
    (D) none of the above

41. Viruses are made of:
    (A) lipoprotein
    (B) glycosides
    (C) nucleoprotein
    (D) lipids

42. The most important character which suggests that viruses are living is:
    (A) viruses multiply only in living host
    (B) their crystals have a definite shape
    (C) viruses grow and multiply
    (D) viruses may be crystallized

43. Bacterial virus is:
    (A) cyanophage   (B) bacteriophage
    (C) mycophage   (D) proteophage

44. Common cold is a:
    (A) bacterial disease
    (B) viral disease
    (C) protozoan disease
    (D) algal disease

45. Virus multiplies in:
    (A) culture medium   (B) dead tissue
    (C) living tissue   (D) none of these

46. Bacteriophage gets attached to the host cell with the help of:
    (A) tail sheath
    (B) tail fibres
    (C) spikes
    (D) collar

47. Which of the following is a viral disease?
    (A) AIDS
    (B) Tetanus
    (C) Whooping cough
    (D) Cholera

48. The vector of malaria fever is:
    (A) culex
    (B) aedes
    (C) anopheles
    (D) all of the above

49. Which of the following is a protozoan disease?
    (A) Tetanus
    (B) Measles
    (C) Filariasis
    (D) Sleeping sickness

50. The disease caused by virus which affects the liver cells and damages the bilirubin releasing cells is:
    (A) influenza   (B) measles
    (C) hepatitis   (D) polio

51. Gastroenteritis, the inflammation of stomach and intestine, is caused by:
    (A) E.coli
    (B) Amoeba
    (C) Bacillus bacteria
    (D) Salmonella typhi

52. The figures given below shows four types of microorganisms P, Q, R and S. What microorganisms are represented by P, Q, R and S respectively?

P	
R	
S	

	P	Q	R	S
(A)	Bacteria	Protozoa	Viruses	Algae
(B)	Protozoa	Viruses	Algae	Bacteria
(C)	Viruses	Algae	Protozoa	Bacteria
(D)	Algae	Protozoa	Bacteria	Viruses

53. Which characteristic cannot be used to differentiate bacteria?
    (A) Shape
    (B) Nutrition
    (C) Size
    (D) Habitat

54. Which industry involves the use of microorganisms?
    (A) The production of chemical fertilizers
    (B) The production of fireworks
    (C) The production of soft drinks
    (D) The production of antibiotics

55. A microorganism X is used in the making of bread. In which of these productions is X also required?
    (A) Cheese
    (B) Vinegar
    (C) Wine
    (D) Yoghurt

56. The figure given below shows the root nodules of legumes such as long beans or groundnuts.

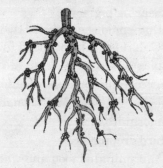

What is the importance of the presence of bacteria in the root nodules of legumes?
    (A) The nitrate salts produced are used by the plants to produce proteins
    (B) The ammonium compounds make the soil more fertile
    (C) The nitrate salts produced help the plants to grow faster
    (D) The nitrogen produced is required by the plants to accelerate the process of photosynthesis

57. Which methods are used in the seafood industry to prevent the growth of decomposer bacteria so that the products can be preserved?

I Drying

II Using common salt

III Freezing

(A) I and II only   (B) I and III only
(C) II and III only   (D) I, II and III

58. What is caused by the harmful effects of certain microorganisms?
(A) Fermentation of glucose
(B) Food poisoning in humans
(C) Heart diseases in humans
(D) Production of antibiotics

59. Infectious diseases caused by microorganisms can be spread through:

I body contact

II the air

III a vector

(A) I and II only
(B) I and III only
(C) II and III only
(D) I, II and III

60. How does a pathogen cause diseases?

I   By producing toxic substances that will destroy the cells or tissues of the host

II By destroying red blood cells of the host

III By releasing a lot of heat to raise the body temperature of the host

(A) I and II only   (B) I and III only
(C) II and III only   (D) I, II and III

61. Which of the following is matched correctly in the table given below?

	Diseases	Spread
I	AIDS	Through sexual intercourse
II	Malaria	Through body contact
III	Hepatitis A and B	Through contaminated food

(A) I only
(B) I and II only
(C) I and III only
(D) II and III only

62. Which useful microorganisms and their activities are correctly matched?

	Microorganisms	Activity
I	Yeast	Ferments glucose to produce alcohol
II	Bacteria in dead plants and animals	Decompose dead materials
III	Nitrogen-fixing bacteria	Convert nitrogen into protein in plants

(A) I only   (B) I and II only
(C) II and III only   (D) I, II and III

63. Which statement on pathogens is true?
(A) All pathogens are non-parasitic
(B) All microorganisms are pathogens
(C) All pathogens are harmful to humans
(D) All pathogens are beneficial to humans

64. Which of the following are represented by P, Q, R and S in figure given below?

| P | Q | R | S |

(A) P – Diatom, Q – Chlamydomonas, R– Spirogyra, S – Volvox
(B) P – Volvox, Q – Chlamydomonas, R – Spirogyra, S – Diatom
(C) P – Volvox, Q – Diatom, R – Spirogyra, S – Chlamydomonas
(D) P – Spirogyra, Q – Volvox, R – Diatom, S – Chlamydomonas

65. Name the microorganism shown in the figure given below.

(A) Virus

(B) Fungus

(C) Bacterium

(D) Protozoan

66. Which of the following is represented by 'X' in the figure given below?

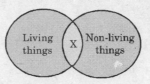

(A) Protozoa   (B) Bacteria

(C) Viruses   (D) Algae

Previous Contest Questions

1. The largest bacteria is of which type?
   (A) Bacillus   (B) Coccus
   (C) Spirillum   (D) Spherical

2. Which of the following substances are produced by an organism to prevent or reduce the spread of microorganisms?

   i. Antiseptics

   ii. Antibiotics

   iii. Antibodies

   (A) i and ii only
   (B) ii and iii only
   (C) iii only
   (D) ii only

3. These organisms have an ability to help in recycling of nutrients and energy. Which organisms are these?
   (A) Bacteria
   (B) Diatoms
   (C) Virus
   (D) Fungi

4. 'Spirogyra' differs with a 'paramoecium' in the presence of:
   (A) mitochondria
   (B) golgi bodies
   (C) nucleus
   (D) plastids

5. Identify the organism that can photosynthesise but lack the cell wall.

(A)

(B)

(C)

(D)

6. Bacteria are used in experiments to study the effects of changing temperature on the growth of microbes instead of viruses because:
   (A) viruses cannot reproduce outside a host
   (B) bacteria reproduce faster than viruses
   (C) viruses do not have cell walls
   (D) bacteria are larger than viruses

7. What microorganisms are used in making antibiotics?

   I Viruses

   II Fungi

   III Bacteria

   (A) I only
   (B) I and II only
   (C) II and III only
   (D) I, II and II

8. What microorganisms are represented by P, Q, R and S?

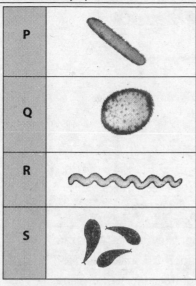

P	
Q	
R	
S	

(A) P–Coccus, Q–Bacillus, R–Vibrio, S–Spirillum

(B) P–Bacillus, Q–Coccus, R–Spirillum, S–Vibrio

(C) P–Bacillus, Q–Vibrio, R–Coccus, S–Spirillum

(D) P–Bacillus, Q–Spirillum, R–Vibrio, S–Coccus

9. Which pair is correct?

	Pathogens	Diseases caused
(A)	Viruses	Dengue fever
(B)	Bacteria	Malaria
(C)	Fungi	Hepatitis
(D)	Protozoa	Syphilis

10. Which of the following exhibit the characteristics given below?

X – Form a green scum over wet soil
Y – Closer to bacteria
Z – Pigments mask the chlorophyll

(A) Lichens
(B) Volvox
(C) Blue green algae
(D) Spirogyra

⊘ Answers ⊘

Multiple Choice Answers

1. D	2. C	3. B	4. B	5. B	6. D	7. C	8. B	9. B	10. B
11. D	12. B	13. B	14. B	15. B	16. A	17. C	18. B	19. A	20. B
21. B	22. C	23. D	24. C	25. A	26. D	27. A	28. D	29. B	30. C
31. B	32. A	33. B	34. A	35. C	36. A	37. B	38. D	39. C	40. C
41. C	42. A	43. B	44. B	45. C	46. B	47. A	48. C	49. D	50. C
51. A	52. C	53. D	54. D	55. C	56. A	57. D	58. B	59. D	60. A
61. C	62. B	63. C	64. A	65. B	66. C				

Previous Contest Answers

1. A	2. C	3. A	4. D	5. A	6. A	7. C	8. B	9. A	10. C

Explanatory Answers

24.　(C) At the 59th minute it is half filled. All the bacteria divide and double. Hence the cup gets filled in the 60th minute.

27.　(A) Cellulose digesting enzyme is absent in the animal digestive system.

31.　(B) The disease known as potato blight had destroyed potato crops on a massive scale in Ireland, resulting in the starvation of many people and emigration of many others to USA.

Chapter 4 Conservation of Plants and Animals

	Common misconception	Fact
1.	Predators chosen for biological control hunt one type of pest only.	Predators hunt any animals which are suitable for food. E.g. snakes used for biological control hunt rats, frogs and lizards.
2.	Conservation is synonymous with preservation.	Conservation involves the use of the earth's resources wisely so that they are not wasted and can last as long as possible, e.g., water and air can be conserved by preventing pollution. Preservation involves keeping some of the earth's resources for future generations, e.g., we can preserve some of our plants and animals by establishing forest reserves.

Waste in the form of hot water from the electric power stations can be recycled. This 'waste' can be supplied as hot water to homes, local offices and factories. Many new power stations today are designed so that the 'waste' is made use of.

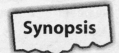

Synopsis

1. The physical and biological world we live in is called our environment.

2. Biodiversity refers to the variety of living organisms in a specific area.

3. Plants and animals of a particular area are known as the flora and fauna of that area.

4. The term wildlife refers to plants and animals living in natural conditions. It serves as a source of genes or a gene bank.

5. Over exploitation of wildlife for economically useful products, deforestation, industrialisation and pollution resulted in extinction of several plant and animal species.

6. Red Data Book contains a record of endangered species.

7. Conservation involves keeping the natural environment in its balanced state as far as possible.

8. Preservation involves keeping some of the earth's resources for future generations.

9. The conservation of wildlife is connected to the conservation of forests and wetlands. India has 13 biosphere reserves, 92 national parks and 500 wildlife sanctuaries to help conserve wildlife.

10. We should save, reuse and recycle paper to save trees, energy and water.

11. Measures for conservation and preservation of organisms.

    (a) National parks. botanical gardens and forest reserves should be established.

    (b) Sanctuaries where endangered species of living organisms can be looked after should be established.

    (c) Hunting of animals for pleasure or for their body parts should be banned.

    (d) Reforestation (i.e. the replanting of trees) should be carried out.

    (e) Selective logging (i.e. the logging of only matured trees) should be practised.

    (f) Enforce the laws which have been enacted to protect our flora and fauna. Some relevant laws are the Wildlife Protection Act, Biodiversity Act and Forest (Conservation) Act.

    (g) Environmental studies should be carried out before a project is started to avoid unnecessary destruction of the environment.

12. In the whole universe we know of only one planet where life exists - our own. The quality of the environment is our concern and our responsibility. There is only one planet Earth. It is our duty to make sure it remains beautiful varied and a worthwhile place to live in.

Multiple Choice Questions

1. The totality of genes, species and ecosystems of a region is known as:
   (A) biosphere
   (B) biodiversity
   (C) bioconservation
   (D) biocommunity

2. Uncontrolled deforestation leads to:
   I the destruction of habitats
   II landslides
   III flooding
   (A) I only
   (B) I and II only
   (C) II and III only
   (D) I, II and III

3. Drought brings about:
   (A) flooding
   (B) volcanic eruptions
   (C) decreased production of food
   (D) increased photosynthesis in plants

4. Which of the following is an abiotic component?
   (A) Cow   (B) Grass
   (C) Temperature   (D) Bacteria

5. The name given to include all living organisms and all life supporting regions of the earth is:
   (A) biosphere
   (B) ionosphere
   (C) stratosphere
   (D) lithosphere

6. Which of the following shows a modern technology measures used to preserve and conserve the environment?
   (A) Practising crop rotation
   (B) Using leaded petrol in motor vehicles
   (C) Using machines in agricultural industry
   (D) Converting industrial wastes into biogas

7. Which of the following are the effects due to the mismanagement of timber logging?
   I Flooding
   II Soil erosion
   III Growing economy
   (A) I and II only   (B) I and III only
   (C) II and III only (D) I, II and III

8. Which of the following must be practised to preserve and conserve the environment?
   (A) Deforestation
   (B) Recycling
   (C) Soil erosion
   (D) Increase in pollution

9. The introduction of exotic species into an area:
   (A) helps to conserve wildlife
   (B) helps to protect biodiversity
   (C) affects native species adversely
   (D) helps native species survive

10. Which of the following is/are the advantage(s) of forests?
    (A) Forests provide us with oxygen
    (B) They protect soil and provide habitat to a large number of animals
    (C) They help in bringing good rainfall in neighbouring areas
    (D) All of these

11. Creation of wild life reserves and enforcement of laws are conservation measures that promote increased:
    (A) use of biocides
    (B) preservation of species
    (C) use of biological control
    (D) exploitation of species

12. The practice of clearing a part of a forest for cultivation and then moving on to a new part is called:
    (A) shifting cultivation
    (B) crop rotation
    (C) step farming
    (D) monoculture

13. How does our government protect the rain forests of our country?

   I Prohibit the felling of trees that are not mature enough

   II Trees that have been chopped down are replanted

   III Discourage the use of pesticides in agriculture

   (A) I and II only   (B) I and III only
   (C) II and III only (D) I, II and III

14. Which of the following are the uses of IUCN Red List?
   (A) Developing awareness about the importance of threatened biodiversity
   (B) Identification and documentation of endangered species
   (C) Providing a global index of the decline of biodiversity
   (D) All of these

15. Special project(s) launched to protect endangered species is/are:
   (A) Project Tiger
   (B) Project Elephant
   (C) Project Crocodile
   (D) all of these

16. Soil erosion can be prevented by:
   (A) allowing herbivorous animals to graze excessively
   (B) growing plants to form a soil cover
   (C) increasing fertility
   (D) making the land slopy

17. Deforestation has an alarming effect on:
   (A) increase in grazing area
   (B) soil erosion
   (C) weed control
   (D) sunlight

18. What is the main aim of conserving living organisms?
   (A) To increase the world's population of organisms
   (B) To prevent extinction of endangered species

   (C) To help students of botany and zoology
   (D) To help in ecotourism

19. Which of the following are living resources in nature?
   (A) Flora   (B) Fauna
   (C) Soil   (D) Both A & B

20. What is an endangered animal?
   (A) An animal on the verge of extinction
   (B) An animal which is extinct
   (C) An animal that is dangerous to humans
   (D) An animal that is dangerous to other animals

21. Which are the factors that pose a great threat to biodiversity?
   (A) Habitat destruction
   (B) Disturbance and introduction of alien species
   (C) Man's interference with nature
   (D) All of these

22. Which of the following is a consequence of Man's interference with nature?
   (A) Increase in natural resources
   (B) Biological imbalance
   (C) Increase in the ozone layer
   (D) Reappearance of some extinct species

23. What is a National Park?
   (A) An area strictly reserved for improvement of wild life
   (B) An area where grazing and cultivation are permitted
   (C) A park where the whole nation can have picnics
   (D) A park which can be privately owned

24. Which of the following are examples of Man's interference with nature that has upset the biological equilibrium?
   (A) Afforestation
   (B) Recycling of paper
   (C) Poaching endangered animals
   (D) Rain harvesting

25. Species which are going to enter the endangered category are called:
(A) endangered species
(B) rare species
(C) vulnerable species
(D) fossil species

26. Energy flow in an ecosystem is:
(A) multidirectional
(B) unidirectional
(C) bidirectional
(D) circular

27. Which of the following is the biodiversity hot spot?
(A) Oceans   (B) Rivers
(C) Deserts   (D) Forests

28. What are the control methods that are to be adopted to restore balance in the ecosystems?
(A) Rain water harvesting for conservation and management of water
(B) Conservation of ocean resources and preservation of marine life
(C) Public awareness programmes concerning conservation of wild life
(D) All of these

29. Which of the following is NOT suitable for the conservation of tigers?
(A) Set up sanctuaries to protect the animals
(B) Establish forest reserve
(C) Establish more recreational and tourist centres in the forest
(D) Increase public awareness on the effects of indiscriminate hunting on the animals

30. Which of the following is NOT the reason for the fall in biodiversity?
(A) Deforestation
(B) Green revolution
(C) Hunting
(D) Environmental pollution

31. Which of the following conservation helps to maintain diversity?
(A) Pollution
(B) Water sources
(C) Gene pool
(D) Forest reserves

32. Which of the following is NOT true regarding the importance of wild life?
(A) Ecological value
(B) Non-commercial value
(C) Scientific value
(D) Aesthetic value

33. Which of the following is NOT a vanishing wild animal of India?
(A) Leopard   (B) Nilgiri langur
(C) The sloth   (D) Fox

34. What is wild life?
(A) All non-domesticated and non-cultivated biota found in their natural habitat
(B) All domesticated and non-domesticated animals
(C) All cultivated plants and non-domesticated animals
(D) All non-cultivated plants and domesticated animals

35. Which of the following regions has a rich flora and fauna?
(A) Deccan plateau
(B) Lofty Himalayas
(C) Slopes of the Himalayas
(D) Thar desert

36. Flora and Fauna are:
(A) renewable and non-living resources
(B) non-renewable and living resources
(C) renewable and living resources
(D) non-renewable and non-living resources

37. Wildlife protection act was passed in the year:
(A) 1972
(B) 1970
(C) 1982
(D) 1990

38. Which of the following is NOT an effective way to conserve living organisms?

(A) Carry out afforestation
(B) Establish national parks
(C) Import organisms from other countries
(D) Establish centres to look after endangered species

39. Which of the following human activities may cause the extinction of species?

(A) Using animal parts as traditional medicines
(B) Encouraging game hunting as a sport
(C) Using animal parts as decorative piece
(D) All of these

40. The species of plants and animals which are found exclusively in a particular area are:
(A) endemic species
(B) endangered species
(C) rare species
(D) extinct species

Previous Contest Questions

1. Deforestation results in:
(A) acid rain
(B) greenhouse effect
(C) increased oxygen content in the atmosphere
(D) decreased carbon dioxide content in the atmosphere

2. Which of the following is true about conservation and preservation?

I Protects the ecosystem from destruction

II Prevents the depletion of natural resources

III Maintains the population of endangered plant and animal species

(A) I only
(B) I and II only
(C) II and III only
(D) I, II and III

3. The enactment passed by the Government of India in 1972 to legally protect the endangered flora and fauna is:
(A) Forest conservation bill
(B) Wild life protection act

(C) Project tiger
(D) Project one horned rhino

4. What is to be done for species preservation?
(A) Protected area for endangered plants and animals
(B) Protection of their breeding grounds
(C) Issuing hunting licence to VIPs
(D) Both A & B

5. Under Man and biosphere programme (MAB), what is a core zone?
(A) A zone where human activity is permitted
(B) A zone where human activity is not permitted
(C) A zone where controlled hunting is permitted
(D) A zone where slash and burn cultivation is not permitted

6. Species restricted to certain geographic regions are called:
(A) rare species
(B) endangered species
(C) vulnerable species
(D) fossil species

7. Conservation of resources means:
   (A) maintaining the earth's resources in their original state
   (B) using earth's resources wisely
   (C) using resources not in a wasteful manner
   (D) both B & C

8. The mass emigration of bees to settle down else where in order to form a new hive is called:
   (A) migration
   (B) swarming
   (C) spawning
   (D) carting

9. Which of these National Parks is not paired correctly with its state?
   (A) Gir National Park - Gujarat
   (B) Corbett National Park - Uttar Pradesh
   (C) Kanheri National Park - Maharashtra
   (D) Bharatpur National Park - Karnataka

10. Proper management of the environment is important so that:
    (A) humans can continue to live
    (B) plants would not become extinct
    (C) animals would not become extinct
    (D) the balance of nature can be preserved

⊘ Answers ⊘

1. B	2. D	3. C	4. C	5. A	6. D	7. A	8. B	9. C	10. D
11. B	12. A	13. A	14. D	15. D	16. B	17. B	18. B	19. D	20. A
21. D	22. B	23. A	24. C	25. C	26. B	27. D	28. D	29. C	30. B
31. C	32. B	33. D	34. A	35. A	36. C	37. A	38. C	39. D	40. A

Previous Contest Answers

1. B	2. D	3. B	4. D	5. B	6. A	7. D	8. B	9. D	10. D

Chapter 5

Reproduction in Animals

Get It
Right

Common misconception	Fact
1. In women, fertilisation of the egg cell usually takes place in the uterus.	Fertilisation usually takes place in the upper part of the fallopian tube. Implantation of the embryo takes place in the uterus.
2. The process of cloning involves only a single parent.	Cloning process involves two animals, a cell is taken from an adult animal (A) and an ovum from another female animal (B) and its nucleus is removed. The nucleus from the cell of the animal A is placed inside the ovum of animal B. The ovum is then placed in a petridish containing nutrient solution, where it divides to form an embryo. The embryo is then transferred into the uterus of another female animal. The young animal born is the replica of the first animal (A).

D Y Kn O u w ?

During the metamorphosis of a tadpole into a frog, lysosomes of the tadpole's tail causes the digestion of tail.

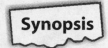

1. Reproduction is the production of new individuals more or less similar to the parent organisms. This may be achieved by a number of means and serves to perpetuate increase of species.

2. There are two main methods in which organisms give rise to new individuals - Asexual reproduction and sexual reproduction.

3. Asexual reproduction is the process of producing new organism(s) from a single parent without the involvement of sex cells or gametes.
    E.g.: Binary fission in Amoeba, regeneration in planaria, budding in hydra.

4. Sexual reproduction is the process of producing new organism(s) from two parents with the involvement of sex cells or gametes. Male sexual unit is known as male gamete or sperm while female sexual unit is termed as female gamete or ova.

5. The fusion of sperm and ovum is known as fertilisation. Thus, the two major processes, i.e., formation of gametes and fusion of gametes constitute sexual reproduction.

6. The reproductive organs of human beings, i.e., testis in male and ovary in female produce gametes and also secrete hormones like testosterone (male hormone) and estrogen and progesterone (female hormones).

7. Fertilisation takes place in the fallopian tube. The embryo develops in the uterus, and receives oxygen nutrients, and so on through the placenta.

8. Animals such as human beings, cows, dogs which give birth to young ones are called viviparous animals. Animals such as hen, frog, lizard which lay eggs are oviparous animals.

9. The transformation from the larval stage to the adult stage in the life cycles of frog and insects is called metamorphosis.

10. The cloning of animals produces offspring with genetic materials which are identical to the parent. The most famous animal clone is Dolly, the sheep.

Multiple Choice Questions

1. What is meant by asexual reproduction?
    (A) New individuals are produced without the fusion of gametes
    (B) New individuals involves the fusion of male and female gametes
    (C) Reproduction which occurs only in plants
    (D) None of the above

2. Which of the following is NOT a characteristic of sexual reproduction?
    (A) It involves the fusion of two reproductive cells
    (B) It is practised by most organisms
    (C) Fertilization may take place inside or outside the body of the female
    (D) The offspring receives its characteristics from one parent only

3. Which of the following is NOT an example of asexual reproduction?
    (A) Reproduction in hydra
    (B) Reproduction in amoeba
    (C) Reproduction in bacteria
    (D) Reproduction in butterfly

4. The figure given below shows the male reproductive system.

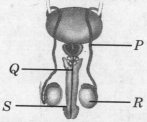

    Which part is wrongly matched with its function?
    (A) P - To transport sperms
    (B) Q - To let out urine or sperms
    (C) R - To make reproductive gametes called ova
    (D) S - To ejaculate sperms into the vagina

5. Which statement about the human female egg cell is incorrect?
    (A) It is produced when a female reaches puberty
    (B) The two ovaries in a female alternately produce the egg cells
    (C) One egg cell is usually produced by a female every 28 days
    (D) An egg cell can live in the body of a female for about a month

6.

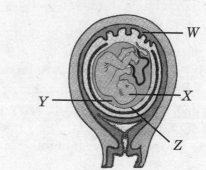

    The above figure shows part of the female reproductive system during pregnancy. Identify the parts W, X, Y and Z.

	W	X	Y	Z
(A)	Placenta	Foetus	Amniotic fluid	Foetal membranes
(B)	Umbilical cord	Embryo	Uterus	Vagina
(C)	Placenta	Foetus	Uterus	Foetal membranes
(D)	Umbilical cord	Zygote	Amniotic fluid	Cervix

7. Where does fertilization of the female egg occur in human beings?
    (A) Vagina
    (B) Uterus
    (C) Ovary
    (D) Fallopian tube

8. What part within the uterus prevents the mixing of the blood of the foetus with that of the mother?
    (A) Umbilical cord
    (B) Uterus wall
    (C) Placenta
    (D) Water sac

9.
   ♦ Baby
   ♦ Embryo
   ♦ Zygote
   ♦ Foetus

   A fertilized egg cell passes through the stages of development shown above. Which is the correct order?
   (A) Zygote → Embryo → Foetus → Baby
   (B) Zygote → Embryo → Baby → Foetus
   (C) Embryo → Zygote → Baby → Foetus
   (D) Foetus → Zygote → Embryo → Baby

10. Which of the following is NOT true about reproduction?
    (A) Unicellular organisms cannot reproduce
    (B) Reproduction is the process of producing young animals or plants
    (C) Reproduction is one of the process of living things
    (D) Reproduction can be divided into sexual and asexual reproduction

11. Figure given below shows asexual reproduction in yeast.

    Which organism also reproduces in the same way?

    (A) Hydra
    (B) Amoeba
    (C) Starfish
    (D) Flatworm

12. Which of the following are types of asexual reproduction?

    I Budding
    II Binary fission
    III Spore formation
    (A) I and II only
    (B) I and III only
    (C) II and III only
    (D) I, II and III

13. Which comparisons are true about sexual and asexual reproduction?

	Sexual reproduction	Asexual reproduction
I	Involves two individuals	Involves only one individual parent
II	Involves a simple process	Involves a complex process
III	Involves the union of two types of gametes	No fusion of gametes

    (A) I and II only   (B) I and III only
    (C) II and III only   (D) I, II and III

14. Based on the figure given below.

    Paramecium   P   Amoeba

    Which statements are true about P?

    I Unicellular
    II Does not have a nucleus
    III Reproduces by binary fission
    (A) I and II only
    (B) I and III only
    (C) II and III only
    (D) I, II and III

15. Which of the following is the function of P in the figure given below?

I   Provides food to the sperm

II Provides energy for the sperm to swim

III Helps the sperm to penetrate into the ovum

(A) I and II only

(B) III only

(C) II and III only

(D) I, II and III

16. What is the function of the scrotum in the human male reproductive system?
(A) To store sperms
(B) To produce urine
(C) To produce sperms
(D) To protect the testes

17. Which is NOT the correct pair about the structure and its function in the male reproductive system?

	Structure	Function
(A)	Penis	Transfers sperms to the vagina
(B)	Testes	Produces sperm cells
(C)	Seminal-vesicles	Holds the testis
(D)	Sperm duct	Transports sperms from the testes

18. Figure given below shows a process which occurs in the human female reproductive sytem.

In which of the following parts of the female reproductive system does the process occur?
(A) Ovary   (B) Vagina
(C) Uterus   (D) Fallopian tube

19. Which of the following processes are correctly represented by the parts R, S and T in the figure given below?

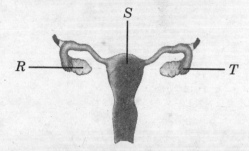

	R	S	T
(A)	Ovulation	Fertilization	Implantation
(B)	Fertilization	Ovulation	Implantation
(C)	Ovulation	Implantation	Fertilization
(D)	Implantation	Fertilization	Ovulation

20. Study the information given below.

W - The ovum dies within 24 hours after ovulation

X - The uterus wall thickens with blood vessels

Y - The uterus wall breaks down

Z - The ovary discharges an ovum

Which sequence is correct about the menstrual cycle?
(A) W, Y, X, Z   (B) Y, W, Z, X
(C) X, Z, W, Y   (D) Z, X, Y, W

21.   Study the information given below.

P - An ovum is discharged by the ovary

Q - An embryo is implanted in the uterus

R - Fusion of male and female gametes

Which processes do P, Q and R represent?

	P	Q	R
(A)	Ovulation	Implantation	Fertilization
(B)	Fertilization	Implantation	Ovulation
(C)	Ovulation	Fertilization	Implantation
(D)	Implantation	Ovulation	Fertilization

22.

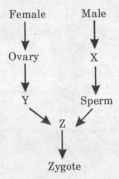

Based on flowchart given above, what do X, Y and Z represent?

	X	Y	Z
(A)	Ovum	Testes	Ovulation
(B)	Testes	Ovum	Implantation
(C)	Ovum	Testes	Implantation
(D)	Testes	Ovum	Fertilization

23.   The foetus in the uterus is enclosed by a sac which is filled with amniotic fluid. What is the function of the fluid?
(A) To provide food to the foetus
(B) To provide oxygen to the foetus
(C) To protect the foetus from shock
(D) To protect the foetus from diseases

24.   The figure given below shows a foetus in the womb of a woman.

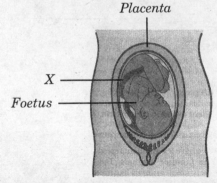

Which substances are transported through the part labelled X?

I Urea

II Antibodies

III Carbon dioxide

(A) I and II only   (B) I and III only
(C) II and III only   (D) I, II and III

25.   Study the figure given below.

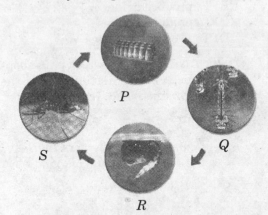

Which of the following stages grow within a case during development?
(A) P   (B) Q   (C) R   (D) S

26.   Fertilisation is external in:
(A) birds and fish
(B) amphibians and birds
(C) reptiles and fish
(D) fish and amphians

27. Binary fission gives rise to:
     (A) two daughter cells
     (B) three daughter cells
     (C) one daughter cell
     (D) three daughter cells

28. . The larval stage in a frog's life cycle is:
     (A) nymph   (B) tadpole
     (D) caterpillar   (D) fry

29. The casting of skin by a caterpillar to
     allow a larger caterpillar to emerge is
     called:
     (A) metamorphosis (B) chrysalis
     (C) moulting   (D) development

30. Which of the following shows the
     correct route, the sperm takes after
     leaving the testis?
     (A) Epididymis - vas deferens -
          ejaculatory duct - urethra
     (B) Vas deferens - epididymis - urethra
         - ejaculatory duct
     (C) Ejaculatory duct - epididymis - vas
         deferens - urethra
     (D) Epididymis - vas deferens - urethra
         - ejaculatory duct

31. Which of the following structures has
     an internal wall lined with fingerlike
     projections?
     (A) Ovary   (B) Vagina
     (C) Fallopian tube (D) Uterus

32. Which of the following is implanted to
     the uterine wall during pregnancy?
     (A) Zygote   (B) Morula
     (C) Blastocyst   (D) Follicle

33. Seminiferous tubules are found in:
     (A) kidney   (B) ovary
     (C) testes   (D) brain

34. Sperms mature in the:
     (A) testes   (B) epididymis
     (C) vasdeferens   (D) cowper's glands

35. The release of ovum from the follicle is
     called:
     (A) ovulation   (B) oogenesis
     (C) capacitation   (D) menstruel cycle

36. Which of the following is an unpaired
     structure?
     (A) ovary   (B) testes
     (C) fallopiantube (D) uterus

37. Acrosome helps the sperm to:
     (A) locate the ovum
     (B) swim to the ovum
     (C) penetrate the ovum
     (D) stick to the ovum

38. The sperm head contains:
     (A) mitochondria   (B) nucleus
     (C) yolk   (D) follicle cells

39. Implantation is:
     (A) attachment of the blastocyst to the
         uterine wall
     (B) release of ovum from the follicle
     (C) development of an embryo without
         fertilisation
     (D) formation of ova from germ cells

40. A specialised structure which provides
     nourishment to the foetus from the
     mother and collects wastes from it,
     passing them onto the mother is:
     (A) fallopian tube (B) placenta
     (C) cowper's gland (D) blastocyst

41. Which of the following are found in high
     concentrations in the blood that passes
     from the placenta to the foetus?
     (A) Urea and carbon dioxide
     (B) Urea and glucose
     (C) Carbon dioxide and antibiotics
     (D) Oxygen and amino acids

42. Cowper's glands secrete a substance to:
     (A) protects sperms
     (B) serve as a lubricant
     (C) make the semen alkaline
     (D) help the sperm in penetrating the
         ovum

43. Which of the following organisms
     reproduces asexually?
     (A) Protozoa   (B) Frog
     (C) Lizard   (D) Housefly

44. Ampluxory pads that help in copulation are present in:
(A) earthworm   (B) frog
(C) fish   (D) butterfly

45. Milt of frog consists of:
(A) ova
(B) sperm mother cells
(C) spermatozoa
(D) both A and C

Previous Contest Questions

1. Which part within the uterus prevents the mixing of the blood of the foetus with that of the mother?
(A) Umbilical cord
(B) Uterus wall
(C) Placenta
(D) Water sac

2. Which statements are correct about menstrual cycle?

I   A girl who has reached puberty will menstruate throughout her life

II Menstruation occurs every 28 days.

III During every menstrual cycle, one mature ovum will be released by the ovary

(A) I and II only   (II) I and III only

(C) II and III only (D) I, II and III

3. Which of the following male sexual organs and its function are correctly matched?

Sexual organ	Function
I Penis	Channels sperms to the vagina
II Testes	Produces sperms
III Scrotum	Protects the testes

(A) I and II only
(B) II and III only
(C) I and III only
(D) I, II and III

4. Which of the following is an oviparous mammal?
(A) Echidna   (B) Kangaroo
(C) Rabbit   (D) Bat

5. Figure given below shows a process. That occurs in the human female reproductive sytem. Identify the process.

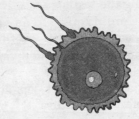

(A) Fission   (B) Fertilisation
(C) Conjugation   (D) Ovulation

6. The mass of eggs of frog is called:
(A) follicles   (B) ostium
(C) both A & B   (D) spawn

7.

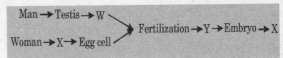

Based on the chart above, identify W, X, Y and Z.

	W	X	Y	Z
(A)	Gamete	Ovary	Foetus	Zygote
(B)	Sperm	Ovary	Zygote	Foetus
(C)	Sperm	Uterus	Foetus	Baby
(D)	Gamete	Fallopian tube	Zygote	Baby

8.   Internal fertilization occurs in:

(A) bird, fish

(B) reptile, frog

(C) mammal, frog

(D) reptile, mammal

9.   Graafian follicles are present in:
(A) fallopian tube   (B) uterus
(C) vagina   (D) ovary

10. Number of ova released at a time in female human beings is:
(A) 4   (B) 3
(C) 2   (D) 1

⊘ Answers ⊘

Multiple Choice Answers

1. A	2. D	3. D	4. C	5. D	6. A	7. D	8. C	9. A	10. A
11. A	12. D	13. B	14. B	15. B	16. D	17. C	18. D	19. C	20. C
21. A	22. D	23. C	24. D	25. C	26. D	27. A	28. B	29. C	30. A
31. C	32. C	33. C	34. B	35. A	36. D	37. C	38. B	39. A	40. B
41. D	42. B	43. A	44. B	45. C					

Previous Contest Answers

1. C	2. C	3. D	4. A	5. B	6. D	7. B	8. D	9. D	10. D

Get It
Right

Common misconception	Fact
1. Boys grow faster than girls.	Girls reach puberty earlier and at this stage they overtake the boys of the same age in weight and height. After puberty, the boys grow heavier and taller than the girls.
2. In human beings, female is responsible for the sex of her child.	Female contributes gametes (ova) with two X chromosomes. Male contributes gametes (sperms) with one X and one Y chromosome. If the sperm with X chromosome fertilises the ova, the zygote would develop into a female child. If the sperm with Y chromosome fertilises ova, the zygote would develop into a male child. Hence, male is responsible for the sex of his child.

Among bees, workers select which fertilized eggs to brood in queen or worker cells, the queen decides the sex of her young. In a mechanism of sex determination known as haplodiploidy, fertilized eggs will become female offspring, while unfertilized eggs will become males.

Synopsis

1. Humans become capable of reproduction after puberty sets in. Between the ages of 11 years and 19 years children are called adolescents.

2. The period of time when a person changes from a child into an adult is called puberty.

3. A boy reaches puberty when he is 13-14 years old. Girls reach puberty earlier than boys at the age of 11-12 years.

4. During puberty, physical and emotional changes take place. These are called secondary sexual characters. In girls, puberty is marked by the onset of menstruation and the development of secondary sexual characters, namely, enlargement of breasts, widening of pelvic girdle and growth of hair in the armpits and pubic region.

    In boys, puberty begins with the production of sperms and is marked by secondary sexual characters, namely, deepening of the voice, growth of hair on the face, armpits and pubic region and enlargement of the scrotum and penis.

5. Menstruation is the periodic discharge of blood from the uterus through the vagina. The discharged blood usually contains a dead egg cell and some tissues from the lining of the uterus.

6. If the egg cell is fertilized, it will form a zygote which will implant itself on the wall of the uterus. It will eventually develop into an embryo. Menstruation does not take place during pregnancy.

7. The onset of puberty and maturity of reproductive parts are controlled by hormones.

8. Hormones are secretions of endocrine glands which pour them directly into the blood stream.

9. Pituitary gland secretes hormones which include growth hormone and hormones that make other glands such of the (testes, ovaries) thyroids and adrenals, secrete hormones. Pancreas secretes insulin, thyroid produces thyroxine and adrenals produce adrenaline.

10. Testosterone is the male hormone and estrogen, the female hormone. The uterine wall in females prepares itself to receive the developing fertilised egg. In case there is no fertilisation, the thickened lining of the uterine wall breaks down and goes out of the body along with blood. This is called menstruation.

11. Sex of the unborn child depends on whether the zygote has XX or XY chromosomes.

12. It is important to eat balanced food and maintain personal hygiene during adolescence.

13. Personal hygiene must be maintained during menstruation to avoid itch, unpleasant odour, bacterial and fungal infection.

Multiple Choice Questions

1. Which of the following statements is true?
   (A) Boys will reach puberty at an earlier age than girls
   (B) At about the age of 12, girls will grow more rapidly than boys
   (C) At the end of rapid growth, girls are normally heavier than boys
   (D) Between the age of 4 to 12, girls will grow faster than boys

2. Why do girls grow faster than boys at the age of 12?
   (A) Girls reach puberty earlier than boys
   (B) Boys reach puberty earlier than girls
   (C) Girls normally take in more proteins at the age of 12
   (D) Boys normally consume less food

The figure below shows a human growth curve. Answer the questions from 3 to 7 based on it.

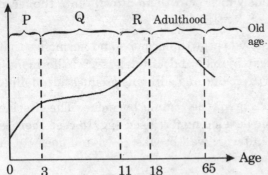

3. Name the periods of growth which are labelled as P, Q and R.
   (A) P-Infancy, Q-Childhood, R-Old age
   (B) P-Infancy, Q-Childhood, R-Adolescence

(C) P-Adulthood, T-Adolescence, R-Old age
   (D) P-Childhood, Q-Infancy, R-Adolescence

4. At what age is the period called adolescence?
   (A) 0 to 3 years   (B) 3 to 13 years
   (C) 11 to 18 years (D) 18 to 45 years

5. Name two different periods which show rapid growth rate.
   (A) Infancy and adolescence
   (B) Adulthood and old age
   (C) Infancy and childhood
   (D) Adolescence and old age

6. Which period shows negative growth?
   (A) Infancy   (B) Childhood
   (C) Adolescence   (D) Old age

7. The growth in height is maximum:
   (A) at the end of adulthood
   (B) before puberty
   (C) at the beginning of old age
   (D) at the beginning of adulthood

8. Which of the following rapid growths in male and female is correct?

	Male	Female
(A)	14 years onwards	12 - 14 years
(B)	0 - 3 years	0 - 12 years
(C)	10 - 14 years	14 years onwards
(D)	4 - 12 years	14 years onwards

9. What is the role of sperms in reproduction?
   (A) To stimulate ovum
   (B) To fertilize the egg
   (C) To form foetus
   (D) To help in puberty changes in male

10. The monthly discharge of blood from the uterus via the vagina in females is called:
    (A) ovulation   (B) menstruation
    (C) fertilisation (D) cultivation

11. Each menstrual cycle usually lasts for about ____ days.
    (A) 7   (B) 14   (C) 21   (D) 28

12. At about the 14th day of the menstrual cycle, a mature egg is released from an ovary. This is known as:
    (A) attraction   (B) fertilisation
    (C) menstruation   (D) ovulation

13. Menstruation will NOT take place if:
    (A) the ovum is released
    (B) the child is given birth
    (C) the hormones are produced
    (D) fertilisation occurs

14. Which of the following statements are correct concerning the menstrual cycle?

    I   An ovum is developed and released during the menstrual cycle

    II The uterine lining becomes very thin immediately after menstruation

    III The fertile period is the period immediately after menstruation

    (A) I and II only   (B) I and III only
    (C) II and III only (D) I, II and III

15. When menstruation stops, the uterine lining is very thin. The repair of the uterine lining takes about ____ days.
    (A) 7   (B) 9
    (C) 11   (D) 13

16. Changes during puberty in females are caused by:
    (A) sex cells   (B) enzymes
    (C) nutrients   (D) sex hormones

17. Which of the following will occur in females at puberty?

    I Ovulation

    II Enlargement of breasts

    III Broadening of hips

    (A) I and II only   (B) I and III only
    (C) II and III only (D) I, II and III

18. A girl has menstruation on the 6th day of the month. When is ovulation most likely to occur?
    (A) 15th - 17th day
    (B) 18th - 20th day
    (C) 23rd - 25th day
    (D) 27th - 28th day

19.

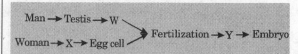

Based on the chart above, identify W, X and Y.

	W	X	Y
(A)	Gamete	Ovary	Foetus
(B)	Sperm	Uterus	Zygote
(C)	Sperm	Ovary	Zygote
(D)	Sperm	Ovary	Foetus

20. Girls overtake boys in height during:
    (A) childhood   (B) adolescence
    (C) adulthood   (D) old age

21. Secondary sexual characteristics of girls develop between the ages of:
    (A) 9 and 11 years
    (B) 11 and 14 years
    (C) 15 and 18 years
    (D) 19 and 21 years

22. At puberty, a diet rich in proteins is essential for:
    (A) supplying sufficient energy
    (B) the formation of new cells for growth
    (C) the formation of strong bones and teeth
    (D) protection from diseases

23. Which of the following is NOT a secondary sexual characteristic of a girl?
    (A) Enlargement of the breasts
    (B) Voice deepens
    (C) Menstruation begins
    (D) Growth of armpit and pubic hair

24. Which of the following is a secondary sexual characteristic of a boy?
    (A) Growth of facial hair
    (B) Bones and muscles develop
    (C) Production of sperms
    (D) All of these

25. The menstrual cycle stops when a women is about 50 years old. The woman is said to have reached:
    (A) puberty   (B) menopause
    (C) menarche   (D) adolescence

26. Which of the following does not take place during the final stage of the menstrual cycle?

    I Further thickening of the uterine lining

    II Repair and growth of the uterine lining

    III Ovulation

    (A) I and II only   (B) I and III only
    (C) II and III only (D) I, II and III

27. Secreted by endocrine glands located on top of kidneys

    Converts glycogen into glucose

    Helps the body to adjust to stress

    The above information refers to the hormone:
    (A) adrenaline   (B) insulin
    (C) progesterone   (D) testosterone

28. Which pair of hormone and mineral is associated with the occurrence of goitre?

	Minerals	Hormones
(A)	Iron	Insulin
(B)	Iodine	Thyroxine
(C)	Calcium	Thyroxine
(D)	Phosphorus	Adrenaline

29. Insufficient production of insulin in the human body causes:

    (A) myxedema   (B) addison's disease
    (C) diabetes   (D) cretinism

30. Incomplete development of male secondary sexual characteristics is due to undersecretion of the hormone:
    (A) estrogen   (B) progesterone
    (C) adrenaline   (D) testosterone

31. Metamorphosis in insects is initiated by the hormone:
    (A) thyroxine
    (B) insulin
    (C) growth hormone
    (D) adrenaline

32. The sex of a child is determined by the:
    (A) chromosomes of the father
    (B) chromosomes of the mother
    (C) Rh factor of the parents
    (D) blood group of the father

33. Chromosomes that determine the sex of an individual are called:
    (A) autosomes
    (B) allosomes
    (C) plasmid
    (D) giant chromosomes

34. What is the legal age for boys and girls to get married in our country?
    (A) 18 years for boys, 21 years for girls
    (B) 21 years for boys, 18 years for girls
    (C) 23 years for boys, 20 years for girls
    (D) 25 years for boys, 18 years for girls

35. Master gland in the human body is:
    (A) thyroid
    (B) adrenal
    (C) islets of langerhans
    (D) pituitary

36. The hormones secreted by the pituitary gland are:
    (A) growth hormones
    (B) hormones for the absorption of water
    (C) hormones which stimulate other endocrine glands
    (D) all of these

37. The menstrual cycle, the ovulation process and the development of the uterus in the females is controlled by:
(A) estrogen   (B) progesterone
(C) testosterone   (D) both A and B

38. Hormones are transported from the place of origin to the place of target by:

| I ducts |
| II blood |
| III nerves |

(A) I only   (B) II only
(C) III only   (D) I, II and III

39. Arjun was losing weight even though he was taking his meals regularly. He felt thirsty all the time. When the doctor tested Arjun's urine, the test showed a high concentration of glucose. What disease is Arjun suffering from?
(A) Goitre
(B) Cancer
(C) Diabetes mellitus
(D) Cirrohsis of the liver

40. Fusion of a male and female gamete which results in the formation of a zygote is called:
(A) fertilisation   (B) fission
(C) implantation   (D) insemination

Previous Contest Questions

1. In humans, sex of the offspring is determined:
(A) through mother's sex chromosomes
(B) through father's sex chromosomes
(C) by enzymes
(D) by hormones

2. A person goes through the following stages of growth. Which is the correct sequence?

| 1. Foetus |
| 2. Zygote |
| 3. Embryo |
| 4. Baby |
| 5. Adult |
| 6. Adolescent |
| 7. Child |

(A) 2, 3, 1, 4, 7, 6, 5
(B) 2, 1, 3, 4, 7, 5, 6
(C) 3, 2, 1, 4, 6, 7, 5
(D) 1, 3, 2, 4, 7, 6, 5

3. Which sequence is correct about the menstrual cycle based on the information given below?

| W - The ovum dies within 24 hours after ovulation |
| X - The uterus wall thickness with blood vessels |
| Y - The uterus wall breaks down |
| Z - The ovary discharges an ovum |

(A) W, Y, X, Z   (B) X, Z, W, Y
(C) Y, W, Z, X   (D) Z, X, Y, W

4. What do X, Y and Z represent in the figure given below?

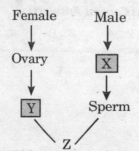

(A) X-Ovum, Y-testes, Z-Ovulation
(B) Testes, Y-Ovum, Z-Implantation
(C) X-Ovum, Y-Testes, Z-Implantation
(D) X-Testes, Y-Ovum, Z-Fertilization

5. What happens during menopause?

I No menstruation

II No maturation of new follicles

III The ovaries will stop the secretion of estrogen

IV Ovarian activity will be induced

(A) I and II only
(B) III and IV only
(C) I, II and III only
(D) I, II, III and IV only

6. Testosterone is secreted by:
(A) tunica albuginea
(B) interstitial cells
(C) germinal epithelium
(D) sertoli cells of testes

7. The endocrine gland nearest to the heart is:

(A) thyroid   (B) pancreas
(C) thymus   (D) adrenal

8. In humans beings, the composition of female destined zygote is:
(A) 22 + X
(B) 44 + XY
(C) 23 pairs
(D) 44 + XX

9. What will happen if personal hygiene is not taken care during menstruation?
(A) Vaginal infection
(B) Fever
(C) Infertility
(D) Pregnancy

10. HIV is generally NOT transmitted through:
(A) blood
(B) breast milk
(C) tears
(D) semen

⊘ Answers ⊘

Multiple Choice Answers :

1. B	2. A	3. B	4. C	5. A	6. D	7. D	8. A	9. B	10. B
11. D	12. D	13. D	14. A	15. B	16. D	17. D	18. B	19. C	20. B
21. B	22. B	23. B	24. D	25. B	26. C	27. A	28. B	29. C	30. D
31. A	32. A	33. B	34. B	35. D	36. D	37. D	38. B	39. C	40. A

Previous Contest Answers :

1. B	2. A	3. B	4. D	5. C	6. D	7. C	8. D	9. A	10. C

CROSSWORD – IV (BIOLOGY)

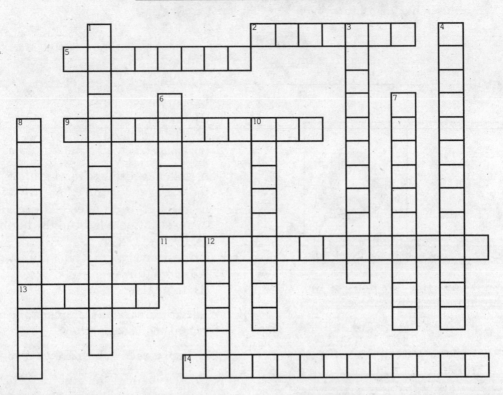

ACROSS

2　The total dry mass or weight of an organism

5　Rod shaped bacteria

9　Plastids that store food and are found in the storage organs of plants

11　The accumulation of fertilizers in water bodies

13　Poisonous substances that cause diseases by destroying living tissue

14　The process of fusion of male and female gametes

DOWN

1　A technique of heating milk for a short time in order to kill bacteria

3　The period of growth, between the ages of 12 and 18 in humans

4　The process by which the zygote is transformed into an adult in the life cycle of butterfly

6　The chemical produced by the endocrine glands

7　The process of providing water to the crops

8　A forest created by planting a particular species of trees for commercial purpose

10　A mutually beneficial association between two different organisms

12　A group of similar cells that perform a particular function

NOTE: Answer to this crossword puzzle is given at the end of this book.

Class VIII — **Biology**

1.

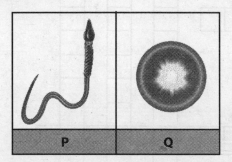

	P	Q

What are the functions of the cells shown in the figure above?

	P	Q
(A)	To transmit impulses	To transport carbon dioxide
(B)	To transport toxins	To form zygote
(C)	To fertilize egg cell	To transport oxygen
(D)	To produce reproductive cells	To engulf and kill bacteria

2. A living cell cannot be without:
   (A) nucleus
   (B) plastids
   (C) mitochondria
   (D) plasma membrane

3. Microorganisms which are widely used in genetic engineering are:
   (A) viruses   (B) algae
   (C) bacteria   (D) protozoa

4. Which of these is known as Adam's apple?
   (A) Larynx
   (B) Pharynx
   (C) Thyroid gland
   (D) Epiglottis

5. A student waiting to receive his results feels nervous and the rate of his heartbeat increases. There is an increase in the release of the hormone:
   (A) insulin
   (B) oestrogen
   (C) adrenaline
   (D) thyroxine

6. Bacteria are useful to humans and other organisms because they:

   I   can be used to prepare antibiotics

   II   are useful in agriculture for increasing soil fertility

   III   can help in the digestion of food in herbivores

   (A) I only
   (B) I and II only
   (C) II and III only
   (D) I, II and III

7. The figure below shows reproduction of a microorganism.

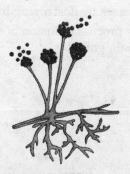

Which of the following combination is correct?

	Microorganism	Method of reproduction
(A)	Amoeba	Binary fission
(B)	Algae	Conjugation
(C)	Yeast	Spore formation
(D)	Mucor	Spore formation

8. Algae is a source of food for humans because it contains useful substances such as:
(A) betacarotene   (B) iodine
(C) vitamins   (D) all of these

9. A bacteriophage is:
(A) a bacterium
(B) a virus which multiplies inside a bacterium
(C) a bacterium which multiplies inside a virus
(D) a fungus infecting bacteria

10. Which of the following is the function of chromosomes?
(A) Producing gametes
(B) Controlling meiosis
(C) Controlling mitosis
(D) Carrying genetic material

11. Which of these is an oviparous animal?
(A) Platypus   (B) Viper snake
(C) Whale   (D) Bat

12. Men may have female characteristics (feminisation) due to the oversecretion of the hormone:
(A) progesterone
(B) testosterone
(C) oestrogen
(D) adrenaline

13. Biosphere reserve is:
(A) a protected habitat for specific endangered species
(B) a place where specific endangered faunal species are well protected

(C) a reserve forest where specific endangered floral species are well protected
(D) a protected area for the whole ecosystem

14. Large scale destruction of forests leads to:
(A) soil erosion during heavy rains and floods
(B) atmospheric pollution
(C) global warming
(D) all of these

15. To evaluate the extinction risk of thousands of species and subspecies this is set up:
(A) The IUCN Red List
(B) The WWF Red List
(C) The IUCN Yellow Pages
(D) The WWF Yellow Pages

16. Arrange the following cell organelles in descending order based on their size.

P - Chloroplast

Q - Ribosome

R - Nucleus

S - Lysosome

(A) QSPR   (B) QSRP
(C) RPSQ   (D) RPQS

17. The characters which differentiate between the Prokaryotes and Eukaryotes are:

i   prokaryotes lack nuclear membrane, while genetic material is enclosed in the nucleus in eukaryotes

ii   ribosomes are present in eukaryotes but absent in prokaryotes

iii   prokaryotes are unicellular while eukaryotes are multicellular

iv   chromosomes of eukaryotes have histones while prokaryotes lack histones

(A) i and iv   (B) ii and iii
(C) i and ii   (D) ii and iv

18. Which of the following is correctly matched?
(A) Levelling - loosens the soil
(B) Fallowing - leaving land uncultivated
(C) Emasculation - sowing of seeds
(D) Harvesting - removal of weeds

19. Which of the following groups represent the bacterial diseases?
(A) Cholera, tuberculosis, malaria, measles
(B) Small pox, tuberculosis, malaria, typhoid
(C) Cholera, tuberculosis, typhoid, measles
(D) Cholera, anthrax, tuberculosis, typhoid

20. Which one of the following is a correct match?
(A) Rabi - sowing (June- July), harvesting (Sep.- Oct.)
(B) Kharif - sowing (June-July), harvesting (Sept.- Oct.)
(C) Rabi - sowing (Oct.- Dec.), harvesting (April-May)
(D) None of these

21. Green revolution in India was possible due to:
(A) Better irrigation, fertilizers and pesticides facilities
(B) Exploitation of high yielding varieties
(C) Intensive cultivation
(D) All of these

22. Wild life is destroyed most:
(A) when there is a lack of proper care and attention
(B) due to mass scale hunting for foreign trade
(C) when its natural habitat is destroyed
(D) when natural calamity occurs

23. Most fungi develop a multicellular mass of filaments that spreads through the organic matter they are using as food. This mass is called:
(A) mycelium   (B) hyphae
(C) sporangium   (D) ascoscarp

24. Read the following sentences and give your answer as per the instructions given below.
In the following question, a statement of assertion is given and a corresponding statement of reason is given just below it.

Assertion (A) : The last step in the preparation of soil is manuring.
Reason (R) : Manure is a natural fertilizer.

(A) Both A and R are true and R is the correct explanation of A
(B) Both A and R are true but R is not the correct explanation of A
(C) A is true but R is false
(D) A is false but R is true

25. In a biology lecture the teacher was dictating the organelles of a cell as - endoplasmic reticulum, mitochondria, nucleus, ribosome, centriole and centrosome. Which cell was she referring?
(A) Prokaryotic cell
(B) Plant cell
(C) Animal cell
(D) It is not possible to predict from the given data

26. Identify the correct sequence in farming.
(A) Sowing → tilling → irrigation → manuring
(B) Sowing → tilling → manuring → irrigation
(C) Tilling → sowing → irrigation → manuring
(D) Tilling → sowing → manuring → irrigation

27. The cell organelle which receives the substances synthesized and released by the ER, condenses, modifies, packs and releases them in the form of secretory vesicles is:
    (A) Golgi complex (B) mitochondrion
    (C) lysosome   (D) ribosome

28. The stomach is made up of:

    I muscle tissues

    II reproductive tissues

    III epithelial tissues

    IV connective tissues

    (A) I and II only
    (B) III and IV only
    (C) I, II and IV only
    (D) I, III and IV only

29. Which of the following substances are produced by an organism to prevent or reduce the spread of microorganisms?

    i. Antiseptics

    ii. Antibiotics

    iii. Antibodies

    (A) i and ii only
    (B) ii and iii only
    (C) iii only
    (D) ii only

30. 'Spirogyra' differs with a 'paramoecium' in the presence of:
    (A) mitochondria
    (B) golgi bodies
    (C) nucleus
    (D) plastids

31. The enactment passed by the Government of India in 1972 to legally protect the endangered flora and fauna is:
    (A) Forest conservation bill
    (B) Wild life protection act
    (C) Project tiger
    (D) Project one horned rhino

32. What is to be done for species preservation?
    (A) Protected area for endangered plants and animals
    (B) Protection of their breeding grounds
    (C) Issuing hunting licence to VIPs
    (D) Both A & B

33. Under Man and biosphere programme (MAB), what is a core zone?
    (A) A zone where human activity is permitted
    (B) A zone where human activity is not permitted
    (C) A zone where controlled hunting is permitted
    (D) A zone where slash and burn cultivation is not permitted

34. Milt of frog consists of:
    (A) ova
    (B) sperm mother cells
    (C) spermatozoa
    (D) both A and C

35. Which part within the uterus prevents the mixing of the blood of the foetus with that of the mother?
    (A) Umbilical cord (B) Uterus wall
    (C) Placenta   (D) Water sac

36. Graafian follicles are present in:
    (A) fallopian tube (B) uterus
    (C) vagina   (D) ovary

37. In humans beings, the composition of female destined zygote is:
    (A) 22 + X   (B) 44 + XY
    (C) 23 pairs   (D) 44 + XX

38. HIV is generally NOT transmitted through:
    (A) blood   (B) breast milk
    (C) tears   (D) semen

39. Cell wall is present in:
    (A) plant cell
    (B) prokaryotic cell
    (C) algal cell
    (D) all the above

40. Minerals required by a plant in small quantity are called:
    (A) macronutrients
    (B) micronutrients
    (C) manures
    (D) fertilizers

41. Nodulated roots contain Rhizobium leguminosarum. Which of these plants lack nodulated roots?
    (A) Pea   (B) Ground nut
    (C) Bean   (D) Castor

42. Baker's yeast is:
    (A) *Saccharomyces cerevisiae*
    (B) *Mucor mucedo*
    (C) *Pencillium*
    (D) *Albugo*

43. The Earth is warm due to the presence of:
    (A) ozone   (B) oxygen
    (C) carbon dioxide (D) hydrogen

44. Fertility of soil is reduced by:
    (A) decaying organic matter
    (B) crop rotation
    (C) intensive agriculture
    (D) addition of N_2 fixing bacteria

45. A fertile hybrid between capture tiger and lioness is:
    (A) mule   (B) hinny
    (C) lige   (D) tigon

46. Storage food of *Euglena* is:
    (A) paramylum   (B) starch
    (C) laminarin   (D) fucoxanthin

47. Most common weedicide used in India is:
    (A) DDT   (B) 2,4-D
    (C) ATP   (D) NPK

48. Rearing of bees is called:
    (A) aquaculture (B) pisciculture
    (C) sericulture (D) apiculture

49. Capsid of virus is made of:
    (A) carbohydrates (B) lipoproteins
    (C) lignin   (D) protein

50. Main cause of deforestation is:
    (A) explosion of human and livestock
    (B) increased requirement of timber and fuel wood
    (C) expansion of cropland and over grazing
    (D) all of these

⊘ Answers ⊘

Model Test Paper

1. C	2. D	3. C	4. A	5. A	6. D	7. D	8. D	9. B	10. D
11. A	12. C	13. D	14. D	15. A	16. C	17. A	18. B	19. D	20. B
21. D	22. C	23. B	24. D	25. C	26. D	27. A	28. D	29. C	30. D
31. B	32. D	33. B	34. C	35. C	36. D	37. D	38. B	39. D	40. B
41. D	42. A	43. C	44. C	45. D	46. A	47. B	48. D	49. D	50. D

❖ ❖ ❖

ANSWERS TO CROSSWORD PUZZLES

CROSSWORD – I (Mathematics)

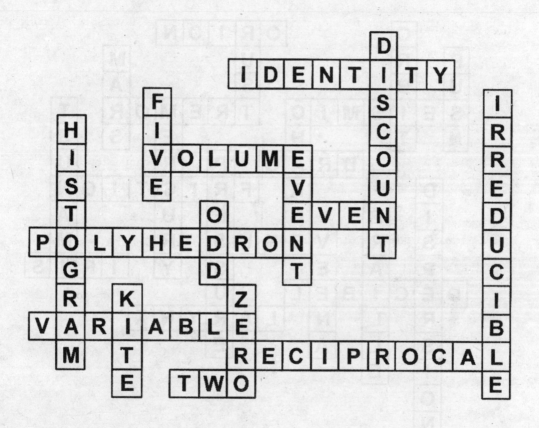

CROSSWORD – II (Physics)

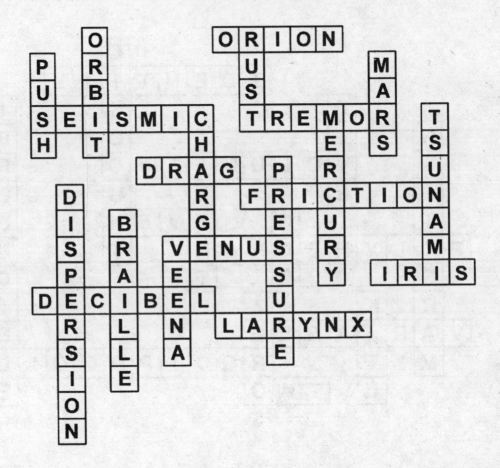

CROSSWORD – III(Chemistry)

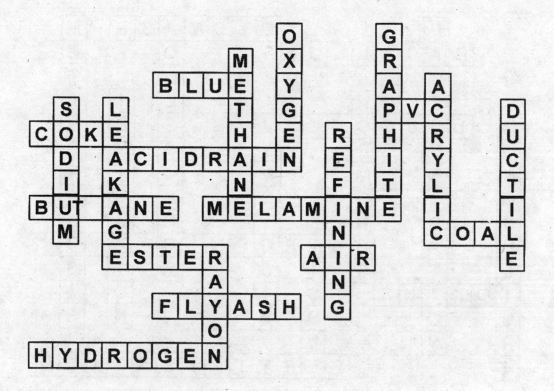

CROSSWORD – IV(Biology)

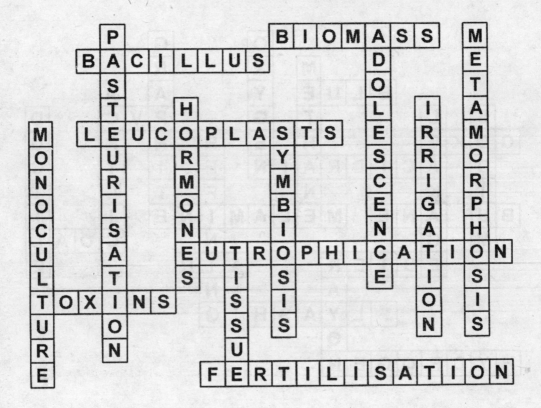

- Enhances the students' reasoning and analysis skills and understanding of subject.

- The exhaustive coverage of mathematics, physics, chemistry and biology give the learners a huge confidence to face the brunt of +1, +2 competition.

- The programme equips the students to post an excellent performance in their regular board exams.

- The extensive assignments pose wide variety of challenges to students in different formats so that they can get accustomed to various competitive examinations.

Assignments

Each lesson in all subjects includes an assignment for the students to answer at home, after studying the lesson carefully. The assignments contain:

✔ Multiple choice questions	✔ Fill in the blanks
✔ Match the following	✔ True or false questions
✔ Reasoning - assertion questions	✔ Short answer questions
✔ Numerical problems	

The solutions to these assignments are provided at the end of the chapter itself so that the student can check his/her progress.

Test Papers

Each set will have four test papers, one for each subject - mathematics, physics, chemistry and biology. The solutions to the test papers in the first set will be sent along with the second set and the solutions to the test papers in the second set will be sent along with the third set and so on The solutions to the last set's test papers will be despatched as a small booklet.

Application based questions

Questions that require the students to apply information to a situation in order to solve a problem or understand something.

Example :

You are part of your school's science team formed to assess the safety of swimmers diving into the swimming pool. You would like to know how fast a diver hits the water. The swimming coach has a diver perform for the observation. The diver, after jumping from a diving board 3 m above the water, moves through the air with a constant acceleration of 9.8 m/s^2. With the stop watch, you determine that it took 0.78 seconds to enter the water. How fast was the diver going when he hit the water?

Reasoning - Assertion Questions

These questions require the students to understand and analyse the reasons or causes of various phenomena. The student must explain the reasons, identify the evidence or draw conclusions.

Example:

Assertion A compass needle experiences more deflection when placed at a point on equatorial line than when placed at the same distance on axial line.

Reasoning Magnetic field induction has more value at a point on axial line than at the same point on equatorial line.

Thinking and Analysing Questions

These questions hone the ability of the students not only to recall the information, but using or manipulating it in someway. They improve comprehension, application, analysis, synthesis and evaluation skills of the students.

Example:

Sketch the path of an alpha particle as it approaches and then passes by the nucleus of an atom. Then, using the same nucleus, sketch the path of an alpha particle that approaches closer to the nucleus but that is not headed directly into it.

Clearing Misconceptions

The popular misconceptions prevalent in the students pose a hindrance in properly under standing scientific phenomena and mathematical concepts. These misconceptions have been discussed in detail and proper explanations have been given to dispel the myths.

Doubt Letter Scheme

Even after going through the solutions provided for questions, if the students face any problem, they can clear their doubts through letters. Your doubts will be referred to our experienced professors and subject experts.

How to apply

Ambition IIT/AIEEE comes for three classes : Class VIII, IX and X. Depending upon your requirements, you can opt for any one of the following courses:

Ambition IIT/AIEEE

Course	Code
1 year individual course for students of Class 10	C03
1 year individual course for students of Class 9	C04
1 year individual course for students of Class 8	C05

The course is divided into 5 sets and will be despatched on a monthly basis in each year, commencing in April. Despatch of lesson material may be at shorter intervals for late entries, in order to complete the course on time. One year individual courses will have 5 sets in a year, year.

Entire programme is offered in English medium and through correspondence only.

Fee

The fee for each one year course (C03, C04, C05) is Rs. 1500

The fee should be paid in full for enrollment. We do not accept fees in installments.

The fee should be paid in the form of a Demand Draft (DD) in favour of

BMA Learning Solutions payable at **Hyderabad.**

For further details contact:

BRAIN MAPPING ACADEMY #16–11–16/1/B, First Floor, Farhat Hospital Lane,
Saleem Nagar, Malakpet, Hyderabad - 500 036.
Ph : 040-65165169, 66135169 Fax : 24542215. E-mail : info@bmatalent.com

♦ **Online payment facility is available at www.bmatalent.com**

E N R O L L M E N T   F O R M

1. I want to subscribe for

   Class : VIII ☐ IX ☐ X ☐

   | Ambition IIT/AIEEE |

   Course Code : C03 ☐ C04 ☐ C05 ☐

2. Name of the student _____

3. Date of Birth _____

4. Parent's/Guardian's Name _____

5. Address for Correspondence
   (Material will be despatched
   to this address) _____

   _____ Pin _____

   Phone No. (with STD code) /Mobile: _____

   E-mail I.D. _____